REGIONS OF THE BRITISH ISLES
EDITED BY W. G. EAST M.A.

SOUTHWEST ENGLAND

LIST OF TITLES

Titles already published

REGIONS OF THE BRITISH ISLES

EDITED BY W. G. EAST M.A.

Southwest England

A. H. SHORTER M.A., Ph.D.

Montefiore Reader in Geography, University of Exeter

W. L. D. RAVENHILL M.A., Ph.D.

Senior Lecturer in Geography, University of Exeter

and

K. J. GREGORY B.Sc., Ph.D.

Lecturer in Geography, University of Exeter

NELSON

THOMAS NELSON AND SONS LTD
36 Park Street London W1
P.O. Box 2187 Accra
P.O. Box 336 Apapa Lagos
P.O. Box 25012 Nairobi
P.O. Box 21149 Dar es Salaam
77 Coffee Street San Fernando Trinidad

THOMAS NELSON (AUSTRALIA) LTD
597 Little Collins Street Melbourne C1

THOMAS NELSON AND SONS (SOUTH AFRICA) (PROPRIETARY) LTD
51 Commissioner Street Johannesburg

THOMAS NELSON AND SONS (CANADA) LTD
81 Curlew Drive Don Mills Ontario

THOMAS NELSON AND SONS
Copewood and Davis Streets Camden New Jersey 08103

———

First published 1969

17 133008 0

C

Printed in Great Britain by
Thomas Nelson (Printers) Ltd, London and Edinburgh

CONTENTS

ILLUSTRATIONS

FIGURES

PLATES

The Plates will be found at the end of the book

TABLES

COLOUR MAP

A full-colour map of Southwest England will be found at the end
of the book, arranged to open out so that it can be consulted
simultaneously with the text.

ACKNOWLEDGMENTS

I acknowledge with gratitude the help I have received from the following: Ministry of Agriculture, Fisheries and Food—the Divisional, District and Advisory Officers. (The Agricultural Returns were consulted by kind permission of the Ministry.) Department of Agricultural Economics, University of Exeter. Milk Marketing Board. Forestry Commission—the District Officers. Chambers of Commerce. Harbour Masters. Industrial and commercial firms. The Clerks, Surveyors, and Engineers of Corporations and Urban and Rural District Councils. Planning Departments—Somerset, Devon, and Cornwall County Councils, and the Corporations of Exeter, Plymouth, and the County Borough of Torbay.

I am much indebted to those who have assisted me by reading and revising substantial drafts of my sections of the book, especially Helen Cole, P. Allington, Dr L. G. Anderson, P. Holmes, E. M. Johns, N. R. Leonard, S. T. Morris, Wing-Commander R. E. G. Van Der Kiste, Professor R. S. Waters, S. C. Wilson, and the officers of many industrial firms. My best thanks are also due to the following for their help in various ways: Janice Arnold, Pauline Grace, Cecilia Greenhalgh, Margaret Jackson, Susan Luther-Davies, Margaret Peskett, Pamela Rowsell, Susan Shakeshaft, Elizabeth Starr, Pamela Suter, Mary Woolley, G. Brown, W. T. T. Davey, H. Dewey, H. L. Douch, M. J. Gandy, R. T. Groves, E. W. Haddon, D. C. Seward, and J. H. Trounson.

A. H. Shorter

I wish to thank Dr E. B. Selwood for reading an early draft of Chapter 2, Dr T. J. Chandler and Dr M. C. F. Proctor for doing the same respectively for the Climate and Vegetation sections of Chapter 4, and Lady (Aileen) Fox for reading Chapter 5; for their many comments and helpful suggestions I am very grateful. Mrs E. M. Minter has kindly made available a photograph and plan of Hound Tor and has provided me with much information on early medieval houses. A long conversation with Mr M. Biddle helped me considerably with the problems of Saxon towns. Miss Helen Rowsell of the Agricultural and Hydrological Branch of the Meteorological Office and Mr S. Patterson of the Devon River Authority were particularly helpful in providing a recent map of Rainfall (Fig. 13), and the map of Woodlands (Fig. 16) owes much to the kindness and hospitality I received from Miss A. V. Child, the Conservator of Forests, South West England Conservancy. I am pleased to record my gratitude to Miss K. M. Dexter who read my contribution to this volume and for whose thorough and helpful criticisms I am especially indebted.

W. L. D. Ravenhill

I wish to record my thanks to Professor R. S. Waters and Mr R. A. Cullingford who very kindly read the draft of Chapter 3, and to Mr A. J. Ward of the Cornwall River Authority who was most helpful in suggesting sources of information regarding water supply in Cornwall. My thanks are due also to Mr B. Clayden of the Soil Survey of England and Wales, who made very valuable comments on the early drafts of the section on Soils in Chapter 4 and was most helpful in providing recent information.

K. J. Gregory

We are all indebted to the following members of the Department of Geography, University of Exeter: Rodney Fry, who drew most of the maps, and to whom we wish to pay a special tribute for his skill, cheerfulness, and stamina in carrying out this task; Andrew Teed and Sandra Isaac, who assisted him in photographic and cartographic work; Miss Marion Bethel and Miss Gillian Stiling, who gave valuable secretarial assistance.

Finally, we are most grateful to our wives for their constant encouragement.

CHAPTER 1

Introduction

THE Southwest region contains the geographical counties of Cornwall and Devon together with part of west Somerset, and the coasts of these areas, washed by the Atlantic Ocean and the Bristol and English Channels, delineate the northern and southern boundaries of England's largest peninsula. The eastern boundary can be recognized with little difficulty. It lies across the isthmus where both the Somerset Plain and the Dorset Downs narrow westwards and quickly give way to more varied landscapes in the hills and valleys of Southwest England. This boundary falls into three parts, each of which is indicated by a hilly, thinly peopled tract and separated from its neighbour by a well-marked gap. The first section runs from Porlock Bay on the Bristol Channel coast southeastwards to the Burlescombe gap which divides the Brendon Hills from the Blackdowns and from which the drainage northwards is to the river Tone and that southwards is to the Culm. The second traverses the northernmost and highest rim of the Blackdown Hills and continues southeastwards to the Axe valley; and the third, and shortest, part doubles back along the hills east of the Axe and reaches the English Channel coast near the head of Lyme Bay.

Although for considerable distances this line approximates to the boundaries of Devon with Somerset and Dorset, it is not wholly coincident with them. The major divergence occurs where the county boundary cuts across the Exe basin and leaves the greater part of Exmoor and the Brendon Hills in Somerset. Historically and economically this area has significant eastward connections, notably with the Somerset towns of Minehead, Wellington, and Taunton; but it is logical that it should be included in Southwest England, for the Exe basin must be considered as a whole, and this involves much of Exmoor and the southern slopes of the Brendons.

As thus defined, Southwest England covers nearly 4,150 square miles. At the base of the peninsula the shortest line from the Bristol Channel to the English Channel measures only 35 miles, but the distension of the mass of Devon increases the north–south distance to a maximum of 75 miles from the Foreland to Prawle Point. Even so, no spot in Devon is more than 25 miles from the sea. For Cornwall, however, the corresponding figure is only 18, and as that county tapers southwestwards and the western half thrusts some 50 miles into the Atlantic, peninsular characteristics become even more marked. Quite as impressive as the size of the region is its length from northeast to southwest. One of the chief routes entering the peninsula penetrates the gap between the Brendons and the Blackdowns and is followed by the A38 road and the White Ball tunnel on the main Western Region railway. There are three other principal entries into east Devon—the crossing of the eastern adjunct of the Blackdowns and on to Honiton (the A30 and A303 roads); the traverse of the Axe valley and the Honiton gap (the A358–A373 and the London–Salisbury–Exeter railway line); and the route of the A35 through Lyme Regis. Whichever way is taken, a lengthy journey lies ahead of the traveller to west Cornwall. Even if he could pursue a straight course to the tip of the peninsula, this would amount to nearly 140 miles. A sinuous route following the north or the south coast would be much longer, for of all the English counties Cornwall and Devon have the highest ratios of coastline to area and the greatest number of estuaries, bays, and coves.

The position and alignment of the peninsula, its protrusion into the Atlantic and its profusion of inlets account for its generally mild, moist climate and its changeable weather. Winters may occasionally be hard, but they are rarely long; spring comes early, and the region enjoys many brilliantly sunny days with remarkable clarity of atmosphere and drying winds. These advantages compensate for the numerous rainy, windy periods and the mists and fogs, which are most frequent on the moors. As it lacks really large towns and heavy industries, the region is, however, free from the pall of 'smokeover'. There are few sharp climatic contrasts but there is considerable local diversity, especially as between high and low, and exposed and sheltered districts. Much of the north coast is open to the full force of the oceanic onslaught. It is a battered but defiant coast of massive cliffs and exposed platforms and beaches, and it has comparatively few inlets and sheltered bays and shores. In some of its high, cliffed sections the south coast matches the grandeur of the scenery of the north, but as a whole it is gentler, with numerous bays screened from the westerly gales and many branching inlets which allow the influence of the sea to penetrate far inland. Although damaging frosts and southeasterly gales are not unknown, in general the climate of the south coast is the mildest in the region, save that of the Isles of Scilly. The wettest areas in the Southwest are the highest moors, which have 80 inches or more of rain during the year and also the largest number of days when snow lies, though this is only 20 to 30 days on the average. The only tract in the region which has an annual rainfall as low as 32 inches lies along the sheltered estuary of the Exe.

In its main trends the structure of Southwest England owes much to Armorican upheavals, which involved the intrusion of granite and provided the vertebrae of most of the terrain, especially west of the Exe.

From east to west there are five major granite bosses—Dartmoor, Bodmin Moor, Hensbarrow, Carnmenellis, and Penwith; and some 28 miles west-southwest of Land's End the sunken, amputated fragments which form the Isles of Scilly bear further witness to the extent of the granite core. The island of Lundy is mostly granite too, but its structural affinities are clearly with the physiographically abaxile mass of Exmoor.

Ancient metamorphic rocks are found in the Bolt Tail–Start Point district of south Devon and in the schists of the Lizard peninsula of west Cornwall, but they are not so extensive as either the granite or the Devonian slates, grits, and sandstones which make up much of Cornwall, west and south Devon, and Exmoor and its margins. The largest area occupied by a single geological series, however, lies within a broad rectangle bounded on the east approximately by the Exe, on the west by part of the Atlantic coast of Devon and Cornwall, on the north by Exmoor, and on the south by Dartmoor. This is the comparatively unknown and unpublicized country of the shales and grits of the Culm Measures, much of it a plateau notched by deep, steep-sided valleys and surfaced by heavy, ill-drained clays.

Red-soil landscapes occur in patches on the Devonian series, but the newer and most famous red rocks of the region are almost confined to the eastern third of Devon. Here a narrow Permian zone extends from the flanks of the Brendon Hills down the valleys of the Culm, Clyst, and Exe—with westward offshoots, notably a long, slender tongue tapering through Crediton to Hatherleigh—and on to the coastlands around the mouth of the Exe and in Torbay. In the valleys farther east, red Triassic marls and sandstones predominate. Much of east Devon, however, consists of plateaux and ridges capped by Bunter pebbles, Greensand, Chalk, gravels or clay-with-flints, and separating the red-soil valleys east of the Exe. Immediately to the west of the Exe estuary the gravel-covered Greensand outlier of the Haldon Hills overlooks the Permian exposure on the lower slopes and the coastal fringe, and forms part of the divide between the Exe and the Teign. Although the whole of this eastern part of the region is akin to the lowland zone of Britain in its rock types and structures, in some respects it has physical affinities with the highland zone, not least in the exposure and the thin soils of its uplands, its fragmentation, and its deep valleys and soaring cliffs.

As is shown in Chapter 3, the regional landforms owe little to glaciation but much to subaerial and marine erosion. Both coastal and inland areas display a great diversity of forms. But even greater variety emerges from topographical studies of the complex human occupancy, rural and urban. Except on the highest moors a close and complicated mesh of field boundaries testifies to various periods, processes, and purposes of enclosure. Much, but by no means all, of this agrarian landscape is of old origin and is characterized by an intricate and—as it remained until fairly recently—

an almost indelible tracery of hedges, earthbanks, and walls. The appearance of the hedgebanked bocage in a zone athwart the isthmian approaches to the peninsula not only accords well with the physical definition of the landward boundary of the Southwest region, but also it emphasizes the broad contrasts between the histories of the field patterns on either side of it. To the east the rural landscapes characteristic of a belt extending from Dorset through the Midlands to Northeast England show much evidence of the Parliamentary enclosure of open fields in the eighteenth and nineteenth centuries, but the bocage of the Southwest portrays the diverse results of the protracted, piecemeal taking-in of fields from forest and waste as well as the legacy from the medieval patterns of open fields. The later reclamations and enclosures here affected mainly the poorer lands, ranging from the plateaux of east Devon to the high moors, and from the lower moors on the Culm Measures to the rough ground in the mining and quarrying districts of Cornwall.

Inseparable from the study of the agrarian landscapes is that of the rural settlements, and here too the Southwest has a remarkable variety of types. Chronologically, the story of the human occupancy of the region contains a wealth of detail extending from the Palaeolithic shelters in the limestone caves of south Devon to the caravan sites of recent years. Dartmoor is particularly rich in evidence of Bronze Age settlements, with the remains of many stone rows and circles, huts and associated cultivation plots and enclosures for stock. The Cornish moors and the Isles of Scilly also abound in early antiquities. Many Iron Age forts have been identified in the Southwest, but the periods of warfare and instability they represent have rarely been paralleled within the later history of the region. The Roman conquerors found no great frontier problem here, and only in Exeter and the few signal stations and fortlets is there evidence of their military work. Nor was the Southwest an unbroken Celtic bastion against the Saxons. Once Devon was opened to them by the successful battles of the seventh century, the Saxon armies and settlers advanced to the Atlantic coast and into east Cornwall, and through their conquests and settlements and the influence of the Church the Southwest was absorbed into England.

During the period between the collapse of the Roman power and the establishment of the English kingdom, however, many of the cultural contacts of the Romano–British people of the Southwest were aligned north–south. Dumnonian emigrants crossed to Brittany and Irish settlers reached Cornwall, while the Celtic saints and their followers maintained strong links between Ireland, Wales, Southwest England, and Northwest France and made a significant contribution to settlement patterns in Devon and, to a much greater extent, in Cornwall. The survival of a great number of Celtic place-names, including those which commemorate the saints, throughout Cornwall—and especially in the western half of the county—draws attention to the part played by the distinctive cultures of the pre-Saxon period in the Southwest. Many of the ancient patronyms of Cornwall have Celtic or religious origins too, and some contain elements which are also common in Celtic place-names. In contrast to the survival of native speech in Wales and Brittany, however, the Cornish language died out in the eighteenth century. For the past sixty years attempts have been made to revive the study and use of Cornish, and recently these have met with some success.

Single farms are found in all parts of the region, and groups of two or three farmsteads also occur widely. In Cornwall these usually bear Celtic names and in some cases they were established earlier than the church, which nevertheless gave Christian unity to them through the parish which was named after it. A feature of numerous parishes in Cornwall, and of some in Devon too, is the 'Churchtown', a cluster of dwellings around the church. Small groups of farmsteads are found in most parts of Devon, but here there are more nucleated villages of the English type than in Cornwall. In both counties there are a great number of secondary settlements, most of them farms and cottages of medieval and later establishment. Many of the old buildings are of local materials, such as the cob and thatch used typically in east and mid Devon and occasionally elsewhere, and the grits, slates, and granite which are more characteristic of the west. As the roots of the settlements go deep into the past and for centuries the rural people were sustained by an almost self-sufficient economy, local customs and loyalties have always been very strong.

Nevertheless the duality of contacts by land and sea and the varied experience resulting from commerce, travel, and migration have frequently counteracted parochialism and have enriched the history of the Southwest. The importance of trade with France as a spur to the growth of Plymouth and Dartmouth, the leadership and initiative of the great sea-captains and explorers who set out from this region, the wealth which accrued from the woollen trade, the development of the Newfoundland fisheries, the overseas settlements by miners, farmers, mariners, and fishermen from the Southwest—these are some of the many themes which give an eloquent reminder of the significance of the former external relations of Devon and Cornwall. During the long adherence of the people to Christianity, traditionalism has been counterbalanced by new enthusiasms, notably in the Methodist movement, which has been strongly supported in both counties, but especially in Cornwall. In politics the conservatism of a predominantly rural region has probably been reinforced by the outlook of many of the elderly retired immigrants, but it has at times been shaken by liberal or, more rarely, even radical opposition from both local and distant sources. Such considerations show that the geographical remoteness of the Southwest, perhaps all too obvious in some ways today, must be kept in perspective by viewing it against the historical background.

Within the region the truly remote settlements lie deep in the rural areas where change has generally been slow. National, political, and religious crises have occasionally disturbed the even tenor of regional life, as during the rising in support of Perkin Warbeck (1497), the Prayer Book Rebellion (1549), the Civil War (1642–6) and the backing of the Monmouth cause (1685). But although there were many small castles and fortified houses, few great embattled strongholds were built in the generally peaceful countryside; and the most powerful permanent fortifications in the Southwest—principally those at Plymouth—were intended to deal with attacks from overseas. Neither the mighty castle nor the magnificent mansion is typical of the regional architecture which, though of great variety and charm, is for the most part small in scale and unpretentious in style.

In terms of land use today the most characteristic holdings in the Southwest are small to medium-sized farms dependent to a considerable degree upon dairying and stock rearing. Some of the pasture, however, is of only moderate or even poor quality, especially on the higher moors and on those parts of the extensive Culm Measures which still suffer from inadequate drainage. Although much wheat was grown under the pressure of conditions during the Second World War, barley, oats, and mixed corn are far more suited to the climate and fit in well with the emphasis on stock feeding. In any survey of the regional arable the broadest distinction is between the really tillable land on the one hand and the high moors and the steep valleysides on the other. But in detail the local patterns of arable farming have often been complex, partly because of fluctuations in the margin and intensity of cultivation and also because of variations within the types of mixed farming practised in the region. Further variety has been added to the agriculture of the Southwest in districts where climate, soil, situation, and aspect favour the production of early or out-of-season vegetables, fruit, and flowers.

The total population of the region is barely 1,250,000, and there are few large towns. Devon's two cities—Plymouth and Exeter—have respectively nearly 250,000 and 93,000 people, and the newly created Borough of Torbay has about 100,000. The character of Plymouth shows a remarkable combination of the functions of a regional and industrial centre and those associated with national and maritime services, but that of Exeter has long borne the stamp of an administrative capital as well as that of a commercial, route, and service centre. By size, growth, and function, Torquay and Paignton have been outstanding among the holiday–tourist–residential towns along the coasts of the Southwest.

Neither the ancient nor the modern capitals of Cornwall—Lostwithiel and Launceston, and Bodmin and Truro respectively—rank among the largest towns in that county, for parts of which Plymouth is in any event a major shopping, distributive, and service centre. About 37,200 people live in the urban district of Camborne–Redruth, whose industrial importance, formerly and primarily based upon tin and copper mining, is now sustained both by old-established and well-developed works mainly concerned with engineering and by new imported factories. The advantages of St Austell's situation in mid Cornwall, as well as its functions as the centre of the largest producing area in the English china-clay industry, account for the growth of the population of the urban district to about 26,300.

Over the region generally, urban growth inland has not kept pace with the expansion of coastal towns, but commercial and industrial development has been a prime factor in the recent increase in the population of several centres. Many towns have remained quite small, even though the loss of markets and old industries which a number of them have suffered in modern times has to some extent been offset by an influx of residents and by the growth of certain service trades, principally those associated with road traffic and the holiday industry.

During several centuries the Southwest had a number of old-established and varied industries of considerable importance. The manufacture of woollens, shipbuilding, fishing, tanning, and paper making were among the most significant, and at various times mining and quarrying flourished. The production of tin and copper rose to a peak during the nineteenth century, but many factors, including the exploitation of ores at a lower cost and in great quantities in several countries overseas, eventually reduced the number of working mines in the Southwest almost to vanishing point. In some ways the decline in mining has been offset by the growth of the china-clay industry. This is not simply an alternative extractive trade, however; it is highly important to the nation as a great producer and exporter of raw materials. The quarrying of stone and the working of ball clay are also significant industries at the present time.

Large tracts of mid and west Cornwall have been scarified as a result of the streaming and mining of ores, quarrying, and the dumping of waste, but no other subregion in the Southwest has suffered extensive spoliation from such causes. Minor blemishes, though numerous, are generally scattered and mostly unobtrusive. Lacking coal deposits, and with very little hydro-electric potential, the region had no basis for the establishment of modern heavy industry. Some of the older manufactures, such as woollens, leather, and paper, underwent a severe geographical contraction during the nineteenth century, and each now has only a few residual sites, although some of these are occupied by firms that have grown considerably. A number of other manufactures and trades were reduced or extinguished as technology changed, as the coalfields, growing ports, and expanding towns in other parts of Britain proved more attractive to industry, and as competition grew from new products and from larger, more concentrated, and better situated factories. No major manufacturing area has developed in modern times, but many small and medium-sized industries have been established in the Southwest, and a few of the older ones have spread or have sprung up again from local roots.

From the eighteenth century the attractions of the region to the retiring, the invalid, the tourist, and the holiday-maker began to be exploited, and they became more widely known as travel by rail and road increased. The immigrant stream of retired people has flowed mainly to the coastal towns, although a subsidiary distribution into many inland settlements has not been insignificant. The holiday and tourist trade is at least equal to agriculture in its economic importance to the region as a whole, and it has brought changes to the character of many districts, not least through the building up of sections of the coast.

Through the National Trust, the Nature Conservancy, the Ministry of Public Building and Works, and—in relation to Dartmoor and Exmoor —the National Parks Commission, as well as by the activities of such organizations as the Council for the Preservation of Rural England and the Dartmoor Preservation Association, much is being done to try to maintain the quality of the region's finest landscapes and the heritage of its many archaeological and historical sites. But constant vigilance is necessary to prevent discordant development and to mitigate the effects of the spread of deleterious exploitation. The preservation of all that is best in the region should have wide support, for through the media of its many visitors the Southwest is far famed for its beautiful coasts, moors and farmland, its ancient settlements, and historic and romantic sites. The affection and esteem with which the region has long been regarded were reflected in the widespread sympathy aroused during the Second World War by the devastation wrought in Plymouth and Exeter and by the hit-and-run raids on smaller towns such as Dartmouth, Teignmouth, and Exmouth, and in the generous response to the appeal for the North Devon and West Somerset Relief Fund after the flood disaster of August 1952.

Many books about the southwestern counties are of particular interest to the tourist and the holiday-maker, and there are also numerous special studies of people and places in the region. The purpose of this volume is to help the general reader as well as the academic geographer to understand the Southwest as a whole, the characteristic features of its component parts, and the fascinating complexity of its topography. The first main section of the book—Chapters 2 to 6—consists of studies of the physical features, climate, soils and vegetation, and of the foundations of the settlements. The reconstruction of formal 'period pictures' in the context of historical geography is beyond the scope of this volume, but the second section—Chapters 7 to 9—outlines the principal changes in the economic geography of the region in the later periods, with special reference to modern trends. In the third section the emphasis is on the portrayal of the contemporary features of the component parts of the Southwest,

1963–7 being generally the date span to which any 'present-day' statistics refer. Figures of employment in industrial concerns are usually given where they are known to be 100 persons or more. For the purpose of the chorographical and topographical studies contained within the last six chapters, the subregions have been grouped as logically as possible without imposing academic definition and artificial unity upon regional and local diversity. It is hoped that this arrangement will prove to be convenient for the general reader, satisfactory for the professional geographer, and realistic for both.

CHAPTER 2

The Structural Basis of Southwest England

MANY geologists have given much time and thought to the structure of the complexly folded and faulted southwestern peninsula of Britain. Although some aspects of the subject remain controversial and uncertain, it is one, nevertheless, not lacking in excitement and interest as new observations and contributions are made. The mere shape of the peninsula foreshows the geological complexity, for it is not a simple promontory extending southwestwards into the waters of the Atlantic Ocean, but one with two components. At first, the land extends from east to west, boldly accentuated by the near-straight north Devon coast and truncated by the western 'points'—Bull Point, Morte Point, Baggy Point, Sharpnose Points, Pentire Point, Penhale Point. At the latitude of St Austell the alignment changes, and to the promontory is added an appendage clearly northeast to southwest in direction, taking Cornwall to Land's End and over the sea to Wolf Rock, Seven Stones, and Scilly. The geological problem consists in reconciling these two alignments, so familiar to us in Britain in our Caledonian and Variscan structures, and of placing them in their correct position in the geological time-scale. The solution to the problem is hampered not only by the complex folding and faulting of different periods, but also by the infrequent occurrence of fossils, and the limited number of beds which are sufficiently persistent to be used as markers.

Controversial though it may be, the structure of Southwest England is, in the main, virtually certain to have been a product of the Hercynian earth movements which in this area gave rise to mountain building—the culmination of the orogeny taking place in Permo-Carboniferous times some 280 million years ago. The main effect of these earth movements was to fold a vast thickness of sediments, which had been accumulating in a geosyncline during Devonian and Carboniferous times, into the huge complex synclinorium which now covers at least the middle of north Cornwall and most of Devon (Fig. 1). For this to have happened, great stresses and pressures must have been exerted; these folded the sediments along east to west lines, and gave a structural trend which can be recognized in parts of the coast and country today. Since these sediments occupy so much of this area a more detailed consideration of them is required. It is

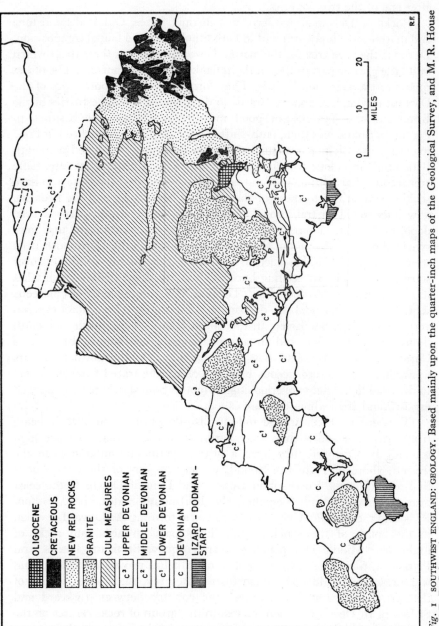
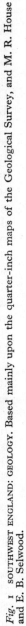

Fig. 1 SOUTHWEST ENGLAND: GEOLOGY. Based mainly upon the quarter-inch maps of the Geological Survey, and M. R. House and E. B. Selwood.

probably most convenient to begin with the system of rocks which is called after one of the two counties.

Rocks of Devonian age have two distinct facies, Old Red Sandstone and marine, strikingly different in both lithological and faunal composition. Devon is the type area for the marine Devonian and it is these rocks which build the greater part of the southern flank of the synclinorium. The oldest rocks are the Dartmouth Beds. They form the cliffs on both sides of the Dart estuary and extend westwards to do the same for the estuaries of the Erme and the Yealm. For good measure they make the bastions to Plymouth Sound and then, fault-shifted northwest, continue through Looe to emerge in anticlinal form on the shore of Watergate Bay. The Dartmouth Beds range in colour from purple to green and in general are essentially arenaceous. Their lithologies and faunas have recently been shown to have striking similarities to those of the Old Red Sandstone, and the beds are now interpreted as transitional (non-marine) lagoonal and perhaps tidal deposits, forming a passage from a narrow shelf environment to a geo-synclinal one. At the end of the period during which the Dartmouth Beds were deposited, subsidence led to a spread of fully marine conditions over south Devon. The succeeding horizon—the Meadfoot Beds—which takes its name from Meadfoot Bay, Torquay, is a dominantly argillaceous sequence in which tidal flat deposits are important. These rocks outcrop very much more extensively in the South Hams on the north and south limbs of an anticline and in a broad, nearly continuous, belt across Cornwall from Whitesand Bay to Perran Bay. On the north they pass upwards into more arenaceous beds, which can be traced from Start Bay to the Staddon Heights overlooking Plymouth Sound, where they are well exposed and after which they are called.

The Staddon Grits are red and purplish-grey grits, some of them being true quartzites, and such is their hardness that they tend to make high ground. In Cornwall they form a nearly continuous outcrop from the western shore of Plymouth Sound, passing by way of the conspicuous St Breock Downs, Rosenannon Downs, and Denzell Downs to the coast near Carnewas Island. Together, the Dartmouth Slates, the Meadfoot Beds, and the Staddon Grits are considered as forming the Lower Devonian in the south of the synclinorium. They pass upwards into rocks of undoubted Middle Devonian age near Torquay, Brixham, Totnes, and Plymouth, thence across Cornwall, though it has proved difficult to find well-preserved Middle Devonian fossils; the grey, shaly slates typical of the series are mapped as forming the country between Liskeard and St Ervan. In Devon the main interest in this group of rocks centres on the limestones, which are best known from their development and their use as a building stone at Torquay, Brixham, and Plymouth. Some of these beds are almost entirely of organic origin and represent vast accumulated masses of stromatoporoid and coral débris. The higher the limestones are in the series the lighter generally is their colour; some are nearly white, but many others are light dove-grey, pinkish, and grey mottled with red. From this abundance of coral remains it would seem that the very special conditions of water depth and temperature suitable for the growth of the coral polyp must have persisted in this part of Devon for a long period. There must also have been reefs and then, as in the modern world, the suitable environment must have been restricted to a coastal fringe washed by relatively shallow, clear, saline warm water free from sediments. These precise conditions did not extend into Cornwall at this time, as there the coral formations are rarely found in the grey slates. A further comparison with our modern world may be made in the association which at times exists between present coral formation and volcanic islands. Volcanic ash in the form of thin bands of tuff is interbedded with the limestones on the coast at Hope's Nose. Inland this extrusive volcanic material thickens, particularly in the neighbourhood of Totnes and Ashprington where the limestones pass laterally into lava and tuff. Since, however, as at Drake's Island in Plymouth Sound, the volcanic rocks are interbedded with the limestones, there are strong reasons for assuming that the lavas are the products of submarine emissions.

Upper Devonian rocks occupy a very large area on this southern flank of the synclinorium. A narrowing outcrop occurs between Dartmoor and the head of the Teign estuary; the main outcrop lies between Dartmoor and Bodmin Moor, making up a good deal of the surface over which the lower Tamar flows. Farther west beyond Bodmin Moor they are to be found again, reaching the coast between the Padstow estuary and Boscastle. Argillaceous grey-green, red, and purple rocks predominate, with shales very often metamorphosed into attractively coloured slates. A very well-known outcrop of these occurs at Delabole, where they have been quarried extensively for roofing slates since Elizabethan times at least. Nearby, metamorphism has continued beyond the slate stage and phyllites have been produced. One striking feature of the Upper Devonian is the appearance of igneous rocks at various horizons; these consist in the main of lavas associated with submarine volcanoes. The 258-foot cliff face at Pentire Point is a very fine example of spilitic lava showing pillow structure.

If minor folds and faults are ignored, the regional dip of the Devonian rocks so far considered is to the north, and in this way they pass underneath the Carboniferous strata which occupy the centre of the synclinorium. When the Devonian rocks emerge again from underneath this later cover on the northern side they are found to have essentially a dip to the south, but this is by no means the only change that has taken place. Three different kinds of thick red sandstones, lithologically quite unlike anything in the south, now come to the surface, while limestones are generally absent and indications of volcanic activity are virtually non-existent. These sandstones are of Old Red Sandstone facies and, as they are interstratified with shale and slate beds, the whole sequence probably represents the alternations of marine and continental deposition; the latter was more persistent farther north and gave rise to the Old Red Sandstone of adjacent South Wales. All the divisions of the Devonian occupy continuous tracts of country in north Devon, running southeastwards from the sea across Exmoor into Somerset. The lowest rocks exposed appear to be the Foreland Grits. They are reddish-brown and grey arenaceous beds forming the sole prominence in this otherwise straight coast at Foreland Point. The accumulation of these sandstones and grits must have occurred when the coastline lay to the south but a marine transgression followed, during which argillaceous materials were laid down to form what are now termed the Lynton Beds; these consist mainly of hard blue-grey slates and are of high Lower Devonian or low Middle Devonian age. A further continental phase is represented in the overlying Hangman Grits; in these the lower beds are fine-grained hard sandstones, giving way to more gritty rocks higher in the sequence. It has been suggested that the Hangman Grits are the Foreland Grits repeated by faulting. The Middle Devonian saw a return of the sea, as a result of which the Ilfracombe Beds were formed. These are mainly composed of slates but are interesting for the abundant fossil fauna found in the few occurrences of limestone. This fauna includes many corals and is clearly the northern analogue of the more widespread limestones already referred to in the south. Overlying these Ilfracombe Beds are the smooth and glossy Morte Slates of Upper Devonian age, and then a thin tuff-band occurs at the base of the Pickwell Down Sandstone. These red, purple, brown, and green sandstones outcrop from Pickwell Down in the west to Wiveliscombe, and represent another continental episode. After they accumulated the sea began to return for the last time in the Devonian of north Devon and stayed for a very long time. The succeeding strata tell a fascinating story of a deepening sea harmonizing with the marine transgression to the north over the Old Red Sandstone continent. Marine sandstones of green and yellow colour called the Baggy Beds were laid down first, followed by the bluish-grey slates of the Pilton Beds, both of which have marine fossils.

The Devonian strata in the north and south of the peninsula pass upwards by insensible gradations and quite conformably into the Carboniferous rocks which are here known as the Culm Measures. They have been christened thus because in a few localities they contain a soft, sooty coal to which the local word 'culm' has been assigned. Although this actual deposit is not widespread and the name is somewhat unrepresentative, these rocks require to be distinguished by name from the other Carboniferous deposits of Britain, since they show little resemblance to them. Nevertheless, they do form an important part of the Southwest peninsula, covering an area of about 1,200 square miles. The northern boundary of the Culm Measures is never very far away from the railway which linked

Barnstaple to Morebath. In the south, the junction running east from Boscastle is much less regular, being broken by thrusts and faults with inliers of Upper Devonian rocks and outliers of the Culm on the Devonian. In this way the Culm Measures occupy the middle of the synclinorium, towards the centre of which younger rocks successively outcrop. Lower Culm Measures are thus found adjacent to the Devonian rocks in two narrow zones both in the north and in the south. They were deposited in a deep trough, the bathymetry and sediment supply of which must have been complex, since dark shales, with slates locally, occur as well as limestones, lavas, and cherts. The Upper Culm Measures outcrop over a very much larger area and consist principally of dark grey shales interbedded with bands of sandstones and grits. The last decade has witnessed the beginning of a systematic survey of these Carboniferous deposits; though much of this work remains unpublished, a recent view is that these deposits accumulated in a geosyncline which received materials from a land mass to the north and turbidities from the south and west.

Of as much importance as the Hercynian folding and faulting which brought into being the synclinorium in Southwest England was the emplacement of large masses of granite. Subsequent events have led to the unroofing of parts of these igneous emplacements so that the granite is now exposed on the surface over a considerable area. A very significant portion of Devon is occupied by the Dartmoor granite; across the county boundary granite again comes to the surface to form Hingston Down and Kit Hill, and then after a short break appears again to form the very much larger granite mass of Bodmin Moor. Farther west, in the neighbourhood of St Austell, is the Hensbarrow, with the two detached small bosses of Castle an Dinas and Belowda on its north side. Near the west coast is a small section of granite cliff at Cligga Head and a quarter of a mile inland in the same area is the upstanding landmark of St Agnes Beacon. These are very small exposures when compared with the Carnmenellis farther south, which also has two detached portions—Carn Brea and Carn Marth. Not far distant to the south is another exposure which builds Godolphin Hill, Tregonning Hill, and reaches the coast at Trewavas Head. St Michael's Mount is an island, for the most part made of granite, from which is clearly visible the Penwith granite country of the Land's End peninsula. It is not known how far this igneous province extends out to sea but at 18 miles is Seven Stones and at 28 miles are the Isles of Scilly, both made of granite.

Surrounding each granite outcrop are the sedimentary rocks which have been in close contact with the heat and migrating fluids emanating from the molten magma and as a result have been altered to form metamorphic aureoles. Combined in this way, the granite masses with their aureoles make a very significant contribution to the landscape of Cornwall and Devon but their significance does not end there. Recent gravity surveys have discovered a belt of large negative anomalies following the line of the granite outcrops. The most satisfactory interpretation of these anomalies is that a continuous batholith exists from the Isles of Scilly to Dartmoor and that the exposed granite bosses are cupolas on it. The idea that an underground connection existed is not new, but it is satisfying to find that evidence from a new technique comes along to support an old hypothesis. Furthermore, the size of the anomalies is of such an order as to suggest a granite thickness of 6 to 12 miles. The mechanism which probably brought the granite into being was emplacement with forcible intrusion and stoping, the magma emerging from a southerly source and flowing nearly horizontally to the north, stoping and assimilating its way forward. This emplacement is usually considered to have taken place in a series of waves rather late in the Hercynian orogeny and to have inherited something of the lineaments of the invaded sedimentary rocks. At a late stage groups of dykes and lodes were emplaced; since some contain minerals of economic value and as many of these have been worked, a considerable amount is known about them. If, therefore, a relationship between the granite and the structures of the invaded rocks is a possibility, an interesting extension of this idea is to investigate whether the lodes and dykes are also in some way related, for, if they are, then their distribution pattern may indicate the nature and orientation of some of the deeper structures of the region. One interesting recent view is that the lodes and dykes are, for the most part, oriented approximately parallel to the long axes of the granite ridges and that these in turn were formed in the 'moulds' provided by the invaded sedimentary rocks. In general, from St Austell to Dartmoor the orientation of the lodes is west to east, conforming with the general Armoricanoid strike of the synclinorium.

The previous paragraph contained a suggested rough date for the occurrence of the granite emplacement. Owing to advances made within the last ten years, much closer dating is now possible, as fortunately many of the rocks have their own built-in radioactive time-keepers. The age of certain rock-forming minerals may be determined by finding in them the proportions of a certain isotope known to be derived from another isotope by radioactive change at a known half-life rate. Such parent and daughter isotopes occur particularly in metamorphic and igneous rocks. The application of this so-called 'isotopic geochronometry' to the granites of Devon and Cornwall gives an age for their emplacements of about 280 million years. Since the geological relationships of the granites in Southwest England are narrowly bracketed within the stratigraphical sequence, this isotopic age—besides dating the intrusion—also defines the boundary in time between the Carboniferous and Permian periods as about 280 million years ago.

This exciting new work may be used to preface what is probably the most difficult and controversial problem of Cornish geology. South of a line running west from St Austell Bay is a series of sediments and structures which is difficult to date and to interpret. The first rocks encountered are the so-called Grampound Beds, which most observers place in the Lower Devonian although there is much difference of opinion as to where in the succession they belong. They have recently been combined with comparable rocks to the south under the name of Gramscatho Beds. These include the Veryan, Portscatho, Falmouth, and Mylor series. Different ages have been suggested for these, but it is unlikely that they are older than Devonian. As to the interpretation of their structures, a hint may well be given by the lode-dyke pattern in plan. It has already been noted that to the north of the latitude of St Austell the orientation of the lodes is clearly east–west, which is also the strike of the synclinorium. To the southwest of St Austell and particularly within the Mylor series, the pattern of the lodes is clearly northeast to southwest, and so, it will be noted, is the general alignment of this part of the peninsula. To the south is a zone in which the strata have been reduced to the condition of a breccia; this, the Meneage Crush Zone, occupies an intermediary position between the sedimentary rocks to the north and the Lizard complex to the south; this consists of schists and gneisses, with plutonic intrusions such as serpentine and gabbro, and numerous basic dykes. The Lizard is not the only metamorphic area to occur on the southern edge of the peninsula. Around Veryan Bay detached masses of gabbro and serpentine, closely resembling the rocks of the Lizard, occur as enormous lenticles in a belt of crush breccia. Farther east, between Bolt Tail and Start Point in south Devon, green schists, mica, and quartz schists outcrop adjacent to the Lower Devonian slates, the junction appearing to be a series of faults. If now these three metamorphic areas are joined up, they tend to align themselves into an interesting arcuate form with a distinctly northeast to southwest trend in the west and an equally persistent east to west trend in the east, as the arc passes south of Plymouth to Bolt Head and Prawle Point. The theory that a connection between these three metamorphic areas exists has found much support in recent years, and the literature now contains frequent references to the Lizard–Dodman–Start Thrust. Fortunately the results of modern gravity, magnetic, and seismic surveys have been found to be consistent with such a concept. It must not go unnoticed that the directions taken up by this supposed thrust-plane are approximately parallel to the pattern of lode-dyke streams and also to the southern edge of the granite batholith.

It would then appear that the major geological events of the region are very closely linked, and the dating of the metamorphism of the rocks in these three areas is a matter of considerable interest. Recent evidence suggests that the metamorphism is of Upper Devonian age, and the rocks must therefore antedate this time. It may be perplexing to find that the two major directions taken by the structures of the peninsula are caledonoid and armoricanoid. In this respect they do not appear to be singular.

'Caledonian and Hercynian movements may be distinguished (but with a merging continuity) by differences in age; but in directional terms caledonoid and armoricanoid trends are equally characteristic of both, and most major Hercynian structures of northwest Europe, including the Armorican arc, have Caledonian cores . . . The Armorican arc was already established in early Devonian times, and it has elements of built-in structure that are long pre-Devonian: in that sense its growth in Devon and Cornwall was Caledonian as much as Hercynian.'[1]

The rocks and structures this far detailed may be regarded as making up the 'Old Land' of the Southwest peninsula. The earth-movements which produced it brought about a complete change in the physique and were accompanied by a change in the climate. The area became a desert hot and arid except for the occasional heavy rains which caused violent torrents to sweep down the steep intermontane valleys into lacustrine areas of deposition. Such aridity, relieved only at infrequent intervals, prevailed throughout two geological periods, the Permian and the Trias. As a result, the rocks of the 'Old Land' were shattered and broken down into sharp angular fragments and sand. These angular rock-fragments would at first accumulate as mountainside screes, but some would be swept on to lower ground by the torrents and, depending on the distance travelled, the material would become angular or rounded, coarse or fine. In Devon from west to east the deposits grade from breccias to breccia-conglomerates to sands and marly sands. They are diachronous but indicate, nevertheless, the general direction of movement, as clearly the larger fragments travelled least and are nearer to their parent rocks, whereas the sand and mud would be carried farther east. In the lower horizons true bedding is difficult to determine; the breccias are single lenses, often representing the residue from a single flood, and the sandstones show large-scale cross-bedding. Whilst the breccias are essentially fluviatile in origin, many of the sandstones, particularly those near Dawlish, are aeolian and represent barchan dune accumulations. These dunes indicate that the wind at the time of their formation was from a northeast direction. The rains, it must be remembered, were but a sporadic interruption in the aeolian scene, the wind and the grilling sun being the constants of the desert landscape.

In Devon most of the Permian rocks are deeply stained by red oxide of iron, a colour which gives much charm to the coast from Paignton to Torquay and again from Babbacombe to a little west of Budleigh Salterton. Inland, the Permian outcrop extends from the Haldons to the foot of the Woodbury Common ridge. The surface of the 'Old Land' on which these deposits accumulated was highly irregular as can be seen by the way in which the red rocks extend at present some 21 miles westwards in a long

[1] George, T. N. 'Devonian and Carboniferous Foundations of the Variscides in North-West Europe' in *Some Aspects of the Variscan Fold Belt* ed. K. Coe (Manchester 1962), 19–49

tongue up the Creedy valley away from the main outcrop aligned north to south. Gravity anomalies suggest that this is a V-shaped trough with a maximum depth of about 1,116 feet. Farther north, a shorter tongue extends west from Uffculme to Loxbeare and a number of outliers between Holcombe Rogus and Stoodleigh are aligned east to west, suggesting the former presence of a third tongue. Where dips are procurable, the dominant inclination is southeasterly off the 'Old Land' and in profound uncon-formity to it. The fragments which collected to form the Permian rocks were clearly derived from the adjacent strata of the 'Old Land'. Thus in south Devon, fragments from the Devonian are abundant, but moving north these diminish, their place being taken by Culm Measures débris and pieces broken off the lofty eminence of the Dartmoor of that day, when no granite was yet exposed. Farther north still, broken and slightly water-worn Old Red Sandstone rocks and shallow-water marine facies, mixed with pieces of Culm grit, go to make up the débris—exactly what the denudation of the then much more formidable Exmoor ridges and Quantocks would be expected to produce. These lithologies do not exhaust the variety of the breccia fragments, as volcanic débris in plenty occurs, particularly around Exeter where as many as fifty-three lava outcrops have been mapped. The stratigraphical position of these lavas indicates that they are a series of Permian extrusives, contemporaneous with the deposition of the red rocks. The history of this very long period—about 45 million years —is one which tells of the destruction of the Armorican mountain chains and their burial in part under the lavas, breccias, and sands of the Permian pediments. The very heart of the city of Exeter may be regarded as a memorial to those far-off days; the warm, red, rough breccias were used to build its churches in the Middle Ages, and the lava hill of Rougemont, the highest point, was made grander with its own stone by medieval castellation and Roman wall.

In the English Midlands, where rocks of the same kind are widespread, it is possible to separate the Permian, which is taken as the last period of the Palaeozoic, from the Trias, which forms the first group of the Mesozoic era. In Devon there is no clear line of division but it is customary to assume quite arbitrarily that the base of the great pebble-bed forming the ridge of Woodbury Common is the first of the Triassic rocks. In other words, Devon persisted as an area of practically continuous sedimentation into and through Triassic times. The Budleigh Salterton Pebble Beds represent what must have been a pluvial period in the otherwise semi-arid continental environment and are best regarded as the débris laid down by a large river —or even rivers—fed by heavy, if seasonal, rainfall on distant mountains, and emptying into a cuvette. The pebbles have survived in an outcrop 70 or 80 feet thick which extends from just west of Budleigh Salterton on the south coast to Watchet on the present Bristol Channel coast in Somerset. From the nature and mineral constitution of the Pebble Beds it is possible to suggest the most likely directions from which they came. In the south the pebbles are composed of lilac-tinted hard quartzite, which cannot be matched in Devon nor anywhere on the English side of the Channel. The Ordovician fauna of the Calvados district is most nearly related to that of our Pebble Beds, and the probability is that they were brought by a large river flowing north from Brittany, or at least from some ridge of the old Armorican range which formerly occupied the present site of the English Channel. To the north in Somerset, between Exmoor and the Quantocks, the pebbles are well rounded, indicating that they have travelled far, and are made of Carboniferous Limestone; this suggests the Bristol Channel and South Wales as the areas from which they were derived. Between the two lies the district around Burlescombe, where the pebbles have a western provenance. A study of the heavy minerals occurring in the sandy matrix confirms this threefold source of the materials whereby the two main currents from the south and the north were joined near Uffculme by a minor current from the west.

From the end of the time during which the Pebble Beds were laid down to the close of the Trias there was a gradual amelioration of the climate, and it appears that the planation of the ancient Armorican continent was becoming more complete, partly by erosion lowering the heights and partly by the filling of the depressions with sediments. With no great changes in level such an area could readily become inundated. East from the Woodbury Common ridge, as far as the Triassic beds can be traced, local evaporites give plenty of evidence for saline lakes which periodically evaporated to dryness; many of the associated sandstones clearly accumulated under a cover of water. Immediately overlying the Pebble Beds are fine-grained Keuper sands and soft sandstones, often false bedded, and these are exposed in a series of impressive river cliffs cut by the river Otter. The total thickness of this deposit may well exceed 400 feet, as, in a boring to obtain a water supply at Dotton Lane, Colaton Raleigh, 338 feet of the strata were pierced before the Pebble Beds were reached. Conformably on top of the sandstones are the Keuper Marls; these form the most persistent division of the New Red rocks and extend over a very large area of east Devon, with a proved thickness of over 1,130 feet. The marls, which most probably represent a wind-blown dust, first outcrop on the upper eastern valley sides in the lower reach of the Otter river; farther upstream they occur on both sides of the valley. Except for the interfluves, the marls outcrop over a very extensive part of the dissected plateau of east Devon; most of the drainage basin of the Sid and the more extensive catchment of the Axe are excavated in them. A group of grey and green marls ends the deposits of the New Red Sandstone. The succeeding Rhaetic Beds give clear evidence that an extensive marine transgression followed. It is only in the extreme east of the county that sediments from this inundation can now be seen, forming the Rhaetic Beds. These form passage beds and reflect, both in their lithologies and fauna, the relatively unstable conditions which followed the initial transgression. By the close of the period, fully marine conditions had been established, the nearest shoreline being recorded around the Mendips, which stood up as an island. The Lower and Middle Lias are now barely represented in Devon but where they are the deposits indicate a fairly deep sea teeming with life.

No further Jurassic deposits are recorded in Devon, these having been removed by erosion during a period of uplift in early Cretaceous times. Following this planation, a widespread subsidence set in once more, accompanied by a steady return of the sea from the east, so that Cretaceous horizons overstep one another towards the west. The lowest member of this series is the Gault, which can be seen in section along the coast from Lyme Regis to Culverhole and inland at the eastern end of the Honiton railway tunnel. A line joining this exposure to Culverhole would appear to mark the most westerly extension of the Gault. To the west the overlying Greensand is in part the time-equivalent of the Gault; it overlaps the Gault and oversteps from the Lias on to the lower part of the New Red Sandstone on the Haldon Hills to the west of the lower Exe. This overmantling of successively older horizons is referred to as the 'Cretaceous overstep'. The overlying Chalk was deposited in water considerably deeper than that of the Greensand, so that the Chalk sea must have spread over a wider area. There is no evidence as to the position of the shorelines in the Greensand and Chalk transgressions, except that it lay to the west of the Haldons, where a thick capping of coarse partially-rolled gravel containing masses of flint, often of large size, is preserved. Considerable interest has been aroused by the deposit of Tertiary gravels at Orleigh Court, 3 miles a little west of south from Bideford, since their discovery in 1808. Here, resting unconformably on steeply dipping Upper Culm Measures, at no less than 400 feet O.D., are both chert and flint gravels. It is certain that some rounding has occurred to these gravels but not enough to suggest that any of the material has travelled far, and this points to the near presence of both Greensand and Chalk. One wonders, therefore, how much, if any, of the Southwestern peninsula remained unsubmerged as islands during the Upper Cretaceous period. If the cover was as extensive as is suggested by this westerly placed deposit, then much indeed has since been removed, as today only the outlier on the Haldon Hills of Greensand and flint gravel, separated from the main outcrop of the Greensand which underlies the so-called clay-with-flints and cherts on the east Devon plateau, is left. In east Devon the term 'dissected plateau' is no misnomer, as the Greensand interfluves make an attractive pattern of spurs and ridges above the Keuper Marl valleys. The extent of removal of the Chalk is even greater than that of the Greensand. In the southeast near the coast all that remains are two small exposures between Lyme Regis and Axmouth and farther west a little Chalk outcrops between Seaton Hole and Branscombe Mouth. It was from the quarries near Beer in the latter outcrop that the stone was obtained for building purposes. In Norman and later times it was used in Exeter Cathedral, while Ottery St Mary, Honiton, and Axminster churches are also built of it. Inland, a small exposure of Chalk again occurs in the faulted tract near Widworthy and a little more to the northeast near Membury and Chardstock.

The point is now being reached in the story of the evolution of our peninsula when the emphasis must begin to move from the realm of geology to that of geomorphology. A suitable transition from the one to the other may be made by some further consideration of the flint and chert gravels, the nature and distribution of which suggest the kind of Britain which now finally emerged from beneath the waves of the Chalk sea. The Tertiary era begins with a widespread upheaval; this restored an eastward sloping country enjoying a warm moist climate, which allowed a dense cover of vegetation to thrive. Erosion and weathering of such a landscape would dissolve the Chalk underground, leaving the insoluble flints comparatively little changed and generally little moved on the flat-topped hills where they have survived. In places this coarse gravel is 30 to 40 feet thick, and if the assumption that it represents the insoluble decalcified residue of the Chalk is correct, then it must have been derived from a very sizable thickness of Chalk. A clue that this was so is given by the fossil record revealed in the gravels. Silicified fossils within the flints reveal that all the zones of Chalk which are present at Beer formerly covered the Haldons also, and point to the enveloping Chalk being eroded, mainly by solution, in a warm-climate cycle of erosion during early Tertiary times.

A short distance southwest of these gravels on the Great and Little Haldon is a low-lying basin some 10 miles long, extending from a little north of Bovey Tracey southeastwards to Kingskerswell. In its widest part the basin is 4 miles and contains lignites and clays which have been known for some considerable time and which have been worked for fuel and for ball clays. The most recent information from both geophysical and bore-hole investigation seems to indicate that the total thickness of the Bovey Beds is of the order of 3,000 feet; this places the bottom of the basin well below present sea-level. Such thicknesses suggest that the deposits accumulated in a very deep rock basin, possibly formed through rift faulting. Since the basin had no outlet, it must have formed a large lake into which rivers flowing from the granite must have drained and formed, where they entered the lake, deltas of granitic sand, and mud. The finer clay remained in suspension longest, to be finally deposited in the southern part of the lake, where it has formed the thick beds of pottery clays so highly prized today. From an examination of the plant-remains in the lignite, it is fairly certain that the Bovey Lake was being filled in during late Oligocene times —a suitable point in the geological time-scale for us to pause before describing the 'epilogue' which moulded the landscape we know today.

CHAPTER 3

The Form of the Ground

THE rapid lateral change of rock type accounts for much of the variation of the physical landscape within Southwest England. Contrasts in rock resistance are in part responsible for the altitudinal variation of the peninsula so that, basically, Southwest England is dominated by uplands such as Exmoor and Dartmoor, underlain by the most resistant rocks, while intervening areas of lower altitude are underlain by less resistant shales, sandstones, and limestones as, for example, in the Culm Measures area of central Devon. In addition to their effect upon general elevation and angle of slope the various rock types are also expressed in the landscape in the nature of the building materials. The granite areas thus contrast vividly with areas of New Red Sandstone and parts of the Culm Measures outcrop where cob is extensively used for building purposes. Rock type is further expressed in the soil colour so that 'Red Devon' contrasts with outcrops of granite, of limestones including Chalk in the southeast, and of Palaeozoic slates, shales, and grits. The peninsula is punctuated by six locally conspicuous uplands which decline in absolute height westwards. Exmoor (Dunkery Beacon, 1,705 feet O.D.) is underlain by Devonian rocks while the other five, founded upon granite, are Dartmoor (High Willhays, 2,038 feet), Bodmin Moor (Brown Willy, 1,375 feet), St Austell Moor (Hensbarrow, 1,027 feet), Carnmenellis (825 feet), and the Land's End area (White Downs, 826 feet). The granite of the Isles of Scilly might be added as a seventh element, rising to 166 feet O.D. on St Mary's.

However, despite this variation in general elevation controlled by lithology, a leading characteristic of Southwest England, as of many other parts of Britain, is that over large areas there is a marked uniformity of summit heights. As early as 1822 it was considered that 'The general character of a great proportion of the County [Devon] is a continued succession of hills of the same, or nearly the same, height'.[1] This impression of uniform summit height is presented by three types of area. Much of Cornwall and the fringes of Devon are composed basically of low coastal plateaux. Although these plateaux are often bounded by steep cliffs at

[1] Lysons, D. and Lysons, S. *Magna Britannia. Volume 6. Devonshire* (London 1822), 252

the coast, and in some cases they have been extensively dissected as, for example, round Torbay, the dominant impression from many viewpoints is one of comparatively level summit surfaces. These coastal plateaux usually range between 200 and 450 feet O.D. in height as in the case of the Lizard, the lower Tamar valley area, and the South Hams. Above this level a second element is represented by plateaux usually developed between 700 and 1,000 feet O.D. and extending over the granite outcrops of Cornwall, the fringes of Dartmoor and Exmoor, parts of central Devon, and the east Devon plateau. A third series of levels occurs on Bodmin Moor, Dartmoor, and Exmoor, and typically extends between 1,000 and 1,300–1,400 feet O.D. (Plate 36).

Despite the first impression of uniformity of summit heights closer inspection shows dissection to be considerable. The typical valley cross-profile of Southwest England is in the shape of an infilled V which varies in character according to the underlying rock type. On the margins of the uplands of Dartmoor, Exmoor, and Bodmin Moor the valleys are often very steep-sided and, on the metamorphic aureoles surrounding the granite outcrops, many of the rivers flow through deep gorges. Equally well-defined valleys dissect the coastal plateaux, and in *Westward Ho!* Charles Kingsley described 'those delightful glens which cut the high tableland of the confines of Devon and Cornwall, opening each through its confines of down and rock, towards the boundless ocean. Each is like the other, and each is like no other English scenery. Each has its upright walls, inland of rich oakwood, nearer the sea of dark green furze, then of smooth turf, then of weird black cliffs, which range out right and left into the deep sea, in castles, spires and wings of jagged iron-stone'.[1]

These deep, steep-sided valleys have profoundly influenced the alignment of routes, they have been an important factor in producing local contrasts in land use, and in some cases they have affected the legacy left by extractive industry as in west Cornwall near St Just and near Lamorna (Plate 53). Although dissection is not so impressive on the softer rock outcrops it is at least as extensive, and in addition to the major flat-floored valleys like the Exe or the Creedy, there are numerous broad and often steep-sided tributary valleys. Eden Phillpotts wrote 'Some of our coombes open gradually, through pastures and orchards from the hills to the plains; some break out in steep gullies and enclosures of limestone or sandstone to the sea; some are concavities where Nature hollows her hand to hold man's homestead'.[2]

The finer detail of the relief of Southwest England is often man-made, as is shown by the many narrow lanes which occur in Cornwall and Devon at levels below the surrounding fields or confined by high hedgebanks. In 'Red Devon' the 'sunken lanes' were gouged out partly by erosion as

[1] Kingsley C. *Westward Ho!* (London 1878), 99
[2] Phillpotts, Eden *My Devon Year* (London 1916), 179

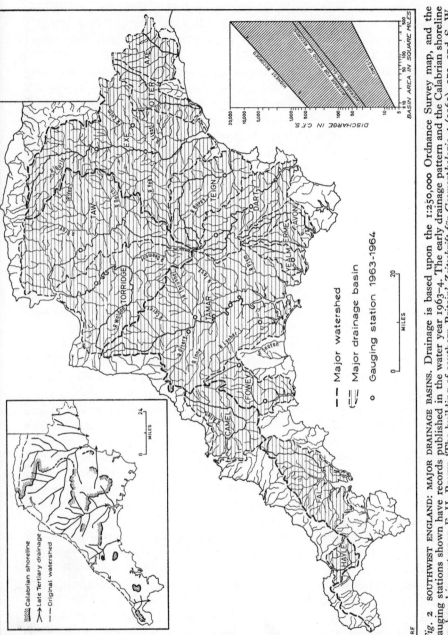

Fig. 2 SOUTHWEST ENGLAND: MAJOR DRAINAGE BASINS. Drainage is based upon the 1:250,000 Ordnance Survey map, and the gauging stations shown have records published in the water year 1963–4. The early drainage pattern and the Calabrian shoreline are based in part upon E. H. Brown 'The building of southern Britain' *Zeitschrift für Geomorphologie* **4** (1960), 272, and S. W. Wooldridge 'The physique of the South West' *Geography* **39** (1954), 232, and "The Radstock Plateau—a note on the physiography of the Bristol district' *Proc. Bristol Naturalists' Soc.* **30** (1961), 156.

'deep grooves left between the cultivated fields for nature to frolic in',[1] whereas on the granite areas the road and field boundaries were often constructed of clitter, originally strewn liberally over the land. These bounding foundations of stone were covered by soil, and trees have often established themselves upon this base.

The general pattern of dissection is based upon major valleys which are drained south, southsoutheast, or southeast. The drainage basins of the Exe and Tamar extend to within a few miles of the north coast of the peninsula and the south or southeast trend of their trunk streams is imitated by parts of the Teign, Erme, Avon, Fal, Lynher, and Fowey (Fig. 2). Basins drained to the north coast also have their dominant trend from southeast to northwest, but some of them such as the Torridge, Camel, and Hayle include anomalous portions which at first drain south or southeast. This dominant trend of the valley pattern imposes a general grain of relief across the peninsula at right-angles to the predominant movement of traffic. There are many instances of this grain decelerating road traffic to and from Southwest England such as west of the Exe valley (A30, A380) and again at the crossing of the Tamar valley at Gunnislake (A390).

The final physical theme apparent in Southwest England depends upon its peninsular nature. In addition to the drowned valleys or rias (Plate 39) the coastline is diversified by the great number of small bays and coves and therefore the ratio of length of coastline (at least 510 miles) to land area (3,937 square miles, Devon and Cornwall) is greater than in many other parts of Britain. The lower parts of valleys drowned by the postglacial Flandrian rise of sea-level have given special problems to communications and have necessitated the provision of numerous ferries and bridges (Fig. 3). Before 1859, when the rail bridge was built by Brunel, the Tamar ria separated the railway networks of Devon and Cornwall, and Plymouth and Saltash were not linked directly by a road bridge until 1961. Expansion of such settlements as Dartmouth, originally sited with respect to the advantages of a ria, has been made difficult by the interposition of an estuary between two steep valleysides (Plate 18). The mouths of many rias have been partly blocked by sand or shingle bars as in the cases of the Exe, Teign, Taw-Torridge, and Otter estuaries, while in other instances the valley has been completely sealed by a bar as at the Loe Pool in Cornwall, and at Slapton in Devon.

These general themes which are apparent in the physical landscape of Southwest England are expressed very vividly in the coastal areas. Variations in rock type are responsible for contrasts in colour, in cliff form, and in the configuration of the coast. Here and there, as in the Devonian rocks of the Padstow area, jointing has influenced the detail of the coastal

[1] White, Walter *A Londoner's walk to the Land's End; and a trip to the Scilly Isles* (London 1855), 89

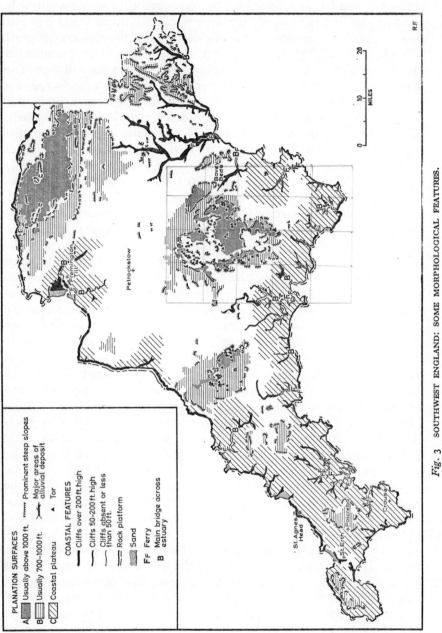

Fig. 3   SOUTHWEST ENGLAND: SOME MORPHOLOGICAL FEATURES.

PLANATION SURFACES

A ▨ Usually above 1000 ft.   ⌐⌐⌐ Prominent steep slopes
B ▩ Usually 700–1000 ft.   ⋏ Major areas of alluvial deposit
C ▨ Coastal plateau   ▲ Tor

COASTAL FEATURES

▬▬ Cliffs over 200 ft. high
─── Cliffs 50–200 ft. high
─── Cliffs absent or less than 50 ft.
═══ Rock platform
▨ Sand
F F Ferry
B   Main bridge across estuary

morphology. Several of the groups of plateaux are truncated by the coast
(Plate 25), and this is reflected in the very sharp cliffs which are usually
200 feet high but occasionally higher, and reach a maximum of 731 feet
o.d. at High Cliff, northwest of Boscastle. Some of the character of coast
and inland areas is shown in Figure 3. One traveller in 1855 contrasted
Devon and Cornwall and commented on arriving in Cornwall that 'The
generally soft features of Devonshire are exchanged for a landscape of a
stern and unfinished aspect. Trees are few and you see a prominent
characteristic of Cornwall—a surface heaved into long rolling swells,
brown and bare, not unlike what we should fancy of waves from the
adjoining ocean, solidified, cut up into squares by thick stone fences
which in many places are covered with brilliant yellow stone crop growing
from the crevices'.[1] Several other authorities have recognized subdivisions
in the Southwest, and some of these are shown in Figure 4.

These general characteristics of the physique of Southwest England
directed early explanations of the evolution of the physical scene. The
uniformity of summit heights impressed many early writers, and the
coastal platform developed extensively throughout Cornwall and Devon
was recorded by members of the Geological Survey working before and
after the turn of the present century. In 1896 Clement Reid described the
430-foot coastal platform in Cornwall and dated it, by reference to the
St Erth Beds, as of early Pliocene age. Earlier references to platforms also
occur, and in 1864 W. Pengelly referred to the plateaux of the Torquay
district as 'terraces of denudation' and interpreted them as the result of
marine erosion. The anomalous drainage pattern, dominated by a watershed
adjacent to the north coast, was also the subject of early speculation and
prompted general reconstructions such as that for Devon as a whole by
Clayden (1906) and in detail for particular rivers such as that by Jukes
Brown (1904) for the river Teign. Jukes Brown suggested that the early
Tertiary drainage pattern was predominantly composed of east-flowing
trunk streams, but that the mid-Tertiary movements subsequently
imparted a southerly tilt which stimulated in late Tertiary times the
development of a drainage pattern dominated by south-flowing streams.
This outline sequence of drainage development has been adopted and
elaborated by more recent workers.

The advent of periglacial studies, long before they were known as such,
was heralded by numerous accounts of the details of superficial deposits
occurring throughout the peninsula. The anomalous deposit of 'clay and
rubble' overlying a raised beach at Porth Nanven near St Just was described
by Borlase in 1758 and the quarryman's term *Head* was first used for this
type of deposit by De la Beche in 1839. He noted that 'A head of angular
fragments is common to all the raised beaches of the coast of the district

---

[1] White, Walter *A Londoner's walk to the Land's End; and a trip to the Scilly Isles*
(London 1855), 167

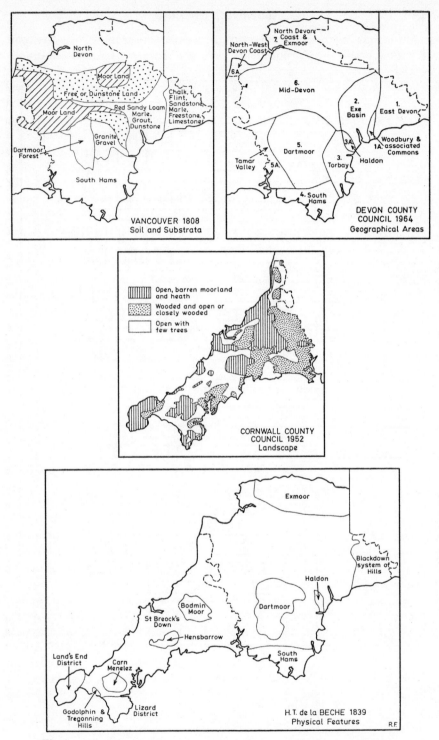

Fig. 4 SOUTHWEST ENGLAND: SOME REACTIONS TO VARIETY OF LANDSCAPE.
S.E.—2*

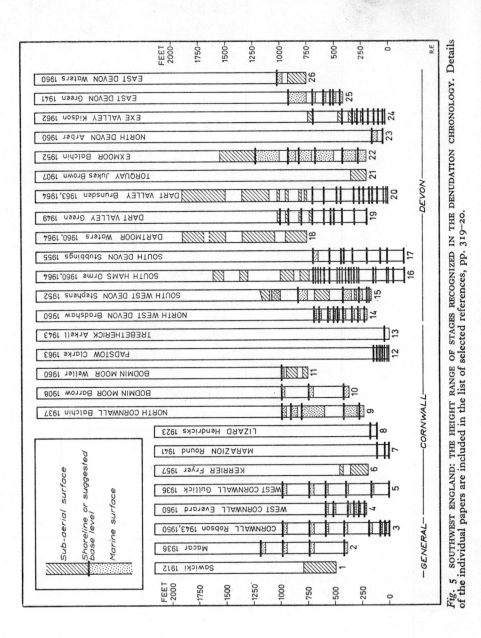

Fig. 5 SOUTHWEST ENGLAND: THE HEIGHT RANGE OF STAGES RECOGNIZED IN THE DENUDATION CHRONOLOGY. Details of the individual papers are included in the list of selected references, pp. 319–20.

[Cornwall and Devon], when hills of hard rocks rise behind them, showing not only that a considerable decomposition of such rocks has taken place since the beaches were elevated above the sea, but also that there has been a great movement of the decomposed surface of the hills downward, covering up all the inequalities that presented themselves and rendering the surface more smooth than would otherwise happen. . .'. Godwin-Austen (1842), in his description of southeast Devon, observed that such head deposits were not restricted to the valleys but 'invest many of the slopes and crown many of the minor ridges'. He recognized that they developed as a result of 'agents' operating for a long period in this district. In many cases the head was first described in association with the raised beaches on the coast, and valuable detailed accounts figure prominently in the Transactions of local societies such as the Devonshire Association and the Royal Geological Society of Cornwall. By 1828 twenty-one occurrences of raised beaches had been recorded along the twenty miles of coast between Pendeen Cove and Mousehole in west Cornwall. The head deposits and related features in Southwest England have occasionally been ascribed to glaciation as on Dartmoor, where they were taken to indicate former glacial action, but it is now generally agreed that they collectively reflect the legacy of phases of 'periglacial' conditions during the Pleistocene. However, some early descriptions of 'glacial action', such as those by Whitley (1882) for west Cornwall, have been substantiated in more recent research, which in this case has suggested that Pleistocene ice sheets impinged upon the north coast of the peninsula, particularly in north Devon and west Cornwall.

Contemporary explanation of the evolution of the relief of Devon and Cornwall is hindered by the lack of any available complete geomorphic study and also by the nature of the physique of the peninsula as correlation from one upland area to the next is necessarily difficult. In view of the amount of attention devoted to denudation chronology, the age and origin of the planation surfaces will be considered first, the views on the development of the drainage pattern will then be summarized, and subsequently the modifications imposed by the Quaternary will be reviewed.

The surfaces of low relief so striking in many of the landscapes of Southwest England have prompted many workers to examine particular areas in detail. However, the general lack of any widespread agreement concerning the number and height range of remnants of planation surfaces in Southwest England as a whole is indicated by the results from particular areas shown in Figure 5. An attempt to present the overall pattern of summit relief is shown by generalized contours in Figure 6, and this illustrates some of the general conclusions of research workers who have been concerned with specific parts of the peninsula. These generalized contours indicate the existence of a summit surface on Exmoor sloping southeast from 1,600 to 1,300 feet, on Dartmoor sloping from 1,600–

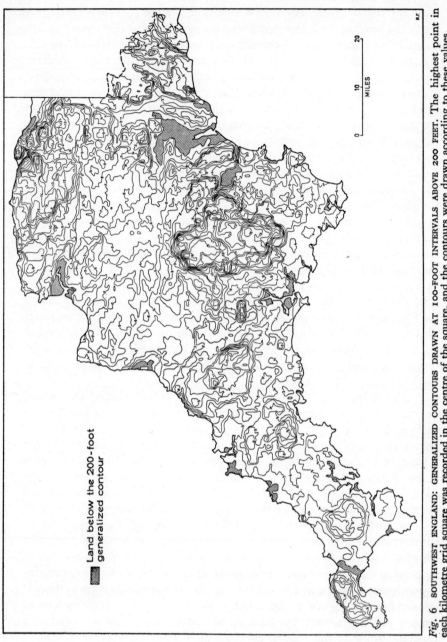

Fig. 6 SOUTHWEST ENGLAND: GENERALIZED CONTOURS DRAWN AT 100-FOOT INTERVALS ABOVE 200 FEET. The highest point in each kilometre grid square was recorded in the centre of the square, and the contours were drawn according to these values.

Land below the 200-foot generalized contour

2,000 feet in the north to 1,500–1,700 feet in the south, in east Devon from
1,000 feet in the north near Staple Hill to approximately 600 feet near the
coast, and southeastwards across Bodmin Moor from 1,370 to 1,200. On
several of these upland areas a second surface of low relief is apparent,
developed across several distinct rock types. This second element occurs
between approximately 1,150 and 1,500 feet on Exmoor, between 1,000
and 1,400 on Dartmoor, and between 950 and 1,100 feet on Bodmin Moor.
A further and more extensively developed group of uniform summit
heights extends across many representatives of the diverse rock types of
Southwest England and occurs between 600 and 1,000 feet on Exmoor
and its margins, between 500 and 750 feet in northwest Devon, and 700 to
1,000 feet in east Devon, whence it continues on Haldon west of the Exe
at 700–900 feet and to the fringes of Dartmoor between 700 and 1,000 feet.
Farther west the same general level is represented on Bodmin Moor
between 800 and 1,000 feet, on Kit Hill between 800 and 900 feet, on
St Austell Moor between 800 and 1,000 feet, on Carnmenellis between
580 and 800 feet, and on the Land's End area between 650 and 800 feet O.D.
The coastal plateau, equally evident in Figure 6, varies substantially in
general height range. In the South Hams it ranges from 400 to 650 feet
east of the river Avon but to the west of that river it occurs between 300
and 450 feet. South of Bodmin Moor it is represented by summits between
380 and 650 feet, between 280 and 400 feet in the Dodman area, between
300 and 500 feet around the lower Fal, between 240 and 370 feet on the
Lizard, and between 300 and 450 feet O.D. on the Land's End peninsula.
The summits of central Devon, between Exmoor and Dartmoor, generally
attain heights in the range 300 to 600 feet. The general characteristics of
the summit relief are illustrated by the watershed profile drawn from
Exmoor southwards across the peninsula over Dartmoor to the South
Hams (Fig. 7), and the generalized distribution of the two high surfaces
and the coastal plateau is indicated in Figure 3.

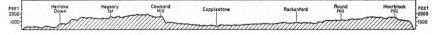

Fig. 7   THE WATERSHED PROFILE FROM EXMOOR TO THE SOUTH HAMS.

The age and origin of these striking remnants of former surfaces of
low relief, largely developed independently of structure, has occasioned
much discussion. Primarily the debate has centred around an explanation
as either subaerial peneplains or as marine surfaces for the origin of those
above 700 feet O.D. (Fig. 5). More recently a third suggestion has been
advanced interpreting some of the surfaces as subaerial pediments or
subtropical surfaces. At lower altitudes many workers have found difficulty
in ascribing the very extensive coastal plateau entirely to erosion during
Pleistocene times. Professor Wooldridge in 1954 and Professor Balchin ten

years later, although not supporting the supposition that the landforms of Southwest England were exhumed intact from beneath a Permo-Triassic cover, contended that the boundaries of Exmoor and Dartmoor may correspond approximately to the sub-New Red Sandstone surface and that the coasts of the peninsula retain in their main features legacies of sub-Triassic physique. The extensive surface developed on the Lizard peninsula has been interpreted as a Triassic pediplain, and Orme (1964) has indicated that erosion and pedimentation during New Red Sandstone times may have been responsible for the outlines of southern Devon and the English Channel margins, thus influencing the Quaternary evolution of the Kingsbridge corridor and the coastal zone particularly around Bigbury Bay. Specific instances of exhumed surfaces in the lower Tamar valley have been suggested. Professor Linton has deduced that the highest point of Dartmoor (High Willhays, 2,038 feet) may approximately represent the basal plane of Upper Cretaceous rocks projected westwards from east Devon, and, in the case of Exmoor, Professor Balchin has concluded that the surface indicated by the present summits marks the level of the former sub-Cretaceous peneplain.

On Dartmoor gently undulating, tor-free summit plains with a relief of the order of one to two hundred feet have been identified between 1,700 and 1,900 feet O.D. north of the Dart basin and between 1,500 and 1,650 feet O.D. to the south (Plate 26). This surface with a southward fall of 40 feet per mile has been interpreted as a warped surface of subaerial origin. It has been suggested that the subaerial Exmoor surface ranging from 1,250 to 1,600 feet O.D. was also tilted, in this case to the southeast. A platform recognized at 1,000 feet on Staple Hill (south Somerset) carries patches of gravels containing beach-battered cobbles of flint, chert, and Eocene silicified sandstone. The accordance between the altitude of these gravels and the underlying Upper Greensand led to the interpretation of this surface as having been deformed by the mid-Tertiary earth movements and bearing the remains of an Eocene formation, probably the lateral equivalent of the Bagshot Beds. Accordingly the warped surfaces described on Exmoor and Dartmoor have been assigned to a similar date in the early Tertiary.

The mid-Tertiary earth movements have long been considered responsible for the downfaulting of the Bovey Basin which includes Oligocene ball clays (Chapter 2). Clays of a similar age and of considerable thickness occur also in the Petrockstow Basin (Fig. 3) in north Devon. More recently a NNW–SSE system of wrench faults on which there has been a cumulative dextral displacement of at least twenty-one miles has been recognized in Cornwall and Devon. A strong zone of dextral wrench-faulting crosses the Dartmoor granite to the northwest of the Bovey Basin. A further extension of this fault line would pass between the offset outcrops of New Red Sandstone near Hatherleigh and then along the long axis of the Petrockstow Basin. This dextral wrench-faulting appears to be largely of Tertiary age, although the structures may have originated much earlier, and the Sticklepath–Lustleigh fault is still active today. Early Tertiary dykes on Lundy are displaced by NW–SE faults which are presumably of similar age. The early Tertiary surface on Exmoor and Dartmoor, and perhaps also on Bodmin Moor, was deformed by these earth movements, and it has been suggested that the same earth movements were responsible for the production of fault scarps, now denuded, as, for example, on either side of the Lustleigh fault zone.

One of the surfaces on Dartmoor, represented in part by basin and tor topography which reflects adaptation to the structure of the granite, may have developed contemporaneously with the sinking and filling of the Bovey Basin. This 'middle surface' occurs between 1,050 and 1,300 feet O.D. and is particularly well developed in the Dart basin and around the headwaters of the North and South Teign. It is separated from the upper warped surface by a zone of variable width which is characterized by steeper, tor-crowned slopes and other isolated and reduced fragments of the upper surface. On Exmoor remnants of the Lynton surface with a similar height range (1,225–1,000 feet O.D.) have been interpreted as marine, and representative of a former base level at 1,225 feet.

Remnants of a third, more extensive surface have also been identified in Southwest England as part of the widely developed planation surface recognizable in southern Britain from Cornwall to Kent. This surface has been described between 750 and 920 feet in east Devon, and between 750 and 950 feet on the margins of Dartmoor and on Bodmin Moor. Although in several areas it has been subdivided (Figure 5, numbers 16, 19, 20) these constituent stages may not necessarily have been caused by base level changes. They may instead have been the result of structural variations in the granite and in the Palaeozoic sediments. These variations were revealed during stream incision and gave rise to a number of minor knickpoints during the creation of the lower surface. Surfaces in this height range occur also on Exmoor and in north Cornwall, but they have been interpreted as the consequence of marine planation related to base levels of 925 (920 in north Cornwall) and 825 (820) feet O.D.

Discussion of the origin of these planation surfaces has long centred on a marine explanation proposed for Exmoor and a subaerial explanation suggested for Dartmoor. However, the absence of relevant deposits and the lack of conclusive indications from the drainage pattern have precluded the achievement of an agreed and widely applicable explanation. In the case of Dartmoor several workers have contended that the first stage of tor production was represented by deep rock rotting by chemical weathering which probably occurred under hot, humid conditions. The climate in the upper Oligocene and lower Miocene times was certainly warmer than that of the present, and subtropical conditions may have continued into the Pliocene. Accordingly Professor Waters has suggested that differential weathering and erosion, producing the basin and tor topography of Dartmoor, could be referred to subtropical, subaerial landscape development during the Miocene. Furthermore, in the case of southern Dartmoor it has been suggested that remnants of the late Tertiary surfaces take the form of broad dissected pediments, and that in view of the warmer, more humid conditions which then operated, it is possible that the surfaces in the 1,000 to 750 feet height range developed at least partly by pedimentation and progressive backwearing of the oldland of Dartmoor.

This suggestion may be relevant to the explanation of surfaces elsewhere in Southwest England. Although on granite outcrops such as Dartmoor the warmer and wetter conditions would have induced deep chemical weathering or the production of an etchplain, on Palaeozoic rocks chemical weathering would have been less effective and therefore slope recession and pedimentation may have been more significant, giving rise to a series of stepped surfaces which morphologically would resemble surfaces produced by marine erosion.

The entire sequence of planation surfaces and their origin should be reflected in the present drainage pattern, but the divergence of opinion over the origin and number of surfaces has retarded the interpretation of drainage development. Explanation of the surfaces, in terms of either marine erosion with attendant superimposition of the drainage pattern, or predominantly subaerial development with associated adjustment to structure, is not completely and universally applicable above 690 feet. Accordingly, even where marine transgressions have been invoked to explain surfaces, it would appear that some drainage lines, in central Devon and north Cornwall for example, can be explained only if they survived the marine transgression.

There is general agreement that the antecedents of the present drainage pattern were superimposed from Cretaceous rocks. This is supported by the evidence that granite débris was not supplied to the Cretaceous rocks of southeast Devon in upper Cenomanian and Turonian times when Dartmoor was probably wholly submerged beneath the sea. Fossil evidence for deep-water Upper Chalk on the Haldon Hills and abundant chalk and flint deposits off the south Devon coast also suggest that Senonian seas covered Dartmoor. Large numbers of flints occur in the beaches of the Cornish coast and represent 86 per cent of the beach material at Gun-walloe. The form of the drainage pattern initiated on the exposed and easterly tilted Cretaceous surface was considered by Jukes Brown (1904) —whose views were elaborated by Green (1949)—to have been composed essentially of east-flowing trunk streams. Remnants of these may still occur in the west to east sections of the upper Exe, Teign, and Dart. The highest surface, now warped and dated as early Tertiary, was fashioned in relation to this east-flowing drainage system which dissected the Cretaceous cover. It is more difficult to reconstruct the drainage evolution of west Cornwall but it has been suggested that the southeast-flowing portion of the Cober is a remnant of the original drainage system. In east Devon the Eocene deposits indicate that the early Tertiary surface was marine-trimmed. Subsequently the mid-Tertiary movements imparted a southerly tilt, attested by the southerly slope of the summit surface of Dartmoor at forty feet per mile, and this stimulated the development of southward draining streams in Southwest England as a whole.

It is thought that the major south-flowing streams, including the Exe, Teign, Tamar, and Fal (Figure 2, inset), were encouraged, if not initiated, by this southerly tilt. In the Dart basin, for example, the south-flowing tributaries of the river Dart were extended but there was no comparable development of the north-flowing streams. Elsewhere further superimposition of the drainage pattern has been invoked in association with the marine platforms described on Exmoor and in north Cornwall. Several major drainage changes may have been introduced in late Tertiary times. In west Cornwall the original southward flowing drainage was reversed in the Hayle–Marazion depression. The present course of the Camel suggests that the former drainage was southwards, and a wind gap at Red Moor at 450 feet O.D. indicates the probable former course. More striking is the course of the upper Torridge, which flows southeast for approximately twelve miles, and formerly continued into the Creedy–Yeo basin and thence into the Exe. Wooldridge (1954) suggested that the lower Torridge from Hatherleigh to Bideford Bay either originated more recently or is the reversed descendant of a parallel stream formerly flowing southeast. Similarly the line of the Taw might mark the line of a former stream flowing southeastwards to join an ancestor of the Creedy.

Although the 430-foot level was the surface most extensively described by earlier workers, evidence of a higher shoreline has been adduced in west Cornwall (600 feet), on Bodmin Moor (675), in central Devon (670–690), around Dartmoor and the Dart valley (690), on southern Dartmoor (690–700) and on Exmoor, where a surface occurs between 500 and 675 feet indicative of a former base level at 675 feet. In the Exe valley the Westermill stage indicates a base level of 690–686 feet. This surface has been identified in all these areas (Fig. 2, inset) on the basis of spur flats and associated terrace stages, and the general consensus of opinion is that the stage can be correlated with the Calabrian stage of southeast England and that it represents a major marine transgression submerging the previous relief, some of which was later resurrected and some of which was not. No unanimous agreement has yet been reached as to the extent of this transgression over the peninsula of Southwest England. One view (Fig. 2, inset) is that much of Cornwall was submerged, whereas Linton (1964) considers that, on the evidence of the drainage pattern, only locally can a shoreline earlier than that at 430 feet be recognized as having transgressed notably within the present coastline. Where the 690-foot shoreline did occur it was represented by a transgression on to the late Tertiary planation surface which was thus trimmed. In some cases, as in the South Hams, the drainage pattern above 690 feet shows some adjustment to structure and contrasts with the superimposed drainage pattern below the level of the shoreline stage.

The legacy of Tertiary time in the physical landscape of Southwest England is therefore one of a series of planation levels. The most extensive surface occurs now between 750 and 950 feet but formerly extended down to 500 feet O.D. or so and had a relief of little more than 500 feet. During the Quaternary this physique, characterized by surfaces of low relief, has been extensively modified as a result of rapid and considerable change of sea-level which in a peninsula induced deep dissection. An intermittently falling sea-level during the Pleistocene, possibly sometimes interrupted by transgressions, has been considered responsible for the production of valley terraces together with associated marine surfaces below which streams were superimposed. The estuaries of many rivers indicate Pleistocene sea-levels considerably lower than at present. The rock floor of the Erme and Taw–Torridge estuaries lies 150 feet below present sea-level. The details of the various stages of Pleistocene dissection of the landscape are shown in Figure 5.

The sea-level changes of the Pleistocene were accompanied by climatic variations which also had a considerable effect upon the physique of the peninsula. The only direct indication of the effect of glaciation in Southwest England is the presence of a deposit of calcareous shelly till near Fremington (Fig. 3) in north Devon. First described in 1864, the till includes small erratics, and overlies a variable thickness of stone-free clay, which was formerly interpreted as a lake clay. In 1964, however, a further deposit of till was exposed below the stone-free clay and so the entire sequence would seem to be a till. Further indication of the effect of glacier ice has been provided by large erratic blocks sealed into the raised beach deposits which overlie the coastal rock platform. At Saunton and Croyde Bay, in north Devon, erratics occur on the rock platform below the raised beach deposit, and at Porthleven in Cornwall a fifty-ton block of microcline gneiss occurs in a similar situation. A possible *in situ* till may be represented by a brown compact clay containing erratic stones which occurs at Bread and Cheese Cove on St Martin's in the Isles of Scilly, and in addition plateau débris and associated solifluction material occurring north of a line from Chapel Down on St Martin's to Gweal Hill on Bryher may be fluvioglacial outwash from a once nearby ice sheet. The till at Fremington in north Devon has been described as Riss/Saale in age whereas the erratics and deposits of the Isles of Scilly probably represent the previous (Mindel/Elster) glaciation. Whether the large erratics were deposited by ice directly or whether they were rafted by ice, remains at the moment the subject of conjecture. The St Erth Beds in west Cornwall, recently reinterpreted as marine clay and sand deposited in the Cromer warm period, may have been disturbed by Lowestoft ice. They are probably early Pleistocene in age, although previous dating has ascribed them to the late Tertiary. Several anomalous valleys, which are now dry, have been explained as glacial drainage channels eroded by melt-water from a Riss/Saale ice sheet which was banked up against the coast of north Devon. These valleys, including the Valley of the Rocks west of Lynton, and four other examples on the north Devon coast between St Catherine's Tor and Clovelly, were previously interpreted as being the result of the truncation of river valleys roughly parallel to the coast, by rapidly receding cliffs. It now seems possible that melt-water could have played a part in their formation. The available glacial deposits have been examined in relation to the coastal rock platforms which they overlie. At present the number of raised rock platforms which occur round the coast is not established and their chronology is not agreed. Within the height range 0–50 feet O.D. there exists at least one such rock platform (Fig. 3), and this is overlain by glacial erratics, a raised beach and occasional fossil sand-dunes, in addition to head deposits. Although parts of this platform may correspond to sea-levels of the present time, or of the last interglacial, several workers have suggested that it was of an earlier date, possibly Cromerian. On the basis of the evidence available, Stephens has suggested the chronology shown in Table 1.

The direct effects of glacial ice in Southwest England are restricted in extent but the results of Pleistocene climatic change, particularly cold conditions, are much more striking and widespread in the present land-scape. Indeed Dartmoor has been described as a relict periglacial landscape. Deposits of head, produced under such cold conditions, were first recognized in coastal sections where they are often 40 feet thick and occasionally 100 feet thick. In some cases two distinct layers are apparent and the head deposits often spread out as an apron or solifluction terrace at the foot of the coastal slope. Although often less apparent in inland locations, the head deposits are equally widespread. Characteristically, head deposits consist of angular fragments embedded in a finer matrix. In many cases they are typified by an anomalous particle size distribution in that there is a large amount of coarse, angular material and much fine-grade material, but very little is intermediate in size. The fine matrix which encloses the larger angular fragments may therefore have been derived from weathering products produced under earlier climatic conditions.

Two head deposits have been widely described at various inland and coastal sites in Southwest England. The lower or main head is usually the thicker of the two and on Dartmoor it has been shown to possess an

TABLE 1

	CORNWALL	DEVON	
	GODREVY-TREBETHERICK POINT	CROYDE-MIDDLEBOROUGH-SAUNTON	FREMINGTON (nr. BARNSTAPLE)
POST-GLACIAL	Soils, hillwash, alluvium, sub-merged peats, sand dunes, limited marine submergence of coasts, strong coast erosion of Pleistocene deposits		
LATE GLACIAL	Increased hillwash? Hawks Tor peat	Increased hillwash?	
WURM/WEICHSEL GLACIATION	Frost cryoturbation Upper fresh head/pebbly clay at Trebetherick	Frost cryoturbation Upper fresh head Coastal buried channels?	Frost cryoturbations of solifluction 'earth'
INTERGLACIAL	Chemical weathering of lower (main) head	Chemical weathering No marine deposits known	Chemical weathering
RISS/SAALE GLACIATION	Frost cryoturbation of lower main head Lower main head 'Boulder Bed' at Trebetherick	Lower main head Coastal buried channels? Sand dunes and head	Solifluction 'earth' of local origin Erosion Fremington shelly calcareous boulder clay Cryoturbation of beach gravels
INTERGLACIAL	Cemented sands Raised beach (with erratics)	Cemented shelly sands Raised beach (with erratics and head)	Raised beach (including erratics)
MINDEL/ELSTER GLACIATION	Large 50-ton neiss erratic greaches Porthleven Old head at Trebetherick	Old head? Large 50-ton Croyde granulite gneiss and Saunton red granite erratics reach coast	
EARLY PLEISTOCENE	Wave-cut rock platforms below 50-60 feet St Erth deposits?	Wave-cut rock platforms below 50-60 feet	Wave-cut rock platform at c.30 feet O.D. Hele-Ellerslie gravels? (=aggrada-tion to a high sea-level?)

inverted weathering profile (Fig. 8) due to the prior existence of a weathered regolith which was inverted as a consequence of its transfer downslope by congelifluction. The upper head is usually thinner, fresher in appearance and possesses fewer structures. On the granite outcrops it is represented largely by a clitter of granite blocks strewn over the surface with little

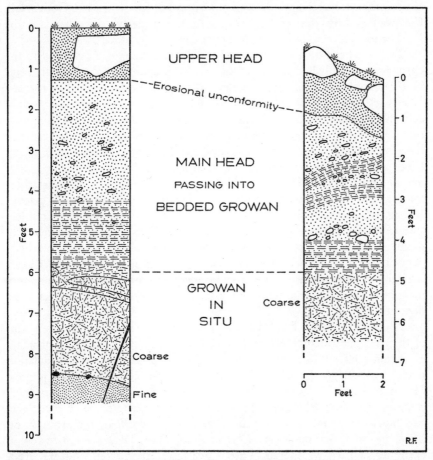

Fig. 8 THE SECTION IN SHILSTONE PIT (SX 659902), DARTMOOR. Redrawn from a diagram by R. S. Waters 'The geomorphological significance of Pleistocene frost action in South-West England' in *Essays in Geography for Austin Miller* ed. J. B. Whittow and P. D. Wood (Reading 1965), 48.

associated fine material (Plate 26). These blocks, representing the upper head, vary considerably in size and shape according to the nature of the granite; the coarse-grained porphyritic granite usually produced large, rounded blocks whereas the fine-grained granite provided angular, elongated gelifracts, generally smaller in size, like those below Haytor.

Structures occur in the head and also in the upper layers of bedrock. Pebbles in the Budleigh Pebble Beds of southeast Devon have been shattered and disposed vertically, sharp-edged stones and slabs are disposed vertically near the surface of the Lynton Beds in north Devon, domelike structures characterize the Oligocene clays of the Bovey Basin, and ice-wedge pseudomorphs have been described from the Pebble Beds outcrop northeast of Cullompton. Involutions and cryoturbation structures are common features and are well shown in the lower head at Godrevy in Cornwall and in the granite head and the underlying growan on the Blackbrook–Cowsic interfluve on Dartmoor.

The two head deposits appear to be of different ages. According to the chronology established for north Devon by Stephens (Table 1) the lower head is dated as of Riss/Saale age and the upper head ascribed to the last (Weichsel) glaciation. On Dartmoor however, it is suggested that the cold phases responsible for the production of the two head deposits followed, but were not interrupted by, a phase of deep weathering, and therefore the deposits both post-date the last interglacial. On Bodmin Moor a lower solifluction layer has been dated as Weichsel and an upper one as Lower Dryas. Traces of older head deposits have been referred to, for example in the Plym valley between Ditsworthy Warren and Cadover Bridge, where the main head rests upon water-worn gravel and boulders (the tin-bearing gravels) which may be relics of an earlier and fluvially modified head. At Trebetherick on the coast of north Cornwall a head deposit has been identified which may be earlier in date (Mindel/Elster) than the main head elsewhere, and in north Devon raised beach deposits include angular material which may have been derived from earlier head deposits.

Whereas the main head deposits of Southwest England are the result of the cold phases corresponding to the last (Weichsel) or the penultimate glaciation (Saale/Riss), some of the landforms produced by periglaciation may have been the cumulative result of a larger number of cold phases. Slopes mantled by upper head, or clitter as it is called on Dartmoor, sometimes possess blocks arranged into distinct patterns on the surface, and block lines and block scallops have been identified, for example on the slopes of Dartmoor west of Great Staple Tor. Over the entire region examples of frost-weathered bedrock are fewer than would be expected. This has been attributed to the fact that the cold phases of the Pleistocene followed milder phases which were characterized by more chemical weathering, and consequently the pre-periglacial land surface carried a residual mantle of weathered rock of sufficient depth to protect the bedrock from initial frost attack. Rock shelters at the base of tors have, however, been identified and have been explained as a result of selective frost-shattering. These are particularly common on granite outcrops where well-jointed and massive granites are in close juxtaposition, as at Haytor and Bench Tor on Dartmoor. Stepped hillslopes or altiplanation terraces have been described on the Hangman Grits of north Devon and at nine localities on the metamorphic aureole of Dartmoor. These small benches, produced by frost-heaving, frost-shattering and the gravitative transfer of débris, may indicate that in some cases cryergic processes have developed rather than eliminated irregularities of slope.

In Southwest England as a whole the effect of each phase of cold conditions was to release vast quantities of frost-weathered or previously weathered materials which were transferred downslope by congelifluction. As a result of the removal of material from the upper slope sections, landforms such as altiplanation terraces and dells on Dartmoor were produced, the head itself was sometimes arranged in definite patterns, and thick accumulations of head occurred on the lower slopes and on the coast. There are several instances where coastal rock platforms were completely obscured by head and are only now being excavated again. There is general agreement, however, that periglaciation, although responsible for many of the minor details of the landscape, was restricted in its effect and was not responsible for the production of extensive planation surfaces in Southwest England. Perhaps the most striking landforms in the area are the tors. These features, which have caught the imagination of many writers and painters, are particularly associated with the granite outcrops (Fig. 3), but tor-like features have been described also on other outcrops, particularly near the coast, as for example the quartzite tors or buttresses of the Dodman headland considered to be analogous to the valleyside tors of Dartmoor (Plate 44).

The tors were formerly attributed to the effects of differential sub-aerial weathering but are now generally considered to have been largely revealed when cold conditions prevailed and the surrounding material was removed by congelifluction. Morphologically the tors are dominated by the structure of the granite, and two major types were distinguished on this basis by Hansford Worth in 1930. The lamellar type has its architecture dominated by sheet jointing or pseudo-bedding planes (e.g. Blackingstone Rock, SX 7885) while the massive type is dominated by strong vertical joints as at Haytor and in the detail of Great Staple Tor. The tors often rise significantly for tens of feet above the bedrock at their base, and Vixen Tor on Dartmoor has a local elevation of 50–80 feet above the surrounding slopes. The tors occur in two types of location. One group rises from summits, ridges, and spurs, and it has been suggested that 70 per cent of these on Dartmoor occur between remnants of the early and late Tertiary planation surfaces. Valleyside tors comprise the second group and are represented by ribs and buttresses at the top of valleysides; they are usually more angular in form than the summit tors (Plate 6).

The tors are usually explained as having been exposed as a result of the action of frost and solifluction recurring throughout Pleistocene times. Although the valleyside tors may owe their existence entirely to periglacial morphogenetic conditions, a two-stage explanation has been advocated for the origin of the interfluve tors (Fig. 9). This explanation involves an earlier period of extensive subsurface rotting by structurally controlled chemical weathering followed by a period of exhumation represented by the removal of the fine-grained products of decay. This explanation

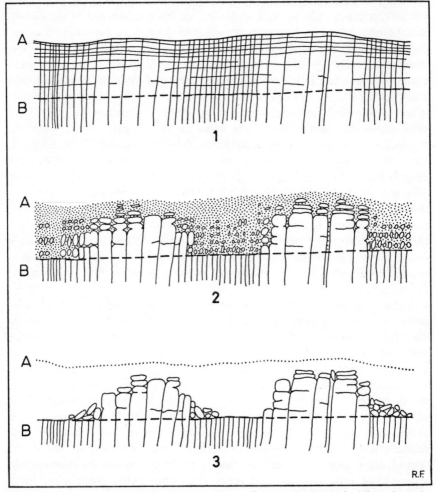

Fig. 9 STAGES IN THE DEVELOPMENT OF TORS. 1. Joints and pseudo-bedding planes in granite. 2. Decomposed rock produced after a period of rock rotting. 3. Tors exposed by the removal of the fine-grained products of decay. Redrawn from a diagram by D. L. Linton 'The problem of tors' *Geog. Journ.* **121** (1955), 475.

receives support from the presence of tors shown in sections and not yet exhumed, as at Two Bridges on Dartmoor, from the rounded nature of many of the blocks in the clitter below the tors, and also from the particle size composition of the head where the fine fraction may be the result of chemical weathering. In an alternative view incoherent granite or growan has been attributed to kaolinization by pneumatolytic processes.

The Pleistocene period therefore transformed the Tertiary landscape of low relief into the landscape of considerable dissection shown by the Southwest England of today. During the warm interglacials stable sea-levels introduced a succession of valley floors which were later to be dissected and left as river terraces or valleyside benches diversifying the sides of major valleys such as the Exe, Teign, Dart, and Tamar. These valley stages have in some cases been related to marine platforms (Fig. 5) and in others it has been demonstrated that the changes of sea-level were responsible for the polycyclic cliff profiles such as those at Ilfracombe and Boscastle. During the intervening cold phases head deposits were distributed liberally over the landscape. The extent of modification which occurred during periglacial conditions may reflect the depth of the regolith cover produced during the pre-cryergic phases. Thus the granite areas would have been more susceptible to modification than the areas of Palaeozoic sediments such as Exmoor and Davidstow Moor. On the dissected plateau country at lower levels, largely fashioned in detail during the Pleistocene, the characteristic slope forms are represented by broadly convex interfluves bounded by slopes convex near the top and concave near the bottom. Waters (1965) considers that convincing evidence of Pleistocene strand flats and valleyside benches is lacking from much of the Culm Measures outcrop, from the Lower Devonian slate and shale terrains of Devon south of Dartmoor and of Cornwall south of Bodmin Moor. Throughout Southwest England the angle of slope of the ground and its morphology varies according to rock resistance and dip. In central Devon the various lithologies within the Culm Measures are reflected in the angle of slope of the valleysides, and many east–west valleys are asymmetrical in cross-section as a result of the prevailing dip of the rocks. In other areas such as southeast Devon, valleys such as that of the Otter are diversified by many small cuesta landforms (e.g. Baker's Brake, SY 0686) which reflect the prevailing eastward dip of the strata. The influence of rock structure has played a varying role during the Pleistocene modification of the landscape so that in some cases it has proved difficult to discriminate between the effects of the various morphogenetic systems that occurred during the Pleistocene. This latter difficulty is illustrated by the nature of the detail of the drainage pattern.

As early as 1839 De la Beche commented that 'In some places . . . as on the slopes of the hills and at variable heights above the present rivers, more particularly in the portions of the county in which the comparatively soft rocks are exposed, we find the ground furrowed, and these furrows filled with transported gravel which also irregularly overspreads the same slopes in patches'. Such infilled furrows or gullies have been recorded more recently on the slopes of the Haldon Hills and in east Devon. Particularly in the upper reaches of drainage basins, some valleys and gullies have been partially infilled by head, giving a flat-floor which has later been dissected, while others have been completely infilled by soliflual deposits. Not all valleys function in the present drainage network, and dry valleys are common on the Permian and Triassic outcrops of Devon as well as on the limestones of Devonian, Carboniferous, and Cretaceous age. Dry valleys occur less frequently on the more resistant outcrops but they have been described in west Cornwall and attributed to erosion by melt-water from snow, which in this case had accumulated on neighbouring Tregonning–Carnmenellis. The detail of the valley pattern in Southwest England thus reflects the culmination of a series of Pleistocene stages as a result of which some shallow valleys have been completely obliterated by an infilling of head, some partially infilled by head and later re-excavated, while others remain as dry valleys in the present landscape.

The physique of Southwest England therefore bears testimony to the effects of several contrasted morphogenetic systems which have operated during the Tertiary and have alternated during the Pleistocene. The Holocene or post-glacial period is particularly relevant to the detail of the coast of the peninsula and also of necessity includes many examples of the direct and indirect effects of man.

During the post-glacial the cliffed portions of the coast have been subjected to erosion which has removed some of the head which formerly accumulated upon a rock platform close to present sea-level. The rias which are so characteristic of Southwest England have all experienced silting as a result of the Flandrian rise in sea-level, but local variations (Fig. 3) may be also the result of the rock types occurring within their catchment areas. In southeast Devon for example, the prevalence of soft rocks may be responsible for the large quantities of silt in the estuaries and lower courses of the Exe and Otter rivers. Elsewhere large amounts of silting can be shown to have been the result of tin streaming, ore mining, and china-clay quarrying. Near St Austell the effects of these extractive industries are reflected not only in the lower river courses such as the St Austell river, but also along the coast where beach material has been increased by these activities. Five kinds of beach material have been identified by Everard on the coast of St Austell Bay, and three of these, including the two largest contributors, are wholly or mainly river-transported mining waste. Vast quantities of 'tailings' have been transported to the Gwithian-Hayle stanniferous beach by the Red river from the major tin, copper, tungsten, and arsenic mining area of Camborne-Redruth.

Silting of estuaries has also been encouraged by obstructions developed across their mouths. There are three major examples of spits— Dawlish Warren across the Exe estuary, the Northam pebble ridge from Westward Ho! across the Taw–Torridge estuary, and a third example, the Den, at Teignmouth. Dawlish Warren is a double spit and, like several others in Southwest England, is accompanied by a minor spit on

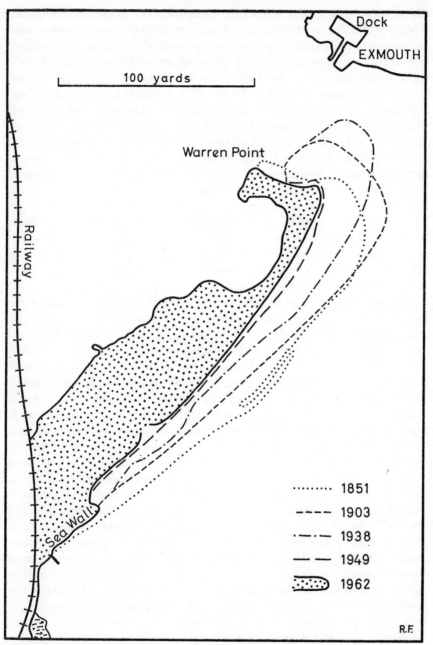

100 yards

Dock
EXMOUTH

Railway

Warren Point

Sea Wall

.... 1851
- - - - 1903
.—.—. 1938
— — 1949
1962

R.F.

Fig. 10   THE RECENT EVOLUTION OF DAWLISH WARREN. Based upon maps by C. Kidson 'The growth of sand and shingle spits across estuaries' *Zeitschrift für Geomorphologie* 7 (1963), 11, and 'Dawlish Warren, Devon: Late stages in sand-spit evolution' *Proc. Geol. Ass.* 75 (1964), 169.

the opposite side of the estuary at Exmouth. The stages of the recent evolution of Dawlish Warren have been traced by Professor Kidson, who has shown that its final destruction is inevitable unless conservation measures are successful (Fig. 10). Many other smaller examples of spits occur as for example across the mouth of the Otter, where the shingle ridge was not large enough to be noted in the middle of the sixteenth century. In several cases, as at Slapton in south Devon and at Loe Pool in Cornwall, a barrier completely seals the irregularity of the coastline. An outlet for Loe Pool, into which the river Cober drains, is now provided by an old adit constructed in the mid-nineteenth century. The coast is further diversified by beaches of shingle or sand, and areas of blown sand such as those near Hayle and at Braunton Burrows in north Devon (Fig. 3). In many cases, however, the amount of material supplied to beaches has been substantially modified in very recent times. The construction of the bathing-pool and the sea wall has resulted in a large decrease in the amount of sand supplied to Summerleaze beach at Bude, and an extension to a car park in 1954 has served to accelerate the loss of sand from the shore, so that the future of Bude as a holiday resort may be threatened.

Inland from the coast the effects of man on the physical landscape are also very apparent. The direct consequences of extractive industry are represented by quarries and their spoil heaps, by the gullies developed by tin working, and by the mounds of waste which diversify many valley floors. Valleysides show accumulations of up to three or four feet of material at field boundaries, and also on the soft rock outcrops many steep valleysides are characterized by terracettes under their present grass cover. More intensive land use, particularly the removal of woodland, together with the further extension of urban areas, improvement of land drainage, and clearance and maintenance of ditches, may have been a contributing factor to occasional high floods of recent years. The most devastating recent floods have occurred in Devon, and include those of Exmoor in 1952 and of the Exeter area in 1960, although high-intensity rainfall and runoff were recorded in the vicinity of Camelford in 1957 (pp. 60–1). The Exmoor floods were occasioned by the very intense rainfall of 15 August 1952, when up to 9 inches of rain fell in 24 hours on catchments with a high relief-ratio and runoff was subsequently accumulated with disastrous consequences at Lynmouth by the confluence of the East and West Lyn rivers. The peak discharge at Lynmouth was estimated at 5,700 cfs (18,000 cfs if two-thirds of the day's rainfall fell within five hours) from a catchment area of 38 square miles. The relationship between catchment area and peak discharge for these exceptional floods of 1952 has been shown by R. I. Smith to be of the form $Q = 2000 \, A^{0.6}$ whereas the 1960 floods involved comparatively lower peak-discharges ($Q = 873 \, A^{0.5}$). The 1960 floods were the consequence of rain which was not abnormal in intensity but was heavy and continued, and occurred at the end of a year in which a total of 50·8 inches of rain fell at Exeter compared with the average of 32·1 inches (1841–1961). As some rain fell on almost every day from July onwards and 22·09 inches fell at Exeter from 27 September to 5 December this culminated in floods on the Exe at Exeter on 30 September, 6 October, 7–9 October, 27–8 October, and 4 December. Damage was extensive in the Exe valley and in other parts of east Devon and 3,000 houses were affected in Exeter, Exmouth, and Tiverton. Flood prevention schemes have since been implemented including a scheme to allow for a design discharge of 25,000 cfs on the Exe at Exeter and a concrete culvert to allow a design discharge of 2,500 cfs on the Withycombe Brook at Exmouth.

There are comparatively few major river-gauging stations in the Southwest which have flow records much before 1960, although Worth provided an analysis of the available discharge data for Dartmoor rivers as early as 1930. Those stations which have data published for the 1963–4 water year are shown in Figure 2, and some general impression of the range of flow at these stations can be gained from the graph plotting catchment area and discharge (Fig. 2). The Exe at Thorverton and the Teign at Preston are two of the major gauging stations with the longest period of records and they can be used to illustrate the short-term average annual regime (Fig. 11). Runoff increases rapidly from September to a peak in December (Exe) or January (Teign) followed by a gradual decline until May when the low summer flows are usually established. May, and to a lesser extent June, are the months with the least variation in flows recorded from year to year whereas October is the month with the greatest variation. The average annual difference between the precipitation and runoff for the Exe at Thorverton for the period 1957–64 is 16·6 inches and the water loss calculated in this way for the Teign at Preston is 18·7 inches. Average annual potential evaporation over the eastern and central part of the peninsula is estimated to be about 21 inches, although values may be higher near the coast and as low as 14 to 16 inches (about 13 inches at Thornmead on Exmoor) on the most elevated areas.

Difficulties are occasionally experienced in parts of the Southwest in meeting demands for water during dry summer periods. Such occasional difficulties are not a reflection of a shortage of water resources in Cornwall and Devon, but rather illustrate the need for more regulating reservoirs which would also incidentally improve river conditions. The possibilities for water supply differ as between the extreme east, particularly on the areas of Permian and Triassic rocks, where ground-water supply is most important, and the remainder of the peninsula where surface water supply is more significant and reliable ground-water supply depends upon the superficial deposits on the valley floors and overlying the granite outcrops. Ground-water supplies in east Devon have concentrated on the Upper Greensand, marls which sometimes include lenticular bands of sandstone, and the Upper Sandstone and Pebble Beds which constitute the most important aquifer. These formations have been exploited to some extent, particularly in the Otter valley, but further development using a large number of small wells is very feasible. Elsewhere direct supply reservoirs together with regulating reservoirs and river and spring abstractions are the main sources of water supply. The largest Devon reservoirs are found on

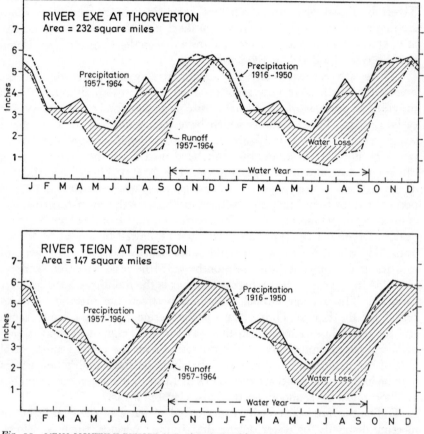

Fig. 11   MEAN MONTHLY RUNOFF AND PRECIPITATION FROM OCTOBER 1957 TO SEPTEMBER 1964.

the upland areas and Dartmoor has eight, including the Burrator reservoir (capacity 1,026 million gallons, yielding 8 million gallons per day) supplying Plymouth and the Fernworthy reservoir (380 mg, 2·2 mgd) supplying Torbay, while on Exmoor the Wistlandpound reservoir is of comparable size (340 mg, 1·7 mgd). The largest reservoirs in Cornwall are found in the west of the county and include the Drift reservoir (300 mg, 2·0 mgd) which supplies Penzance and much of Penwith, Stithians reservoir (1,112·5 mg, 2·7 mgd) and Argal reservoirs (400 mg, 1·92 mgd). In 1966

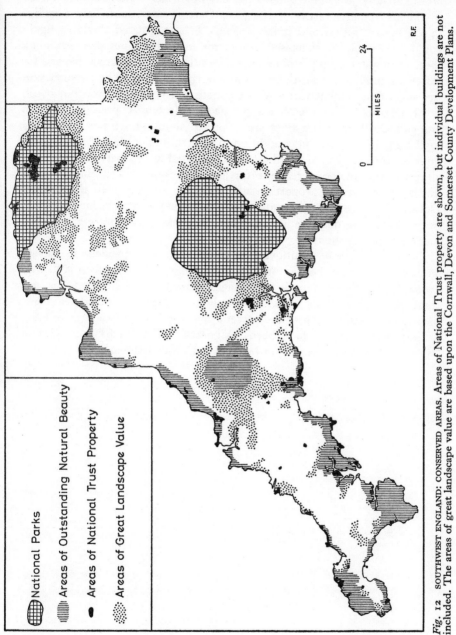

Fig. 12 SOUTHWEST ENGLAND: CONSERVED AREAS. Areas of National Trust property are shown, but individual buildings are not included. The areas of great landscape value are based upon the Cornwall, Devon and Somerset County Development Plans.

approximately 50 million gallons per day of surface water were abstracted in the hydrometric areas of the Exe, Dart, Tamar, and Taw-Torridge (3,000 square miles) and it has recently been estimated that this figure could very easily be increased to 440 million gallons per day. Although there is no water supply problem in the Southwest and no great demand for water for industrial use, there is some irrigation need. The frequency of irrigation requirement varies with location, soil type, and crop but it can be of the order of between five and nine years in ten. At present in Devon and east Cornwall 3,067 acres are irrigated (about 0·0016 per cent of the total area) in a dry season in addition to 97 acres under glass. An estimated limit for the area which could easily be irrigated in this part of the Southwest is over 10,000 acres but further expansion will probably occur unevenly. A greater proportion will probably be required in southeast Devon where the average annual precipitation is below 35 inches per year, but an extension of irrigation elsewhere is unlikely to require any special measures during the next twenty years.

The physique of Southwest England with its considerable variety affords an attractive background for the holiday industry which is further encouraged by the climatic advantages described in the next chapter. Increasing dependence upon the holiday industry necessitates some measure of conservation of the present landscape, and already large areas of Southwest England have been designated National Parks or Areas of Outstanding Natural Beauty, or taken over by the National Trust (Fig. 12).

CHAPTER 4

Climate, Soils, and Vegetation

Climate

MILD, equable, soft, and moist are the traditional adjectives used to describe the climate of Southwest England. How inappropriate they are to depict the scene of unrelieved whiteness of snow and ice outside the room in which these words are being written in February 1963! Yesterday 'Cornwall was cut off by blizzards; 50 people spent the night in a train on the edge of Dartmoor and 70 lorry drivers took refuge in a school at Whiddon Down, between Exeter and Okehampton, after being surrounded by deep drifts'.[1] The contrast in these two statements does much to express the scatter of individual days' weather about the long-period climatic mean, yet both, in their different ways, are essential to an appreciation of what this corner of our island is really like.

The climate of any area is determined in broad outline by its setting within the patterns of the atmosphere's general circulation and its geographical position in relation to the form and distribution of land and sea. In the British Isles, the weather is dominated for much of the year by the mid-latitude westerlies, but most of the essential day-to-day and seasonal variety of weather reflects Britain's marginal position between the Atlantic and the large continental land-mass to the south and east. The more specific regional factors affecting the climate of Cornwall and Devon are their southerly latitude, the projection westward of Cornwall into the Atlantic between Ireland and Brittany, and the considerable difference in height within the peninsula. Climate, since it depends on the accumulated records of the past, expresses the persistent underlying rhythms and patterns of the weather phenomena as well as its extremes, and climate can most usefully be thought of as an aggregate of the weather rather than as a simple average of weather conditions. This aggregate is perhaps best expressed as the frequency and periodicity of the recurrent weather types associated with a particular synoptic situation and wind-direction.

Some indication of how often and at what months of the year these weather types are likely to be present in the Southwest may be obtained from Table 2, which lists month by month the average percentage frequency

[1] *The Guardian*, 3 February 1963

of occurrence of air-mass types (as defined by J. E. Belasco) at the surface over Scilly at 1800 hours G.M.T.

TABLE 2

	J	F	M	A	M	J	J	A	S	O	N	D	YEAR
Polar Maritime	49	34	33	41	45	43	49	50	40	41	43	41	41·7
Polar Continental	3	6	0	0	0	0	0	0	0	0	0	2	0·9
Tropical Maritime	17	20	13	9	8	11	15	11	9	12	19	18	13·5
Tropical Continental	2	2	4	3	2	1	1	2	3	5	6	1	2·7
Frontal	9	12	11	11	15	13	13	13	12	10	12	11	11·8
Anticyclonic	11	15	30	30	20	29	20	19	34	21	14	22	22·1

A simplified version of the data collected from an examination of records for a period of 12 years 1938–49 by J. E. Belasco 'Characteristics of Air Masses over the British Isles', Geographical Memoir No. 87, H.M.S.O. 1952

The values on this list indicate the extent to which maritime air is experienced at all seasons; it appears to be over the Southwest for more than half the year, and the polar variety from source-areas in Greenland and the north Atlantic is very much the more frequent visitor. On the other hand, Continental air appears to be fairly rare, though this rarity may, in fact, enhance its significance. Not all the air reaching Scilly could be identified, which is the reason why the percentages in any one month do not sum to the 100. Frontal weather is common in Scilly in all months of the year whilst air in or near the centre of anticyclones is over Scilly for about a fifth of the year, March, April, and September being the most favoured months.

Polar and Tropical Maritime air-masses are modified in their lowest layers by their journeys over the Atlantic Ocean. Off Cornwall the sea temperatures of the coastal waters fall from averages of 16·6° C (62° F) in August to 8·8° C (48° F) in late February; in harmony with this fall the average temperatures prevailing during the onset of Atlantic air, whether tropical or polar in origin, steadily decrease through the winter months. This air then loses its heat, gradually in transit eastwards and rapidly when forced to ascend the western hills. Thus the average January mean temperature of 7·9° C (46·3° F) at Scilly becomes 6·3° C (43·4° F) at Torquay and 5·6° C (42·2° F) at Exmouth. Inland over high ground the fall-off in temperature is more brisk; at Tavistock the January mean is 5·4° C (41·7° F) and at Princetown 3° C (37·4° F). The recording station at Princetown is at 1,359 feet above sea-level, and a good deal of Dartmoor extends above this height. As, unfortunately, there are few recording stations on the more elevated parts of the moorlands, the weather gradient for the Southwest is known merely in descriptive terms. Too often, perhaps, we in Britain consider as typical of Devon and Cornwall the subtropical plants growing in the sheltered Morrab Gardens at Penzance or on the promenade at Torquay, forgetting the notoriously sharp deterioration with altitude, so that close by—at 2,000 feet above sea-level inland—the climate and accompanying vegetation may equally well be described as subarctic. In western districts of the British Isles a correction of 1° C for every 450–90 feet (1° F for every 250–70 feet) is typical. As a result, conditions in many ways are not markedly dissimilar from those found in southern Iceland, and it needs to be stressed that, height for height, the uplands of Britain experience a much more rapid reduction in potentialities for plant life than many of those on the Continent. Again, it is the lapse-rate within the prevailing westerlies which is responsible for this, more particularly the sharp fall of temperature within the first few thousand feet of Polar Maritime air-streams after their long sea-travel. Such cold air flowing over a relatively warm sea is extremely unstable, particularly in its lower layers, and the additional ascent required on its passage over our western hills gives increased cloudiness and vigorous showers. In common with other upland areas of Britain, the elevated parts of the peninsula are coolest in periods of cloudy, windy weather accompanying Polar Maritime air which, as we have seen from Table 2, is the most frequent invader of these western shores. Under warm, dry, calm anticyclonic conditions, the uplands suffer less as compared with the lowlands; it is, then, the least favourable aspects of the oceanic climate which are markedly accentuated on high ground.

Maritime influence is seen also in the retardation of the lowest and highest temperatures for about six weeks after the solstices. Most stations record their lowest mean average temperature in February, and August is on average as warm as July and in many cases slightly warmer. Compared with other parts of Britain away from the coast, both the diurnal and yearly ranges are small, particularly in the extreme Southwest, but quite considerable increases of these two ranges have occurred by the time east Devon is reached. The mean daily range, for instance, at Scilly is as low as 4·2° C (7·5° F) but it is 8·8° C (15·8° F) at Cullompton. Similarly the range of average monthly temperatures is respectively 8·6° C (15·4° F) and 11·9° C (21·4° F) for the same two stations. One of the most striking features displayed by the temperature maps is the way in which the isotherms roughly parallel the coastline in Southwest England. More Continental conditions seem to intrude in a long tongue extending over southern Somerset across the Blackdown Hills and mid Devon, to encompass north Dartmoor and Bodmin Moor. Locally, aspect is very important; south-facing slopes receive the highest annual insolation amounts, and on the south coast, especially near the time of sunrise and sunset, a good deal of solar radiation is reflected off the sea to raise early morning and late evening temperatures in south-facing valleys and coves.

Fronts, which are of fairly frequent occurrence in the Southwest, are zones of steep thermal and other weather gradients and of intense dynamic activity, so that it is by no means rare for the temperatures at any one season to revert to those of a previous season, or even to anticipate those of the season to come. It is not unusual for temperatures of 13·8° C (57° F) to be recorded in what, on average, is our coldest month of February.

When the long-term range of variation between the highest and lowest monthly mean temperatures is scrutinized for Britain, it is seen that the winter months December to February show the greatest range of variation. In other words, the most striking kind of thermal abnormality to which our climate is liable is a spell of very cold weather in winter. The explanation of this is that normally the prevalence of the westerly winds which form part of the maritime air gives these islands winter temperatures abnormally high for their latitude. We find ourselves on the edge of the European continent, whose air-masses we do not normally share, although we are liable to share them when the westerly winds break down. In this context the Southwest is no exception, and consequently, when air-streams are drawn from the northeast and east, a large fall in temperature is to be expected, and little amelioration can come by way of solar radiation in the winter months, owing to the low noon-altitude of the sun and the reduced length of daylight. Furthermore, winds from this Continental quarter blowing over an ice- or snow-covered England can arrive in the Southwest bitterly cold. Unguarded statements about a freedom from frost, which appear in so many descriptions of the West Country, can be very misleading as few parts of the peninsula are immune from occasional very hard frosts. It may come as something of a surprise to learn that in the decade 1950–9 the average number of days a year on which ground-frost occurred at Exeter was 89, a figure not much below the 93 days for Ross-on-Wye and 99 days for Cambridge. A few more illusions may be shattered by the report that on the morning of 25 January 1958 the observer at Princetown recorded a minimum temperature of −6·6° C (20° F). His colleagues on the very same occasion recorded −8·8° C (16° F) at Exmouth, −12·7° C (9° F) at Starcross, and almost unbelievably −15° C (5° F) at Exeter. Places of low altitude suffer more frequently from temperatures below freezing point than stations at higher elevation, because of the drainage of cold air into valleys and hollows. Some of the valleys in western England appear to be particularly susceptible, as can be seen from Table 3. It must not be forgotten that frost, though linked here for convenience with temperature, also has close affinities with wind and cloudiness, both of which are considered below.

It is often emphasized that snow falls more frequently and lingers longer in eastern Britain than in the west. Though this is, in general, true, we would be wrong to regard the whole of the Southwest as equally blessed in this respect. For the decade 1950–9 the average number of days with snow falling at Exeter was 13, which is not much fewer than at Cambridge, which had 17. The reason for this difference is that eastern England is more subject to cold, showery winds from the Continent. Nevertheless, the quantity of snow may not diminish, as the frequency of snow falling does, from east to west; the quantity may, and often does, increase to the west. This is not due only, or even largely, to the higher relief, but to the presence, during some of our winters, of a vast bulwark of high pressure which extends from Siberia to Greenland and brings persistently cold, easterly winds over Britain. Depressions on the southern edge of this high

TABLE 3

Number of days on which ground and air frost occur

		EXETER 106 feet	STARCROSS 29 feet	DARTINGTON 120 feet	PRINCETOWN 1,359 feet
1957	Ground	71	68	104	68
	Air	41	36	60	59
1958	Ground	63	63	96	60
	Air	41	29	45	31
1959	Ground	68	76	97	62
	Air	49	41	59	51
1960	Ground	59	67	98	47
	Air	33	32	46	31

Air frost is entered when the screen minimum temperature is 0°C (32°F) or less. Ground frost is entered when the grass minimum thermometer is −1·1°C (30°F) or less.

pressure normally take a southerly course and bring heavy snowfalls to the west. Such a situation is often made worse by accompanying strong winds with particularly dangerous blizzards and drifting of the snow. Exactly thus did the blizzard of 25 December 1927 bring the level of snow up to the bedroom windows of the two-storey houses at Princetown, and so strong were the winds that great clouds of snow were blown out to sea from the high cliffs of south Devon. It was thought that great quantities of snow were driven from the heights of southern Dartmoor towards the coast, and this, with the local snow, helped to build up immense drifts around Salcombe. Just as the warm, moist air-streams are often associated with heavy rain on the western side of Dartmoor, so cold, easterly air-streams on the eastern flank can give exceptionally heavy falls of snow in winter. During the winter of 1928–9, no less than 6 feet of snow fell in 15 hours over Holne Chase. This was no blizzard—just a mighty downfall, a cloud-burst of snow which fell in enormous flakes and in such amounts that even great oaks were uprooted by the weight. This fall of 16 February 1929 may well be the deepest single fall of snow ever actually measured anywhere in the British Isles at so low an elevation as 1,000 feet above sea-level. The need to stress further the susceptibility of the West Country to heavy snowfall is not necessary, as the memories of the great winter of 1962–3 are still fresh and vivid.

In comparison with the whole of Britain, the Southwest peninsula must be regarded as one of its wetter provinces. The map of distribution of mean annual rainfall for 1916–50 (Fig. 13) indicates a close relationship between relief and rainfall. The 40-inch isohyet encircles the Land's End peninsula; the 50-inch isohyet does the same for the Carnmenellis, the Hensbarrow, Bodmin Moor, and the Hartland plateau, and the 60-inch isohyet for Exmoor and Dartmoor. The drier parts, those with less than 40 inches, are of lower relief and include the Isles of Scilly, the north-facing and extreme southwest-facing coasts of Cornwall; in Devon a large area extending from Barnstaple along the Taw valley is equally blessed, and this area of low rainfall continues southeastwards to the Exeter area, where totals drop as low as 32·5 inches. To the northeast of Exeter the rainfall increases again and a substantial area on the east Devon plateau is ringed by the 40-inch isohyet. If under 40 inches of rain a year marks off the drier areas, it is convenient to think of more than 60 inches as depicting the wetter ones. Only the three uplands of Dartmoor, Exmoor, and Bodmin Moor qualify for entry into this wetter group. Dartmoor has by far the largest area over which more than 60 inches of rain falls. The isohyet for this amount coincides roughly with the 1,000-foot contour in the north of the moor, but heights of 800 feet and even lower receive this amount in the south— in all an area of about 260 square miles. On the evidence so far collected for Dartmoor, it would appear that the rainfall increases significantly with elevation. For instance, at Princetown Prison (1,359 feet) the annual average rainfall is 87·63 inches; at 1,560 feet on Beardown Hill (SX 605767) it is 90·83 inches; quite a large area in the south of the moor is ringed by the 80-inch isohyet and an average of 90 inches of rain falls over a fairly extensive part north of Princetown. In any particular year the actual amount of rain which falls may vary considerably from the average figure as given by the isohyets of Figure 13. The greatest percentage-variability of rainfall in Britain is found in the English Midlands, but a close runner-up is the Southwest peninsula and particularly Dartmoor. An indication of the range of this variability may be seen in the rainfall for 1912, when Princetown recorded the very large amount of 112·5 inches. From the records it can be assumed that more than 100 inches have fallen somewhere on Dartmoor in at least 20 out of the last 114 years.

Before 1950 there were few rain gauges on Exmoor and none on the

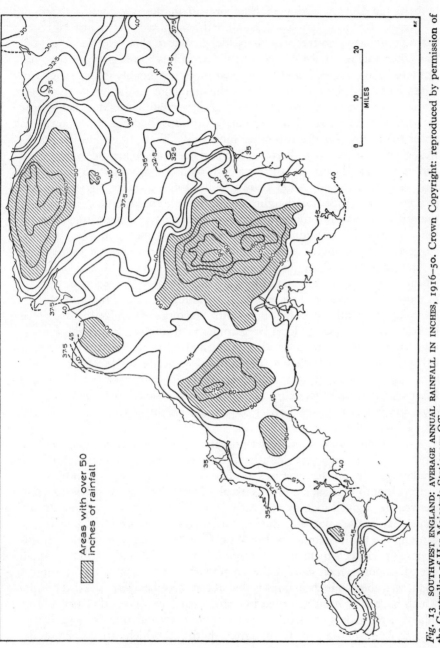

Fig. 13 SOUTHWEST ENGLAND: AVERAGE ANNUAL RAINFALL IN INCHES, 1916–50. Crown Copyright: reproduced by permission of the Controller of Her Majesty's Stationery Office.

higher parts of the moor. Since then, records of rainfall have been kept both in the Devon section of Exmoor and in the neighbouring part of Somerset. By 1960 an average rainfall computed for Kinsford Gate (SS 745365) at 1,500 feet was 79·93 inches, but in that year the actual fall was 96·41 inches. It would seem as if Exmoor is a wetter place than has hitherto been imagined, and the wettest piece is probably in the vicinity of The Chains and Span Head—that is, the high land on the west of Exmoor. Dunkery Beacon (1,705 feet), though the highest eminence, does not appear to be the wettest part. The rainfall records for Bodmin Moor are even fewer than those for the two other moorlands. Two gauges on the north-western side of the moor, between 850 and 900 feet, collect on average 59·3 and 60·1 inches, but in 1960 77·87 and 81·05 inches were actually collected. East of these two gauges lies Brown Willy, some 400 feet higher; this, on analogy with comparable heights on Dartmoor, could have something of the order of 20 inches more rain on average a year. A gauge at 990 feet on the southeast side of Bodmin Moor recorded 81·11 inches in 1960, and this suggests that the higher eastern flank may well be somewhat wetter than the rainfall-maps so far published lead us to believe. The correlation of altitude with greater precipitation is usually explained in terms of the rise of moist air-streams, but observations are tending to show that this may be an oversimplification and that many other factors are involved. It may well be that some of the very local large amounts of rain occur through funnel-ing, whereby moisture-laden air is concentrated in its flow up converging valleys, where it is forced to rise almost vertically up the valley-heads. This phenomenon, it is thought, accounts for the 'wet patch' around Princetown: in 1960 its gauge at 1,359 feet recorded 106·54 inches, while close by, North Hessary Tor, at the greater height of 1,401 feet, received only 86·83 inches.

In common with other western oceanic localities, Cornwall and Devon have some rain in every month of the year and the records show the predominantly greater wetness of late autumn and early winter. The wettest month at most stations is usually December, and the driest part of the year is enjoyed in May and early June. The two following months are somewhat wetter, but it is during these holiday months that odd things can happen to the rainfall in the West Country. The most terrific down-pours experienced in Britain give some 8–10 inches in a day. The rainfall over Exmoor, which caused the Lynmouth flood disaster on 15 August 1952, was about 9 inches. This is one of the three heaviest falls in 24 hours which have ever been recorded in the British Isles. The other two were a fall of 9·56 inches at Bruton on 28 June 1917 and one of 9·40 inches on 18 August 1924 at Cannington, both of which are in adjoining Somerset. These exceptionally heavy rainstorms in summer are usually accompanied by thundery weather. A similar downpour occurred in the Camelford area on 8 June 1957. The actual amount collected at Roughtor

View (700 feet) during the rainfall day was 7·09 inches, but some 5·43 inches of this fell within two and a half hours, and possibly an inch of equivalent rain may have been lost from the gauge during the hail-showers. If this estimation is correct, the total rainfall was probably very close to the greatest hourly intensity yet known or estimated for Britain. A particularly bad flood occurred in Camelford on 30 August 1950, and on 16 July 1847 the flood resulting from a downpour over Bodmin Moor destroyed the bridges on the rivers Camel and Inny. When the last previous destructive flood at Lynmouth in 1796 is taken into account, an impressive list of outstanding daily rainfalls can be made for the West Country.

Closely associated with the incidence of rainfall is the cloudiness of the sky and the amount of sunshine which may be received. Cornwall and Devon are among the sunnier counties of Britain and receive on the average some 1,600–1,700 hours of bright sunshine around their coasts. For the period 1921–50 Torquay was favoured most by the sun with 1,733 hours a year; Scilly, with 1,725 hours, was a close runner-up. Only farther east along the south coast of Britain are higher amounts received in this country. Movement inland quickly leads to increased cloudiness and a reduction in sunshine-amounts. In the five miles from Teignmouth to Newton Abbot, the number of hours falls from 1,711 to 1,605, and in the sixteen miles from Exmouth to Cullompton the amount falls from 1,616 to 1,516 hours. It may come as something of a surprise to find that June is the Southwest's sunniest month, with an average of between seven and eight hours a day, and that May is the next best month. The usual holiday months of July and August are, in that order, less bright than May or June, but it is really in September that sunshine-amounts markedly decline, making December the gloomiest month, with January not much better. Sunshine-amounts have an inverse correlation with cloudiness and fog. These visible results of the condensation of water vapour in the atmosphere are known to all. Clouds in their various forms and shapes are an integral part of the southwestern scene, thickening towards sundown with golden hue, blanketing the land for days in winter and casting their drifting shadows over the rounded granite domes in summer. In the lee of Dartmoor where air is warmed by descent the clouds disappear and the sun breaks through, much to the pleasure and delight of those who visit the resorts around Tor Bay and the Exe estuary.

Fogs occur when moist air is cooled by night-time radiation, by heat losses, or by contact with a cooler surface beneath. In such an event condensation in the form of radiation or advection fog occurs. Radiation fogs are seen most frequently inland and more particularly are found accumulating over valley-floors and spreading horizontally. A most interesting sight is the horizontal outflow of fog in a narrow band from the Axe valley for some miles seaward. This drainage of fog goes far to improve visibility on the higher ground and keeps down the incidence of radiation

S.E.—3*

fog on the east Devon plateau, while filling its dissected valleys. Maritime Tropical air flowing over a relatively cold English Channel provides the necessary ingredients for the production of advection fog over the sea. This occurs fairly frequently in late summer and early autumn, and the fog which results drifts over the coast and inland up the estuaries. The tendency for this type of fog to occur at this time of the year rather than in winter may be explained by the air-temperatures being more frequently higher than sea-temperatures during the warmer part of the year. It is not easy to give a comprehensive account of the occurrence of fog over the two counties owing to the scarcity of records, particularly for stations in the more elevated parts. Moreover, the entry of fog in official records implies a range of vision less than 1,100 yards at 9 a.m. G.M.T. On this basis Princetown is, without any near rival, the foggiest part of the Southwest.

It has long been known that the wind blows more strongly and is less gusty over the sea than over the land. In Cornwall, and somewhat less in Devon, one is never very far from the sea so that, except for the well-sheltered districts, the two counties form a windy peninsula and are surpassed in Britain for windiness only by the northwest of Scotland. The records point to the high wind-speeds around the coasts; the anemometers at Scilly, Lizard, and Pendennis at times record the strongest gusts for the year of the British stations. To the best of our knowledge, the speed of 111 miles per hour recorded on 6 December 1929 at Scilly has been exceeded only twice (by a small amount) anywhere in Britain. Over land, the increased frictional drag reduces the near-surface speeds, particularly in the first 1,000 feet. It is thought that thereafter speeds increase again but to what extent is difficult to assess, as the data available for winds over the highlands are most fragmentary. As on the coasts, so on the exposed uplands, the effect of the high wind-speeds is writ large in the stunted hedgerows and trees leaning from the wind. To man, the wind is not merely something with speed and direction; it is also a feeling and a sound, which linger long in his memory. More than 300 years ago the village church of Widecombe-in-the-Moor occupied an unlucky position in the path of a tornado. In quaint old spelling a contemporary recorded the disaster thus:

A most prodigious & fearefull storme of winde
lightning & thunder, mightily defacing Withcomb- church in Devon, burneing and slayeing diverse
men and women all this in service-time, on the
Lords day Octob: 21—1638.

The tablet beneath the church-tower, recording the death of the sixty churchgoers, no less than the graveyard of ships wrecked around the coasts, will do much to remind us that just as the landscape of the Southwest has elements both grand and quiet so, too, does its climate have storm and calm, severity and mildness, inextricably woven.

Soils

Climate in conjunction with the other soil-forming factors of parent material, relief, vegetation, and time collectively dictate that the most frequently encountered soil profiles in Southwest England are classified as brown earths. The brown earth group includes acid brown soils which dominate over large areas, intermixed with very thin soils that may be classified as rankers which commonly occur on eroded sites. The second division of the brown earths, known as leached brown soils and characterized by soils with clay-enriched subsoil horizons, is represented by soils on the Permo-Trias vales and on the plateau surfaces of east Devon. Surface-water gley soils are also widely distributed and represent the dominant type of soil profile in parts of central Devon. Peaty gleyed podzol soils occupy many upland areas and are the most important representatives of the group of podzolized soils in the Southwest, humus-iron podzols being restricted to small areas of coarse-textured parent materials. Organic soils are confined to the high moorland summits and moorland basins, and calcareous soils occupy only limited areas owing to the paucity of calcareous parent material.

The importance of parent material as a factor governing soil characteristics was emphasized by early workers in the Southwest and it is equally acknowledged in recently completed soil surveys. Referring to the connection between geology and agriculture in Cornwall, Devon, and west Somerset, De la Beche in 1842 stressed that variations in fertility largely correspond to differences in rock type, and Worgan in 1810 commented that 'The soils of Cornwall chiefly consist of three species; first the black growan or gravelly; second the shelty or slaty; third various loams which differ in texture, colour and degree of fertility'. Vancouver in 1808 distinguished eight areas on his soil map of Devon (Fig. 4, p. 29): these were partly based upon different parent materials and also recognized further subdivisions on the outcrops of granite and Culm Measures. Solid rock is not always the parent material for the soils because overlying superficial deposits have often provided the basis for soil development. The most extensive superficial deposits in the Southwest are undoubtedly the head deposits which, in some areas, extend well beyond the parent outcrop. East of Exeter and the Exe estuary the Permian marl outcrop is usually overlain by about 15 inches of loam containing stones from the Pebble Bed outcrop farther east, and near the Pebble Bed scarp the thickness of this head deposit increases to 3 feet or more. A similar mantle of Cretaceous débris overlies the outcrop of Trias marl at the foot of the east Devon plateau, and the distribution of soils on the Oligocene ball clays of the Bovey Basin is strongly influenced by the thickness and nature of the head deposits. Elsewhere, as for example on the sandstone, shale, and slate outcrops, it may be difficult to decide whether the soil profile is developed on the underlying rock or on material which had been previously transported. On the granite outcrops the soil parent materials are usually represented by head deposits which overlie the 'growan' or rotted granite. Distinct soil types have been recognized by the Soil Survey on flood plain deposits, and also on the often adjacent colluvial deposits which are represented by the relatively stoneless material that has accumulated at the base of slopes as a result of soil creep and local wash during the Holocene period.

The texture of the parent material is sometimes influenced by the presence of depositional layers occurring within 3 to 5 feet of the surface. On the Isles of Scilly a relatively stone-free layer of silty material occurring between two distinct layers of gravelly head deposits was interpreted as wind-blown loess by Barrow in 1906. The presence of several feet of loess mantling the serpentine outcrop of the Lizard area has been demonstrated and this deposit is not associated with solifluction material. Superficial pockets of loess-like silty material or brickearth are reported from several other localities notably on the flint gravels capping the Cretaceous outcrop of the Haldon Hills, on the Pebble Bed cuesta, and on the margins of the Bovey Basin. The presence of such silty lenses has been taken to indicate local rearrangement of loess-like material by wind, frost, or water during the last cold phase of the Pleistocene. The effect of cold conditions which were responsible for the production and distribution of head deposits and the overlying patches of loess may also be retained in certain profile characteristics. In many sections, but particularly on the loamy granite head, Clayden (1964) has noted discontinuities at about 20 inches from the surface which separate upper layers of friable consistency and crumb or blocky structure from lower layers of extremely compact or indurated material with a marked platy structure. Sometimes a thin seam of iron accumulation may pick out the contact of these two zones. It is thought that the two zones still retained in soil profiles may represent the former active and permafrost layers which were present during the last cold phase. In other cases, as at Harpford Common in east Devon, discontinuous seams of iron accumulation which occur about 7 feet below the surface have been attributed to frozen and unfrozen bands which occurred in the surface layers under permafrost conditions.

The effect of relief, particularly as it influences climate, is well illustrated by the distribution of the four major soil types of Dartmoor (Fig. 14). The gently sloping summits usually above 1,500 feet O.D. with an annual rainfall of more than 80 inches have peaty soils classified either as blanket bog or peaty gley soils. The second group is represented by peaty gleyed podzols which are characterized by a peaty surface layer and a horizon of iron accumulation in the form of a very thin iron pan. They occur where rainfall is between 65 and 80 inches, on uncultivated moorlands of *Molinia* grassland or wet heath surrounding the plateaux. The third group is typically developed in the height range 750 to 1,100 feet O.D. and is particularly

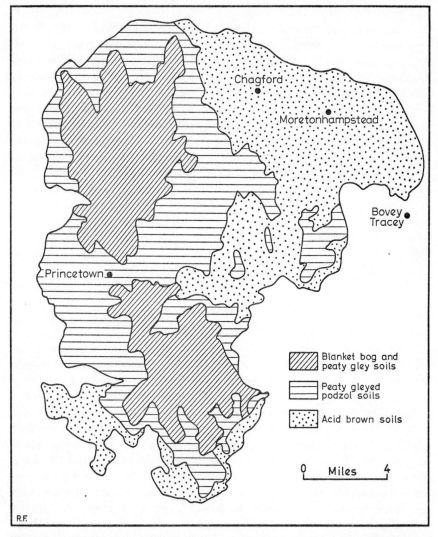

Fig. 14 PROBABLE DISTRIBUTION OF THE MAIN SOIL GROUPS OF THE DARTMOOR GRANITE. Redrawn from a map by B. Clayden and D. J. R. Manley 'The soils of the Dartmoor granite' in *Dartmoor Essays* ed. I. G. Simmons (Devon. Ass. 1964), 122.

frequent in the northeast of Dartmoor where there is a greater proportion of farmland. There are fewer wet-loving and heath species in this area which is essentially one of acidic grassland with bracken and gorse. The soils have the characteristics of free drainage and they lack a surface layer of peat and are classified as an upland variant of acid brown soils. The finer details of topography are reflected in further variations in the distribution of soils on Dartmoor. The basins and the valley floors which occur between the tor-crowned ridges, particularly of the higher areas, possess valley bog and peaty ground-water gley soils.

Land-form influences the amount of water received and lost by different sites and this is reflected in the detailed distribution of soil series. A hydrologic sequence has been identified on the Culm shales between Exeter and Okehampton, where both weathering and soil development are closely related to site conditions (Fig. 15). Well-drained, acid brown soils (Dunsford Series) are associated with steep or moderate slopes. These soils are shallow, weakly weathered, and possess little horizonation. Much of the heavy rainfall received runs off directly instead of draining through the profile. On flat or gently sloping sites surface-water gley soils are found and these are deeper and more strongly weathered and they possess thick

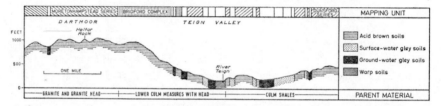

Fig. 15   A TRANSECT ACROSS THE TEIGN VALLEY. Information derived from the soil map by B. Clayden 'The soils of the Middle Teign valley district of Devon' *Bulletin of the Soil Survey of England and Wales* No. 1 (Harpenden 1964).

subsoil horizons of dense silty clay that cause severe drainage impedance. The surface-water gley soils include the Tedburn Series which is associated with the receiving sites of lower slopes and possesses a thin surface horizon of grey-brown silty clay loam overlying 2 feet or more of plastic silty clay; and the Halstow Series, developed on gently sloping ridge-tops, in which gleying is less pronounced. It appears that clay formation, or the release of clay material from the shales, is considerably greater on subdued slopes than on steep slopes which allow more rapid runoff. Surface-water gley soils are therefore especially widespread in central Devon where there are extensive remnants of planation surfaces of low relief. However a similar hydrologic sequence of soils does not occur on the Devonian slate outcrops of the South Hams where acid brown soils of silt-loam or silty clay loam texture (similar to the Dunsford Series) occupy both the gently sloping interfluves and the steep valleysides—gley soils being mainly confined to basin sites. North of Dartmoor gently sloping interfluves underlain by Culm shales are usually occupied by poor pastures on gley soils contrasting with similar sites on the slates of south Devon, which have well-drained, acid brown soils commonly used as arable land. The reasons for the contrast between the soils of these two argillaceous parent materials awaits further mineralogical investigation, but the more pervious nature of the slate is probably a contributory factor. Ground-water gley soils are also mapped on sites where topography exercises a predominant control and are mainly confined to the alluvial deposits of the valley floors.

One further effect of land-form upon the soils of the Southwest is shown through the effect of angle of slope. Whereas on some steep slopes the soils are suitable for arable cultivation but the slope angle has proved to be a limiting factor, on others ploughing has taken place. This has allowed the gradual movement of soil downslope so that accumulation has occurred at field boundaries transverse to the slope. Pack-horses were originally used for carting the soil from the base of sloping fields to replace that lost from the top, and today recovery of soil is still practised on steeply sloping fields. The need to recover and redistribute soil on steep slopes is a reflection of slope angle emphasized by the removal of the original vegetation and the introduction of different forms of land use. There are other ways in which man has modified the soils of the Southwest. Profiles of arable soils have a distinct plough layer (Ap) in the top six inches or so. Manures and fertilizers are added to this layer today and in the past, as well as lime, marl, dung, and ashes, several writers referred to the application of 'maritime manure' derived from fish, ore weed, and shelly sea-sand which was carried inland for up to 15 miles.

The effect of much earlier vegetation changes, which sometimes reflected changes of climate, is recorded in many soil profiles. In the case of the peaty gleyed podzols of the Hexworthy Series on Dartmoor, the evidence from their morphology and chemical analysis suggests that iron pan formation was superimposed on soils of acid brown rather than podzol type. Studies of the post-glacial sequence of vegetation development (pp. 70–1) in relation to early settlement have demonstrated that the present areas of peaty gleyed podzol soils were formerly forested. Acid brown soils were probably more extensive on Dartmoor during the Bronze Age and occupied much of the ground below about 1,500 feet. Heath vegetation probably colonized former woodland, and after the end of the Bronze Age this vegetation change, combined with the cooler and wetter conditions of the Sub-Atlantic phase, may have initiated a change from acid brown to peaty gleyed podzol soils. The Hexworthy peaty gleyed podzols and the Moretonhampstead Series of acid brown soils thus developed from acid brown soils that were at an earlier stage of development, but the latter developed further as sesquioxide-rich acid brown soil profiles whereas the former developed to peaty gleyed podzols and now characterize the higher rainfall areas where surface waterlogging is more likely to occur. This hypothesis, that the iron pan soils and the acid brown soils are both derived from profiles of acid brown type, may be applicable to parts of the South-west beyond Dartmoor. On Exmoor, for instance, peaty gleyed podzols

occur largely above 1,300 feet O.D. and their podzolized and gley characteristics have been ascribed to development since the Bronze Age. Below
1,300 feet acid brown soils occur, but analyses of some of these soils suggest
that some movement of iron has also taken place to a limited extent. The
soils of Southwest England thus reflect a variety of factors manifested in
soil development since the last cold phase. Parent material, directly or
indirectly as derived head deposits, provides perhaps the dominant control,
but further and more detailed variations are introduced by relief, and the
differentiation of soils in space and time is further explained by changes in
climate and in the activity of man. Although the effect of any one of these
factors is inseparable from that of the others, parent material affords a
convenient basis for a summary of the character of the soils which exist
today in the region. Necessarily this summary relies heavily, as the fore-
going account has done, upon the work done by the Soil Survey of England
and Wales, particularly that by B. Clayden.

Although peat occurs on the Dartmoor plateau and a shallow peat can
be found on the moorland areas of Exmoor, blanket bog is virtually absent
from the granite uplands of Cornwall. This is the result of the lower
elevation and consequently lower rainfall of the more westerly uplands.
Valley bogs, where the ground-water table is high, are frequent in the
basins of Bodmin and St Austell Moors, but otherwise peaty gleyed podzols
cover much of Bodmin Moor and acid brown soils are the most significant
types on the lower, more westerly granite outcrops. These acid brown soils
have a thick surface horizon of dark brown to almost black, often humose,
gritty loam giving way to a dark brown layer 3 to 9 inches in thickness
which is transitional to the orange-brown, gritty loam B horizon which has
a fine crumb structure and a pronounced, very friable consistency. An
indurated layer often occurs at a depth of about 24 inches, but the loamy
texture and free drainage of the soils allows cultivation during much of the
year. The peaty gleyed podzol soils have a thin iron pan in the profile
normally at a depth of 10 to 15 inches and this provides an effective barrier
to root penetration and also to water movement so that surface waterlogging
is experienced for several months of the year.

The soils on the pre-Devonian and Devonian slate terrains of Devon
and Cornwall often include numerous slate fragments (or shillet) near the
surface and consequently were described by many early workers as slaty or
shelty. The soils on these outcrops are typically acid brown soils with free
soil drainage and most of them have a moderately fine texture (silty clay
loam, clay loam) and a clay content which is fairly constant in all horizons.
On agricultural land the organo-mineral A horizon is dark brown in colour
indicative of well-incorporated organic matter, and it usually extends to a
depth of 10 to 15 inches before merging to bright orange-brown subsurface
horizons. The distribution of these soils is interrupted by very shallow soils
classified as rankers, by gleyed acid brown soils, by surface-water gley soils

in occasional depressions, and by peaty gleyed podzols which occur on upland sites under a semi-natural vegetation of wet heath or grassland as on Davidstow Moor.

Shale outcrops of the Culm Measures are noteworthy for the extent of poorly drained land which they possess, the better drained soils being confined to steep slopes. Surface-water gley soils occupy gentler slopes, particularly on the remnants of planation surfaces in central Devon and east Cornwall. Peaty gleyed podzols occur together with peaty surface-water gley soils on areas of higher ground as for example above 750 feet O.D. on uncultivated land between Launceston and Davidstow. These soils are thus some of the most difficult to manage in the Southwest as they dry out in periods of summer drought, and in the subsequent wet period water moving downwards through the desiccation cracks is arrested by the dense clayey subsoil and the shale parent, and this inflicts periods of surface waterlogging. Where sandstones form a more important part of the Culm Measures succession as in the area around Bude, the soils often contain more fine sand. On parent materials of sandstone or sandstone head, shallow loamy soils occur but these also vary according to slope angle with well-drained soils on steep slopes and poorly drained soils on gentler slopes.

The outcrop of the red rocks was described by De la Beche in 1842 as 'one of considerable fertility'. A number of soil series have been established around Exeter and these are largely in sympathy with the extent of the outcrops of breccia, sandstone, marl, and pebble beds shown on the geological map. On the breccias reddish brown gravelly loams overlying red gravelly loam which merges to compact breccia at about 2 feet are common. These soils often lack changes in texture with depth, and well-defined horizons are often absent, although variations in the nature of the breccia allow some lateral subdivision to be made. Sandy acid brown soils, with a loamy sand or sandy loam texture and also lacking marked horizons, predominate on the Permian and Triassic sandstones of the Exe and Otter valleys. Their distribution is interrupted by occasional patches of humus-iron podzols which occur especially under woodland occupying the sites of former heathland. The most extensive series on the Permian marl is represented by a moderately well-drained profile which shows about 15 inches of reddish brown loam above brownish red, silty clay. Two complexes have been recognized on the outcrop of Pebble Beds. The Budleigh complex consists of strongly podzolized soils and is largely restricted to ungrazed commons whereas the second complex is mapped on agricultural land and includes soils which lack evidence of podzolization. These variations in soil type on this part of 'Red Devon' are emphasized by variations in land use. Tillage with some market gardening dominates on the soils of the Permian sandstone and also on the soils of the breccia despite the high content of hard angular stones in the plough layer. On the marl outcrops dairy farming with emphasis on permanent pasture and long leys is predominant.

The broad pattern of soil types reflecting these four groups of parent material in Southwest England is diversified further by the presence of soils developed on other rock outcrops. On rock outcrops restricted in areal extent distinct soil types may often be detected so that four main soil groups have been identified on the serpentine rocks of the Lizard, of which two are derived directly from the serpentine and two are developed partly from the loess that overlies much of the plateau. A very complex pattern of soil types exists on the Devonian limestone outcrop, and the igneous rock outcrops, other than the granite, although often restricted in area produce distinct local relief features and give rise to distinct soil series. Along some valley flood plains warp soils, often sandy loam in texture, with horizons weakly differentiated, may be distinguished from the more commonly occurring ground-water gley soils. The variety of the geological map is reflected in the diversity of textures and drainage classes of the soil types and not least in the numerous soil colours. Although the red soils of 'Red Devon' are particularly striking, the saying 'Gold under bracken, silver under gorse and copper under heather' is one other vivid instance of reaction to the variety of soil colour. Although soil parent material exercises a major control on soil character, further variations are accounted for by contrasts in relief and in land use and it is the character of the vegetation pattern and its evolution which can now be considered.

Vegetation

The hand of man has lain heavy on the vegetation of Southwest England; even the moorlands, wild though they may appear, can lay claim to few, if any, truly natural plant communities, as nearly all show varying degrees of adjustment to widespread grazing, swaling, or other activities. In view of this, it will be valuable, within the limits of the evidence available, to look for a moment not at the vegetation as it exists today but at the stages by which it has come to its present form. From the investigation of many sites in Britain a scheme of pollen zones has been built up, each zone characterized by a distinctive suite of tree-pollen types. These pollen zones outline the main changes of forest cover since the end of the Pleistocene glaciations. The zones have now been given an absolute chronology by the method of carbon-14 dating. Such pollen analyses undertaken in the West Country suggest that our vegetation, in common with that of southern Britain as a whole, changed with the climatic oscillations from late glacial times to the present.

An early phase in the progressive amelioration of climate is indicated by the spread of birch trees together with a smaller number of pines. The warm, drier (boreal) climate which occurred around 7000 B.C. encouraged the immigration of warmth-demanding trees such as oak, elm, and alder, and hazel became abundant. About 5000 B.C. a wetter climate set in and during the early part of this so-called Atlantic phase the oak, elm, and alder forests reached their most widespread lateral and altitudinal development, possibly reaching 1,500–1,600 feet above present-day sea-level. Large areas of our western moors would therefore have been covered with deciduous trees during the 'forest maximum'; vestigial remains of such forests survive, albeit stunted and eerily distorted, in such famous oak copses as Wistman's Wood (1,250–1,350 feet), and Black Tor Copse (1,150–1,450 feet), both of which grow amid clitters of boulders strewn on the hillsides. Subsequently a recession of the forests occurred, particularly over the more elevated parts, and blanket bog covered large areas above 1,500 feet. By 3000 B.C., when men first appear on the scene in any considerable numbers, the valleys and lower hills of the Southwest were covered with this broad-leaved, deciduous forest which thinned out on exposed coasts and on the higher hills where ultimately bogland reigned supreme. The recession of the forests, which began as the natural result of the onset of wetter oceanic weather, has been ruthlessly continued by man during the long history of human settlement which the region has experienced. Since Neolithic times the woods have been felled to satisfy a variety of human needs. Much of the original woodland cover was cleared to provide land for cultivation and for pasture, on which the grazing of animals has prevented regeneration and encouraged the growth of grass. Large areas were felled to provide timber for constructional purposes and for the needs of industry; this is particularly so in those areas rich in minerals, where the cutting of wood on a coppice system for charcoal to smelt ores has outstripped regrowth. Associated with this coppice working was the harvesting of oak bark for the local tanneries.

So much natural woodland has been removed that a present-day map of vegetation may most usefully be compiled by plotting the boundary of the cultivated farmland; this, the 'in country' as it is called in the vernacular, may then be distinguished from the 'out country' of wild or semi-natural vegetation—the heathlands, moorlands, and rough pastures—and the present-day woodlands. It is on the more elevated parts of the granite and on Exmoor that the large and continuous areas of moorland now exist. Much has already been written about the very rapid rate with which our weather deteriorates with increased elevation, but this in itself is not the full explanation of the sharply defined limit of cultivation and of the great contrasts which occur in the vegetation within short distances as the hills are approached. As a rough guide, we can assume that plants begin and continue to grow whenever the mean temperature exceeds about $5.5°$ C ($42°$ F) and that the intensity of that growth depends upon the amount by which the mean temperature of the warmest month exceeds that figure up to an optimum somewhere between $15.5°$ C ($60°$ F) and $26.6°$ C ($80°$ F). Hence in our oceanic climate, with its relatively cool summers, a change in altitude brings not only a very sharp decline in the length of the growing season but a decrease in the rate of growth. On Scilly, even in mid-winter, though growth may be slow it rarely ceases altogether, while at Princetown the growing season may not begin until April and closes in late November.

Although it is convenient to use the term moorland for that land which is too poor to be cultivated, there is immense variety in the plant communities which it sustains. We shall therefore consider three major types of moorland vegetation, all of which indicate close affinities with the moisture-content of the soil and the drainage. The higher and wetter parts of Dartmoor with more than 70 inches annual rainfall are covered with blanket bog, areally one of the most important types of British peat-land. Peat is formed when conditions are such as to inhibit the activity of micro-organisms which normally lead to the breakdown of organic matter. Of the 215 square miles of wild vegetation on Dartmoor, about half is covered with such bog vegetation growing on waterlogged terrain. It occurs in two large areas, one to the north and one to the south of the diagonal road across the moor from Moretonhampstead to Princetown. Where slopes are gentle the blanket of peat may vary from a foot or so to as much as 15 feet in thickness. The general form of such bog vegetation is a surface mat of bog-mosses (*Sphagnum*) through which project scattered shoots of purple moor grass (*Molinia*), cotton sedge (*Eriophorum*), heather (*Calluna*), and deer sedge (*Scirpus cespitosus*). Wherever such a moss carpet is growing, active peat formation is still taking place. In some places the peat is deeply eroded and isolated hags stand 6 feet or more above the levels of the channels. In such dissected parts, drainage is improved, with the result that the moss carpet is much less in evidence and the balance of the various species very different: heather and cotton sedge (*Eriophorum vaginatum*) frequently dominate the vegetation.

Surrounding the blanket bogs on Dartmoor are drier moorlands which are usually classified according to the dominant species of plants, but their delimitation cannot be rigidly defined as they merge into one another. Visitors to Dartmoor soon discover the more obvious contrasts between the heather moors and grass moors, while the more local but still extensive growths of bracken, gorse, and bilberry are readily identified. The heather moors, brown coated in winter and gently purple with the budding of the flowers later on, are quite extensive, with the common ling or heather as the most prominent plant. Heather, intolerant of poor drainage, forms a ring of vegetation around the periphery of the moor and on most lines of approach it quickly gives the visitor the feeling that a new landscape is being entered. If undisturbed, the heather will grow to become a cover as much as two feet high beneath which little else can survive. Such a cover is, however, rare owing to the practice of swaling, which, when completed, leaves an intertwined mass of burnt and charred twigs. If this burning is done to leeward so that the flames work up the wind, the roots are not damaged and a dense growth of tender, highly nutritious, and floriferous young shoots is stimulated. On the other hand, too frequent and uncontrolled swaling damages the heather roots, at the same time allowing the deep-seated rhizomes of bracken (*Pteridium aquilinum*) to survive and spread. As a consequence, areas formerly clothed with good heather have become covered with bracken which, by its leaf shade, prevents most other plants from growing and this takes place on the drier, better parts of the moor.

With better drainage, a bog-land on Dartmoor quickly changes to grassland. The soil may still be peaty and persistently wet but if there is a slow movement of the water and consequent aeration *Molinia* will establish itself, particularly on near-level or slightly undulating ground. On such soils it develops large tussocks some 3 feet or more across. It provides a good spring feed for stock, but it is extremely sensitive to grazing and quickly disappears when heavily grazed. The valley-sides and spurs around the margins of the blanket-bog are often dominated by mat-grass (*Nardus stricta*) or 'white bent'; this flourishes on a damp peaty, acid soil which is not permanently wet. It is unpalatable to stock and forms a thick mat that ousts all but a few rivals in a whitish sea of waving grass. Still better drainage favours the spread of bent-fescue grassland on grazed well-drained slopes with shallow soils of moderate acidity, especially around the dry margins of the moor.

Although the boundary of the moorland encompasses a considerable area in what is loosely called Exmoor, only a small part actually lies in Devon. This consists of the fringing commons on the west side of Exmoor such as West Anstey, Molland, Shoulsbarrow, Brendon, and Challacombe, to which must be added those areas of wild vegetation bordering the coast, like Countisbury and Martinhoe Commons, Trentishoe and Holdstone Downs. Exmoor has the same broad types of moorland vegetation as Dartmoor but is more heathery and has hardly any true blanket-bog, though there are some extensive bogs in shallow valleys on the uplands. Heather moorland occurs most frequently on the commons and downs near the coast, including the large Brendon Common, but locally gorse and bracken may become dominant, both yielding to oak woodland down the valleys. Grass moors, both *Molinia* and *Nardus*, occur on the west-facing commons such as Challacombe, Shoulsbarrow, and Whitfield Down.

Cornwall has a considerable acreage of moorland, but large, continuous areas are found mainly on Bodmin Moor—with its extension northwest on to Davidstow Moor—the Penwith peninsula, and the Lizard. The Carnmenellis and the Hensbarrow have been nibbled into to such an extent that wild vegetation now grows only in a number of scattered patches between the china-clay workings and between those areas which have been 'taken in' for cottage cultivation under the leases-for-three-lives system. Bodmin Moor, like Dartmoor, has a vegetation which tends to vary with the wetness of the soil. Bog vegetation is very local and restricted in area.

Where very wet spots do occur they are called 'piskie pits' and are emerald green in colour; 12 feet or more of sphagnum peat may be found in some of them. Developed over the peat in all but these wetter parts is a purple moor grassland, and this may be considered the main vegetation of the moor, within which rushes and heather may be abundant and locally sub-dominant. On the drier and less peaty soils, a considerable area in all, *Festuca-agrostis* grassland becomes dominant. Recently it has been shown very clearly that more productive grasses and clovers can be grown, pro-vided certain soil deficiencies are artificially rectified. Lately some 2,000 acres were substantially improved after the application of sea-sand, rich in calcium carbonate, from the beaches of northwest Cornwall.

Semi-natural vegetation also occurs on less elevated ground than the granite and in a fringe of varying extent around the coast—the landscape so covered must add up to a very considerable acreage. It is important to associate with these areas the highly oceanic nature of the climate and the southerly position. Close floristic affinities may be expected with southern and western oceanic parts of the neighbouring Continent—indeed, many southern and oceanic species occur, which are local or entirely absent in other parts of Britain. In east Devon there is a considerable amount of wild vegetation but continuous large areas are not frequent. The Woodbury Commons on the Budleigh Pebble Beds aligned north to south make quite an impressive landscape of dry heath with occasional groups of conifers. Farther east, the wild vegetation of the flat-topped Greensand plateaux contrasts markedly with the cultivated fields downslope on the Keuper Marls. For example, the main part of Gittisham Common is covered with heather, gorse and bracken, the dwarf gorse (*Ulex gallii*), and *Erica tetralix*, expressive of the western oceanic element in the vegetation. Where the Greensand underlies a thin layer of Chalk the calcareous soil bears a scrubby ashwood; away from the Chalk the flat surfaces can have a highly acid soil and this bears oakwood of the heathy type. Bovey Heathfield in south Devon is another heathland of low elevation. In the northeast of this basin common furze (*Ulex europaeus*) and bracken flourish but as the ground slopes westward they are superseded by *Ulex gallii* and the fine-leaved heath (*Erica cinerea*). Bristle-leaved bent grass (*Agrostis setacea*) is dominant in drier localities and where damper ground occurs the cross-leaved heath (*Erica tetralix*) becomes abundant—all quite typical of the oceanic western European element. In many areas of poor drainage, especially on the heavy clay soils derived from the Culm Measures, rushes frequently flourish so that pasture fields often grade into reedy and open *Molinia* cotton grass moors: particularly is this so in north Cornwall and central west Devon, but a statement such as this should not pass without recording the con-siderable improvements made on several farms in the area. The almost universal ownership of the versatile tractor to which can be attached hydraulic digging and draining equipment has changed **many** erstwhile reedy, boggy acres into rich pasture. The find of a bronze bowl embedded deep in the peat of Crooked Moor, Munson (SS 766220) during one such draining operation goes far to suggest that some land now being improved has not been farmed since the end of the first century B.C. at least.

In contrast to the rocks which surround it, the serpentine of the Lizard has proved unsuitable for agriculture, so that much of the Goonhilly Downs and Lizard Downs remains unenclosed, unploughed, and unimproved. This is not to suggest that these Downs are undisturbed; few have not at one time or another been burnt in the recent past. Afterwards a heathy vegetation becomes established, especially over large areas of the plateau surface away from the coast and above the river valleys. There is some correlation with the degree to which the soil derived from the weathered serpentine is mixed with foreign material weathered out of the adjacent granites under periglacial conditions and deposited as a wind-blown loess over the serpentine. Where there is a fairly thick accumulation of soil over the rotting serpentine a mixed heath grows, in which Cornish heath (*Erica vagans*) and gorse become dominant. Soils which have a considerable amount of granite-derived loess tend to be badly drained, compact, and of a silty-clay texture and to support a tall heath in which the Cornish heath is co-dominant with bog rush (*Schoenus nigricanus*).

A strip of land bordering the coastline has also largely escaped the attentions of man and his animals, and patches of maritime vegetation can frequently be found approximately in the natural state. On low coasts, sand dunes occur in several places, particularly along the Atlantic-facing coasts. The chief areas of blown sand are north of Hayle in the Upton and Godrevy Towans; Penhale Sands north of Perranporth; around the beaches west of Padstow, Bude, and the very large area of Northam and Braunton Burrows. The coastal dunes at the latter extend for nearly three miles north of the Taw–Torridge estuary and in places are as high as 100 feet above O.D.; they thus rank as one of the high dune-systems in the British Isles. Since it is here that dune vegetation reaches its very best expression in the Southwest we may, with advantage, explore its flora and make passing reference to the other dune areas mentioned above. At Braunton, as in the Cornish examples, the dune system is built up from calcareous shell-rich sand, and the flora has developed in a subtle variety of plant habitats. The fresh-water table under the dunes has a dome-shaped profile so that dry and exposed mobile dunes on the one side contrast sharply with the sheltered slacks, where the level of ground water is maintained for a considerable part of the year at or near the surface. A marked zonation of vegetation bears witness to the decisive operation of these two physical factors—shelter and accessibility of water. The seaward side of the Burrows is composed of irregular lines of dunes running approximately north to south, the building and stabilization of which depend largely on the growth of marram grass (*Ammophila arenaria*). On the more mobile dunes nearer the sea this grass forms a pure community of irregular tussocks. On the more sheltered of these dunes a mixed plant community establishes itself, in which the chief species are rest harrow (*Ononis repens*), many small annuals, and other low-growing plants in a carpet of moss (*Tortula ruraliformis*). Marram grass is still usually present but is less vigorous and few, if any, well-marked tussocks are formed. Farther to landward, the lower dune-slopes and sandy hillocks are much more stable and on these fixed dunes a more complete vegetation cover exists. It takes the form of a dry dune-pasture of short turf, in places infested with bracken, or a dune scrub which, on the extreme landward edge, becomes dense and woody. A rapid change in vegetation occurs in the slacks between the dunes and in the hollows to landward, where increased shelter, ground-water, and occasional flooding give rise to a great variety of plant communities. Again there is an irregular zonation in a landwards direction. The hollows among the foredunes tend to have a sparse cover of such halophytes as sea rocket (*Cakile maritima*) and prickly saltwort (*Salsola kali*). Farther inland an almost continuous carpet of vegetation covers the slacks with a predominance of rosette-forming species such as buck's-horn plantain (*Plantago coronopus*) and hairy-headed hawkbit (*Leontodon leysseri*). An even denser and more varied flora covers the sheltered hollows east of the main line of dunes, forming a damp pasture of grasses and sedges.

A very different kind of coastal vegetation grows on the expanse of broken ground in southeast Devon (Plate 1). Landslips have occurred along this stretch of cliff for centuries—small slips almost yearly and massive ones periodically. The rocks which make this broken terrain contain calcium carbonate so that the soils and drainage water are strongly calcareous. A dense scrub frequently covers this ground, mainly composed of privet, dogwood, and wayfaring tree and other calcicoles. Drainage water which emerges by seepage or springs on the lower cliff levels is sufficiently calcareous to form a tufa-coating over dead twigs and mosses. Sallow (*Salix atrocinerea*) is the dominant shrub of these wet patches, together with giant horsetail, rushes, and sedges.

Of all the maritime habitats, it is the spray-washed rocks and cliffs which present plant-life with its greatest struggle for survival. Most of the plants found on the lower portions of cliffs are halophytes but the upper parts, frequently less steep and with more soil, carry in addition many of the inland plants belonging to the ground above. The amount of vegetation is fairly closely related to exposure. The more protected a stretch of cliff land is from the wind, the thicker is the vegetation, and the lower it grows; east-facing cliffs usually have more vegetation than those with a westerly exposure. The area of uncultivated land on the tops of cliffs varies greatly but almost everywhere exposure is the important factor influencing vegetation.

Mention has already been made of the long period during which forest

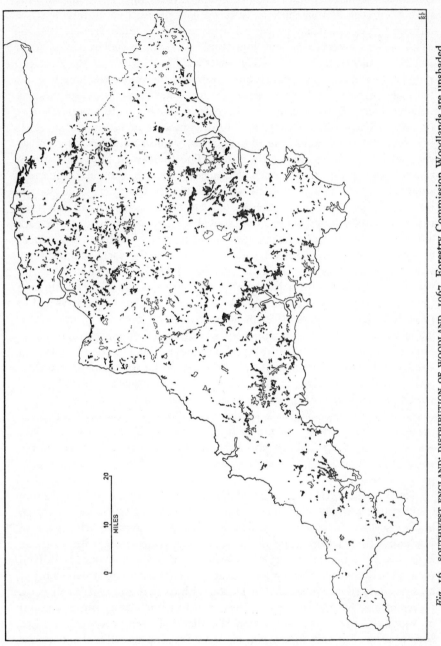

Fig. 16 SOUTHWEST ENGLAND: DISTRIBUTION OF WOODLAND, 1967. Forestry Commission Woodlands are unshaded.

clearance was actively pursued. For much of this time the woodland must have been regarded as the enemy to be conquered; how different is our outlook at present when we regard it as an indispensable friend. Historically, and to a certain extent topographically, the woodlands shown on Figure 16 may be grouped into three classes. Firstly there are the scattered remnants of woodland most frequently found on very steep valley sides, too steep and unprofitable to clear for any other agricultural activity, on which oak coppice and scrub predominate, commonly with an understorey of great wood-rush, bilberry, and heath grasses; on rather deeper soils bracken, bluebells, and brambles flourish, while on higher sites moss-covered boulders are frequently found. The Southwest bore its share in the culture of the woods and planting which was general throughout England during the eighteenth and nineteenth centuries. The second broad class of woodland therefore consists of those planted at this time mainly around country houses; they show the characteristic features of park and amenity-planting familiar elsewhere in Britain whereby an assortment of species, both broad-leaved and coniferous, in the form of individual trees, small clusters, shelter belts, and small formal plantations enhance the view from and give a backcloth to the great house. Nearer our own time there have been the unavoidable ravages of the First World War, but these have had the good effect of emphasizing the need for strong action if the forests are to be re-established. The Acland Committee reported on the state of our woodlands in 1917; the sequel to this was the formation of the Forestry Commission in 1919. It was not to be very long before their activities became obvious in the landscape of the Southwest, for in the same year they took over Eggesford, their first acquisition in Devon. The third class therefore consists of the plantations established during the present century, mainly on the moorlands, by the Forestry Commission, the Duchy of Cornwall, certain private landowners, and water supply authorities. These plantations are largely of conifers with the spruces predominating.

Despite the further fellings of the Second World War, the Devon countryside, with its tall lush elms and sturdy oaks, gives the impression of being a well-wooded county. This is an illusion common to other parts of England where a very large number of fields resplendent with so many hedgerow trees deceive the eye into believing that there is more woodland than actually exists. The national average of land area wooded—6·6 per cent—is only slightly exceeded in Devon with its percentage of 7·1 in 1959. Nevertheless, Figure 16 shows a scattered but not unsubstantial amount of woodland. In the 1924 Census of Woodland of over 5 acres, Devon had 80,610 acres, but this figure had risen to 101,574 acres by the time the 1949 Census was taken; ten years later in 1959, the last year for which we have a total, it stood at 118,895 acres. By far the greater part of this woodland is still in private hands, and a good deal of it is found scattered throughout the county, more related to slope than to soil conditions. Steep valley sides are frequently wooded; the woods give way to grassland above, and good examples of this type of reversed land use can be seen in the Taw and Torridge valleys, along the upper Exe, and beside several of the streams draining the east side of Dartmoor, of which the upper Dart as it flows through Holne Chase is a fine example. In west Devon similar forested sites exist along the Tavy and Tamar valleys. The thirteen estates of the Forestry Commission (Fig. 16) can usually be recognized by their larger size and by their location; with the three exceptions of Molton, Plym, and Erme, which are mainly on steep valley slopes, they are either on the exposed moorlands, the Culm clays, or the gravel-covered Greensand hilltops of east Devon. On the exposed moorlands are the two estates of Dartmoor and Fernworthy, where at elevations of over 1,500 feet Sitka Spruce trees 70 feet in height are growing vigorously. On the Culm Measures in ascending order of size are Bampton, Okehampton, Lydford, Eggesford, Hartland, and Halwill, which, with its 4,590 acres, is the largest estate in the Southwest. The two important gravel-covered hilltop areas which have forests are at Haldon (where the woodland is continuous) and in the Honiton area, where eleven acquisitions give an attractively discontinuous pattern of waste and woodland amid rich agricultural land. The total acreage of woodland in the Forestry Commission estates is about a sixth of the total in Devon; it mainly consists of soft woods rather than hardwoods. Nevertheless, over the county as a whole broad-leaved trees still predominate in the high forests of Devon.

In the long, narrow peninsula of Cornwall, exposure to winds coming straight off the sea appears to have a more discouraging effect on tree growth than does the exposure at high elevations. Travellers to Cornwall frequently remark on the contrast between the treeless windy uplands and the lush vegetation wherever there is protection from the sea and the wind. This impression is borne out by the very low acreage of woodlands recorded for the county in the 1949 Census, the total amounting to 34,528 acres which is only 4 per cent of the land area. As in Devon, a good deal of the woodland is on valley slopes; most of this is in south and east Cornwall where the Fal and Fowey, with their tributary valleys, are notable. The corollary of this location is that by far the larger amount of woodland is in private hands and for the year 1949, which is the last occasion when the Census of Woodlands was taken, over 30,000 acres were so owned. At that time oak was by far the predominant hardwood of the high forest, followed by beech, ash, and sycamore, the two last in very much smaller numbers. As in Devon, the Forestry Commission early acquired land in Cornwall. Its first acquisition was in the Glynn valley in 1922 and now there are six estates. Four of these are located in valleys—Glynn in the Fowey valley, Bodmin in the vale of the river Camel, Herodsfoot in the deep valleys of the Looe and West Looe rivers, and the small St Clement estate within the valley of the river Allen. The remaining two estates are mainly on the exposed moorlands; the larger, Wilsey Down, is on high ground where exposure from all directions is severe and where the trees show remarkably poor growth. At the much lower height of 350 feet on the Lizard planation surface is Croft Pascoe, a small experimental forest of just over a hundred acres, the object of which is to observe tree-growth under conditions of extreme exposure.

CHAPTER 5

The Early Settlement of Southwest England

WHILE there are some important sites in the Southwest where evidence of Palaeolithic and Mesolithic life can be found, it is with the more developed and settled Neolithic culture that our consideration of early settlement can begin. The Neolithic way of life with its techniques of agriculture and stock raising, as well as its early beginnings of trade, was brought to the Southwest by immigrants from western France probably somewhat before, rather than after, 3000 B.C. This cultural phase was to last some 1,500 years but, surprisingly, there are few visible remains of a domestic character to show for this great passage of time. Authentic finds of Neolithic houses even in the whole of Britain are few, but of these, two are located in the Southwest. On an open site at 740 feet near the Belvedere on the Haldon plateau a roughly rectangular house—the first of its kind to be discovered in England—measured some 20 feet by $17\frac{1}{2}$ to $14\frac{1}{2}$ feet. Rather differently, within the causewayed camp at Hembury an almost perfect hut site was discovered; it consisted of stake holes for the support of an oval or sub-rectangular hut of wattle and daub 28 feet by 12 feet. To the same culture belongs the settlement at 470 feet on Hazard Hill near Totnes, and recent finds on Peak Hill (SY 10338593) near Sidmouth at 499 feet suggest another dwelling-site of this period. There are as yet no authenticated Neolithic houses in Cornwall but the hill-top settlement at Carn Brea (SW 686407), and the open sand-hill site near the coast at Gwithian, are Neolithic on the basis of the pottery evidence. The presence of Neolithic communities is also strongly suggested by surface finds near East Week at 900 feet on the northeast corner of Dartmoor; on Mutter's Moor at 500 feet near Sidmouth; at Orleigh near Bideford, and near Dainton. From the finds of grain seeds and querns there is little doubt that the Neolithic settlers in the Southwest were arable farmers; from the few sites so far discovered it is possible only to postulate a settlement in which sub-rectangular and oval houses may have been constructed on open and enclosed sites at both high and low elevations.

Before 1550 B.C. the, by now, mixed Neolithic peoples came under the influence of new leaders who heralded the establishment of a Bronze Age culture throughout the Southwest—a phase which was maintained over a long period down to about 450 B.C. and even later in some parts. Until fairly recently the principal evidence for Bronze Age settlement in this area came from the very numerous hut circles which survive on the high

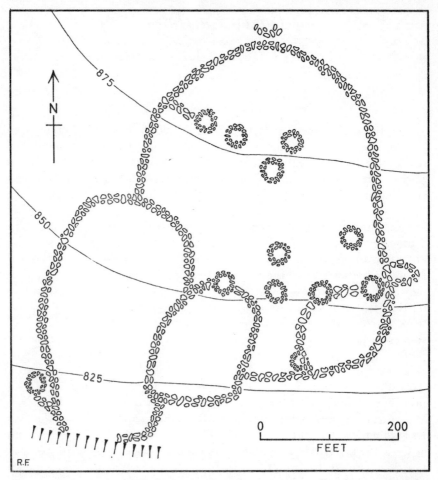

Fig. 17   LEGIS TOR (SX 573654), DARTMOOR: HUTS AND POUNDS. Based upon a drawing by R. H. Worth 'The Prehistoric Pounds of Dartmoor' *Trans. Devon. Ass.* **75** (1943), 285.

moorlands. The distribution of these on Dartmoor is uneven and later cultivation may well have led to the destruction of many such huts; nevertheless, the pattern which emerges is one which indicates an appreciation of the local topography in so far as the higher and more exposed parts of the moorlands are avoided. On the less elevated parts it now appears as if two types of settlement existed simultaneously in different locations, and in all probability reflected two types of economy. An economy in which stock-keeping was significantly more important than cereal growing seems to be found on the wetter southwestern and southern parts of Dartmoor at heights between 1,000 and 1,300 feet. The settlement expressive of this economy consisted of round huts varying from 10–25 feet in internal diameter, with substantial dry-stone walling 4–5 feet thick and about the same number of feet high. Enclosing the huts are roughly circular walls of granite boulders which are locally called pounds— Grimspound (SX 701809) is a particularly well-known example of this type of settlement. Some pounds are irregular and very large; in several

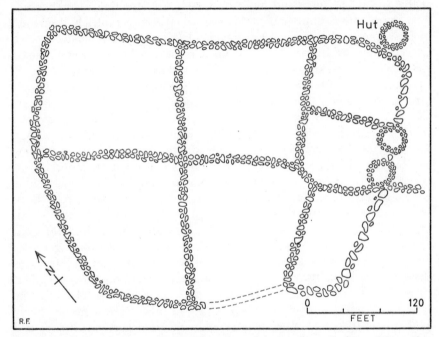

Fig. 18   HUTS AND FIELDS EAST OF BLISSMOOR (SX 7380), DARTMOOR. Redrawn from a plan by A. Fox 'Celtic Fields and Farms on Dartmoor' *Proc. Prehist. Soc.* **20** (1954), 92. See also Plate 2.

cases there are two or more enclosures conjoined to form a complex pound, as at Legis Tor (SX 573654), where there is an aggregation of four enclosures (Fig. 17).   In contrast is the settlement on the drier eastern part of Dartmoor associated with farmers whose economy was predominantly arable. Huts are again round but somewhat larger, 20–35 feet in diameter; they occur singly or in groups but their most interesting characteristic is that they are integral with rectilinear 'celtic' fields (Fig. 18, Plates 2 and 3). Analogues of what has been described for Dartmoor can be found on the Cornish granite masses, particularly on Bodmin Moor and on the Penwith, where Rough Tor (SX 144803) and Trewey Foage (SX 465373) are respectively good examples. Since a large number of

Bronze Age barrows are also conspicuous on the more elevated parts of the Southwest, we must be warned against incautious generalizations from negative evidence about Bronze Age settlement being confined to particular rungs in the altitudinal ladder of the landscape. Houses are a great deal more difficult to find than graves, and the excavation of Trevisker at 390 feet on the St Eval plateau and the comparatively recent exposure of Bronze Age ploughed fields at the lowland site of Gwithian are not only a most significant addition to our knowledge of this period but a timely corrective to any claim of exclusiveness for a high-level form of settlement at this time. The moorland hut circles attracted attention early, because their sturdy stone-built structures have never been completely destroyed in an area which has become marginal land. That they have tended to give a false picture of Bronze Age settlement must now be clearly emphasized and it must be recognized that occupation of lower levels did occur.

The earliest of the Early Iron Age peoples may have differed but very little in their way of life and initial settlement from those of their Bronze Age predecessors. At Bodrifty (SW 445354) near Penzance and at Kynance in the Lizard, the Early Iron Age culture is present above the Bronze Age levels on the very same sites, and the evidence from such sites as Garrow on Bodmin and Kestor on Dartmoor also indicates this continuity of occupation by the two farming communities. For the most part these people lived in open, undefended sites, and their sturdy stone-built huts, set in the corners of small sub-rectangular fields, appear to be the typical farmstead arrangement. At Bodrifty saddle-querns were used for corn grinding, while the finds of spindle whorls and leather-working stones denote the keeping of sheep and cattle as well. What really differentiates these people from their Bronze Age predecessors is not so much their house forms and agriculture as their pottery and the use of iron. The transition from the use of the one metal to the other came about gradually as it was introduced by bands of immigrants from northern France and Brittany, arriving at first in small numbers, after 400 B.C. for the most part, by way of the then well-established cross-channel sea-ways. These immigrants, labelled by archaeologists Iron Age A, can be recognized at coastal sites such as Mount Batten near Plymouth and Harlyn Bay (SW 877754) near Padstow. Few settlements between the coast and the moorland are yet known, but this may well be owing to the lack of recognition of such sites or to their obliteration by subsequent farmers. These immigrant settlers were clearly following in the wake of merchant adventurers who knew well the sea-ways to places where tin was available and who, like Pytheas about 320 B.C., found the Britons in the Southwest very numerous, hospitable, ruled by many chiefs, but usually living at peace with one another. Some of the immigrants, however, even as early as the third century B.C., were becoming uneasy in their newly acquired homes, and their fortifications of earth and stone, probably owing to their more frequent survival, have come to be regarded as the most notable contribution of the Iron Age peoples to the landscape of southern Britain. These fortified places differ markedly both in site and form.

A clearly recognizable group is seen in the cliff-castles. These may be conveniently defined as defended headlands at which—on two sides at least—sea cliffs, the sea, or an estuary are used as natural defences. The man-made features consist of banks and ditches constructed across the necks of headlands in straight lines, in arcuate form, or in combinations of both. From north Devon west along the Cornish coast including Scilly and then east to south Devon, cliff-castles are to be found. A very early one constructed in Cornwall was at Maen near Land's End on the wind-swept granite cliffs above Sennen Cove. The extensive field-system nearby and the absence of minerals in the area suggest that the builders of this earthwork were agriculturalists. Subsequently cliff-castles were built with multivallate defences and it is in this form that Caesar described those on the coast of Brittany occupied by the tribe known as the Veneti. 'The sites of the forts were almost of one kind, set at the end of tongues and promontories . . .' (*De Bello Gallico*, III, 12) Caesar's conquest of this part of Gaul in 56 B.C. put an end to a long period of Venetic trading contacts with Southwestern England. The influence of these people from Brittany is clearly seen in the cliff-castles in general and at the Rumps (Fig. 19) in particular; here the settlers brought with them their pottery styles—if not actual pottery—from their homeland. The evidence seems to point to cliff-castles being introduced by the Veneti, not as refugees after the disastrous events of 56 B.C., but as traders and colonists, decades before.

In the arrangement of the ramparts of the multivallate forts found inland there appear to be some quite distinct differences. Probably most familiar are the forts with closely set banks and ditches, occupying positions in which the natural features contributed to security. Hill-tops (Plate 4) and spur-ends with marked breaks of slope are favoured sites and the massive man-made banks are added to make an already difficult position more formidable to attack and subdue. Somewhat different is a group of forts which do not use the most obviously defensive position, whose banks are not close set but widely spaced: these forts are found frequently on hill slopes, sometimes overlooked even by higher ground. This arrange-ment is seen to perfection at Burley Wood hill-fort, Bridestowe (Fig. 20) and would appear to satisfy the need for several separate enclosures; it has been suggested that their function was to contain herds of animals and to provide grazing and water for them for short periods. Such an interpretation would fit the traditional view of Celtic social oganization, which is based on the early epic literature and the law codes of Ireland and Wales. In them is revealed a warrior society in which wealth was counted in cattle and heroism in daring in cattle-raiding and stealing.

Something of this tradition may well be preserved, albeit telescoped with the passage of time, in the Cornish peasant-tale of Tom the giant-killer. This story relates how the hero passed through the outer gate of the Giant's castle and saw nothing but cattle feeding in the fields, until he came to a double door in the wall surrounding the castle proper. Also in keeping with this warrior aristocracy is the excellence of the decorative metal work which adorned the weapons and trappings of martial splendour, such as the shield mount from St Mawgan in Pydar, and which gave pleasure to the noble lady who fondled the lovely St Keverne bronze mirror. Mention

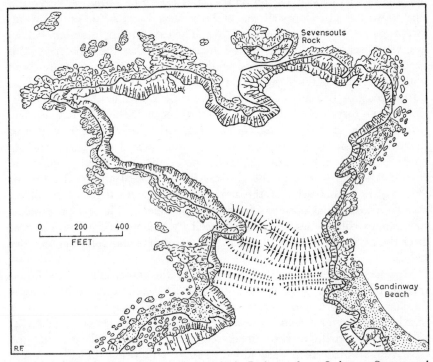

Fig. 19   THE RUMPS CLIFF-CASTLE (SW 934812). Redrawn from Ordnance Survey and D. J. Bonney *Cornish Arch.* 3 (1964), 27.

of these is essential to convey the ferocious restlessness and the sophistication of the later centuries of the Iron Age, but no less important is the appreciation of the economic background which supported them. The large multivallate hill-forts may well have housed the chief and his retinue of warriors, and provided security for his cattle and the stud farm; the tribe too, may well have sought refuge within the ramparts in times of stress. Nevertheless, these hill-forts imply a great communal effort and the force of authority—an authority which required division of labour and an agricultural surplus. Once again the relict in the landscape may well be focusing our attention in the wrong direction.

Far more conspicuous in the landscape of later Iron Age times must have been the earthworks known to us as 'rounds' from the name given to them in Cornwall, where they are reflected in the toponomy by caer-, car-, ker-, or -gear. They were enclosed agricultural homesteads rather than hill-forts of a military character, probably built by a kin group, and consisted of a single bank and ditch—sometimes circular, more often

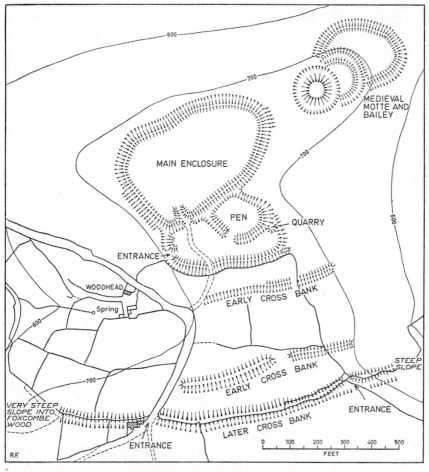

Fig. 20   BURLEY WOOD HILL-FORT (SX 495875), BRIDESTOWE, DEVON.

irregular in shape—enclosing in most cases less than three acres. Few have been scientifically explored to date, but Castle Gotha (SX 027496), which has been excavated recently, may be taken as an example. Here, the enclosed ground, roughly oval in shape, measured 293 feet by 228 feet inside the simple univallate defences, but the ditch has long since been partly filled, and the rampart for part of its length has been incorporated in the existing field hedge. The pottery found suggests that the earthwork was erected about 100 B.C. and that some of the buildings inside were occupied down to the first, and possibly the second, century A.D. Of the 'rounds' so far located, many are situated on ground of moderate elevation between 200 and 400 feet and on a variety of sites; several of them are just above the convex break of slope between the planation surfaces and the valley sides. They were a form of nucleated hamlet settlement with attached field systems. In the two western hundreds of Cornwall, Penwith and Kerrier, the known density of 'rounds' must approach one per two square miles. It is very likely that they were equally numerous at lower and middle levels in both Cornwall and Devon, but as they are frequently found on land which has a long history of cultivation, their ditches must have long since been levelled and parts of their banks been incorporated in hedge banks. Many of them have in this way either been removed or disguised but there is little doubt that 'rounds' and open settlements surrounded by arable fields were the significant settlement forms in the landscape of Iron Age times.

The Iron Age inhabitants have become known to us by the name of Dumnonii, a Celtic people whom the Romans found settled and ruling over Devon and Cornwall. It is worth recalling that in the summer of A.D. 43 a reluctant Roman army set forth across the English Channel and, after a single but hard-fought battle on the Medway, the Imperial armies were soon made ready for a breakout to the west. Vespasian with Legio II Augusta was given the task of annexing southern Britain. Apart from the brief statement made by his biographer Suetonius that Vespasian 'reduced to subjection two very powerful tribes, more than 20 hill-forts and fought 30 battles', little was known of his advance to the south and southwest until recently. It is now almost certain that the Romans had reached Exeter and built a fort there in the late 'forties. They were certainly in occupation of the fortlet at Old Barrow, in north Devon, in the 'fifties and—more remarkable still—had pushed on to Nanstallon, just west of Bodmin, in the 'fifties or 'sixties. It now seems very probable that this early advance resulted in the annexation of the whole of the peninsula. As yet, more is unkown than known about the Roman occupation of Southwest England, but already there are some pointers to the attitude of the invader to the invaded, and to what happened to the native settlements. The speed of the advance and the garrisoning of small numbers of Roman soldiers in isolated fortlets surrounded by native settlements would suggest that the Dumnonii showed themselves peaceably inclined to the invader and in general were allowed to remain in possession of their existing lands and settlements. Even at the hill-fort of Hembury, finds indicate that the occupation continued down to A.D. 65–70 and, at more and more native dwelling sites less formidable in construction, recent excavations have revealed finds dateable to the second and third centuries A.D.

On present evidence, four forms of native settlement have been recognized in the landscape of Roman times. At Porth Godrevy (SW 583428) a single isolated hut of irregular plan 30 feet by 22 feet with internally rounded corners was found to be integrated with a rubble-filled bank that probably formed an enclosure around it. Slight remains of small square fields are almost certainly associated with it. Perhaps this find indicates that the Iron Age circular hut was losing its monopoly during the Roman era and that many more such single homesteads remain to be found—it seems unreasonable to invest the single stead at Porth Godrevy with uniqueness. A single dwelling within an enclosure such as this is far removed from the cellular courtyard house villages of the Land's End area. The classic example of this settlement form (Plate 5) is Chysauster (SW 473350), where the walls of eight houses, in a compact group of two rows of four each, still stand several courses above ground level. The thresholds, which face away from the prevailing southwest wind, give onto a narrow passage in the thick outer wall of each house; this leads into a courtyard which presumably was uncovered. A round room used as the main dwelling was built opposite the entrance with a long room for industrial use on the right of it. This arrangement is repeated with minor variations in each house. The finds indicate that the village was built in the first or possibly as early as the second century B.C. and that here, once more, occupation continued during the presence of the Romans into the third century A.D. The houses were abandoned piecemeal and nothing was found to suggest destruction or a violent end. At Mulfra Vean (SW 454350), there seems to have been a mixture of courtyard houses and the more familiar circular or sub-circular huts, while at Goldherring, Sancreed (SW 4128) a courtyard house has been located in a 'round'. Courtyard houses thus occur singly, in pairs, or in clusters; they are found on quite open sites or more rarely they are surrounded by a kind of stone cashel, but most, if not all, appear to be associated with or adjacent to field-systems. On archaeological grounds it seems that the occupants of the courtyard houses shared in the general culture of west Cornwall at this time, and it is very likely that this kind of dwelling evolved in this particular environment of granite uplands where boulders were plentiful and to hand. The distribution of courtyard houses may well turn out to be very limited, and they must not, therefore, be regarded as the only or even the typical type of native settlement in the Roman period, even in west Cornwall. In Devon a native farmstead with its field system has been excavated at Stoke Gabriel (SX 864575). This, for the greater part of its existence, was an apparently open site; it was occupied during the first and second centuries A.D. and life there may well have continued into the fourth century. A mixed type of farming was practised; corn was grown, cattle, sheep, goats, and pigs were kept and a find of shells may indicate that the diet was varied with edible marine molluscs. Only one ruined round hut was uncovered, but the possibility of there having been others is not excluded. Sites similar to Stoke Gabriel must have existed in many parts of our peninsula, but the intensive cultivation of later times may well have temporarily covered or permanently obliterated them. Certainly there was a variety of settlement forms, and the inescapable conclusion is that for the earlier part of the Roman era, at least, many of the natives continued to live in their 'rounds', probably replaced and added to by open settlements as the *pax romana* became established. As continued field-work seems to reveal more and more native sites both in Devon and Cornwall, the implication is that a considerable breakage of new ground on the lower part of the landscape must have taken place during the Roman occupation; this clearance must have begun to set the pattern for the rural settlement of later times.

Settlements of deliberate Roman origin in Cornwall and Devon were either few in number or have as yet eluded discovery. Of these, by far the most important was the cantonal capital of the civitas Dumnoniorum at Exeter or, as it was then called, Isca. The site on which it stands is part of an extensive flat (Fig. 21) about 120 feet high, with the river Exe to the west some 100 feet below. Lateral streams flowing from the east to find their base-levels at the trunk river have cut this surface into a number of spur-flats. The early Claudian fort was almost certainly established on the spur-flat between the stream rising near the Cathedral—which flowed along the line of Coombe Street (*La comba c.*1260)—and the Shutebrook. The earliest buildings of the later Roman town were erected on the larger spur-flat between the deep Longbrook valley and Coombe Street, and later spread onto both of the spur-flats and down the slope towards the Exe. About A.D. 200 the Roman town of 92½ acres was enclosed by an impressive stone wall built from the Permian purplish-red volcanic rocks of the neighbourhood. In this way Isca assumed the attractive shape and aspect which can be clearly seen on the maps of the late medieval period and even on the maps of Rocque and Donn in the middle of the eighteenth century. Apart from the cantonal capital at Exeter, the only non-rural Roman sites yet identified are coastal; perhaps a port at Seaton (Moridunum); another which may have been a naval base at Topsham, and some large but uncertain settlement at Plymouth which has produced coins covering most of the Roman centuries.

Away from Exeter, Roman-style buildings are rare indeed. In Devon they have been found on Seaton Down overlooking the Axe estuary at Honeyditches, and at Holcombe, Uplyme; in the far west of Cornwall an isolated lop-sided little villa has been discovered at Magor. It is inconceivable that there were not many more in the pleasant productive lands of the Southwest. Where indeed was the home of the 'clarissima femina, civis Dumnonia'? Since this is an official title borne by the wives of wealthy senators, the source of her wealth presents an interesting problem; if it was in real estate, where was that land? If in industry what was the economic activity and where was it situated? The tombstone at Salona near Split in Yugoslavia on which the above inscription is engraved does not assuage our curiosity on either of these two points, but the very fact of this lady's presence there in A.D. 425—so far away from her place of birth—indicates what aristocratic level could be attained by one, at least, of the natives. She was born hereabouts in A.D. 395 when Dumnonia

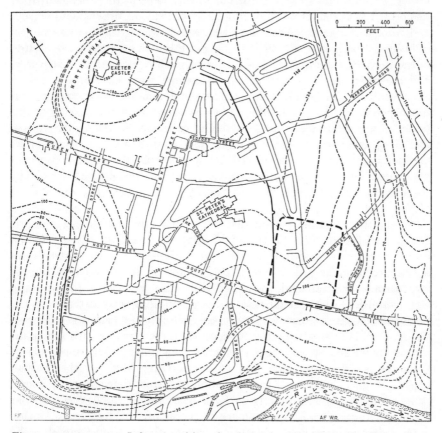

Fig. 21   ROMAN EXETER. Inferred position of early fort in pecked lines; later Roman town walls in solid lines.

was still part of the ordered and secure Roman world, with freedom of movement within it. Alas! this security and freedom were soon to be harassed by assailants from without and conspiracies from within.

Although the end of Roman rule is frequently associated with the year A.D. 410, when Honorius instructed the civitates of Britain to arrange for their own safety, there are signs of the decline of Roman civilization some time before this in the West Country. About A.D. 380 there was decay in the cantonal capital of Isca (Exeter), where pits had been dug in the gravel of the Roman Forum and where wind-blown dust and rain-wash from rubbish heaps was being allowed to cover what remained of the grandeur of the Roman town centre. On the administrative side there are indications of growing independence among the native states, and in place of local councils subordinate to Roman power the Dumnonii began to elect their own rulers, at first called *princeps* or protectors, but later to be regarded as kings. Some of these are known by name such as Constantine who, about A.D. 540 ruled Cornwall and Devon, and who, if the genealogies are to be trusted, was by no means the first of his line. Much of what was happening in this area between the departure of the Romans and the arrival of the Saxons still remains to be discovered, and though in terms of settlement an outline can be attempted, future investigations will undoubtedly modify and amplify what is now but dimly perceived. An initial difficulty to be overcome is the naming of this period; since it witnessed the growth and expansion of the Celtic church, and since the word Celtic has undergone considerable extension of its original linguistic meaning, this label is probably the most convenient one to use. The evidence for settlement in this period is derived principally from two sources, the results of archaeological excavation and the analysis of place-names.

One of the most remarkable discoveries made by excavation is that the Iron Age hill-fort at Castle Dore (SX 103548), deserted early in the first century A.D., was re-occupied. Within the original ramparts post-holes of a large rectangular aisled hall of timber and those of other subsidiary structures were unearthed, associated with finds dateable to the fifth and sixth centuries. The spaciousness of these buildings is consistent with the re-use of this old defensive site as the enclosure for the palace of a Cornish Celtic king. It is also tempting to associate these remains with the sixth-century inscribed stone nearby, which commemorates Drustans, son of Cunomorus—plausibly identified with the King Mark of the Tristan legend. Similar evidence of re-occupation of former defensive sites comes from Chun in Penwith and High Peak near Sidmouth. A very peculiar feature of these sites is the presence of pieces of fine, hard, wheel-made pottery dateable to the late Byzantine Empire, that is from the end of the fourth century to the end of the seventh century A.D. The sherds are those of fine red table-ware and buff amphorae for wine and oil which can be matched with pottery made around the eastern Mediterranean. The trade-route along which this merchandise travelled was probably through the straits of Gibraltar along the Atlantic coast to landing places near the estuaries of rivers, such as Bantham on the Avon or Mothecombe on the Erme in south Devon, where this pottery of eastern Mediterranean provenance has been found in association with encampments made by the merchants or their customers. Literary confirmation of this trade-link appears in the early life of John the Almsgiver, who lived at the end of the sixth century and recorded the sailing from Alexandria to Britain of a ship laden with corn and its return with a cargo of Cornish tin.

The same imported pottery has been found in a very different type of Celtic settlement on the Tintagel headland. Here several buildings were unearthed and a sequence of occupation established which lasted from the fourth century A.D. to the erection of a medieval chapel. Beneath the chapel are parts of buildings which survive from four phases of construction and in this period 'only a monastery would provide all the conditions suggested by the remains'. The word monastery as applied to the Celtic period should not call to mind stately buildings such as the Benedictines loved to erect at a later date. Celtic monasteries were far simpler. They belong to a tradition emanating from the hermits of the Theban desert in Egypt and passing by way of Gaul to Britain. Celtic asceticism developed this tradition on extreme lines and several inaccessible islands and headlands in the west of Britain were peopled by communities who had withdrawn from the world. The close links between the Celtic shores of Britain and the eastern Mediterranean, which are defined by the pottery, go some way to explain those puzzling features of early Celtic Christianity which differed from Roman Christianity and which can now be seen to be more reminiscent of the Eastern Church.

Palace and monastery contributed but few of the settlements to the landscape of Celtic Cornwall and Devon. Where did the much more numerous common folk farm and live? The most outstanding archaeological find which helps to answer this question comes from Gwithian, where the imported wares were found in association with native pottery of this period. At first this native pottery of the fifth century was derived from Romano-British copies of Roman coarse wares. Subsequently, the pottery form changes in so far as the undersides of the bases bear the impressions of chopped dried grass, resulting from the practice of standing the newly-made pots on this material to dry. The impressions thus made on the bases have provided a convenient label for this pottery—grass-marked ware. The practice can with considerable confidence be traced to a centre of diffusion in the northeast corner of Ireland. This discovery points to a migration of people from what is now Ulster to the northwest coast of Cornwall, towards the end of the fifth century A.D. Grass-marked pottery has now been found on some twenty sites, whose distribution indicates a marked coincidence with a group of west Cornish parishes dedicated to Celtic saints long known to be of Irish origin—Phillack, St Ives, St Erth, Gwinear, Gwithian, Breage, Germoe, and Crowan. The archaeological evidence seems to point to the occupation of a number of low-lying sites —many of them actually on the coast—the remains of which have been preserved by being overwhelmed by sand. In form the settlements appear to have consisted of a group of small round houses of dry-stone walling derived from the type known in Roman times; even so, the uppermost

S.E.—4*

level at Gwithian revealed a house rectangular in plan with rounded external corners and angular internal ones. It seems as if the rectangular house was being built more frequently in the course of the Celtic period, and this type has been best exposed archaeologically at Mawgan Porth (SW 852673). Between Trevose Head and Berryl's Point the Cornish coast runs nearly north to south; here the cliffs are broken by sandy coves where the streams draining the coastal plateau reach the sea. On land sloping down to such a stream was built the settlement of Mawgan Porth, consisting of a number of rectangular houses, independent of each other but grouped to form a hamlet. Over the centuries blown sand has formed high dunes hereabouts and this encroachment was the reason for the abandonment of the dwelling-site (as indeed it was for Gwithian and other sites along the coast). This implacable invasion of the sand at Mawgan Porth ruined pasture and made life impossible for the inhabitants. Excavation suggests that they abandoned their houses without haste some time in the ninth century; then, slowly but inexorably, these former homes were covered. Subsequent removal of the sand by excavation has made possible not only the tracing of the ground plans of these houses but also the method of their construction. The turf was first removed and carefully laid on one side to be used as a roofing material. The underlying red clay was then pared off and the rotted rock of the slope cut into to form a level platform, the spoil being heaped downhill to extend the available level surface. Two wall-faces were then built two and a half feet overall and the intervening space filled with stone and clay. The roofs, supported by centrally placed timber uprights, had their rafters meeting on these wall-tops, and were made weatherproof by branches and turves. The whole house measured internally 33 by 15 feet and clearly consisted of a part for humans and a part for animals. Adjacent and linked by a courtyard were other structures, the whole being reminiscent of the earlier courtyard house plan translated into rectilinear form. On the hillside above the houses was the cemetery containing the remains of the hamlet dwellers who had been given Christian interment.

To date, most of the archaeological evidence has been derived from coastal or near-coastal sites, the most prolific in finds being those settlements which have been 'preserved' by inundation of sand. Inland, where no such calamities occurred, the archaeological evidence is more difficult to disinter and for clues to the nature of the Celtic settlement in these parts we must perforce turn to the place-name evidence which can go some way towards filling this gap in our knowledge.

The examination of the place-name evidence in Southwest England bristles with difficulties and problems for a variety of reasons, not the least of which is the nature and date of the Saxon conquest as it proceeded from east to west. In Devon, conclusions arrived at in the 'thirties based on the meagre survival of Celtic place-names spoke of migration to Brittany, extermination, and a sparsely populated county. In vogue then was the firm belief that a fundamental distinction existed between the Celts, an upland-loving people, and the Saxons who farmed at lower elevations on valley sides and floors. Fortunately, even in Wessex—where these ideas were nurtured and pronounced with great authority—they have been proved wrong. Until the possibility of a significant Celtic contribution is at least put to the test, no convincing explanation of settlement history is likely to be advanced. With this in mind it seems most appropriate to attempt to recognize dwellings of Celtic and English origin in the landscape, and to subject their topographical siting to some kind of analysis and classification. The early Celtic settlement of Cornwall is clearly the point at which to begin such a study, but the problem there is that the Cornish language persisted in use and it is possible that Celtic place-names were given to settlements at any time down to the seventeenth century. An exception may be made of those places which, anciently, were called after Celtic saints and to whom the local church is dedicated. These churches are considered to have been founded by the saints whose names they bear or by some of their immediate followers; since the saints alluded to flourished during the fifth to the eighth centuries, the occupation of the sites almost certainly extends back to about the same period. Although the subject is here treated only in its geographical aspects, it must be emphasized that the emergence and expansion of Celtic Christianity was the principal element in the cultural setting of the last centuries during which the Dumnonii existed as an independent people. There is little doubt that some of the Celtic saints in their missionary zeal would set up their places of worship near contemporary settlements. No significant differences, therefore, need be envisaged between ecclesiastical and secular sites. Investigation reveals some 200 sites in Cornwall rewarding of study and classification as examples of Celtic settlements, and site and altitude analyses are summarized in the form of percentages on the graphs (Fig. 22).

The existence in Southwest England of a polycyclic landscape with planation surfaces is largely accepted. This is revealed in a systematic staircase morphology of 'rises' and 'treads'. It is, in the last resort, these units of relief, more familiar to us as 'flats' and 'slopes', which offer a variety of habitats to man; they are grouped here under the generic name of sites. Although in detail no two of these units of relief need be exactly alike, the following categories of sites are suggested as appropriate for the discussion of our problem: hill-top, spur, valley-head, valley-slope, valley-floor, and coastal. As one descends the 'physiographic staircase' in Cornwall, few dedications crown the exposed hill-tops and ridges. Very much more attractive were the spurs and even more attractive were the heads of valleys. The graph (Fig. 22) also shows the occupation of land on valley sides and (very much more important to our argument) on valley-floors as well. That the native Cornish lived on the lowlands is also evident in the large number of dedications on the coast and alongside the many estuaries and creeks which delve deeply into this tapering land mass. Further evidence as to the nature of the Celtic settlement is revealed by the graph (Fig. 22) which shows the number of sites within each 50-foot contour interval, expressed as a percentage of the whole. The preponder-

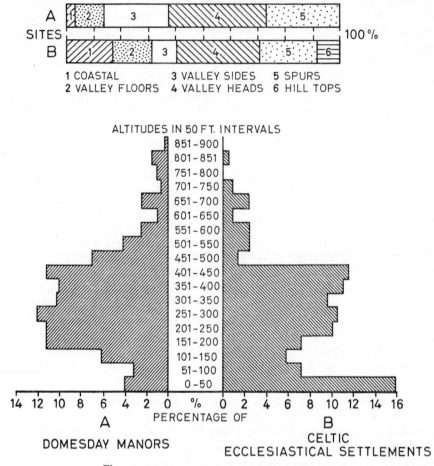

Fig. 22   ALTITUDE AND SITE ANALYSES: CORNWALL.

ance of sites below 500 feet is very marked. If now to this argument the archaeological testimony is added, particularly the sites of the 'rounds' and those where grass-marked pottery has been found, the evidence, although allowing only a partial reconstruction of the landscape of settlement, is sufficient to dispel once and for all the myth that the Celts were exclusively an upland-loving people; that they occupied a variety of sites over a wide range of height and were also numerous on the ground appears to be the most appropriate conclusion to draw for the settlement of Cornwall during the Celtic period.

In Devon, the surviving dedications to the Celtic saints are far less

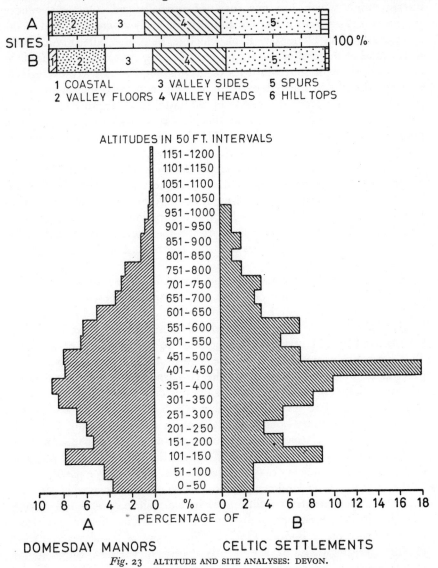

Fig. 23   ALTITUDE AND SITE ANALYSES: DEVON.

numerous than in Cornwall. Owing to the very much earlier date and nature of Devon's conquest by the Saxons which led to an eclipse of the native tongue, Celtic place-names which appear in early charters provide additional examples of native settlements. In site and altitude (Fig. 23) they show a similar variety to those of Cornwall. Nevertheless, the number

of examples remains incredibly small and the Place-Name Society reached
the conclusion that in the middle of the seventh century '. . . no considerable
native population remained to complicate the life of the new settlers', an
interpretation which has not survived unchallenged. One particularly
pertinent fact emerges if the site and altitude analyses are extended to the
manors named in Domesday Book which is, of course, virtually a survey
of England at the end of the Saxon period. They reveal that the English,
after some three or four centuries of occupation, did not live exclusively
in lowland farms in the valleys. Sites on spurs and valley-heads are in the
majority, while a gradual increase in the number of manors occurs from
sea-level to a maximum between the 300- and 500-foot contours. The
graph also reveals that before the end of the eleventh century, farming was
being practised at heights of nearly 1,200 feet. We may well ask what
prompted the English to own such elevated sites on Dartmoor and Exmoor?
When the Cornish Domesday manors are examined in like fashion,
similarities with the Devon graphs can be seen, even though in Cornwall
only about a century of effective English occupation had elapsed by 1086.
The inescapable conclusion is that there was no difference in the habitation
sites chosen by the two peoples and that the Saxons took over or settled
alongside the Celtic folk.

Since the early charters and Domesday Book make unmistakably clear
the extensive expropriation of Celtic ecclesiastical properties in Cornwall
by the Saxons, and later by the Normans, we could hardly expect the
secular dwellings not to have suffered a similar fate, and what holds good
for Cornwall would certainly have applied to Devon at an earlier date.
The most likely explanation of the significant difference between the
survival of Celtic place-names in the two counties is that there was a
substantial influx of people and a considerable take-over of Celtic dwellings
in Devon in the late seventh and early eighth centuries, an influx which
spread over the county boundary in the north and southeast of Cornwall;
this explains the relatively more numerous English place-names existing
in these two localities. In the rest of Cornwall the final eclipse of independence in the ninth century may well have been followed by a parcelling out
of the land to Saxon landowners, most of whom were probably absentee
landlords, the peasantry continuing to be Cornish in speech and culture.
This is the impression created by the manumissions of slaves recorded
in the tenth-century Bodmin Gospels. The names of the slaves and those
of the clerical witnesses are mostly Cornish, whereas those of the
manumittors are Anglo-Saxon. In Devon the few Celtic place-names that
are found haphazardly distributed in the county have survived because
they represent properties which remained in British hands until approximately the same time, namely the reign of Athelstan. This is certainly so
in the case of the valley-head farm of Treable (SX 720928). By two
charters of 739 and 976, a very large area now amounting to some thirteen

parishes was conveyed to the monastery of Crediton. The boundaries are described in detail and a perambulation of them is straightforward except for one anomaly which excludes from an otherwise compact estate the Celtic farmstead of Treable. Clearly it must have been a property with which the government of Wessex was loath to interfere. It is not known why the Celts who lived at Treable were allowed to hold their land while others were absorbed into the Anglo-Saxon settlements. 'It is at any rate clear that they (the Celts) were a far from negligible element in the population of Devon.' [1] They were still an important element in the population in Exeter as late as the reign of Athelstan where, William of Malmesbury tells us, they had inhabited the city on a footing of legal equality with the English. The parishes of St Petrock and St Kerrian, with their Celtic dedications, have long since been cogently argued as marking the nucleus of the British enclave. In many cases there could have been no abrupt end to Dumnonia and equally no abrupt beginning to Saxonia but both Celt and Saxon must have lived alongside each other on inextricably mingled lines.

In 1085 King William decided to enquire over the whole of his conquered kingdom, how it was settled, what lands constituted the Royal Demesne, what had been granted to the Barons or by them granted to lesser folk. The results of the enquiry were collected together into the volumes known to us as Domesday Book. As to settlement, the total number of separate places mentioned for Cornwall is about 330 and for Devon about 983, most of which can be topographically pin-pointed in the landscape and which therefore provide the most comprehensive picture of settlement we have so far been able to obtain. As will be seen later, incautious generalization should not be made from negative evidence but the positive presence of these dwellings is worthy of some further site analysis as indicating some aspects at least of the now combined Celtic and English settlements. Figures 22 and 23 indicate in the form of percentages an analysis of the sites of the identified names. In Cornwall, not unexpectedly, only two manors were found on the exposed hill-tops and ridges; such a number makes a percentage too small to appear on the graph. A substantial number of manors exists on the spur type of site, and the largest number is to be seen in the heads of valleys. There are fewer situated on valley-sides, and fewer still on valley-floors, and remarkably few on the coast; this is to be expected in view of the feeling of insecurity engendered by the Danish raids. There is no doubting the significance of the valley-head and spur sites, as these two groups account for some 66 per cent of all the Domesday manors. Not dissimilar are the results for Devon where 36 per cent of the manors are on spurs, 27 per cent in valley-heads, 17 per cent on valley-sides, and 16 per cent on valley-floors. It must be stressed how very significant are the residual remnants of the inter-

[1] Finberg, H. P. R. *The Early Charters of Devon and Cornwall* (Leicester 1953), 31

fluvial flats and the valley-heads below those flats in the siting of our early settlements and—since nearly all the Domesday places have continued in occupation—how significant these sites are in the present rural landscape, too. Equally revealing is the height-range within which these 1,300 or so manors are located. In Cornwall, a modest number of named manors lies between sea-level and 150 feet, while the landscape between 150 and 500 feet accounts for no less than three-quarters of the total. Domesday names continue above this level to heights of over 800 feet. On a north-facing valley-side on Davidstow Moor at 870 feet stood Treslay, where one Berner farmed, assisted by three bordars who had three ploughing-oxen. In Devon the number of Domesday manors begins to fall off above the 600-foot contour line, but some farms are found at quite surprising altitudes. High up in the head of a south-facing valley at 1,200 feet stands Natsworthy (SX 722800) north of Widecombe, one of the very high recorded manors in the Southwest where a certain Richard was farming and, incidentally, growing grain, for there was 'arable for two ploughs which are there'. Similar heights were being cultivated on Exmoor where Lankcombe (SS 771456) stood at 1,200 feet and, at about the same height, Radworthy (SS 696428) on the south-facing valley-head of the river Bray. Here one Rainald had a plough on his demesne farm and the villeins had two ploughing-oxen. The occurrence of these manors at such high points in the landscape raises very many interesting problems not least the necessity for the English to cultivate such elevated land. Surely the 330 named farms in Cornwall and the 983 in Devon did not absorb all the land of lower and more attractive relief?

Since the time of Maitland it has been suspected that Domesday Book does not name all the settlements which existed in the eleventh-century landscape. In Devon, Domesday Book itself tells us that some manors which were in existence before the Conquest had by then been absorbed into named manors. We should not assume that Pawton, the largest of the Domesday manors in Cornwall with 44 hides, and the only one mentioned in the Hundred of that name, was the sole inhabited place, particularly when there is no evidence to suggest that there has ever been anything more than an episcopal barton on the site. Then again there are several places mentioned in pre-Conquest charters which do not appear in Domesday Book but they did not go out of existence, because they appear in later documentary material. The numerous sub-tenants in the extensive manors of Tavistock and Hatherleigh are unlikely to have been situated actually at these two sites. A map of Domesday settlements makes this very clear, as around most of the very large manors there are spaces on the map without symbols, apparently devoid of settlements. Domesday Book frequently mentions ablations from manors but omits to give them their place-names. This deficiency of place-names has been well known for a long time and various estimates have been made of the total number of farms; the figure of 3,000 for Devon was suggested as long ago as 1932. Professor Hoskins,[1] in an exploration of what lies buried in the shorthand formulas of Domesday Book, calculated that some 9,000–9,500 farms existed in Devon between the years 1066–1086. This figure, which may appear inordinately large, is based on the argument that, in addition to the demesne farm which the Domesday statement described, we should allocate some kind of farm to each of the villeins as well. The vast majority of Domesday entries for both Cornwall and Devon contains a note about the demesne and this is almost invariably followed by the statement that the villeins have the remaining lands. Can the realities in the landscape be worked out from these and other fiscal statements in Domesday Book?

There are, both in Devon and Cornwall, some descriptions in Domesday Book which can be referring only and obviously to small single isolated farmsteads such as the purely pastoral farm of West Curry (fo. 264), where one serf looked after 100 acres of pasture, or Killogorrick (fo. 236b), where another lone serf had two ploughing-oxen. Only a small percentage is described in this way. Other descriptions when related to the ground imply the existence of a demesne farm and other territorially separated farms as well. After identifying the individual farms of manors with 5 to 10 villeins, Hoskins proceeded to the immensely more complicated larger manors. In some he claimed to recognize hamlets, where he was tempted to place some of the bordars of Domesday Book. In the large manors which contain true villages the process of allocation becomes insoluble as there is nothing in the formula of Domesday Book to suggest how many villeins lived in farmhouses in the village street and how many in farms in the outlying parts of the parish.

It now looks as if the Domesday Book formulas are really subsuming both in Cornwall and Devon the three main settlement forms—the single farm, the hamlet, and the village. Single farmsteads were probably quite common, particularly on the hills and in the combes where water is often readily available on the surface or not far below it in sufficient quantities for the needs of men and animals Excavated examples of these early medieval peasant houses in Southwest England were, until recently, few in number. However, enough have now been explored to suggest that the actual building was rectangular in form and in many respects a development from the tenth-century houses at Mawgan Porth. An early example to be excavated was the rectangular house (Fig. 24) which stood on the break of slope between valley-floor and valley-side at 500 feet at Beere (SS 689033). It is in the parish of North Tawton and may well have been included silently in the Domesday assessment of the Royal manor of Tawetona (fo. 83), though the pottery found is twelfth century. The excavated foundations were of a long-house divided into three parts; in the middle

[1] Hoskins, W. G. 'The Highland Zone in Domesday Book' in *Provincial England* (London 1963), 15–52

was the living-room with central hearth to the left of which was the sleeping-room. On the right-hand side beyond the cross-passage between the two doors was the byre. The only structural post-holes found were those for the two doors, and it must be assumed that the roof was carried on trusses resting on the low walls. A mixed economy was practised, as in

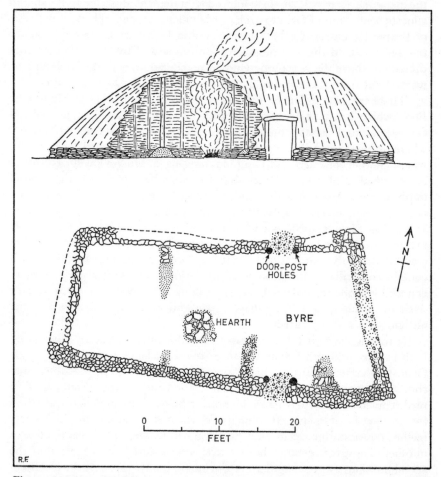

Fig. 24   MEDIEVAL FARMHOUSE AT BEERE, NORTH TAWTON, DEVON. Redrawn from a plan by E. M. Jope and R. I. Threlfall 'Excavation of a Medieval Settlement at Beere, North Tawton, Devon' *Medieval Arch.* 2 (1958), 119.

addition to the byre, there was a barn adjacent and, most interestingly, a corn-drying kiln. A house of the same type and date was excavated as long ago as 1891 at Trewortha (SX 2576), a site at 900 feet two miles west of North Hill in east Cornwall. A much earlier example of a rectangular house, found underlying the Celtic monastery at Tintagel and dated to the period A.D. 350–450, extends this form of building back in time, while another long-house excavated at Lanyon (SW 422337) in West Penwith extends the area in the Southwest in which this kind of house has been found; it is likely to have been the characteristic house form in the Southwest throughout the Middle Ages and early modern times.

For very many of the single farms, the emphasis in the farming economy must surely have been on pastoralism. This is the most suitable use of a landscape of many small well-watered valleys, slopes, and hills. In this economy of animal husbandry no problem presents itself of sharing plough-teams and little pooling of economic resources is required. Buildings need be only of the simplest when animals can remain in the fields for most of the year, though the cattle would be brought into the long-house or barn in the worst times of the winter. Such single farms would be surrounded by their own independent enclosed-field system of small closes held in severalty, their shapes and massive hedgebanks—many of which survived to be placed on modern maps—reflecting the manner in which they were cleared piecemeal by hacking down the forests.

When we come to consider forms of settlement next in size to the single farmstead, we are immediately confronted with the problem of nomenclature and definition. Most people recognize a difference between the hamlet and the village but the actual line of demarcation can never be precise in all cases, particularly when we try to imagine their forms in the eleventh century. We will not be far wrong if we imagine the hamlet as a cluster of farm houses and associated cottages and outbuildings usually grouped without any formal plan and without function in the administrative sense. In recent years much new information about the hamlet form of settlement has been made available by archaeological investigation and documentary analysis.

At about 950 feet on a south-facing hillside at Garrow Tor (SX 146780) on Bodmin Moor were probably nine rectangular platform houses, their shorter sides cut into the slope at right-angles to the contours. These platform houses are a variant of the long-house in that they provided shelter both for man and his beasts under one roof. Here the living quarters, which measured 20 feet by 11 feet, were separated from the byre by a paved passage connecting the entrances in each of the long sides of the house. A hearth was placed centrally in the living-room with a fire-back similar to the 'pentanfaen' of the Welsh long-houses. The walls were at least six feet high, supporting a roof probably of simple truss construction with tie-beams at roof level. At Hound Tor (SX 745789) on an east-facing Dartmoor hillside at 1,200 feet was a hamlet (Fig. 25, Plates 6 and 7) which consisted of five long-houses, two smaller houses and three barns with corn-drying kilns. In their last period of occupation these long-houses, which here also had centrally placed cross-passages and opposite entrances on their longer sides, were built of undressed granite boulders. Beneath the floor of one house was an earlier floor revealed by a number of takes holes. This earlier house had its entrance in the same position as its successor. Further lines of stake holes were recognized as yet an earlier floor, but on the opposite alignment and between two houses were remains of even earlier floors. The sequence of occupation at this site began with small buildings with sunk floors, succeeded by turf-walled houses on the same northwest to southeast alignment; these were replaced by similar turf-walled houses, but on the opposite alignment. The turf walls of two houses were replaced by stone walls which showed two periods of con-

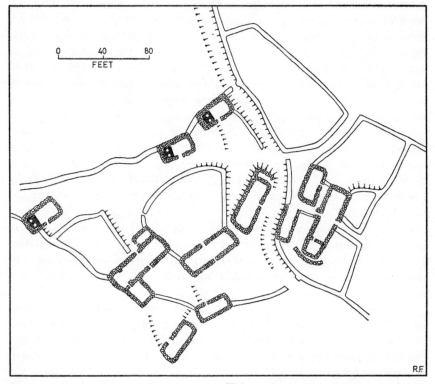

Fig. 25   HOUND TOR (SX 745789), DARTMOOR. Thirteenth-century stone houses and corn-drying barns. Redrawn from a plan by E. M. Minter *Medieval Arch.* **8** (1964), 284. See also Plates 6 and 7.

struction. That Hound Tor was no exception is revealed by a similar sequence of events at Treworld (SX 124903) near Boscastle in Cornwall, where beneath a long-house, 72 feet by 22 feet, were earlier rectangular structures built and rebuilt on the same site and on the same alignment. These again had turf walls faced on the inside with wattle hurdles, which were replaced by stone facing in the last phase of occupation. In the three excavations mentioned the pottery found has been thirteenth century but the sequence of structures in the case of the last two must surely suggest occupation as early as the eleventh, if not the tenth, century.

From the presence of byres and corn-driers there can be no doubt that the people who lived in these long-houses practised a form of mixed farming. In the case of Garrow Tor there is evidence that alongside the hamlet there was an arable field with strips 200 yards long and 6 feet wide running up and down the hillside. Unenclosed rectangular arable fields with cultivation ridges resulting from four or five journeys up the whole length of the ridge and down again were also found at Gwithian, dated to the period A.D. 850 to 1100. Whether these arable fields were divided, share-land fashion, amongst the cultivators of the hamlet is something as yet beyond the technique of the archaeologist to prove. Nevertheless the forces which brought houses together into clusters would seem to have had a technological as well as a social aspect: that some form of co-aration was practised is a distinct possibility.

Archaeological excavation is proving the existence, house type, and methods of construction of our medieval farms and the grouping of these into clusters or hamlets. An ingenious analysis of a collection of documents allows us to visualize the degree to which these farms were clustered or agglomerated in three different parts of Cornwall. Professor Beresford has discovered that the documentation for the Duchy manors is unusually good for the period 1300–1330 and that the records are cast in a form which allows the tenantry to be assigned to their geographical location; furthermore, the information which the documents contain is the totality of settlement for the period in question. In a sample of five parishes— Lanteglos, Advent, Michaelstow, St Stephens, and Creed—located in three quite separate parts of the county, there were 203 messuages scattered in 57 different places, grouped as follows:

Messuages	1	2	3	4	5	6	7	8	9	10	over 10
No. of groups	11	16	8	9	6	0	1	2	1	0	3

The largest number, 16 or 28 per cent, were in groups of two farms and no less than 50 of the 57 places or 88 per cent lay in clusters of up to five dwellings. If the groupings of these messuages are a representative sample of the settlement pattern as a whole, there is no doubt of the significance of the hamlet in the landscape of the period 1300–1330. Furthermore, in these three parts of Cornwall at least, the common belief that Cornish settlement was typified by isolated farms is unfounded, only 11 or 19 per cent being so. Three of the 57 places had a grouping of over 10 messuages, so that the larger agglomerations or villages also existed and it is to these that our attention must now be directed.

Since a warning has been given of the imprecision which surrounds the distinction between hamlet and village, and since a reference has been made to the former as an amorphous grouping of farms, it would appear as if some formal plan is the essential requirement of a village. Such a clear-cut distinction is far too facile, because a scrutiny of village forms as they were drawn on our early maps exhibits a great variety of shapes which clearly are the outcome of organic growth and particular local influences, both social and topographic. This is not to say that similar influences did not bring about a village-shape that is repeated. Since we must envisage the growth of some hamlets into villages, and with this growth a rearrangement of fields and farmsteads, it is in such rearrangements that regularities in the shapes of villages are perhaps best explained. We may thus sharpen the difference between hamlet and village if we regard the latter as a nucleation of a large number of houses in a setting of streets, crofts, and lanes. Can this medieval scene be recognized from our distant point in time? There has been some criticism of accepting any considerable antiquity for the village forms as they were drawn on our earliest maps. A good deal of evidence indicates, however, that very few radical changes have taken place in the internal lay-out of villages over the period 1300–1800. Individual houses have of course been rebuilt and not always on the former foundations, but the 'crofts' on which they stand have been very resistant to change. To alter the boundary of a croft meant encroachment on to the street in the front or the open field at the back, an intrusion which involved the community as a whole. Thus strong barriers of property rights and custom were present to thwart great changes, and many villages show extreme conservatism in the alignment of their crofts, streets, and lanes. Much that was medieval had undoubtedly survived, albeit in modified form, to be put on the earliest of our large-scale maps, and the recognition and recent interpretation of these maps has meant that much of what was written with confidence, even twenty years ago, about the southwestern villages can no longer be accepted. Perhaps foremost to be disclaimed is the notion that the nucleated village so familiar in England, with its open-field form of agriculture, was never introduced into Devon and Cornwall.

In recent years cartographical and topographical investigation has added considerably to our knowledge of the character and distribution of the open field in Devon. Cartographic recognition is possible because a strip—or group of strips (Figs. 26 and 27)—was subsequently enclosed and such closes perpetuate and, as it were, fossilize the ancient strip-pattern. On the tithe maps of Devon they are frequently associated with the field name *landscore*, or its local variant *landscove*. Topographically, too, some can still be recognized by micro-relief features occasioned by medieval ploughing and the survival of baulks and strip-lynchet boundaries. This work of recognition was substantially underpinned in 1949, when Finberg found documentary proof that the long-disputed field pattern at Braunton was the legacy of open-field agriculture dating from at least 1324. The ancient strips were recognized on the estuarine flats and on Braunton Down 350 feet above sea-level—an area of quite strong relief.

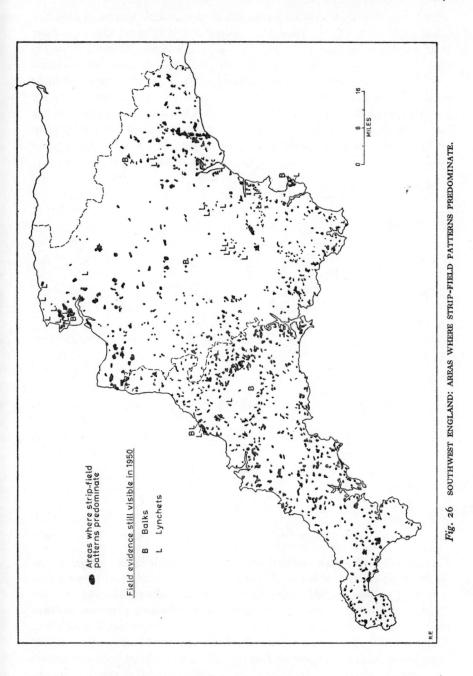

Fig. 26 SOUTHWEST ENGLAND: AREAS WHERE STRIP-FIELD PATTERNS PREDOMINATE.

In the 'thirties Charles Henderson recognized in Cornwall that the place-name Gweal Hellis meant the open fields of Helston and argued for their existence around the other towns in Cornwall. Carew too, in his *Survey of Cornwall*, compiled in 1602, declared how 'These [the husbandmen] in times not past the remembrance of some yet living rubbed forth their estate in the poorest plight; their grounds lay all in common or only divided by stitch-meal . . .', i.e. in strips. The documentary references, extremely valuable though they are, have not been found nor are likely to be found in sufficient quantity to give us an idea of what the overall

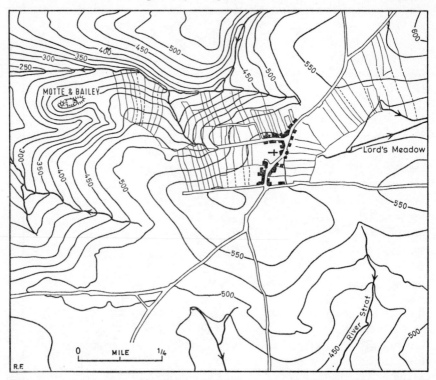

Fig. 27   KILKHAMPTON: SITE, EARLY SETTLEMENT NUCLEUS, AND MEDIEVAL FIELD PATTERN.

distribution of this field system was. Nor can much light be shed as yet on the problematic nature of the less regular and small, but nevertheless strip-like, enclosures which are found in most parts of Cornwall except the east and north of the county, where the strip-field patterns conform more closely to the furlong-strips typical of the open fields in Devon. Those parts of Devon and Cornwall where strip-field boundaries and sets of enclosed fields with patterns reminiscent of strips have been recognized are shown in Figure 26. In spite of the known fact that many hedgebanks have been thrown down in the last 200 years and the strip-field evidence ploughed out or built over, the map shows how generally widespread this form of field system must have been in both counties. As a map depicts only the strip patterns which survived down to modern times, caution is required in its interpretation, but at least it suggests that open-field systems were formerly commonplace in Southwest England.

Integral with the arrangement of strips in the open-field were the villages with their meadow, a reconstruction of which is attempted for Kilkhampton (Fig. 27). Here in north Cornwall, at just over 500 feet on the western and northern sides of the village, the map shows several small enclosed fields; their size and the elongated shape of their hedgebanks irresistibly suggest that they are fossilized remnants of medieval strip cultivation. To the east of the village is an extensive area in the gently sloping valley-head of the stream called Abbery Water into which this arrangement of hedgebanks does not penetrate and which to this day is called 'Lord's Meadow'. Domesday Book records that King William and Harold before him had 30 acres of meadow in his manor of Kilkhampton, the largest amount assigned to any one manor in the whole of Cornwall. Medieval meadow, since it provided the hay-crop, would have been near to water-courses and preferably on valley floors where the grass would grow most luxuriantly. In Cornwall, extensive low-lying river meadows are not of frequent occurrence and this is the reason why about half the Domesday meadow is at a high level on the floors of wide, open valley-heads excavated but feebly in the remarkable sequence of planation surfaces for which the Cornish landscape is renowned. Inside the boundary of the open fields and the meadow were the tofts and crofts. John Norden, who surveyed and wrote *The General Historie of the Duchie of Cornwall* in 1584, defined a toft as 'a little peece of land upon which sometimes was situate a dwelling house', and a croft as 'a small plot . . . neere a dwelling house'. The houses, which in modern parlance would be described as detached, lay alongside the street, and the crofts, usually long and narrow, ran back to the edge of the open fields and meadow from which they were usually separated by a back lane. It was, and in some cases still is, this arrangement of tofts and crofts with their attendant pattern of streets and lanes which gave our villages their form and fabric.

We may then visualize the landscape of medieval Devon and Cornwall as made up of single isolated farms surrounded by their enclosed fields; hamlets, sometimes with enclosed fields, sometimes with miniature open-field systems; and villages of different shapes, some regular, some irregular, with their common arable fields and meadow around them. These were the ingredients of the rural landscape; but is it possible to estimate the extent to which they filled the available land? A recent estimate of between 9,000 and 9,500 farms has already been quoted for Devon, something over 1,000 demesnes and over 8,000 farms of one kind or another being worked by the villeins. This figure is based on the frequent coincidence or near-coincidence of ploughlands and villeins in the Devon Domesday.

Hoskins suggests that when Domesday Book mentions the ploughlands on a manor it is stating the number of farms from which rents or services could be expected apart from the demesne farm. Where ploughlands do not equal the number of villeins it would seem sensible to take the smaller figure as indicating the number of farms which were actually there. Applying this formula to the Cornwall Domesday there would be 263 demesnes and the count of ploughlands/villeins sums to 1,553. On this basis then we should think of a total in the order of 1,800 farms. If these figures approximate to reality, then much less emphasis must be placed on the so-called 'Golden Age of Labour 1100–1330' which hitherto has been regarded as the great era of colonization and multiplication of settlements. It has acquired this description because the number of new place-names recorded for the first time in documents such as the Assize Rolls, Book of Fees, and the early Lay Subsidy Rolls, is large when compared with the number of separate places named in Domesday Book. In the Devon volumes of the Place-Name Society some 7,500 names are considered; about 1,000 are names of places known to have been in existence by 1086, while a further 3,700 represent dwellings mentioned in documents by 1350. Even so, the total only sums to about half the number of the now postulated Domesday farms. It does begin to look as if Devon and Cornwall were settled to a remarkable degree, both on low-lying ground and on the quite elevated parts, by 1086 and that most of the farms which we see on our modern maps would have been in the landscape by 1350 at the latest. This is not to say, of course, that all the land belonging to a particular farm was being utilized to the full in a modern sense. To our eyes there would still have been much woodland and waste, but these formed an essential element in the economy of a medieval dwelling, providing not only fuel and the timber necessary for construction purposes but also ensuring pasture for pigs, cattle, and sheep. Such an interpretation goes part of the way to explain why farms existed on the elevated parts of Exmoor, Bodmin Moor, and Dartmoor at this time—clearly, available land was becoming scarce. It must be remembered that conditions of life on our moorlands were not quite so severe then as they are today. The years 1100 to 1300 are considered to be the most favourable climatic phase known in the written history of our islands. It was a time when the wine from the vineyards of Gloucester and Hereford was considered the equal of French wine, and the old Norse colony in Greenland was burying its dead deep in ground that has since been permanently frozen.

By 1350 the vast majority of place-names which we know today could have been written on a map of Devon and Cornwall, and around the settlements were the small irregular enclosed fields, with open-field farming adjacent to some of the hamlets and villages. Already, however, there are signs, even in the mid-thirteenth century, of a tendency towards the enclosure of some of the open fields. The juxtaposition of the different field systems in many parishes must have made apparent the superior advantages of individual farming over communal farming and was probably a contributory factor in the early enclosure of the open fields in the South-west. Already in the middle of the thirteenth century the documents tell of tenants complaining of the curtailment of pasture rights and of landlords consolidating their strips of arable by purchase and exchange. The Black Death in 1348, the subsequent plagues of the mid-fourteenth century, and the contemporary deterioration in the climate transformed even further this relation of men and land. Settlements and fields had multiplied in conditions of growing population and land-hunger but now the moving frontier of cultivation was halted, particularly in the marginal areas. The land-hunger of the thirteenth century was replaced by a glut of land and a hunger for men to till it. The arable open fields were increasingly enclosed and put down to grass: to such an extent was this so that Carew in 1602 could describe Cornwall as falling 'everywhere from commons to en-closures' and Hooker could state in 1590 that Devon for 'the most part is inclosed'. It might well be asked why it was that pasture supplanted ploughs when there was so much grass available on the moorlands. The answer lies principally in the temptation to have larger and larger flocks to satisfy the growing demands for wool made by the developing and profitable Tudor cloth industry, particularly in Devon.

CHAPTER 6

The Origins and Early Growth of Towns

IN the recognition of the early phases of town life in Southwest England it is not profitable to seek too precise a definition of what constituted a town: the same applies with even more force in this early period to that growing and developing institution, the so-called burh or burgh, a word which, after undergoing semantic change in the tenth century, became borough. To deal with a living institution such as this much patience is required, but initially we shall not go far wrong if we are able to recognize the concentration of exceptional numbers at certain settlements, and the presence of some inhabitants who are not concerned exclusively with the agrarian round of common tasks. Indeed, one of the distinguishing characteristics of a town is that its people are not primarily food-producers. A town's survival, therefore, depended markedly on the strong links which it was able to forge with the countryside around it. In fact, it was the ability of rural communities to farm more efficiently, to increase their numbers and still to produce a surplus, which made possible the urban revival of medieval times.

At Exeter there is little doubt that life of a sort survived the departure of the Romans, and the presence of dedications to Celtic Dark Age Saints within the walls goes far to support such a view. Later in the seventh century the Saxons had taken over a good deal of Devon by peaceful infiltration and by force, and it was not until the Kingdom of Wessex was in turn threatened by the Danish assaults that anything resembling town life is revealed for Devon in written sources, of which the two principal are the Anglo-Saxon Chronicle and a curious document which, in the absence of any known title, has been called the Burghal Hidage (911–19). Mainly as a consequence of the Danish raids, the Kings of Wessex, and—in the case of Devon—Alfred (871–99) in particular pursued a policy which both recognized the importance and accelerated the growth of town life. In the campaigns against the Danes a most effective military device proved to be the burh, a fortified place for whose upkeep and garrisoning the men from the surrounding district were made responsible.

Initially the burhs served well as a deliberately organized means of defence but in the course of time the security and accessibility of some of their sites allowed them to function in roles other than those of a purely military character; the burhs therefore represent only a stage, but a vitally important one, in the evolution of the medieval English borough and the medieval town. The four burhs in Devon listed in the Burghal Hidage were Exeter, Pilton, Halwell, and Lydford.

The choice of Exeter and Pilton can be readily explained in terms of military exigences, for both are situated near estuaries that give access to the interior of the county: these the seafaring Danes would be expected to use. Alfred was clearly not choosing new sites for his burhs—the men and the means of supporting them had to be at hand. Furthermore, no fortress which was intended to form part of an ordered system of national defence could safely be allowed to stand vacant until an emergency arose and required its occupation. The Burghal Hidage, therefore, lists alongside the name of the burh the number of hides in the surrounding countryside required for the repair and garrisoning of its defences. The burh at Exeter was given 734 hides for its maintenance and defence. As every hide supplied one man and four men were needed for every pole of wall, the length of wall to be manned was $734 \div 4$ poles, i.e. $183\frac{1}{2}$ poles or 1,009 yards. The length of the Roman walls of Exeter is about 2,566 yards. This lack of coincidence could be explained in various ways; it may mean that the Saxon burh only occupied a part of the area enclosed by the former Roman walls, or that only certain sections of the wall required actually to be manned. Topographically the southeast and northeast sides of the city are the least formidable in their natural state, and it is there that the 1,009 yards of walling which needed manning may have been. In some versions of the Burghal Hidage, Pilton is described as 'pis bearstaple', which again indicates that Pilton probably, and Barnstaple certainly, were already in existence. The actual burh at this time was most likely to have been built on the end of the narrow spur where the church and village now stand and it did not include Barnstaple, for the burh was given 360 hides and the length of the defence would therefore have been of the order of 90 poles, or 495 yards only. It is not so easy to explain the choice of Halwell and Lydford or to see how they resolved the military problems which faced Alfred in his defence of the western part of Wessex against the Danes. It may be suggested, however, that Halwell was something of a military economy—one stronghold to command two avenues of entry, the Dartmouth and Kingsbridge estuaries. Men garrisoned at Halwell could be deployed along the ridge roads which meet at this point on high ground and they could thus counter any advance up the two estuaries. The allocation of 300 hides—which would give about 413 yards of defences—points to the earthwork to the east of the present village as the actual site of the burh. For southwest Devon a defensive site somewhere near the Tamar estuary would appear to have been more ideal than Lydford (SX 585416), but the excavation of early Christian pottery and the dedication to St Petrock are pointers to an already occupied site on the ravine-bounded interfluvial spur-end (Fig. 28). Only 140 hides were allocated to

Lydford; this would be sufficient for 193 yards of defences. The upstanding rampart and ditch (Fig. 28) is longer than this, and so it looks as if the early burh may have occupied a somewhat smaller part of the spur-end; it seems to be a very small burh for such a large area, particularly if parts of adjacent Saxon Cornwall were also under its surveillance.

On the analogy of Alfred's arrangements for the building of the burh at Worcester between the years 889 and 899 it is highly probable that the

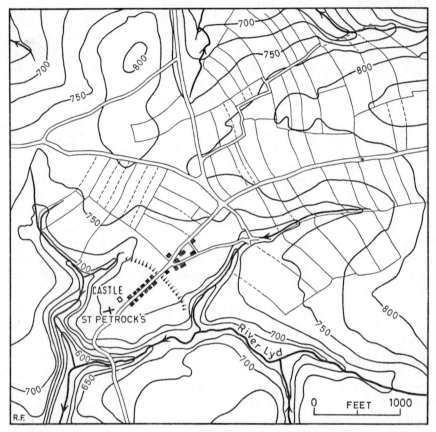

Fig. 28   LYDFORD: SITE, EARLY SETTLEMENT NUCLEUS, AND MEDIEVAL FIELD PATTERN.

burhs were intended, or by virtue of the security they afforded, had become, centres for trade as well as places of defence. This combination of military and commercial factors in the burhs of Devon can first be recognized at Exeter where a mint was opened some time after *c.*895. An early surviving law relating to coinage forms part of Athelstan's Ordinance issued at Grately; a section of this dealing with trading regulations forbade the purchase of goods outside a town. Such a regulation should not be interpreted as an attempt to hinder trade—quite the contrary. The restriction of trade to the burhs simplified the collection of dues and by the greater publicity of the transactions and the presence of the portreeve made fraud much more difficult. The effect of these regulations was to concentrate this growing trade in the burhs and this in turn fostered their growth and further differentiated them from rural settlements. Athelstan's laws also decreed that there should be one coinage over the King's Dominion and that no one was to mint money except in a town. In the quota of moneyers for each mint Exeter was assigned two and the other burhs were allowed one each.

The coin sequence for the burhs of Devon, other than Lydford and Exeter, demonstrates that the mere fortification of a place was not in itself sufficient always to ensure the growth of a town. If the ascription of Darents Urb on a coin of Athelstan's reign to Totnes is correct then this town had by 939 replaced Halwell as the settlement of significance in south Devon; it certainly had done so by the reign of Eadgar (959–75). Similarly in north Devon the earliest known Saxon coins to be minted locally are known from the reign of Eadwig (955–9) and these were minted at Barnstaple, which had supplanted Pilton in importance. Surprisingly, Lydford maintained its importance in southwest Devon, and coins were probably minted there soon after the reform of the English coinage which occurred c.973 under Eadgar. This reform tried to reduce hardship by ensuring that few people would need to travel more than a reasonable number of miles to a mint. Circles with radii of 15 miles—the upper limit that a man could be expected to walk to a mint and back again in a day—when drawn around the four mints of Exeter, Totnes, Barnstaple, and Lydford, embrace fairly adequately the county of Devon, but leave almost untouched the adjoining county of Cornwall. It is probable that a mint was opened at Launceston soon after the Eadgar reform, but the first coins indicate that the place being referred to was the original Launceston—the 'Lanscavetona' of Domesday Book, the St Stephens by Launceston on our modern maps. It now seems likely that for a period of about forty-five years the work of the Launceston mint may have been taken over by Castle Gotha (SX 027496) because on stylistic grounds the small group of problematic late Saxon pence with the remarkably consistent mint signature Gotha (byri) must have emanated from a centre in the Southwest.

When we attempt to assess the importance of late Anglo-Saxon towns, the percentage of the output from any particular mint and the number of moneyers actually minting give an approximate indication of relative size. Within the two counties pride of place clearly goes to Exeter, but in terms of the country as a whole it frequently held fifth place to the four major mints of London, York, Lincoln, and Winchester.

Alongside the important evidence of coins and that derived from the law codes, information on the late Anglo-Saxon burhs comes from fragmentary references to guild regulations and other local institutions. For instance, Guild Statutes in the Exeter of the tenth century make provision for corporate payment in money and in spiritual observance on various occasions such as the death of a member or when a member's house burned down—a fire insurance of early date. Obscurely but steadily, an essentially non-agricultural community of traders and artisans formed the residential population of the town—a new local community which in time was to receive special treatment in the form of tenure, local government, and legal status. That this administrative quasi-municipal function was present in the four Devon burhs is made clear in the letter which Bishop Eadnoth of Crediton sent in 1018 to the burhwitan of Exeter, Totnes, Lydford, and Barnstaple, informing them officially of a life-grant of a piece of land near Crediton in return for a loan. The significance of this letter lies in the very clear intimation that at each of these places the burhwitan formed some kind of constituted body, able to preserve the record of a transaction brought to its notice.

Soon after this date England was disturbed yet again, this time by the uncertainty of the succession on the death of Edward the Confessor—a confused situation which culminated in the Norman Conquest. Twenty years later in 1085 King William caused to be carried out a general *descriptio* over the whole of his newly conquered kingdom, the edited results of which form that most important document known later by the name Domesday Book. Cornwall shares with Somerset, nearly all Devonshire, some of Dorset, and a single Wiltshire manor, the distinction of having a parallel but earlier and fuller text called the *Exon Domesday*, which is preserved in the Cathedral Library at Exeter. In order to carry out this nation-wide survey the country was divided into a number of circuits, one of which almost certainly covered the five southwestern counties: the actual material appears to have been compiled in four stages—the returns from the local inquests; the conflation of these into a draft; a fair copy of this; and finally the abbreviated report, the Exchequer Domesday. *Exon Domesday* represents the second stage of this process, made without much doubt by the commissioners at Exeter and left behind them when the contents in revised form had been sent forward to the Treasury at Winchester. That the making of Domesday Book was an immense undertaking no one can deny, and in *Exon Domesday* the commissioners and the scribes can be seen at work, giving order and shape to a vast collection of facts. That Exeter made a valuable contribution to its compilation is particularly significant for our understanding of Exeter's administrative function, both locally to the south-western shires and also to the country as a whole at this time. Besides this piece of information garnered incidentally, Domesday Book itself provides further details about the boroughs, and at the same time affords material for retrospect.

The four pre-Conquest burhs, Exeter, Barnstaple, Totnes, and Lydford were recorded as boroughs in Domesday Book, where they are linked by the fact that 'if an expedition goes forth by land or sea Barnstaple, Totnes and

Lydford between them pay the same service as Exeter pays'. They, too, paid geld only when Exeter did and, in the time of King Edward, Exeter did not pay except when London, York, and Winchester paid, a fairly clear indication of royal support and patronage. Exeter, which is referred to as a city, *In civitate Essecestrae*, seems to have had just over 450 burgage tenements, some 333 of which belonged to the King. The borough (burgus) of Barnstaple had 107 tenements, Totnes 110, and Lydford 109, but—with the exception of those in Totnes—not all these tenements were occupied in 1086. Strangely, only one castle is mentioned directly in Domesday Book and that is the castle at Okehampton, where it is described in association with four burgesses and a market—surely a sign of an incipient town, if one did not exist already. Only one other place with a market is recorded for Devon and that is at Otterton, where the church (Abbot of St Michael of the Mount) held one on Sundays.

This far in our consideration of the origins of towns in Cornwall we have been able to point to only two possible contenders and of these only one 'Lanscavetona' survived. As in Devon, so also in Cornwall, the Abbot of St Michael's Mount features as a holder of a market and fairs. Into the cartulary of the priory of St Michael's Mount has been copied a charter on which the name of King William I appears as a witness, and by which Robert, Count of Mortain, grants St Michael's Mount in Cornwall to St Michael in Normandy, together with half a hide of land and a Thursday market. The suggested date for the original charter is *c.*1070. In another charter, to which the date 1087–91 has been assigned, the same Count of Mortain gave to St Michael and the monks the manor of Ludgvan, a holding in Truthwall, and both fairs of the Mount, *et ferias ambas de monte*. Without attempting to underestimate the considerable difficulties which have for so long beset the full interpretation of these charters, there can be very little doubt that a market or a fair (or both) existed at the Mount or, more likely, on the mainland near the Mount, at a date roughly contemporary with the taking of the Domesday Inquest. Domesday Book itself makes no reference to this particular market but is quite eloquent about five others, most of which were owned formerly by the church. At the time of the Inquest these were falling, by devious means, more and more under the control of the Count of Mortain. An interlineation in *Exon Domesday* makes it clear that at Methleigh Bishop Leuric had a yearly market in 1066: in 1086, even though the manor was still held by the Bishop of Exeter, the Count of Mortain had taken possession of the market 'unjustly'. The Count also held a market at Liskeard and another at Trematon. There is little doubt that it is this particular market which is being referred to in the account of St Germans which informs us that there was in 1066 a Sunday market held there by Bishop Leuric. In 1086 this Sunday market was being reduced to nothing, *ad nichilum redigitur*, as the Count had set up in competition another market on the same day at his castle nearby. From associated evidence it is clear this market of the Count's was at Trematon, which, like St Germans, is near the head of a tidal creek on the north bank of the river Lynher but closer to the river Tamar, the trade across which it was deliberately placed to control and monopolize. Economic pressure of a more direct kind was being exerted in roughly similar circumstances farther north near another crossing of the river Tamar.

In 1066 the Canons of St Stephens, the 'Lanscavetona' previously noted as having a mint, had a market at their manor but here again the Count of Mortain had taken it away from them and placed it in his castle at Dunhevet, the former name of present Launceston and the strategic place of entry to the county. This market was quite the most valuable one in Cornwall, rendering 20 shillings yearly compared with Liskeard, which rendered only 4 shillings, and Trematon (3 shillings). This precious glimpse of a squabble for local markets tells more than many lengthier documents about what was really going on, because Domesday Book, by enabling us to look retrospectively to the time of King Edward, bears certain witness to the existence of early towns, albeit small ones, control of which the Norman Lord was successfully wresting from the church, and in so doing was at Trematon and Launceston in the powerful position of surveilling almost the entire landborne external trade across the county boundary. Indeed the market of Bodmin was the only one left to the church, and as to the existence there of a town Domesday Book is most specific. In the principal *descriptio* of Bodmin we are told there are 68 houses but it has not been emphasized hitherto that in the summary of certain fiefs in folios 527b–531, St Petroc is described as having 68 burgesses. Since St Petroc held Bodmin, there is little doubt, owing to the coincidence of the number of houses and burgesses, that it was at Bodmin that these burgesses lived. Although this is the only place in Cornwall to which the Domesday Book assigns burgesses, the other places with markets or fairs referred to must have functioned as small towns, even though they were not formally accorded burghal status in the record. The same must be true also of Helston, where there is a curious reference to 40 *cervisarii*; this word has been variously translated but is most likely to have been a derivative of the Latin word for ale (*cervisia*). It is unlikely that the *cervisarii* were actually brewers; more probably they were burgesses who held their tenements in return for the rendering of ale to the lord. The record of 10 salt-pans at Stratton also hints at something more than a mere agricultural vill and perhaps justifies the addition of this settlement to the list of places which in the eleventh century show signs of being towns.

The Norman Conquest, by linking England with the Continent, stimulated the economy and, as trade expanded, so did the towns. In the twelfth and thirteenth centuries the Southwest shared in the movements common to the whole of England which led to the founding of boroughs by both king and powerful baron. The stage was now reached where, by a stroke of a pen, a lord could convert a settlement into a borough, and his *villani* into burgesses. The most liberal grantor of charters for the founding of royal boroughs was King John, whose coffers welcomed the sums which the burgesses were prepared to pay for their privileges. The motives for the creation of a borough by the feudal lords, lay or ecclesiastical, were not only financial but also strategic. They quickly appreciated the value of urban centres in the administration of newly acquired territory as sources of larger incomes than could be raised from purely agricultural communities. In Devon the movement was as active as anywhere in England, and the term seignorial borough has been applied to those foundations which owed their inception and subsequent vigour to the patronage of the great and wealthy. The process by which a settlement received this enhanced status can be traced in the case of Tavistock, where c.1105, the first official step was taken when Henry I issued the following writ: 'Henry, King of England, to Geoffrey de Mandeville and all the barons of Devon and Cornwall, French and English, greeting. Know that I have granted to St Mary of Tavistock and the monks there that they may have a market in Tavistock every week on Friday. And I grant to merchants that they may sell and buy whatever they please; and no one is to do them wrong on that account.' Allowing for the inevitable imperfections in the documentary record (but at the same time eliminating dubious cases) there were 91 places in Devon which were styled boroughs or had markets by the middle of the fourteenth century. At these settlements would be found burgesses who held their tenements in free burgage, or markets and—as a rule—courts distinct from those of the rural manors out of which the burghal terri- tories had been carved. These 91 places must therefore represent the larger nucleated settlements and nodes and as such they have been used to express in map form (Fig. 29) the growth of towns in the post-Conquest period in Devon. Such settlements cannot be appreciated and evaluated except in terms of communications and sites.

Distance and the means available at any one period of negotiating it are factors of major importance in limiting the effective tributary area of a node and its market potential. Taking into account the slowness of medieval road transport, there was much sense in the old law which forbade the establish- ment of a market within six and two-thirds miles of an existing legal market, but the actual market area must have varied considerably according to local circumstances. If allowance is made for the hard going on foot in a hilly county such as Devon, a five mile hinterland to a market would perhaps represent a reasonable area of countryside, within a day's return journey on foot, from which a centre could be expected to draw trade. For instance, in a Survey of the Duchy manor of St Austell carried out as late as the 1630s the distance of six miles to the nearest market is complained of 'There is neither markett or faire within the mannor, but the towne is fitt for both especially being soe remote from markett townes. The nearest markett towens are Lotwithiel 6 myles, Tregney 6 and Grampound 6 myles'. When circles with radii of five miles to scale are drawn around the early boroughs and markets plotted on Figures 29 and 32 a very interesting pattern emerges.

The only areas in Devon for which there seems to be a long journey to a borough or market centre are Dartmoor and the portion of Exmoor within Devon. Were it not for the circle around Holsworthy quite a large portion of west Devon on the cold clay soils would appear blank on the map. This

Fig. 29   THE EARLY TOWNS OF DEVON. Dots denote places which had been styled boroughs or had markets by the middle of the fourteenth century; the circles are drawn with radii of five miles to scale.

is an isolated area, its remoteness somewhat mitigated towards the southwest by coming within the circle for Launceston. Of equal interest in the pattern of circles is the area between Teignmouth and Dartmouth, where considerable overlapping of circles occurs; this emphasizes the richer and consequently more closely settled lands in the lee of Dartmoor. With slightly less overlapping but quite well-endowed with markets and medieval boroughs were the South Hams and east Devon.

The site for a successful borough had to be chosen with some care, preferably at a point where topographical accessibility was good, a water supply ensured, and where a reasonable amount of flat or gently sloping land made building relatively easy and provided space for the market. Of the total of 91 medieval towns, 35 are on spur sites. A good example is South Molton (Fig. 30); there, Broad Street, part of the through west to east road from Barnstaple to Taunton, runs along the spine of the inter-fluvial flat and widens out to form the Market Place, where roads from the north and south also enter the town. Whether the means of communication follow valley or ridge, the spurs, and particularly the interfluvial spurs, are

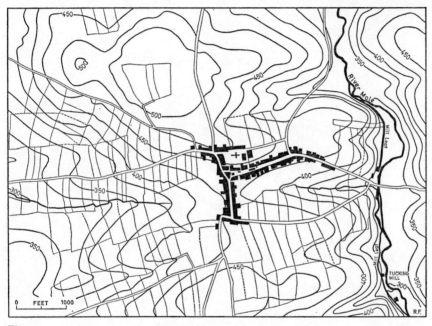

Fig. 30   SOUTH MOLTON: SITE, EARLY SETTLEMENT NUCLEUS, AND MEDIEVAL FIELD PATTERN.

readily accessible. Quite frequently they are the meeting-points of roads which have followed the valleys and those which have crossed the ridges. There are 16 coastally located medieval towns but most of these are on estuarine sites (Fig. 31) where two kinds of accessibility and harvest meet— those of the sea and those of the land. Plymouth, Dartmouth, and Fowey, to give a similar Cornish example, prospered when the rich harvests of south-western France were shipped to England, after the marriage of Henry II to Eleanor of Aquitaine in 1152 had placed the seal on commercial as well as connubial ties. The presence of a physical barrier such as a creek or an estuary can have an interesting effect on early town development, often bringing two boroughs close together. It is not easy to explain the nearness of Noss Mayo and Newton Ferrers or of Barnstaple and Bideford, expect

in terms of the estuaries separating their respective hinterlands. In the cases
of Totnes and Bridgetown Pomeroy and of Kingsbridge and Dodbrooke,
where the riparian lands were in different manors, the lords were,
seemingly, eager to carve out boroughs on their own territories. Thirty-
one towns are located on valley-side and valley-bottom sites but within
these two broad site categories the vast majority are near to the change of
slope between the highest river terrace and the valley sides. Many of these
settlements now take the form of long villages or small towns with their

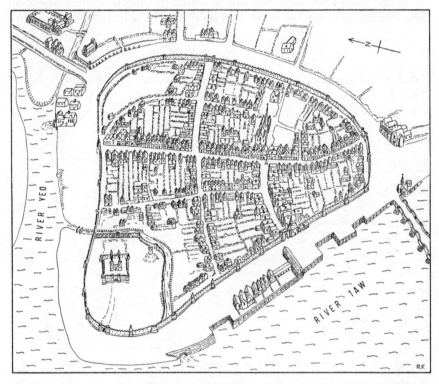

Fig. 31   BARNSTAPLE. A reconstruction of the seventeenth-century townscape with much
of the medieval town plan still visible. Redrawn from a plan by O. W. Davis *Architectural
Rev.* 4 (1898), 99. Approximate Scale one inch to 175 yards.

houses on different levels bordering the main street, the latter having at
times a disconcertingly uncomfortable valleyward tilt. Such dry points on
gravel terraces have a considerable degree of accessibility, besides the other
attractive qualities and amenities inherent in the site itself; a good example
is Tavistock, a borough outside the gates of the richest medieval monastic
house in Devon. Valley-head sites are not necessarily the dead-end which
they might at first sight appear to be, and from the point of view of access
may not be at a disadvantage. If the valley-head is in isolation it could be
something of a cul-de-sac, but numerous valley-heads give rise to cols easily

reached both from roads leading up the valleys and from those coming down from the ridges. Crediton began as a settlement within a small valley-head but its subsequent growth has involved a spread over the col into an adjacent valley-head.

It would be rash to assume that all the places styled boroughs and plotted on Figure 29 developed into towns of any size. Many of the medieval lords did not appreciate the discipline of distance and over-estimated in some cases the richness of the areas tributary to the would-be towns. Some of the places such as, for example, Sampford Peverell, Rackenford, Aveton Gifford, and Chillington did not succeed as boroughs nor grow sufficiently to warrant the status of towns. In the Assize Roll of 1238 18 boroughs were sending delegations of their burgesses to meet the justices in eyre and 22 boroughs only of the large number in Devon regularly appear on the taxation lists of the early fourteenth century. Interestingly of these, 6 are on sites near the coast or on estuaries and 10 on spur sites and all were recorded in Domesday Book; however, this is true for nearly all the markets and boroughs and is the logical outcome of the medieval lords wishing to enrich themselves by the deliberate found-ing of markets and boroughs near their caput manors and not on new sites.

As in Devon, so in Cornwall, many of the medieval boroughs were fostered and cherished by the great landlords as profitable sources of revenue. The foundation stone of a borough was its charter. It was this which made it a self-contained community and protected it from outside interference. Many charters in Cornwall were granted not to the burgesses but to the lord who held jurisdiction over the town. It was often the lord who took the first step in the negotiations to secure such a charter, as his power and influence made this possible. Moreover, some of the charters were not granted by the King himself; the Earls of Cornwall—by virtue of their quasi-palatine powers—exercised the right to grant charters them-selves. Thus by the middle of the fourteenth century the number of places which were either boroughs or market towns had grown from the 5 of Domesday times to around 37 and these are plotted on the map (Fig. 32). Since one is seldom far from the sea in Cornwall and since there are so many drowned estuaries deeply piercing the land, it was comparatively easy for one and the same place to be a market and a seaport. The Tamar, the Helford, the Fowey, the Fal, the Camel, all large estuaries, brought the sea well into the interior. This was more a strongly marked feature in medieval times than at present, for many of the estuaries which were formerly navig-able have been gradually silted up with the immense quantities of sand and gravel washed down from the granite moorlands. Thus the town of Tregoney, which now lies high and dry, was formerly a flourishing port. Soon after the Conquest the Norman baronial family De la Pomeroy built a castle here and in 1306 the settlement was a borough for taxation purposes, but by 1600 it was forced to give up its maritime role. Lostwithiel was

another example; Leyland in 1533 could describe it as being 'scant a mile
on the principal streame of the Fowey river. It hath ebbid and flowen above
Lostwithiel; but now it flowith not ful to the toun . . .'. Likewise Helston, a
town whose antiquity has already been mentioned and which received its
borough charter from King John in 1201, combined the functions of market
town and seaport until the formation of the shingle Loe Bar forced it to

Fig. 32   THE EARLY TOWNS OF CORNWALL. Dots denote places which had been styled
boroughs or had markets by the middle of the fourteenth century; the circles are drawn
with radii of five miles to scale.

surrender this role. In 1182 one Godric of Helston was fined ten marks for
exporting his corn out of England without a licence but at an eyre of 1302
the burgesses were claiming considerable jurisdiction over the adjacent port
of Gweek at the head of the Helford estuary, when no mention was made of
ships at Helston itself.

    The exploitation of a coastal site by local initiative led to the founding of
several other boroughs, including a number on the sides of the sheltered

tidal creeks which drain to the Tamar estuary. Cornwall's north-facing
coast is not well endowed with similar suitable sites; it is craggy and wild,
dune-fringed at intervals, difficult to approach from the sea, and open to
the full force of the Atlantic gales. The symbols of Figure 32 also point out
how few were the inland towns in Cornwall. Launceston and Bodmin we
have already alluded to. The bridge over the Fal was instrumental in the
rise of Grampound and in giving it its name Grand Pont, because this
bridge formed part of the highway through south Cornwall. Mitchell and
Camelford were similarly placed as halts on the north road. Kilkhampton
(Fig. 27) and Week St Mary at the junction of ridge roads from the southwest and southeast on a 450 foot high spur-flat, served the needs of north
Cornwall. In the south were Callington—500 feet up on a valley-side—and
Liskeard athwart a stream in a delightful valley-head, just below a considerable area of land around 450 feet high, traversed by numerous ridge
roads. In spite of the large number of places for which evidence has been
found for burgesses and markets, there are still some parts of the county
which do not appear to be adequately covered by the five-mile circles on
Figure 32; more particularly their absence is noted for the Bodmin Moor
area and the Lizard peninsula. By c.1350 something like 37 places in
Cornwall had acquired the title of borough or had markets, but in order to
survive, the geographical conditions had to be conducive to the growth of
trade, and many places, lacking these, did not develop into towns worthy of
the name. Some received a setback when the tides no longer reached their
quays; others failed when the economic endowment of their hinterlands
changed. Even as early as 1603 this was obvious to Carew, who noted
waspishly: 'I will conclude with the highest jurisdiction, namely the Parliament, to which Cornwall, through the grace of his Earls sendeth an equal,
if not larger number of burgesses to any other shire. The boroughs so
privileged, more of favour (as the case now standeth with most of them)
than merit are these following: Launceston, Liskeard, Lostwithiel, Truro,
Bodmin, Dunheved, Helston, Saltash, Camelford, E. Looe, W. Looe,
Penryn, Tregoney, Callington, Bossiney, St Ives, St Germans, Mitchell,
St Mawes.' By the time Carew was writing, however, great changes had
occurred in the economic life of the two counties and town growth had
become closely associated with two important but differently organized
activities—the winning of metals and the making of cloth. Though both of
these industries were to be found to some extent in both counties, cloth
manufacture had a proportionately greater influence on the towns of Devon
than on those of Cornwall; in mining the reverse was equally true.

To appreciate the way in which mining led to the growth of towns in
this early period, it is important to remind ourselves of the provenance of
the ores—in particular tin ores; they occur either in lodes in the rocks or in
the detritus derived from the weathered lodes, which has been deposited
downstream—the so-called stream tin deposits. These were the first to be

s.e.—5*

discovered and worked, since they were exposed when rivers swollen by rain cut gulleys in the detritus. What was shown to occur in one valley would be sought in similar situations elsewhere. From the shallowness of the stream tin deposits and the comparative ease with which the ore could be shovelled out and washed, it follows that all discoveries of ancient tin-workings have been made in alluvial ground and that this method of winning the ore prevailed down to the sixteenth century. These stream tin deposits were, by the nature of their formation, of limited depth and with the exhaustion of one stream the miner sought his ore elsewhere. Such settlement as resulted directly was of the ephemeral type, quickly to be forsaken when fortune failed. Indirectly the effect on certain towns was considerable. In 1198 tin-working in Devon was placed under the supervision of a warden appointed by the King. From this early date the importance of the stannaries as a source of revenue was appreciated by the Crown, and several charters were issued which regularized stannary administration. One of these demanded a strict adherence to a system of coinage or stampage by virtue of which the tin, directly after smelting, had to be taken to one of the legalized coinage towns to be assayed, stamped, and taxed before sale. The medieval coinage towns in Devon were Chagford, Tavistock, Ashburton, and Plympton. Besides these four coinage towns which served different sectors of Dartmoor, there was the grim prison of Lydford to which transgressors against the elaborate code of stannary laws were committed. From the coinage towns the block tin was carried the length and breadth of England and some legally, some illegally, shipped overseas. There were intermittent attempts from the thirteenth century to establish tin staples by Act of Parliament and Ashburton was made the official point of departure for Devon. Nevertheless shipments went out as well from Plymouth, Dartmouth, and Exeter, not to mention considerable quantities which were illicitly and clandestinely put on board at other small Devon ports.

In addition to tin-working there was the mining of silver and lead, two metals which were also a favourite province for royal enterprise. In the thirteenth century, mines, if they could be dignified by this term, were operated in southwest Devon between the Tavy and the Tamar rivers, and it was then that Bere Alston developed into a market town and a borough. A roughly similar situation can be gleaned from the records of the silver mines near Combe Martin; the presence of these played no small part in the growth of this elongated coastal town contained within a faulted valley. The Devon landscape bears the scars of many mining ventures; many of the settlements associated with them were small and, like them, transitory. On the other hand, the towns, strategically placed or chosen to handle and market the tin and silver, thrived between the thirteenth and seventeenth centuries.

Between these centuries a significant technical development occurred in mining. Stream works could not be long in operation without showing their link with the lodes in the adjacent hills above. As the miners worked upstream they could not fail to discover some traces of the veins from which the stream tin had been derived. The exhaustion of the stream tin rendered necessary the mining of the lode itself and the introduction of shaft mining probably occurred soon after the middle of the fifteenth century. Such a development required more equipment and, if the lode were a rich one, gave a permanence of location and had a significant effect on settlement growth. With very few exceptions the lodes of Devon were not rich in ore and the erection here and there of a line of miners' cottages is about all that the landscape received. How very much in contrast was Cornwall. As was noted in Chapter 2 (p. 16), the lodes are intimately associated with the vapours and solutions which arose from the solidifying granite. These emanations affected not only the granite but also the country rock close to it. The subterranean continuity of the granite can then be linked with a zone of mineralization 10 miles wide, extending from Tavistock in Devon southwestwards to Land's End. Although some streams and lodes were quickly exhausted, the deposits in Cornwall were far richer than those of Devon; in 1220 the Devon stannaries were farmed for 200 marks only, whereas those of Cornwall were valued at 1,000 marks. The bigger scale of production, together with shaft mining and smelting in Cornwall, had a greater influence on the growth of towns.

The two counties did nevertheless have similar restrictions on assaying and stampage and the choice of coinage towns gives a good indication of how the prospecting, streaming, and mining moved ever westwards. In 1305, it was Bodmin and Lostwithiel that featured in the 'coinage' of tin, with a fair quantity at Truro and a small amount at Helston. By 1577 Bodmin's place had been taken by Liskeard, and Truro and Helston were receiving each about three times as much as Lostwithiel; in 1607 Helston and Truro were coining between six and seven times as much each as was Lostwithiel. In 1663 Penzance was first made a coinage town and soon rose to a position of pre-eminence. The influence of mining on town growth in Cornwall was not restricted, as it was in Devon, to the coinage towns; mention must be made of Callington in the east of the county and St Austell to the south of the Hensbarrow. Associated with the tin in the Carnmenellis intrusion, the settlements of Camborne, Redruth, and St Day grew to importance and farther to the southwest St Just—which was associated with the Penwith granite—increased in size. In addition to the town growth resulting from the administrative and residential aspects of mining, there was growth at the seaports which exported the tin and imported the requirements of the mines. The shift of emphasis from east to west is again clearly discernible, particularly during the seventeenth century, when exports generally appear to have increased about threefold. In the first half of the century the most important ports were those in the east of the county—in particular Fowey, Looe, Millbrook, and Saltash—but by the end of the century they had been surpassed by the ports in the centre and the west, those of the Falmouth Haven—Truro, Penryn, Falmouth— Penzance, St Ives and Padstow.

There is little doubt that in later medieval England and in the West Country in particular, many settlements grew as the manufacture of cloth and its export developed. During the twelfth, thirteenth, and fourteenth centuries both Cornwall and Devon made cloth, but almost all of it was for local and home consumption, and little was exported. The distribution of this activity from the thirteenth century onwards may be partially recon- structed by plotting the fulling mills or tucking mills, as many of the West Country scouring and fulling mills were called (Fig. 47). The two essential requirements for water power which drove these mills, namely a constant flow of water and breaks of slope, could be found almost anywhere in the Southwest. It comes as no surprise to find that there were many fulling mills in Cornwall spread fairly evenly throughout the county; even so, between the years 1394–9 the Devon merchants sold 8,235½ cloths com- pared with Cornwall's 205 only, a clear reminder that the industry in the two counties was of an entirely disparate magnitude. The effect of the industry on the growth of towns comes about by the manner in which it was organized. The division of labour is described precisely by Westcote writing *c*.1630: 'First the gentleman farmer, or husbandman, sends his wool to the market, which is bought either by the comber or the spinster, and they, the next week, bring it thither again in yarn, which the weaver buys; and the market following, brings that thither again in cloth; when it is sold either to the clothier (who sends it to London) or to the merchant who (after it hath passed the fuller's mill and sometimes the Duyer's vat) transports it.' This particular form of organization involved considerable distribution and collection of the raw materials and semi-finished goods, so that old lines of communication were enhanced. In long-settled lands this is an important principle in the study of settlement, a feature which tends to give con- tinuity of site occupancy, for routeways once established (and they are so established to link habitation sites) tend to follow the same lines from period to period. There must have been constant comings and goings along the roads leading to the towns from their groups of contributing villages and cottages. In this way the woollen industry brought new life to many of the existing market towns and particularly to those that were near to water power where the fulling and dyeing could be done.

The earliest reference yet found to a fulling mill in Devon is that for Dunkeswell in 1238, probably connected with the abbey, but thereafter the fulling mills are for the most part near the larger settlements and towns. In 1244–5 there were mills at Honiton and Tiverton, in 1292 at Chulmleigh, 1295 at Sampford Courtenay, and two at Hartland and one at Harpford by 1299. Other early mills were at Slapton in 1307, Crediton 1308; there were two at North Molton and one at Chudleigh in 1317. By 1327 Barnstaple,

Bovey Tracey, Moretonhampstead, and South Molton could be added to the list and soon afterwards Matford, Aylesbeare, and Uplowman. The customs accounts show that during the Breton War of Succession substantial quantities of grey and russet cloth were being exported from Dartmouth, Exmouth, and Topsham. Towards the end of the fourteenth century the accounts of the Aulnager, whose duty it was to examine all cloth for sale 'to ease the buyer of trouble and to secure him from loss' lists sales of cloth at Bampton, Barnstaple, Honiton, Culmstock, Torrington, South Molton, Totnes, Plympton, Crediton, Ashburton, Plymouth, Tavistock, Okehampton, Chulmleigh, Newton Abbot, Kingsbridge, Cullompton, Dartmouth, and South Tawton. Towering above all these was Exeter, for which a separate Aulnager was appointed, a clear indication of the way in which the city was emerging as a manufacturing and marketing centre for the finished cloth. The list goes far to show the surplus for sale—over and above that for home use—and the wide distribution of the industry throughout the county, but there was more to come. Devon made relatively coarse woollens and it was not until a change of fashion and a demand for this type of cloth in Western Europe occurred that Devon got its great chance. Thus there developed a marked expansion of trade in the 1430s and 1440s for kerseys made of Devon's own coarse wool, lightly milled, brightly coloured and destined for the foreign as well as the home market. Though subsequently the export cloth trade had its ups and downs, the industry brought prosperity to Devon and particularly to its towns, about whose specializations Westcote could enthuse:

> The late made stuff of serges, or perpetuanos wherewith the market at Exeter is abundantly furnished. Tiverton hath also such a store of kersies as will not be believed. Crediton yields many of the first sort of kersies. Totnes, and some other places near it, hath had, besides these a sort of coarse cloth which they call narrow-pin-whites. Barnstaple and Torrington furnish us with bays, single and double; and Pilton adjoining, vents cloths for lining. At Tavistock there is a good market for cloth. At Axminster you may be furnished with fine flax thread there spun. At Honiton and Bradnige with bone lace. Ottery St Mary hath mixed coloured kersies, Cullumton kersey stockings; and Combe Martin serves the whole county, and other places, with shoemakers' thread.

About this time there are records of fullers in many places besides those already mentioned and in terms of the seventeenth century many of these can be regarded as towns (Fig. 47).

The cloth industry did not lead to the creation of many new sites; the majority of the places plotted on Figure 29 are recorded in Domesday Book and, since the topographical accessibility of a site was a factor of importance for the survival of a borough, the same quality was significant for the growth of a woollen town, owing to the nature of the early organization of the industry. Of the broad categories of settlement sites it is those on spurs which may appear least promising in terms of water-power, but one is never far away from running water in Devon and several of the Domesday settle-

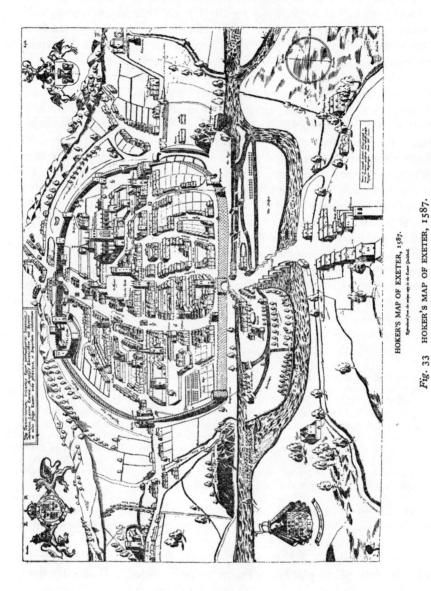

HOKER'S MAP OF EXETER, 1587.

Reproduced from the unique copy in the Exeter Guildhall.

Fig. 33   HOKER'S MAP OF EXETER, 1587.

ments on spur sites subsequently had their mills close by. Thus North Molton and South Molton (Fig. 30) had mills at the end of the spur where it met the valley floor; likewise the mills of Crediton, Modbury, Holsworthy, Chagford, Hatherleigh, Great Torrington, Moretonhampstead, and Exeter (Fig. 33) were not distantly separated appendages to the earlier established nuclei.

From the later Middle Ages the cloth trade held its place as incomparably the most important activity in Devon. The trade enriched the inland towns where the cloth was collected and the ports whence it was shipped. For centuries it occupied men's daily thoughts and energies and eminent townsmen like John Greenway of Tiverton and John Lane of Cullompton so embellished their respective churches from their wool-derived wealth that they have remained places of pilgrimage for church-lovers ever since. Men such as these were in business in a big way and their home towns were, for the period, large manufacturing centres requiring considerable quantities of water. Water resources of this magnitude were available in Devon, for the watershed lies far to the north of the county and there are some large river catchments. Towns downstream in such catchments, like Tiverton and Cullompton, were thus able to stand elevated in the hierarchy of woollen towns in the county, but Exeter, farther downstream in the Exe river catchment, was paramount in the county and high in rank among the provincial manufacturing cities of England.

CHAPTER 7

Rural Landscapes and Agriculture

Estates

THE seventeenth-century landscapes of Southwest England inherited little from the deer parks of medieval times. Some large estates had been created, notably those of the Earl of Bedford (derived from monastic lands) and the Rolle family who, originally settled at Stevenstone near Torrington, had acquired land in various other parts of Devon. In the eighteenth century the building of large mansions and the laying out of extensive parks were exceptional occurrences. The more typical estates were those of landholders of substantial means, who had large farmhouses or 'bartons' dating from earlier times, or country houses which were built, rebuilt, or extended during the seventeenth and eighteenth centuries. These account for most of the hundreds of 'seats' which are listed or shown on the county maps by Thomas Martyn (Cornwall, 1748 and 1784) and Benjamin Donn (Devon, 1765). Many had a walled garden with lawns or a 'green', an orchard, and a small plantation near the house. The newer of the small estates were commonly well sited for aspect and view, for example those adjacent to the Exeter–Topsham–Exmouth road, and a number of those in the southern valleys of Devon and Cornwall.

Although some landscaping of estates was carried out earlier than 1700 —as at Mount Edgecumbe in Cornwall—much more was done in the eighteenth century. The Italian gardens on the Clinton estate at Bicton (Devon) were originally laid out in 1735 according to designs by André le Nôtre, who was best known for his planning of the gardens at Versailles. The work of the 'landscape manipulators' of the period is represented on a number of estates, including Filleigh near South Molton (planned by William Kent), the gardens at Sharpham near Ashprington and the grounds of Mamhead in Devon (laid out by 'Capability' Brown), and the Port Eliot and Catchfrench parks near St Germans in Cornwall (designed by Humphrey Repton).

In modern times a considerable number of country houses have been taken over by the National Trust or are occupied by schools, hospitals, or commercial firms. So many estates have been broken up that, as far as farm holdings are concerned, the tenancy system generally has been reduced in significance. The tenanted farm is less typical of the holdings in the South-west today than is the owner-occupied farm of small to medium size. There is, however, a tendency for the average size of farms to increase. If continued, this may have some effect on the landscape through changes in the layout of farms; but its economic implications are a more contentious subject, as is also the future of the small farms and the part-time holdings, which are a considerable proportion of the total, especially in Cornwall.

Agrarian landscapes

By the seventeenth century there were only scattered survivals of open-field landscapes in Southwest England, so that most of the enclosures from then until the latter part of the nineteenth century took place in a context quite different from that of the open fields of the English Midlands. The main forces behind this late enclosing movement in the Southwest were the demand for wool in the serge-making industry and the need for more food to supply the people engaged in the woollen, mining, and quarrying industries. To these were added the requirements of the naval base at Devonport and the pressure on the land during the wars with France. Resulting from these forces, the changes in the agrarian landscapes took several forms.

Especially along road verges and on the fringes of towns and villages engaged in the woollen industry, numerous patches of waste ground were appropriated by cottage dwellers. Although it contributed only a small total area to the enclosed land, this kind of appropriation was widely practised. Its characteristic pattern of elongated roadside plots is still easily identified, as in places along the Okehampton–Launceston road. Far more important, however, was the addition of new fields to existing farms; as in many cases this process extended over waste ground which lay in one main direction from the farmhouse, it often accentuated the asymmetrical pattern of the holding. Another main form of enclosure, less common than in medieval times but nevertheless already well under way again in the seventeenth century, was the creation of new farmsteads and fields, a procedure which culminated in such large-scale enterprises as the reclamation of parts of Exmoor in the nineteenth century. Taken together, these two forms of enclosure affected a considerable area of the Southwest and, especially in upland districts, are often attested by field names of such late type as Newtake, Broom Park, and Furze Close. The other chief patterns of new enclosures took shape in the mining and quarrying districts, especially in Cornwall, where numerous cottage-holdings were carved out on the downs, commons, and wastes, particularly on and around the granite masses.

Occasionally the boundaries of old farmlands were remodelled according to a geometric plan, but by and large it was the newly enclosed lands which were characterized by straight-sided fields and plots. Here and there, and especially on and around Exmoor, these embodied long stretches of beech-lined roads. Many of the new fields were demarcated by walls and hedge-banks of the traditional Southwestern types, but the quickset hedge was also used, notably in parts of east Devon. Straight-sided fields are parti-cularly well represented on the poor soils on the hills of east Devon, on Exmoor and its margins, on the local moors dispersed throughout the Culm Measures country, and on the Cornish moors and downs (Fig. 34). Other patches of geometric pattern occur on reclaimed heathland, as in the Bovey Basin, and on marshes, for example along the estuaries of the Taw and the Exe; and, extensively, in the mining and quarrying districts of Cornwall. In contrast, the richer lands such as the valleys of east Devon, the Permian soils of the Exeter district and the Torbay area, and south Devon generally, have few straight-sided fields; and most of what there are indicate small patches of poorer soil which were the last to be reclaimed and enclosed.

The agrarian landscapes of Southwest England, as displayed during the nineteenth century, contained elements derived from many periods of enclosure, notably the legacy of strip-like patterns, the irregular patchwork around many old single farmsteads, and the more rectilinear texture of the later field boundaries. By virtue of one or more of these enclosures, some areas showed a closely meshed bocage of small fields defined by tree-dotted hedges. In the 1840s a survey made of the fields and hedges of ten parishes in east Devon revealed that more than half of the 8,000 or so fields were less than four acres each. Nevertheless by that time considerable changes were occurring in localities where small farms were being absorbed or amal-gamated, and old closes were being thrown together into larger fields by the removal of hedges and earthbanks. The process of opening out the agrarian landscape went on gradually until the advent of mechanized farming, but it has speeded up in recent years.

Particularly where infield–outfield systems were practised, and on the poorer soils and waste ground, it was an old-established procedure (gener-ally known as beat-burning) for farmers periodically to pare off and burn the turf together with furze and straw. The ashes, supplemented by sand and any locally available manures, were used as a soil dressing, and a corn crop was taken for two, three, or four years, after which the land was allowed to revert to grass or a more or less wild state for several seasons. Temporary cultivation of marginal land was, however, particularly exten-sive in wartime; and it left a distinctive, albeit minor, imprint on the land-scape. During the late eighteenth and early nineteenth centuries, many tracts of moorland, heath, and grassy commons were temporarily cropped for oats, wheat, and potatoes. For the most part the ridge-and-furrow pro-duced by this cultivation was quite shallow and narrow, but the width of the ridges varied considerably from about 5 to 18 feet. Traces of this type of ridging are still visible on Dartmoor, on the moors and commons of the Culm Measures country, in isolated patches in east and south Devon, and here and there on commons and in permanent pasture in Cornwall. Examples

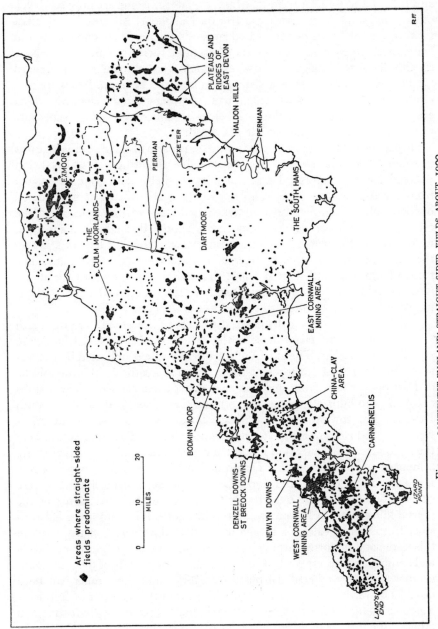

Fig. 34 SOUTHWEST ENGLAND: STRAIGHT-SIDED FIELDS ABOUT 1900.

occur in widely separated districts from the south Devon coast to Lundy, and from Land's End to the east Devon plateau. Some are near sea-level, others are found as high as 1,400 feet on Dartmoor. All these are distinct from two other forms of corrugated surface which are occasionally seen in fields in Southwest England—sets of straight furrows which were made specifically for drainage, and ridges which were thrown up in orchard grounds for the purpose of assisting drainage and aeration. They are also easily distinguished from the alignments of water-meadow channels which are still traceable along the floors and sides of some of the valleys, especially in the southern and eastern parts of Devon.

Proximity to the sea meant that in various parts of the Southwest it was possible for the farmers to use considerable quantities of seaweed and decayed fish as manures. Large amounts of shelly sand were abstracted from the beaches, particularly in north Cornwall, whence it was carried overland along 'Sandingways' or taken in barges to 'Sandplaces' in the estuaries. Of greater general importance almost throughout the region, however, was the use of lime in agriculture; and this has left its mark on the landscape in the large number of limestone quarries and kilns. The ruins of limekilns still dotted about the region, together with the documentary evidence of lime burning, testify to the widespread activity in this industry from the seventeenth to the twentieth century (Fig. 35).

Within the Southwest the greatest sources of limestone were the south Devon quarries, especially those in the Plymouth, Ashburton, Chudleigh, and Torbay districts. The extent of the inland trade is indicated by the fact that lime from Ashburton was used on farms at Postbridge, in the middle of Dartmoor. Stone from quarries near the sea was carried in small ships and barges to kilns along the coast and on tidal rivers and canals in south Devon and south Cornwall. The kilns at Topsham and Exeter, for example, were supplied from quarries at Babbacombe and Berry Head. Elsewhere in the region the local sources of limestone varied considerably, but there were a number of quarries in east Devon and in the Culm Measures and the Devonian rocks of mid and north Devon. In many cases limekilns were situated adjacent to the quarries, but some were on farms. Some of the coastal kilns in north Devon used local limestone, but many were fed with stone from South Wales. Barnstaple and Bideford were particularly active in this trade, and imported large quantities of stone from the Gower peninsula and Pembrokeshire, especially Caldy Island. By the middle of the nineteenth century a variety of artificial-manure factories and bone mills had been established in the Southwest. Competition from their output of fertilizers was one factor which adversely affected the lime-burning industry, and others were the use of guano, the later concentration of lime production in fewer centres, and the modern working of ground limestone on a large scale. The spread of the railways and thereby the possibility of obtaining fertilizers in bulk from distant sources, the agricultural depression of the 'seventies

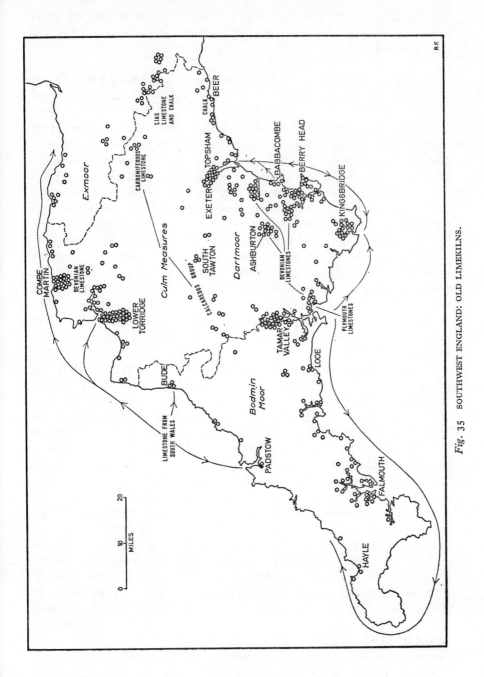

Fig. 35 SOUTHWEST ENGLAND: OLD LIMEKILNS.

and 'eighties, and the distribution of ground limestone by road transport were other reasons why the activity of the local kilns waned and has now almost ceased.

Trends in agriculture from the eighteenth century to the Second World War

DEVON

In the seventeenth century Devonshire agriculture was commended for its careful preparation and manuring of the arable, its orchards, and, especially, its sheep farming. The demand for wool was met not only from the extensive pasturing on the upland areas, but also from the lower lands where sheep were grazed on both rough ground and enclosed fields and were folded on the arable, to the general benefit of the crops. Devon was not always self-supporting in food grains, but was able to supply provisions for the merchant ships and fishing vessels which thronged its harbours.

Observers during the late eighteenth and early nineteenth centuries were generally less favourable in their comments on agriculture in the county, finding that there was room for considerable improvement and that the farming needed a better system of convertible husbandry. Standards and management varied, however, and some improvements had certainly been made or were in progress. Turnips had been introduced into the rotation by about 1750. For a time, appreciable quantities of flax were grown in east Devon, where the red soils on the Permian and Triassic rocks were very suitable for this crop. Farming in southwest Devon responded to the demand for meat and vegetables to supply the naval base at Dock. Important progress was made in stock breeding, including the production of the North Devon breed of cattle by the Quartlys of Molland. The Devonshire Nott, a longwool sheep, was linked with the Leicester to produce the Devon Longwool breed. Probably the Dartmoor and South Devon breeds also became established from the eighteenth century onwards, while the Devon Closewool evolved by the crossing of the Exmoor Horn with the Devon Longwool. During the nineteenth century there was much progress in the breeding of the Devon and South Devon cattle. Shorthorns, however, were pre-eminent in the important dairying area of east Devon.

The war period from 1793 was a comparatively prosperous one for agriculture, but it was followed by a great fall in prices after the peace of 1815, and there was a considerable exodus from the land. By the mid-nineteenth century Devonshire farming generally was considered mediocre, a state of affairs which was in part bound up with the fall in prosperity caused by the decline of the woollen industry and the diminution in trade. Despite the effects on local corn-growing of the wider availability of grain brought in by rail, in the 'sixties wheat was still the most important cereal crop. As a result of the great depression of the 'seventies and 'eighties, however, the acreages under wheat and barley greatly decreased, and a considerable proportion of the arable was laid down to permanent grass, especially on the poor soils such as those of the Culm Measures country. Oats, the cereal crop of greatest significance to the stock farmer and best suited to the damp climate of much of Devon, more than maintained its position and there was an overall increase in acreage to the First World War, after which it too fell. In 1938, however, oats occupied a larger acreage than the sum of the other grain crops. The increase in the arable during the First World War was followed by another steady decline and conversion to grass and even much rough grazing, especially again on the poorer lands of the Culm country. Acreages under all cereal crops increased greatly during the Second World War, when the ploughing up of permanent grass was undertaken on a large scale.

CORNWALL

In the early eighteenth century the Cornish moorlands, still largely unenclosed, were extensive grazings for cattle and sheep, but in the eastern half of the county an appreciable emphasis was put on pasture, partly in response to the demands of the Devon and Somerset graziers, and partly to meet the needs of the spinners who provided yarn for local weavers as well as for the Devonshire woollen industry. Considerable quantities of wheat and barley, however, were grown in southeast Cornwall, and in parts of the middle and western areas of the county crop-growing was stimulated by the demand for food for the increasing population in the metalliferous mining districts, the towns and ports, and later in the china-clay area too. The best soils in Cornwall were used for wheat growing, and the poorer for oats and rye. Barley occupied large acreages, especially in a tract on the northern side of the county from about Newquay through the Padstow district to Port Isaac. This area was long known as 'The Granary of Cornwall'. Among the noteworthy tracts of arable farther south and west were the district of the Fal and its tributaries, and the land east of Penzance, where large crops of grain and potatoes were usual.

Until the nineteenth century was well advanced, much of the farming in Cornwall was essentially of a subsistence character, and on the generally small farms the standard of management was low. In the late eighteenth and early nineteenth centuries there was still a considerable proportion of 'inarable lands', perhaps as much as one-quarter of the county being unenclosed. The system of working the arable for a succession of two or three corn crops, possibly followed by a single root or green crop, then grassing down for a period of three to eight years, was gradually varied, notably by the regular inclusion of turnips and mangolds in the rotation, so that by the third quarter of the century Cornish farming was showing some improvement. The depression of the 'seventies and 'eighties resulted in much land being switched from corn growing to mixed farming and pasture. Except for a sharp but temporary increase during the First World

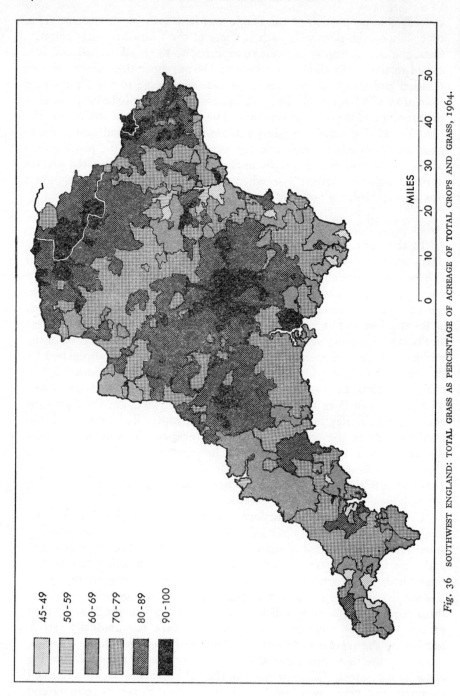

45 - 49
50 - 59
60 - 69
70 - 79
80 - 89
90 - 100

MILES

0   10   20   30   40   50

Fig. 36 SOUTHWEST ENGLAND: TOTAL GRASS AS PERCENTAGE OF ACREAGE OF TOTAL CROPS AND GRASS, 1964.

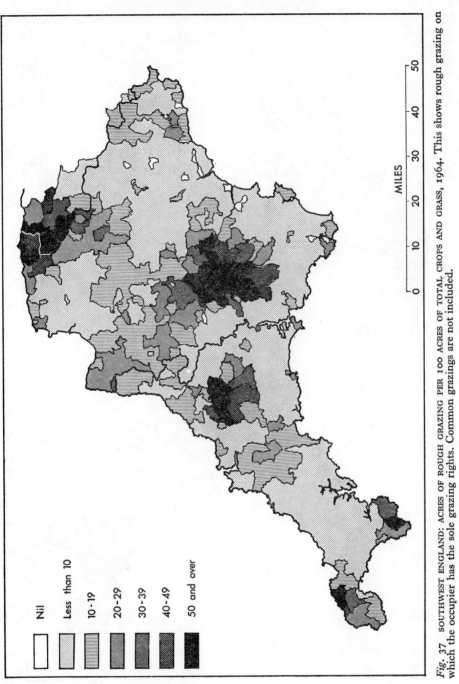

Fig. 37 SOUTHWEST ENGLAND: ACRES OF ROUGH GRAZING PER 100 ACRES OF TOTAL CROPS AND GRASS, 1964. This shows rough grazing on which the occupier has the sole grazing rights. Common grazings are not included.

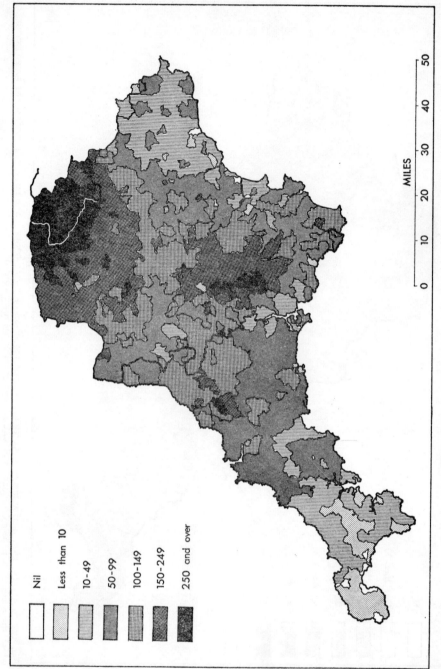

Legend:

Nil

Less than 10

10–49

50–99

100–149

150–249

250 and over

MILES

0   10   20   30   40   50

Fig. 38   SOUTHWEST ENGLAND: SHEEP PER 100 ACRES OF TOTAL CROPS AND GRASS, 1964.

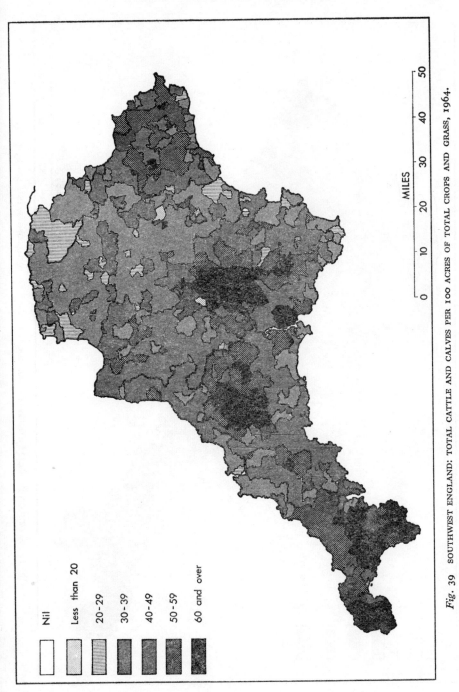

Fig. 39 SOUTHWEST ENGLAND: TOTAL CATTLE AND CALVES PER 100 ACRES OF TOTAL CROPS AND GRASS, 1964.

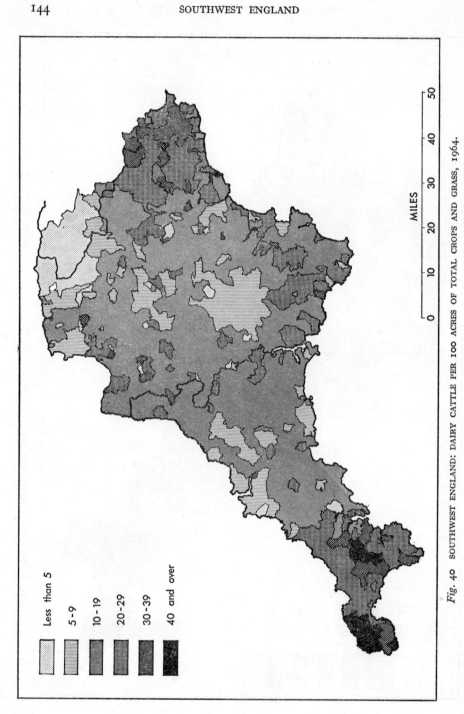

Fig. 40 SOUTHWEST ENGLAND: DAIRY CATTLE PER 100 ACRES OF TOTAL CROPS AND GRASS, 1964.

Less than 5

5 - 9

10 - 19

20 - 29

30 - 39

40 and over

MILES

0   10   20   30   40   50

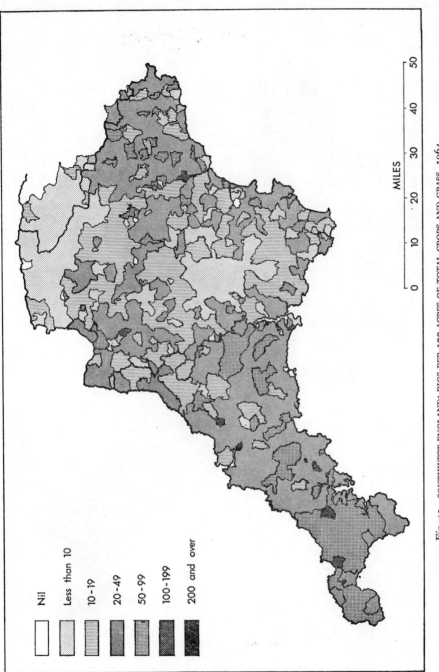

Nil

Less than 10

10 - 19

20 - 49

50 - 99

100 - 199

200 and over

Fig. 41 SOUTHWEST ENGLAND: PIGS PER 100 ACRES OF TOTAL CROPS AND GRASS, 1964.

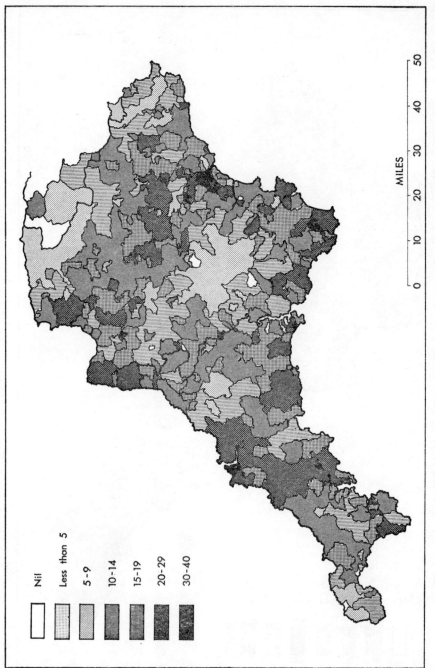

Nil

Less than 5

5-9

10-14

15-19

20-29

30-40

MILES

0   10   20   30   40   50

Fig. 42   SOUTHWEST ENGLAND: BARLEY AS PERCENTAGE OF ACREAGE OF TOTAL CROPS AND GRASS, 1964.

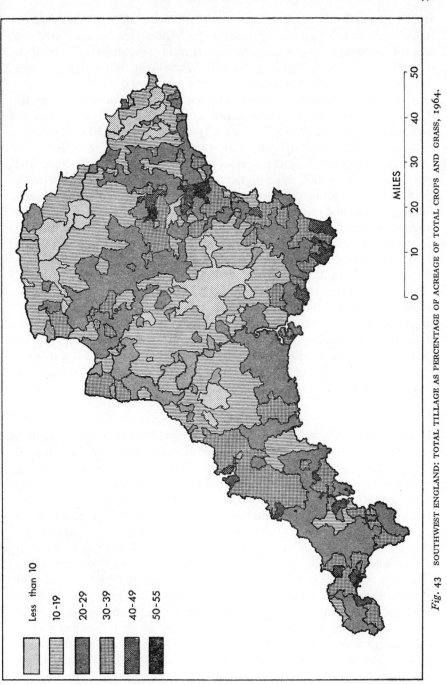

Fig. 43 SOUTHWEST ENGLAND: TOTAL TILLAGE AS PERCENTAGE OF ACREAGE OF TOTAL CROPS AND GRASS, 1964.

War, a generally downward trend in the acreages under all cereals continued until the ploughing-up campaign of the 1940s. From the 1870s onwards the area under permanent pasture at first expanded quickly, then remained fairly steady until the Second World War; but rough grazings increased considerably too, especially in the poor-soil districts.

Other marked trends, however, were occurring in Cornish agriculture during the second half of the nineteenth century. Dairying had not hitherto been very significant, although Channel Island cattle were already common in parts of the county early in the century. The later switch to an emphasis on dairying was aided by the development of the distant milk-trade and eventually also by the establishment of a number of milk factories in Cornwall. Guernsey cattle remained of outstanding importance in the west, although for a time other breeds such as the Cornish Shorthorn had some success. In the late nineteenth century the increase in pig keeping in Cornwall was very marked, especially in the dairying districts. From the 'sixties the completion of the main railway link stimulated the production of special crops in the far west, and large dispatches of potatoes, broccoli, and flowers to markets in London and the Midlands soon became an established feature of the trade. In the Tamar valley the decline of mining and of shipbuilding caused many part-time growers to concentrate on horticulture as their sole occupation, and their trade was helped very considerably by the construction of the Lydford–Devonport section of railway line in 1890 and by the completion of the branch line from Bere Alston to Calstock and Callington in 1908.

Modern trends in agriculture

The series of maps which refer to this section have been compiled on a parish basis from data in the Agricultural Returns of June 1964 (Figs. 36 to 43). They may be used for studies of both the general geographical picture of farming in the Southwest and the features of agriculture in the subregions which are described in Chapters 10 to 14. As the use of pasture is the basis of much of the farming in the region and as high standards of grass management are one of the keys to its future prosperity, the economist will probably agree with the geographer in giving pride of place to the map of grasslands. Particularly because of the systems of long leys practised in various parts of Southwest England, it has proved difficult to make an absolute distinction between permanent and temporary grass; and in order to appreciate the importance of pasture generally in the modern patterns of farming in the region, it is more realistic to map all grass together and to add a map of rough grazing. The latter, however, shows only the rough grazings on which the occupier has the sole rights. This gives a basis for an understanding of the relative importance of rough grazings in the various subregions, but the addition of the commons would emphasize their significance on and around the moorland areas.

In recent years there has been a general increase in the numbers of sheep and cattle in Southwest England (Fig. 44), especially sheep, which have been comparatively profitable. With the Government aid given, for example, by the hill-cow subsidy and the supplementary grant for winter keep, stock ratios on the hill farms have risen appreciably. The main role of the upland areas is the rearing of beef cattle and sheep, the latter most notably on Exmoor and in north Devon. Most of the store-raising farms which do not sell milk are in the upland districts on and around Exmoor, Dartmoor, and Bodmin Moor. A considerable part of the farm output of Southwest England as a whole, however, consists of the production of sheep and cattle as stores and for fattening; and the two stock enterprises are not uncommonly found together on the same farm. Large numbers of young cattle are sent to other regions of England for fattening.

Dairying is outstandingly important in four subregions—east Devon, west Cornwall, and the Lizard and Land's End peninsulas—but it is the predominant enterprise in many other districts too. During the past twenty-five years the emphasis on dairying has greatly increased in Southwest England. The trend quickened noticeably after 1955, and it has been accompanied by a spectacular rise in the numbers of Friesian cattle. Whereas in 1955 this breed accounted f ust over one-quarter of the dairy cattle in Devon and Cornwall, in 1965 the proportion was well over one-half. The Ayrshire and Channel Island breeds have increased appreciably, but the number of Shorthorns has fallen sharply and the South Devons have also decreased. In Devon, Friesians make up 57·3 per cent of the breed distribution in the milk-selling herds, but Cornwall, where Guernsey cattle are strongly represented, has a considerably lower figure, 42·1 per cent.

While it is true that many of the dairy herds in Southwest England are small—in Devon one-half and in Cornwall two-thirds of the total number of herds are of less than 20 cows—taking the two counties together the average size has steadily increased from 10 cows in 1942 to 20 in 1965; and the very small herd is no longer so typical of the region. In this period herds numbering less than 10 cows decreased by three-quarters from the 1942 figure of about 10,000, while at the other end of the scale herds of 50 or more increased from 40 to 467. The upward trend in the size of herds is one aspect of a significant change that is still proceeding in the dairying enterprises in the Southwest. Another is the reduction in the number of herds and in the total of milk-selling farmers. In recent years Devon and Cornwall together show a considerable fall in the number of registered milk-producers—from 17,900 in 1955 to 12,799 in 1966. This fall is attributed partly to the elimination of much of the side-line dairying of former years and partly to the fact that some farmers have changed to the production of meat and crops, even in such strongholds of dairying as east Devon. Other important aspects of modern developments in dairy farming are the increased intensity of stocking and the greater yields and sales of

S.E.—6

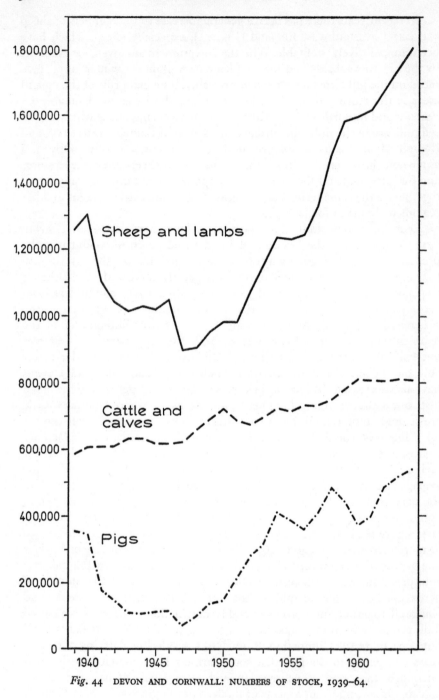

Fig. 44   DEVON AND CORNWALL: NUMBERS OF STOCK, 1939–64.

milk. The several markets for milk, cream, and butter—the all-the-year-round local trade, the holiday-season demand, and the distant market—all now play a significant role in the economy of Southwest England. With few exceptions the locations of the creameries are also those of the main points of dispatch of milk, which are, in Cornwall, St Erth, Camborne, and Lostwithiel; and in Devon, Great Torrington, Lifton, Lapford, Totnes, Crediton, Hemyock, and Seaton Junction. For the distant markets, the milk is sent out mainly by rail tankers, but to some extent road transport is also used, especially where the destination has no rail connection or where special milk, for example Channel Island, is required at a particular time and place. The milk is sent predominantly to the London bottling centres of the major dairy companies for distribution in the metropolitan area.

Although Southwest England is not of great importance for poultry, there are at present about 5,500,000 in the region; and there is a considerable number of chick hatcheries and intensive poultry-units. Egg-packing firms are widely distributed, but the largest group has recently centralized its organization in Exeter. Of the 25 parishes where poultry ratios are between 10 and 20 per acre of crops and grass, 15 are in the eastern third of Devon. Densities higher than this, however, are recorded in only a few parishes in east Devon and are rare elsewhere. Most of the greatest densities are accounted for by the presence of large specialist and intensive enterprises. Trends in poultry keeping in the Southwest since the Second World War have not been uniform. The numbers of poultry in both Devon and Cornwall quickly recovered from the wartime trough; and in Devon, although there have been minor fluctuations, the later increase has been so marked that the county now has nearly one and a half times as many poultry as in 1939. In Cornwall, however, the post-war recovery in numbers reached a peak in 1950, since when there has been a general decrease. From 1962 onwards there have been fewer poultry than there were in 1939. Whereas in 1959 there were about 16,000 registered egg-producers in the county, in 1965 there were only 9,500. This decrease is generally attributed to the inability of small-scale producers to withstand a succession of low returns.

Pig keeping is of special importance in half a dozen subregions of Southwest England—the west Cornwall district, the Land's End and Lizard peninsulas, mid Cornwall, southeast Cornwall, and east Devon. In the first three and the last of these areas there is an obvious and long-standing association of high densities of pigs with the principal dairying districts, even though in modern times, and mainly for economic reasons, the part traditionally played by local supplies of skim milk and whey to pig producers in Devon and Cornwall has diminished in importance. A contributory factor which has fostered pig keeping in most of these areas has long been the small size of the agricultural holdings. In southwest Devon–southeast Cornwall the availability of large quantities of swill from the Plymouth district was another factor favourable to this enterprise, and in the Tamar valley and east Devon it was advantageous and beneficial for the soil to use many of the orchard grounds as pasture for pigs. As with poultry, the development of large intensive breeding-units in recent years has emphasized the densities in certain localities. A high proportion of the pigs in Southwest England are classified as mixed or crossed types, but the Large White, the Wessex Saddleback, and the Landrace breeds are all important. With the demand for quality pork and the high standards required by the bacon factories, there was already in the 1930s a tendency for the white breeds generally to increase at the expense of the black. In recent years, however, there has been a more marked degree of specialization in breeding, production, and marketing by 'pig groups' as well as by individual farmers in certain areas, for example southeast Cornwall. The Southwest supplies large numbers of store pigs to other regions for fattening. The pre-war importance of pigs in the region was not numerically restored until 1953–4, but the total for Devon and Cornwall is now much larger than in 1939—539,771 in 1964 compared with 352,844. This increase, which has been particularly marked in Cornwall, has been stimulated by the greater demand for bacon and pork and has been aided by the availability of both local and imported feedingstuffs.

Following the upsurge in production during the Second World War, the acreages under most cereal crops were much reduced in the late 1940s (Fig. 45). The contraction was most marked in wheat, which is the least suited to the damp climate of many parts of the Southwest. For a time the acreage under barley stood fairly steadily at the diminished figure of the early post-war years, but there was an appreciable increase in mixed or 'dredge' corn which, in Southwest England, usually consists of oats and barley sown together. Mixed corn has long been a popular crop in parts of Devon and, more especially, in Cornwall, for one grain supports the other against wind and rain, they draw nutrients from different soil levels, and it is not usual for both to fail at the same time. Now, however, this crop has been reduced considerably, in Cornwall to one-sixth of the wartime acreage. Since 1955 the great and successful competitor in grain growing has been barley, a crop which in pre-war years was grown chiefly in areas of comparatively low rainfall and light soils in Devon, and especially in the redland districts around Exeter and in the South Hams. In most parts of the region it has now assumed great importance, and in many it occupies a large proportion of the total tillage. While it is true that the greatest recent increases within the region have occurred in the Exeter district, the South Hams, southeast Cornwall, and the Truro–Padstow area, much barley is grown on poorer land. The casual observer might think that this is an uneconomic proposition, unless it is realized that the crop is important not only for feeding to stock but also for a supply of straw, which would be very costly to purchase from distant merchants.

The trend in which barley has been largely substituted for oats and

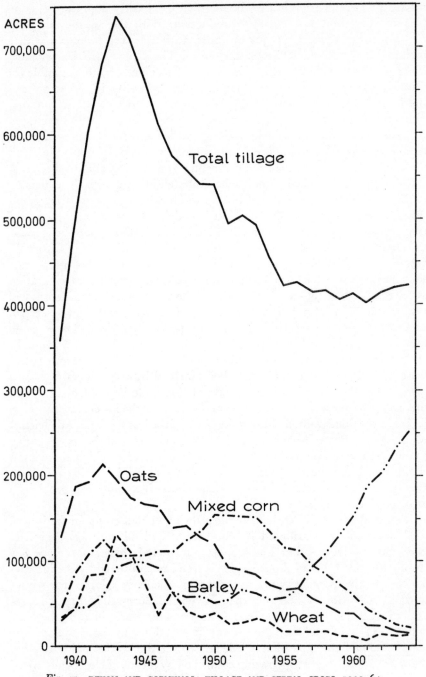

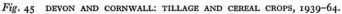

Fig. 45 DEVON AND CORNWALL: TILLAGE AND CEREAL CROPS, 1939–64.

mixed corn draws attention to the fact that even fairly high rainfall is no longer a deterrent to successful production. With the advance in plant breeding from the early 1950s onwards, varieties were produced with a high yield potential and disease resistance. These new varieties—notably the generally reliable 'Proctor'—have proved to be much more suitable for growing conditions in the Southwest. They are stiffer in the straw and much less likely to be severely lodged during windy, rainy spells in summer. Other factors, however, have also been important in spurring on the rapid advance of barley. These include the great demand for feedingstuffs in a region where stock farming is not only important but is still expanding, and the improvements in mechanized harvesting, grain drying, and weed control. But the greatest financial stimulus was initiated in 1954 with the extension of the cereal deficiency payment to all growers who harvested barley grain. Acreages reached a peak in 1964, but it is debatable whether the upward trend of previous years will really be reversed. A decline cannot be forecast merely from the fact that in very recent years, and noticeably in Cornwall, barley is being grown on rather fewer farms, for usually this means that some farmers are giving up small acreages of cereals and are concentrating on livestock production. Some believe, however, that mixed corn will recover much of its popularity, at least in Cornwall, and that, as certain varieties of oats are greatly improving in quality and yield, this crop too may be re-established in importance, perhaps particularly in Devon. In 1965–6 barley growing in England generally was still a prosperous enterprise, the disposal of record crops being helped by a considerable export market. On the other hand, the future of this trade is problematical, and there have been some slightly ominous portents for the immediate future of barley in the Southwest, including the effect of the less favourable deficiency payment and the variation in crop yields. In some parts of the region barley has suffered from fungus diseases such as *rhynchosporium* which, though not confined to Devon and Cornwall, is exacerbated by mild, humid conditions. It is significant that one of the sites where research work on this problem is to be carried out is in Cornwall.

Before the Second World War the growing of root crops for feeding to stock was widely distributed in Southwest England and was especially important in Devon; but in the post-war period their importance has steadily declined. From about 1947 this trend was initiated by the increasing competitive popularity of green crops, particularly kale, for the winter feeding programme. Whereas in 1939 Devon and Cornwall had 47,497 acres under turnips, swedes, and mangolds as crops for stock, in 1964 they had only 23,111 acres, and the figure is now (1966) down to about 19,000. The main reason for the expansion of kale acreages in the 'forties and 'fifties was the wider adoption of strip grazing controlled by means of electrically wired fences. This method of grazing kale was used principally for dairy cattle, and was a popular advance on the old laborious method of cutting the crop by hand in winter. The peak of the acreage under kale in Devon and Cornwall (49,311) was, however, reached in 1960, since when there has been a gradual reduction to less than 32,000 acres now (1966). Some farmers assert that, in view of the simplification of their farming systems, it is difficult to maintain a proportionately large acreage of kale; but the main reasons for its recent decline are probably the readier availability of other winter feeds and the problem and cost of cleaning dairy cattle after they have been feeding on kale in muddy fields.

Potatoes played an important part in the increase in tillage during the Second World War, but whereas in Devon the acreage reached a peak in 1943 (35,929 compared with 6,200 in 1939), in Cornwall, where the crop continued to be widely grown, the maximum figure was attained in 1948 (28,537 acres against 4,678 in 1939). In the reduced areas of the present time, Devon has about 5,500 acres and Cornwall has 6,400, of which 5,000 are under 'earlies'.

The micro-climatic advantages possessed by certain districts in South-west England are their principal asset for the growing of 'special' crops, for they permit the emphasis on early production and on high-value crops that is necessary economically to overcome the disadvantage of distance from the chief markets. The risk elements, however, in these enterprises are in particular the occasional occurrence of frost and cold winds and the coincidence of high humidity and warmth, which may induce *botrytis* disease in anemones and strawberries and give poor travelling conditions for broccoli and flowers. The impact of competition from elsewhere, though variable, can be serious, and for bulb flowers arises not only from imports from many different sources but also from the use of pre-cooling and forcing techniques by growers in other parts of this country. Markets for early potatoes from the Southwest are chiefly affected by supplies from Pembrokeshire and imports from the Channel Islands, Cyprus, and Italy. For broccoli growers the main competition comes from shipments from Italy, France, and the Channel Islands, and—when there is a seasonal overlap in output—from producers in Kent and Lincolnshire.

By no means all of the special crops for which Southwest England is so well known are essentially 'early'. It is more realistic to classify them as (i) out-of-season and (ii) really early crops. Broccoli and anemones, low- and high-value products respectively, come in the first category, while the second group consists of narcissus and strawberries as high-value crops and early potatoes and spring cabbage as those of low value. In some districts, as around Calstock in the Tamar valley, cultivation under glass has increased considerably, and in the 'sixties growers have had assistance from the Horticulture Improvement Scheme in installing and extending glasshouses. The largest concentration of glasshouse cultivation in Devon is at Elburton (Plymouth), where there is a marked specialization in tomatoes. There appear to be possibilities for the further development of this branch of production in localities which have a high incidence of sunshine. While in some horticultural districts in Southwest England special crops have for various reasons declined somewhat in acreage and importance, certain other recent trends have been encouraging, notably the diversification of flower growing, the improvement in quality, and the organization and co-operation of growers, for example at St Erth and in the Tamar valley, Elburton and Yealmpton areas.

CHAPTER 8

Industries

THE principal industries which were carried on in Southwest England between medieval and modern times fall into three groups—manufacturing and processing industries, most of which were largely based upon regional resources; mining and quarrying and their auxiliaries; and fishing and shipbuilding. Most of these have contracted geographically in modern times; some have declined in absolute or relative importance, and others have changed in emphasis or character. On the other hand, the extraction of clay has rapidly increased, and a variety of manufacturing and processing industries has been developed in the region and some have been newly brought in. This chapter deals with the chief industries in these groups; but the holiday industry, which is essentially concerned with the movement and accommodation of people, is logically assigned to Chapter 9.

Until they began to thin out as a result of the advent of the steam engine, many hundreds of old-established mills were profusely distributed over Southwest England. Wind and tide mills were used mainly for the grinding of corn, and horse mills were employed on some of the farms as well as for grinding malt and colouring materials in the towns. All these, however, were far outnumbered by water mills, for the siting of which the broken physique, the copious rainfall, and the multitude of streams in the region afforded abundant possibilities. Some rivers, such as the Kennall in west Cornwall, averaged as many as seven wheels to each mile of their course; and there were numerous other concentrations. About 1815 the Tavistock Iron Works, for example, had nine water wheels which drove boring, turning, and grinding mills; and in the heyday of the Devon Great Consols mine thirty-three wheels were used in connection with the working of copper and arsenic. The majority of the water wheels in Southwest England were employed in corn or grist mills, but a considerable number were devoted to other uses such as the textile industries (especially in fulling mills); sawing timber, marble, and slate; metal working; pressing rape seed for the extraction of oil; and pulverizing or grinding ore, china stone, bark, ochre, powder for mining and quarrying purposes, and bone and gypsum for manure. While some of the water mills, and even some of the steam mills that displaced them, were of only transient significance, in general and together with the crafts which accompanied their activity they were for long the industrial life-blood of many localities. Very few water wheels are in use today. The eventual cessation of each factory, mill, and craft marked a stage in the transformation of the local economy and sometimes also of the social cohesion of a hamlet, village or town as people left to seek employment elsewhere. The same is true of several other industries, such as foundries, brickworks and breweries, which were widely represented in the region but are now reduced to a few sites on which production has been consolidated and increased.

Tanning and leather working

As stock farming has always been a mainstay of the regional economy, a plentiful supply of hides and skins provided the materials for a number of trades and crafts including fellmongering, tanning, saddlery, and the making of boots, shoes, and gloves. During the eighteenth and nineteenth centuries this supply was augmented by imports from Ireland, Western Europe, and South America. Many of the small tanyards, which were numerous and widely distributed until well into the nineteenth century, used local oak bark for the preparation of the tan-pit liquor. The 'bark harvest' in the wooded valleys of Southwest England took place in May, and the bark was ground in poundhouses or water mills which in some cases were adjacent to the tanyards. Bark was exported and, by means of coastwise shipments, was traded to localities which were deficient in oak woods, for example to west Cornwall from Exeter; but there were also imports of tanning materials, such as sumach and valonia. Tanning was particularly important in the area tributary to Exeter, and there too were most of the chamois-leather mills (Fig. 46).

About the middle of the nineteenth century there were still 75 tanyards at work in Devon and Cornwall, but in recent years only half a dozen have been active, and one of these—at Swimbridge near Barnstaple—closed in 1965. In common with many other rural regions, the Southwest has lost a great number of small tanneries, while the industry has become concentrated and has grown in Lancashire and Cheshire, the Midlands, the London area, and the West Riding of Yorkshire. With three exceptions —at Plymouth, Cullompton, and Topsham—glove making is now mainly carried on in north Devon. It has long been established in that district, and still provides employment not only in the factories but also for female outworkers. A proportion of the output, however, now consists of fabric gloves.

Textiles

As in medieval times, but by no means according to the same pattern of distribution, a high degree of dispersal of fulling mills was a character-istic feature of the woollen industry after 1600 (Fig. 47). From then

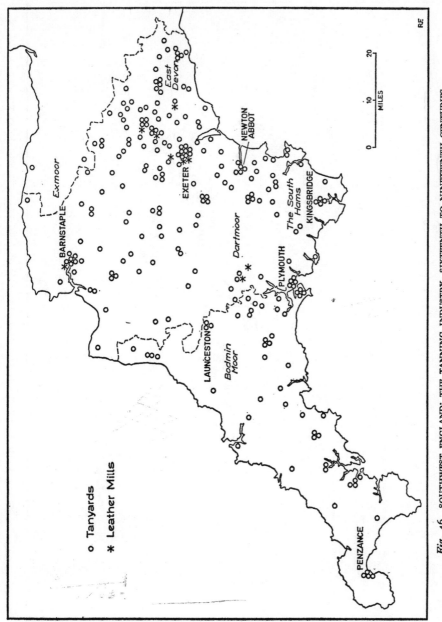

Fig. 46 SOUTHWEST ENGLAND: THE TANNING INDUSTRY, SIXTEENTH TO NINETEENTH CENTURIES.

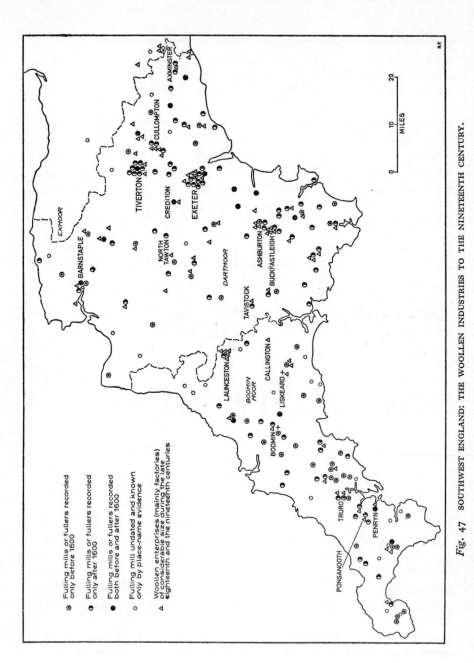

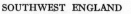

Fig. 47 SOUTHWEST ENGLAND: THE WOOLLEN INDUSTRIES TO THE NINETEENTH CENTURY.

onwards, however, important changes occurred in the nature of this industry in the region, especially since the emphasis moved almost entirely from the production of straits and kerseys to the manufacture of serge, a cloth woven from both long and short wools and requiring considerable, but not heavy fulling. Until the nineteenth century most parts of the Southwest were in one way or another concerned with the woollen industry, for there was a wide distribution of the combing, spinning, and weaving of the local wools together with supplies of long wool imported from Ireland (mainly via Barnstaple) and short wool from Southeast England and Spain (brought in at Exeter). Tiverton was the most important manufacturing centre, with a largely independent trade. Exeter had several fulling mills, but it was primarily the great focus for commerce and for finishing, dyeing, packing, and exporting cloth to its principal overseas markets in Holland, Germany, Spain, Portugal, and Italy. In south Devon the most noteworthy concentration of the woollen industry was in the Ashburton–Buckfastleigh district. The industry in Cornwall was widely dispersed, but in the area from Bodmin eastwards considerable emphasis was put on the production of yarn. Although the Cornish manufacture was far less important than that of Devon, credit should be given to several enterprises there which made various branches of the woollen industry of more than purely local significance. These included the carpet factory at Truro and the mills which, during the late eighteenth and early nineteenth centuries, were at work at Launceston, near Liskeard, and in the Truro and Penryn districts. There was even an attempt to establish a Cornish broadcloth industry at Camelford.

Much of the great woollen trade of Southwest England was crippled by a series of wars which resulted in the diminution or loss of the overseas markets for serges, and by competition from Norwich cloths, the growing factory industry of Yorkshire, and cheap cotton goods. It was chiefly during the late eighteenth and early nineteenth centuries that a number of spinning mills or factories were established in Devon and Cornwall in an attempt to arrest the decline of the industry. The Napoleonic Wars, however, delivered a staggering blow, and although for a time the East India Company provided a considerable outlet for woollens from Devon and Cornwall, the ending of the Company's monopoly of the China trade in 1833 was another severe shock. In the 1830s there were still about 40 woollen mills in Devon and some 3,000 looms employed in weaving serges; but many of these ceased production later in the century. One of the last mills to close was a sizeable factory at North Tawton, which was at work until 1930. Today Devon's principal representatives in the woollen industry are the carpet factory at Axminster, mills in the Culm valley and at Buckfast and Buckfastleigh, and the Dartington Hall weaving and tweed-making enterprises. In Cornwall eight mills were at work in the 1830s but the industry gradually thinned out and only one factory—at

Ponsanooth, and chiefly concerned with the manufacture of tape—survived as late as the end of the First World War.

During the seventeenth and eighteenth centuries the hand-made lace industry flourished in many parts of east Devon, but was especially centred upon Honiton and Ottery St Mary. For a time it had considerable markets in London and Bath, but it was adversely affected by vicissitudes in fashion and by the machine manufacture of net lace. This last industry was brought to Devon by John Heathcoat who, after vainly seeking a suitable factory site near Exeter, moved from Loughborough to Tiverton in 1816. A few other lace factories were tentatively established in Devon, but of these only the enterprise at Barnstaple was successful. Most of the several attempts to set up cotton and silk industries were very short-lived. Cotton spinning was carried on at Exeter for several years from 1796, and about 1840 a large factory at Ottery St Mary was being used for the manufacture of silk ribbons and handkerchiefs. Until the advent of steamships, the demand for sailcloth supported numerous small-scale industries in and near the harbour towns such as Penryn and Padstow, where the manufacture was described as that of 'poldavy', a coarse canvas or sacking.

Paper making

At various times during the seventeenth and eighteenth centuries the paper-making industry in England was stimulated by the cutting off of supplies of paper from Continental countries as a result of wartime conditions. Until the spread of the use of the paper-making machine from 1804 onwards, the English industry responded to the increasing demand mainly by multiplying the number of vat mills, which were still almost entirely water-driven. Devon's first paper mill, at Countess Wear, was established by 1638, but nearly 80 years elapsed before paper making began in Cornwall, at a mill near Truro. Throughout the eighteenth century, and especially in the second half, the number of mills in Southwest England showed an overall increase, and a peak was reached in the 1820s (Fig. 48). Most of these were converted from corn or fulling mills. Although some, particularly in the Exeter district, produced good-quality writing and printing paper, and although there were considerable shipments of paper out of the region, especially from Exeter, it is probable that until the later part of the nineteenth century a substantial part of the output consisted of common wrapping or shop papers for local sale. While the woollen trade of the Exeter area was still active, some mills specialized in the production of glazed paper for use in the hotpressing of cloth and of pasteboard for packing serge.

Except for a steam-driven factory at Penryn and a board mill near Calstock, no paper mill was founded in Southwest England after the 1830s. Almost all the mills that have ever existed have been situated south of a NE–SW axial line through the region. The marked concentration in the

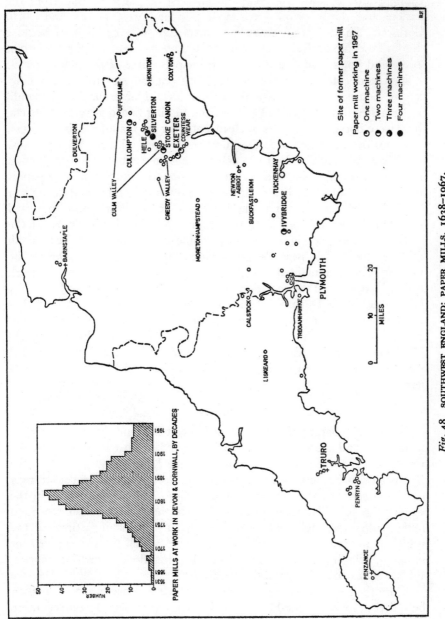

Fig. 48 SOUTHWEST ENGLAND: PAPER MILLS, 1638–1967.

trading focus of the lower Exe valley and its tributaries, especially the Culm, contrasts with the complete absence of paper making from the remote and thinly peopled tracts of mid and west Devon and north Cornwall. The southern areas were attractive to paper makers because they were comparatively well populated, they had most of the important towns and ports, and they were the principal source of the raw materials —linen and cotton rags for good-quality papers, and disused sacking, canvas, netting, and ropes for the poorer sorts. Numerous streams could be harnessed for power, and save in the mining and quarrying districts, there were bountiful supplies of clean water for the manufacturing process.

From the 1830s onwards the number of paper mills in the Southwest was inexorably reduced by the trend towards concentration of production based upon the machine and the steam engine, the growth of large paper-making units elsewhere in Britain—especially near London and in some of the industrial regions—and the increased competition from imported paper. Such factors were instrumental firstly in eliminating most of the vats and later in deleting the remote machine-mills. The last of the Cornish mills—Kennall Vale near Penryn—ceased work in 1900. In Devon the number of mills remained at eight after the closure of the Buckfastleigh factory in 1940 until the cessation of Head Weir Mill (Exeter) in July 1967. Today most of the Devonshire mills are owned by group firms. All together they employ about 1,100 people and produce a wide range of papers, from common sorts to good-quality papers made from wood pulp and esparto grass. The cheaper grades, such as brown and sugar papers, wrappers, and boards, are manufactured in the smaller mills, and chiefly from waste paper.

Mining

In the long history of mining in Southwest England tin and copper are paramount, and the subregions which have been most important for the production of these ores—west Cornwall, the Land's End peninsula, the St Austell district, and east Cornwall–west Devon—appear most strongly on a map showing the comparative densities of mines and shafts in the region (Fig. 49). The intensity of working in these areas is also expressed in the numerous, and now mostly relict, surface manifestations of the results of mining activity—pithead structures which housed engines for pumping, winding, and stamping; ore-dressing floors, smelting houses, and waste heaps; and adits and watercourses.

From the sixteenth century, mining in the true sense began to outstrip the old tin-streaming methods, and the balance of activity moved more markedly to the western parts of Cornwall. Shafts were sunk deeper, and by about 1700 some of the copper lodes below the tin were being exploited, notably in the Redruth district. During the eighteenth century the pursuance of mining at really deep levels became practicable by reason of the

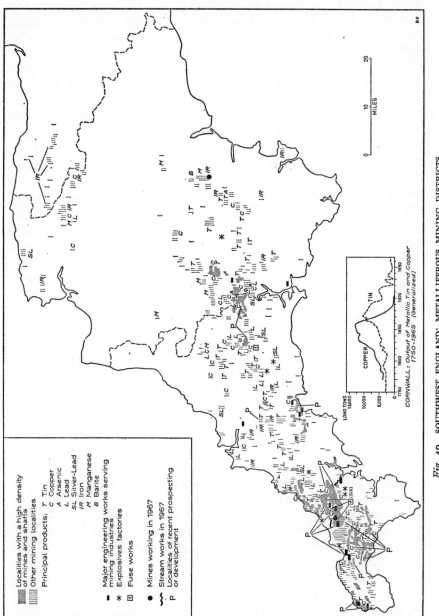

Fig. 49 SOUTHWEST ENGLAND: METALLIFEROUS MINING DISTRICTS.

application of steam power to pumping machinery used for drainage. Mainly because of the cost of bringing in coal, steam engines at first came slowly into use, but from 1777 Watt's more efficient engines superseded those of Newcomen, and the rapid development of Cornish mining was further aided by the work of such notable engineers as Hornblower, Bull, Trevithick, and Woolf.

Tin mining on Dartmoor declined in importance from the seventeenth century onwards. The last mine to work on a commercial scale—Hen Roost near Hexworthy—closed in 1916, although small workings three miles northeast of Postbridge were carried on as recently as the 'thirties. Changes of fortune in Devonshire tin-mining were, however, of small significance compared with those in the industry in Cornwall where, together with the vicissitudes in copper mining, they greatly affected the lives of thousands of people. Cornish tin-mining reached a peak in 1871 with a yield of about 10,900 tons; but shortly afterwards, and largely because of the increase in output overseas, there was a catastrophic decline in the number of mines at work in the county, and an exodus of tin miners. There followed the disastrous slump of the 'nineties, when the working out of easily accessible ores coincided with the large-scale marketing of cheap Malayan tin. Between then and 1950 the trend in Cornish production, though in general downwards, was uneven, three phases of partial but ever-diminishing recovery being cleft by two plunging troughs. In 1918 nine mines employed 3,566 people, but as a result of the calamitous fall in the world price of tin and the high costs in the post-war years, mining had almost ceased by 1922. The great Dolcoath mine closed in 1920, and two years later Cornwall produced only 370 tons of tin. In Camborne and Redruth about 2,750 miners were out of work, a tragic state of affairs that was to be repeated within ten years. A reversal of the price trend during the 'twenties, however, pushed employment up temporarily, although most of the output—now barely 2 per cent of the world's annual total—came from only half a dozen mines.

Following the great depression of 1930–1 there was a brief uplift in production before the onset of the Second World War, during which mining was carried on at Geevor (for tin), South Crofty (tin and arsenic), and East Pool and Agar (tin and wolfram); the last-named closed in 1947. None of the smaller wartime workings is now in operation; nor is New Consols near Luckett (east Cornwall), which in 1947 was re-opened for a few years for the mining of tin and the extraction of wolfram from pebbles. In recent years, however, the increasing prospect of a world shortage of base metals has resulted in renewed attention being given to several of the old mining areas in Southwest England. Despite the lack of Government interest, much systematic surveying has been proceeding in Cornwall. Any development in the locality of flooded workings will present major problems of drainage, but the formerly haphazard nature of some of the small-scale mining will not be repeated. It is likely that in the near future the output from Cornish mines will at last be augmented by the yield from new shafts. Although there must be appreciable reserves of arsenic and wolfram, development will probably be focused upon tin.

The principal phase of copper production in Southwest England during the eighteenth and nineteenth centuries was intercalated between periods of marked concentration upon tin, but overall it was of far greater economic importance. In the 1770s cheap Anglesey copper began to flood the market, but although this inflicted great hardship on Cornwall it proved to be only a transitory challenge, for by 1800 the Anglesey ores were largely worked out. In the first decade of the nineteenth century Cornwall accounted for two-thirds of the world's production of copper, and this branch of mining was predominant until the 'sixties. Towards the end of this period the peak output was reached, of about 13,000 tons per annum; but the west Cornwall subregion, earlier outstanding in copper production, especially from the Camborne–Redruth–Gwennap area, was declining in importance. Meanwhile Levant (near St Just) and the mines between Charlestown and Par made a significant contribution, but the main transfer of emphasis was to east Cornwall and west Devon. From the 'thirties the Caradon district north of Liskeard, and from the 'forties the Devon Great Consols mine near Tavistock also yielded large quantities of copper. During the 'sixties, however, a general decline in copper production set in. The effects of the rapid increase in output overseas, accentuated by cheaper transport by steamship, together with the exhaustion of many of the most lucrative copper lodes in Cornwall, were so severe that copper mining had virtually ceased by 1900. Although Cornish miners were already emigrating much earlier in the century, it was the collapse of copper mining that caused many thousands of people to move from Cornwall. Of temporarily better fortune for the county, however, was the discovery of tin at greater depths; and some of the most important copper mines became the greatest producers of tin. Dolcoath (Camborne) led the way in mining tin underneath the shallow copper zone and, with workings more than 3,000 feet down, became the deepest mine in Cornwall. From the 'seventies stream works too were especially active, and the Red river alone had 41 concerns engaged in the recovering of tin.

Of the 30 principal tin-smelting houses which formerly existed in Southwest England, 24 were situated west of a line from Truro to Perranporth. There too were most of the major foundries and explosives works which served the mining industries. In its heyday Harvey's foundry at Hayle employed more than 1,000 people. Several mills placed in remote or thinly peopled valleys in Southwest England produced powder for blasting purposes, but from the 1870s this was supplanted by dynamite. One of the last of the explosives works was built in 1889 on Upton Towans, a large inexpensive site sufficiently isolated from settlements but near the mines of west Cornwall. At the peak of its activity it employed about 700 persons. The safety fuse was invented in 1830 by Bickford of Tucking-mill. In its busiest period the fuse factory there gave work to nearly 300 people; it was the last to close, in 1961. At least five other fuse works were situated in west Cornwall.

Appreciable quantities of wolfram and arsenic have been produced in Southwest England, chiefly subsidiary to the mining of tin and copper; but in its latter years, from 1880 to 1903, the Devon Great Consols mine concentrated on the output of arsenic and had the largest of these works in the region. The history of the working of other minerals extends over many centuries, but it was especially during the nineteenth century that considerable amounts of lead, iron, and manganese were mined. Significant yields of silver, a by-product of some of the lead lodes, came from mines north of Truro, in southeast Cornwall, and at Bere Alston and Combe Martin. Iron was worked in several parts of Cornwall (there are still large reserves in the Great Perran Iron Lode near Perranporth), on the fringes of Dartmoor (where a micaceous haematite mine is still active at Hennock), near Brixham, and in west Somerset, and north Devon, whence ore was shipped via Combe Martin to South Wales. The working of manganese in the Lower Culm Measures was important during the late eighteenth and early nineteenth centuries. Barite mining at Bridford on the eastern margin of Dartmoor was carried on for several years until 1956.

Quarrying

Despite the prevalence of bricks, concrete, and tiles in modern con-struction, the building stones formerly used in Southwest England bear witness to the geological variety in the region and help to maintain the historical character of many localities. Thus the red sandstones, breccias, and traps of the Exeter area, the Devonian limestones of Plymouth and the Torbay district, and the slates of Cornwall and south Devon contribute much to the distinctiveness of the vernacular building in the subregions. In the Culm Measures country hundreds of small quarries yielded stone for local use, but here the sandstones and grits give comparatively little variety. Certain specially attractive stones have imparted charm to local buildings, as with the green volcanic ash from the Hurdwick quarries, used in and around Tavistock; others have been worked for ornamental or monumental purposes. Examples are the dove-grey hornblende picrite of Polyphant (north Cornwall) and the 'Catacleuse' stone (from Cataclews Point west of Padstow), a hypabyssal basic igneous rock which lent itself to carving.

Historically, stone quarrying on the largest scale in Southwest England has been carried on in the slates, the igneous rocks, and the limestones.

By the sixteenth century slate was almost certainly being produced in quantity in the northwest and the southeast of Cornwall. Numerous slate quarries have been worked in the district between Camelford and Tintagel, the greatest of all being at Delabole (Plate 41); and in south and west Devon appreciable quantities were produced for both local use and export, especially during the eighteenth and nineteenth centuries. About 1750 the Mill Hill quarries near Tavistock employed as many as 200 persons. The great demand for granite for constructional work, including large public contracts, during the nineteenth century stimulated the intensive working of this stone in several parts of Cornwall—Lamorna Cove (Plate 53), the Penryn–Constantine district, Luxulyan, the Callington–Gunnislake locality, and the western and eastern sides of Bodmin Moor (De Lank and the Cheesewring). Granite was also quarried on Dartmoor and the east coast of Lundy. The nearness of many of these quarries to points of shipment favoured the development of an important granite trade, both coastwise and overseas. Compared with the highly mechanized quarries of today they were great employers of labour; in its heyday Pearson's quarry at Gunnislake (1808–1905) gave work to about 700 men.

In modern times Welsh slates, tiles, and asbestos have competed with slate production in Southwest England, and granite working has suffered from competition from Norway and the widespread use of bricks and concrete. Limestone, on the other hand, has been much in demand for both agricultural use and the manufacture of cement, and the several quarries in Devon now produce over 2,000,000 tons per annum. As a quarrying enterprise, the production of sand and gravel is carried on mainly in the eastern third of Devon (Fig. 50), but other major sources are the waste dumps of the china-clay industry, and coastal and estuarine deposits, especially those of the Taw and Torridge where, by the turn of the century, much was already being extracted for use in constructional work in the Bristol Channel ports. In view of the modern demand for road-making materials, the Southwest is fortunate in the widespread occurrence of igneous rocks and sandstones, so that roadstone quarries for both commercial firms and the local authorities can be fairly well dispersed. Excluding clay, Devon's quarry output now totals about 4,250,000 tons per annum, and that of Cornwall nearly 1,500,000 tons.

During the nineteenth century numerous brickworks were active in Southwest England, many of them using local deposits of clay, as on the granite in the Gunnislake district. The industry is now carried on in only half a dozen localities. Fremington clays have been used in the north Devon potteries, including those at Bideford which lasted from the seventeenth to the twentieth century. Early in this period the working of the Devonshire deposits of ball clay began to assume importance, firstly those of the Petrockstow district and then those of the Bovey Basin, which by

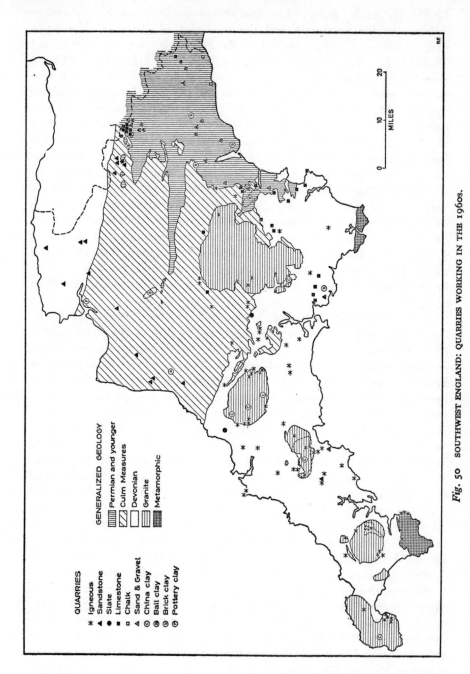

QUARRIES

* Igneous
▲ Sandstone
● Slate
■ Limestone
□ Chalk
▲ Sand & Gravel
◉ China clay
◎ Ball clay
⊗ Brick clay
⊕ Pottery clay

GENERALIZED GEOLOGY

Permian and younger
Culm Measures
Devonian
Granite
Metamorphic

MILES
0   10   20

Fig. 50 SOUTHWEST ENGLAND: QUARRIES WORKING IN THE 1960s.

the middle of the eighteenth century had a significant output and a convenient outlet via Teignmouth. In the early decades of the nineteenth century about 20,000 tons per annum were being shipped, destined mainly for Staffordshire; but a proportion of the output was taken by the local potteries at Bovey Tracey.

Kaolinization affected most of the granite masses of Southwest England, but in varying degrees. The search by Cookworthy, a chemist in Plymouth, for china clay and china stone as materials for the manufacture of porcelain was rewarded just before 1750 in one of the smaller masses—Tregonning Hill in west Cornwall. Shortly afterwards his discoveries were extended to the St Stephens locality near St Austell, in the area which later became the greatest producer of china clay and stone. The china factory established by Cookworthy at Plymouth was short-lived and was transferred to Bristol. But following this monopoly in the early stages of china-clay working, the next phase, which lasted until about 1820, was dominated by the interests of Staffordshire potters. By that time a dozen works were in production.

For the next forty years the industry was carried on mainly by local adventurers. Commensurate with their modest resources, small 'setts' were typical of the partitioning of the ground for clay working; and because of the expense and problems involved in deepening the pits, development proceeded largely by areal expansion. In the Hensbarrow district the landscape has been so greatly changed by modern working that it is not possible to discern the boundaries of many of the early pits. During this period there was renewed interest in Tregonning Hill, and clay was also worked at Towednack and near Sancreed in the Land's End peninsula. From the 'sixties onwards, pits were opened at more than a dozen sites on the western half of Bodmin Moor, where at present three are in production—Stannon Marsh, Hawkstor, and Parson's Park. In 1830 development began at Lee Moor (Dartmoor), a site later renowned not only for its great extent and scale of output, but also for the fact that it was the first china-clay work where bricks and tiles were manufactured from the waste material.

On Hensbarrow the china-clay industry was injected into an old mining district, and indeed in some cases the open-cast production of tin and clay was carried on in the same works. Activity in clay was stimulated when the price of tin sagged and, especially from the 'seventies, clay firms were able to take over the pumps and steam engines of abandoned mines. They also absorbed part of the labour made redundant by the collapse of copper mining in the 'sixties and the later decline of tin. Despite the depressed economic conditions of the 'seventies, output increased rapidly in the following decade. Clay working was now assuming much greater importance, with more capital investment, a wider variety of uses for the products, a larger demand, and a steady technical advance.

In 1885 the yield of china clay and stone amounted to 312,413 tons, and by 1912 the figure had risen to 860,649. In later years, major setbacks were caused by the two World Wars and the general trade depression of the 'thirties; but since 1946 the advance of the industry has been unimpeded.

During the latter part of the nineteenth century the principal producers were already moving towards a common policy for development and distribution, and from about 1912 there was a strong trend in the direction of closer association, integration, and concentration. In 1932 the three main firms amalgamated, and in more recent years the industry has become even more consolidated, with fewer pits but a far greater volume of production.

Fishing

Southwest England's interest in the Newfoundland fisheries lasted from the late sixteenth to the early nineteenth century, and the trading of salted cod from Newfoundland to Mediterranean countries was an important element in the commerce of several Devonshire ports. At one time or another Topsham, Bideford, Dartmouth, and Teignmouth were among the leading participants. No other far-distant fishing grounds have been of such significance to the Southwest, although during the nineteenth century Cornish fishermen sailed to Ireland and around the coasts of Britain in search of herrings.

By the early nineteenth century the few pilchard fisheries along the Devonshire coast west of Bolt Tail had declined or had been abandoned, while in Cornwall there was a great increase in fishing, with a general shift of emphasis to the western harbours. The fishing stations of St Ives and Mount's Bay were particularly well placed for dealing with migratory shoals along the shores, but during the nineteenth century drift fishing gradually replaced the long-used seine-net methods. Whereas in 1827 Cornish seining employed 2,672 men and the drift fishery 1,599, in 1870 the numbers were 1,510 and 2,462 respectively. Already long dominant in the Cornish trade in fish, pilchard exports reached a peak in the 'forties. These were the greatest years of employment in curing and packing, and dispatching pilchards to the Italian market. In modern times pilchard shoals are fewer and more variable. The virtual cessation of demand in Italy and the importing of canned pilchards into this country have also made it difficult to achieve a large, constant market for the Cornish product. In the summer of 1967 only seven boats were engaged in pilchard fishing, and five of these were at Looe. The mackerel fisheries, especially those based upon Mount's Bay, were also formerly of more considerable importance, as was drifting for herrings, which at one time or another was carried on from many harbours in Cornwall and Devon. Mackerel shoals, however, have become rather more wayward, and herrings virtually deserted the southwestern waters in the 1930s, since when they have made only fitful appearances, and rarely in great numbers.

Irregularity in the supply of fish and alternations of scarcity and glut are, however, only one of many factors which have affected the fishing industry of Southwest England. Much of the overall decline this century is attributable to such general causes as the competition from larger and better-equipped vessels and the large-scale development of deep-sea fishing. The First World War dealt a severe blow, for many young fisher-men went into the forces and by the end of hostilities most of the local boats and their gear were out of date. Over-fishing by foreign vessels and the cost of sending fish from Cornwall by rail have been other adverse factors. The future of the industry is uncertain, but the progress made in recent years—especially at Newlyn, Brixham, and Plymouth—fosters the hope that the long decline has been arrested. At present Newlyn and Brixham hold the leading positions among the few harbours where the sea fisheries are of more than local importance. Numerous small harbours rely considerably on the shellfish catch, but here a new element has arrived in the activities of skin divers who compete with the pot fishermen. Commercial salmon-netting is carried on in several estuaries of Southwest England, and the region is well known for its facilities for sportsmen's rod-and-line fishing in rivers and reservoirs.

Shipbuilding

Fostered by the requirements of trade and fishing, the construction of small ships was formerly carried on in numerous harbours in Southwest England. During the nineteenth century shipyards were dotted around the coasts and estuaries from Exmouth to Barnstaple, with a few major concentrations as in the twelve yards at Falmouth. Many produced wooden-hulled sailing ships for the coastal traffic and several, including yards at Falmouth and Penzance, built ocean-going vessels. The launching of a wooden ship of 1,220 tons at Bideford, the largest built in the port, took place in 1855; and from the 'fifties to the 'seventies many yards in Southwest England were active in building schooners. Employment ancillary to the construction, fitting out and repairing of ships was provided in sail lofts, timber yards, anchor smithies, and block, chain and nail works. Rope making was not universally directed towards shipping, for it also served the needs of agriculture, mining and transport; but while some of the rope-walks were thereby situated in inland towns and villages, they were most numerous in the ports. The Plymouth–Devonport area had over a dozen, and in smaller settlements such as Topsham the sites of rope-walks can be identified from the former names and the lengths and alignments of some of the streets.

Much of the activity in the building and equipping of wooden ships came to an end in the last decades of the nineteenth century. The general substitution of steam power for sails, the increased size of vessels, and construction in iron and steel were the principal causes of this decline. Today, small boats, mostly pleasure craft, are built at numerous places, but few commercial yards are engaged in the construction of vessels of larger size. Appledore is one of the most active centres. Naval building at Devonport, begun in 1714, has passed through several phases determined by changes in policy and strategy and in the types of vessels, and in recent years has been concentrated upon frigates.

The modern industrial accession

Apart from those concerned with agricultural products and constructional work, few of the manufacturing and processing industries which have been introduced into the region in modern times are directly dependent upon a local market or indeed upon local materials. In several districts engineering firms and clothing factories have been prominent in the accessions of recent years. Mechanical engineering has been particularly suitable for Plymouth, with its background of engineering at the Royal Naval Dockyard and a number of firms capable of undertaking sub-contract work. Even including the largest of the engineering factories which have been started in Southwest England since the Second World War, however, there are very few manufacturing firms in the region who employ more than 2,000 persons. Many of the factories and workshop units are of small to medium size, and in Cornwall one-fifth of all the people engaged in manufacturing industry are in establishments with staffs of less than 20. Almost throughout the towns of Southwest England there is a desire to attract more industry in order to widen the range of employment, halt the outward drift of young people, and provide work during the periods when the holiday trade is at its lowest. The last of these tasks is indeed difficult, for by itself the acquisition of industry may simply involve the immigration of new workers or the permanent absorption of local labour rather than the provision of work specifically to solve the problem of seasonal unemployment. Added to these difficulties is that of making full use of both male and female labour in any given area.

It is commonly said that, from the industrialist's standpoint, the two greatest disadvantages of the Southwest are the comparatively poor communications and the scarcity of skilled labour. A variety of factors has, however, led to the importation of new industries. A few firms, situated in districts which were bombed during the Second World War, moved to the Southwest and have remained because of certain special conditions. An example is one which manufactures piano ivory at St Ives, where the high light-intensity is advantageous to this industry. A considerable number of factories have been set up in the Development Areas in Cornwall and north Devon, and a marked increase in industrial establishment at Plymouth took place in 1960–1, when the city too had the

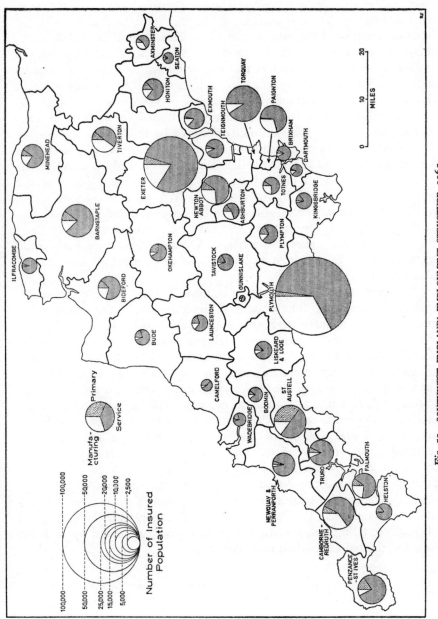

Fig. 51 SOUTHWEST ENGLAND: EMPLOYMENT STRUCTURE, 1965.

status of a Development District. In these instances, primary encouragement was available in the provision of factories and Government grants for buildings, plant, and machinery. Loans from local authorities for building purposes have also helped. The cheapness of land, low rates, comparatively low wage scales, and the provision of housing for key workers have been other factors which have influenced a decision to move to the Southwest. Some firms have come because in their original situation they had reached their limit both as regards space and availability of labour. Although industrialists generally want an improvement in communications, not everyone is unduly deterred by the 'remoteness' of the Southwest. Some firms rely almost entirely upon special road transport for bringing in lightweight materials which are worked up into a high-value product, and for dispatching their finished articles. Three of the greatest assets possessed by the region are its record of good industrial relations, the attractiveness of the area for residence, and the cleanliness of the atmosphere. The last of these may yet be important in developing or attracting a higher proportion of 'clean-air' industries, such as the manufacture of electronic and photographic equipment and medical and pharmaceutical products.

As is shown in Figure 51 (compiled on the basis of the employment exchange areas), the 'service trades' predominate in the structure of employment throughout the Southwest. In such regional centres as Exeter, Plymouth, Barnstaple, and Truro, high places in this group are taken by the distributive trades, transport, education, administration, and professional services; while in the resorts, work in hotels and catering accounts for a large proportion of the total service employment. In the Newquay–Perranporth area it is as high as 60 per cent. The 'primary' employment categories amount to one-quarter or more of the insured population in the areas of St Austell, Camelford, Okehampton, and Gunnislake. China-clay working is pre-eminent in the first of these, and quarrying makes an important contribution in the others. Eight areas have one-quarter or more of the insured population in manufacturing industries—Camborne-Redruth, Plymouth, Ashburton, Totnes, Paignton, Newton Abbot, Tiverton, and Axminster. In Chapters 10 to 14, dealing with the subregions of Southwest England, attention is given to the part played by both the new and the old-established manufactures.

CHAPTER 9

Transport and Population

SINCE the seventeenth century five main trends have occurred in the systems of transport in Southwest England—the increase in activity in numerous but by no means all ports until well into the nineteenth century; the improvements in road traffic and conditions in the period 1750 to 1850; the development of the railway network; the modern decline in the part played by the ports and railways generally (there are exceptions); and the great increase in motor traffic by road.

Ports and harbours

Many of the Devonshire ports suffered as a result of the succession of wars overseas during the eighteenth century and the decline of the woollen industry. The great exception was the naval base at Dock (later renamed Devonport), which was built in the 1690s. For many Cornish ports the transport by sea of people as well as cargoes remained important until the advent of railways; good roads were few, road travel was expensive, and there were numerous harbours near the principal centres of mining and quarrying. Smuggling activity took full advantage of the long and intricate coastline of Southwest England and its remoteness from the central authorities.

Until the rise of Falmouth in the seventeenth and eighteenth centuries, Truro and Penryn were among the most important trading ports in Cornwall. In 1661 Falmouth was granted its charter, and in 1688 was appointed a mail packet station. It developed a considerable general trade, and also became very important as a port of call where sailing vessels, outward or homeward bound, replenished their stocks of water and food and received fresh orders. At the peak of activity, 40 packets were based on Falmouth, but the functions of the mail port were transferred to Southampton in 1852, and as steam replaced sail and wireless was installed in ships, Falmouth's value as a port of call diminished.

An important phase in the history of Penzance was inaugurated by the granting of her coinage charter in 1663, for in addition to fishing, the mining and general trades became significant. A number of other harbours, such as Newlyn, Mevagissey, and Polperro, concentrated upon fishing, while at St Ives, Newquay, and Padstow this activity was varied by other trade. A remarkable development in Cornwall during the late eighteenth and early nineteenth centuries, however, was the creation or expansion of harbours and quays with the specific purpose of serving the mining and quarrying industries. This was the *raison d'être* of Portreath, Hayle, Devoran, Pentewan, Charlestown, Par, and the quays along the lower part of the Tamar valley. Portreath exported copper ore to Wales and imported coal and lime; and Charlestown and Par were established in the interests of the copper mines and china-clay workings of the Hensbarrow district. Pentewan, re-created especially for the shipment of china clay, eventually suffered greatly from silting, and both the harbour and the railway which fed it were closed in 1918. Meanwhile Fowey, where new jetties for the clay export trade came into use in the 1870s, re-emerged as an important port. At one time or another, china clay has been shipped from about a dozen Cornish harbours other than the present main outlets of Charlestown, Par, and Fowey, but nowadays the only such activity is at Penzance, where there is an occasional dispatch of clay from the Lower Bostraze pit near St Just.

The decline of mining was a primary cause of the diminished importance of many ports in Cornwall, eliminating the export of ores and the import trade in supplies of timber, coal, machinery, iron, tallow, candles, and hemp for the mines. Devoran lies derelict, and although Portreath continued for many years to import coal for the Camborne–Redruth area, this trade has ceased. The intake of coal into Devon and Cornwall generally is still, however, an important item in transport, amounting to about 1,300,000 tons per annum. Between one-half and two-thirds of this comes by sea, but is now discharged at only about a dozen points. Apart from the shipping of clays and stone, which have been the major increasing elements in the maritime trade of Southwest England in recent years, and the general commerce of the port of Plymouth, the numerous harbours in the region have a comparatively small total of imports and very few exports. The hinterland offers little for shipment. Many of the harbours are too shallow for large vessels and some suffer considerably from silting.

Canals

A pound-lock canal was cut down-river from Exeter as early as the 1560s, but it had to compete with the traffic carried by road between the city and Topsham. In the eighteenth and early nineteenth centuries the canal was improved so that vessels of 150 tons could reach the quay at Exeter, and in the 1820s it was extended from Topsham to Turf Lock, which is still the point of ingress from the Exe estuary. Almost all the other work of planning or providing canals in Southwest England was done during the period 1770 to 1830. Desirable though canals may have been, the physique of much of the region presented difficulties for their construction. Fortunately the Southwest had numerous harbours and navigable estuaries to serve the coastwise and foreign trades; and the important sites of most of the heavier industries—mining, quarrying, and their ancillaries—were not far from the coast.

Numerous canal schemes were considered, however, including at least four which would have created long transpeninsular routes—from Bude to the Tamar near Calstock; from Axmouth to Uphill (Somerset) via Chard; 'The Public Devonshire Canal' from Topsham to Barnstaple; and 'The Grand Western Canal' from Topsham to Taunton, with branches to Tiverton and Cullompton. Only the last of these was seriously started, but it was never completed; one section, however, from Burlescombe to Tiverton, was used for the limestone trade. In Cornwall, several plans for shorter links between the north and the south coasts, for example from Wadebridge to Lostwithiel, came to nothing, as did also canal schemes to bring in coal for the western mining districts, for instance along a route from Hayle to Troon.

The principal functions of the short canals which were constructed in Southwest England were to take out ores, stone, and agricultural produce, and to bring in coal and fertilizers. Their success was ephemeral, however, for the coming of the railways and the decline of mining and, in some cases, of quarrying also, put an end to their trade. The Stover canal, north of Newton Abbot, carried lime and coal inwards, and clay, lignite, and granite outwards. By means of a canal from Tavistock to Morwellham on the Tamar there was a considerable carriage of copper ore and slate, with return cargoes of coal and lime. Farther north, canals from Bude to Holsworthy and along the Tamar above Launceston supplied agricultural sand from the beaches, imported coal and lime, and exported oats and slate. The fortunes of the Liskeard–Looe canal were mainly bound up with the output of granite and copper ore from the Cheesewring and Caradon localities north of Liskeard, but it also brought in lime, sand, and coal.

Roads

A concomitant of the dispersal of settlement over much of Southwest England was the formation of a close mesh of roads and lanes, especially in Cornwall, where the ratio of roads to area is probably the highest in England. Until a measure of amelioration began in the eighteenth century, most of the roads in the region were in a poor state, many of them being narrow, unsurfaced lanes bounded by high, wide banks. The stimulus to improvement was the spread of wheeled traffic which, notably in the Exeter district, increased as the carriers, who hitherto had used only teams of packhorses, gradually turned over to wagons, and as private and public coaching developed. Exeter's high degree of nodality and her position on the main routes from London, Bristol, and Bath ensured that she would play an important part in the turnpike era, and the first of the trusts in Devon were those of Exeter, Honiton, and Axminster, formed in 1753. In order to cope with the constant increase in traffic, the city of Exeter between 1760 and 1840 cleared away its medieval gates, provided new roads, and built a new bridge over the Exe. In the peak phase towards the end of this period, the coach, post, and wagon traffic provided a major means of employment in several parts of the city, especially in the parish of St Sidwell.

West of Exeter the height and extent of Dartmoor determined the bifurcation of the main routes which, from the late seventeenth century, became vitally important because of the function of Falmouth as a packet station and the creation of the naval base at Devonport. The Truro–Falmouth turnpike (1754) was the first in Cornwall, and in 1769 most of the route from Launceston via Bodmin to Truro was turnpiked. This 'great northern' road was one of the two principal coach routes through Cornwall; the other, linked with Devonport by the Torpoint ferry, ran through Liskeard and Lostwithiel and met the northern road at Truro, which was the chief coaching town in the county. In 1820 the mail-coach service was extended to Penzance (Fig. 52).

By the 1830s many additions and improvements had been made to the turnpikes in Southwest England, not least in the gentler curves and easier gradients of the new roads, of which a well-known example is the Exeter–Barnstaple road, as re-aligned along the Taw valley in 1830. In essence, the network of the present system of major roads in the region had been achieved by 1850; but already the arrival of the main railway was having an adverse effect on the turnpike traffic in Devon. The toll income of the Devonshire trusts in 1854 was over 20 per cent less than that in 1837. In Cornwall, however, where the main railway link was not completed until 1859, the income over the same period increased by about 10 per cent. Although, especially in Cornwall, coaches were late in disappearing altogether from the scene, the main railways in the region speedily took away the through traffic; and as branch lines were added, the 'feeder' functions of the local coaches and wagons diminished, together with their dependent crafts and trades.

In large measure the road system has had to be gradually and laboriously adapted to the ever-increasing volume of motor traffic during the present century. Heavy congestion in the holiday season is but one of several problems now much in the minds of planners and local authorities, Members of Parliament, and commercial and industrial firms. How can the accessibility of the Southwest be increased with the least disturbance of its essential character and with the greatest benefit to the economy of the whole region? As the contribution from other forms of transport can only be comparatively small, road programmes take up much of the discussion. The by-passing of more of the towns and villages on the main routes, the provision of relief roads through large towns and of new circulatory systems within them, the construction of a spine road through the region, and the radical improvement of the two main routes into

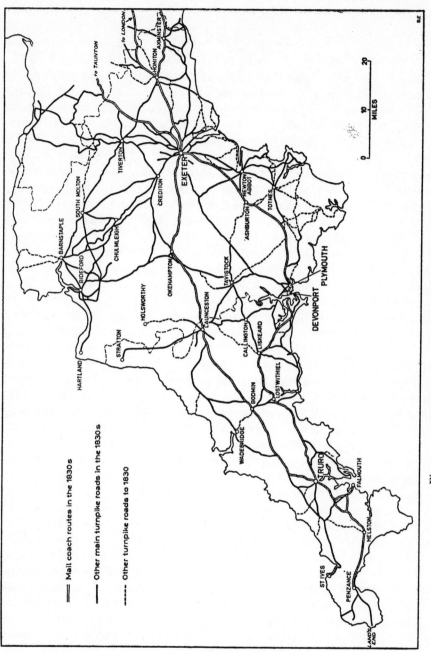

Fig. 52 SOUTHWEST ENGLAND: TURNPIKE ROADS TO THE 1830s.

and through Cornwall are topics that are currently and constantly being debated.

Railways and their effects

At various times during the nineteenth century, tramroads and mineral railways were brought into the service of mining or quarrying localities. A few of the tramroads were reconstructed to take locomotives, but most have long been abandoned. Noteworthy among the earliest were three in west Cornwall, linking the Redruth–Gwennap mining district with the harbours of Portreath, Hayle, and Devoran. Dartmoor had two early lines, one of which connected the Haytor granite quarries with the Stover canal, and the other—from Plymouth to Princetown—carried coal, fertilizers, and lime in return for the downward loads of granite. From the 'forties the mines and quarries on the southeastern margins of Bodmin Moor were connected by rail to the Liskeard–Looe canal, and in 1872 the East Cornwall mineral railway, running from Calstock Quay to Callington, began to serve a number of mines, quarries, and brickworks. In the Hensbarrow district and on southwestern Dartmoor, mineral lines and tramways were constructed for the transport of china clay.

The first locomotive railway in Cornwall was the Wadebridge–Bodmin line, built in 1834. This carried sand inwards and, later, granite and ores out. The West Cornwall railway, connecting Hayle and Redruth, was inaugurated in 1844 and soon afterwards was extended west to Penzance and east to Truro. Meanwhile, on the eastern side of the region, the main railway from Bristol had reached Exeter in 1844, and by 1849 it stretched as far as Plymouth. By means of the railway eastwards from Truro and the construction of Brunel's bridge at Saltash, the link between Plymouth and west Cornwall was finally established in 1859. In the following year the line from Waterloo to Exeter was opened, and by 1900 the railway network in Southwest England was complete except for a few branch lines, the last of which—from Torrington to Halwill Junction—was added in 1925. The passenger lines of the network are shown on Figure 53.

One of the most important results of the spread of the railways to the coast was the stimulation of the holiday trade. The early construction of a line to Torbay—it reached Torre in 1848—together with the provision of through trains gave that area an advantage over other watering places in the Southwest; but the completion of many of the branch lines—for example, Falmouth (1863), Newquay (1876), and St Ives (1877)—heralded the modern development of numerous resorts. The impact of the railways was, however, strong in many other directions, including its effects on industry and agriculture generally. Moreover, the pattern of railway development had important local results, for instance in assisting the spread of settlement in and around Plymouth, and in enhancing the nodality of Barnstaple in comparison with that of other north Devon towns.

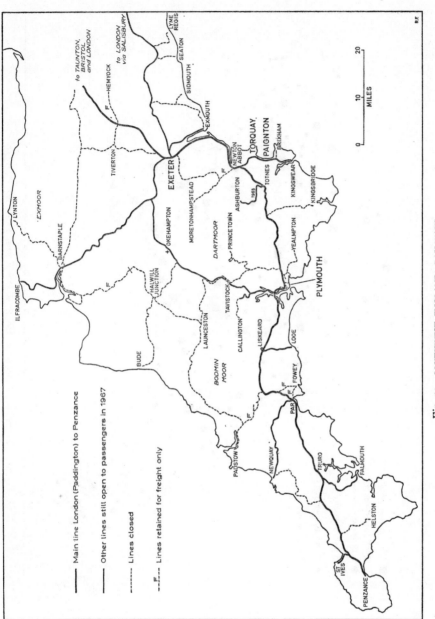

Fig. 53 SOUTHWEST ENGLAND: RAILWAYS.

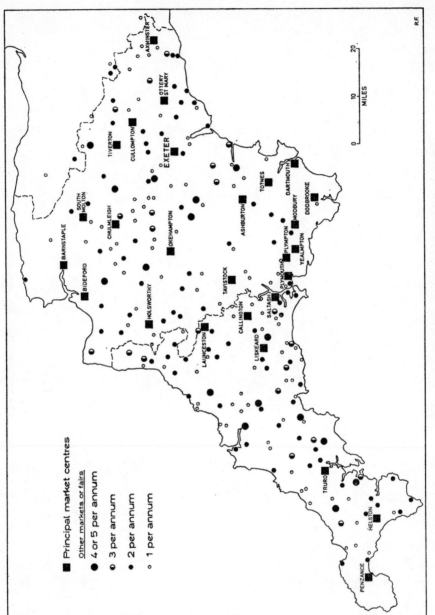

Fig. 54 SOUTHWEST ENGLAND: STOCK MARKETS AND FAIRS ABOUT 1850.

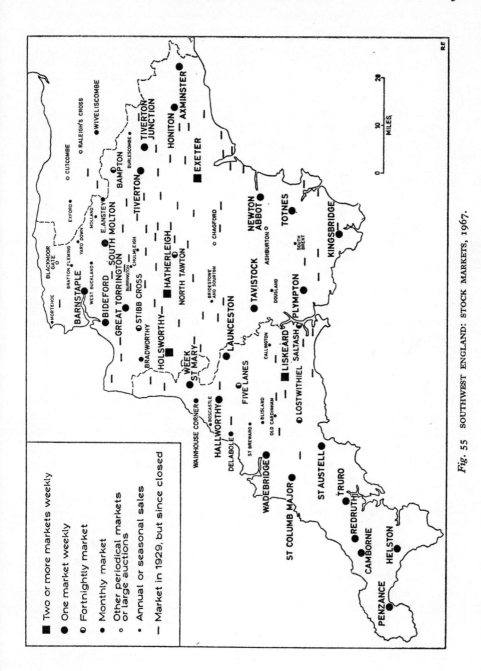

Fig. 55 SOUTHWEST ENGLAND: STOCK MARKETS, 1967.

In the recent process of pruning the railway network most of the branch lines have already been lopped, and comparatively strong emphasis now rests upon the main route through Exeter, south Devon, and Plymouth. Livestock and goods traffic is now relatively light, but the railways still play an important part in the transport of clay, stone, fuel, and agricultural products and equipment. The sections of line that have been retained for freight only, are concerned with these types of traffic. In addition to those indicated on Figure 53 there are freight tracks which serve the china-clay industry in the Hensbarrow district and north of Bodmin, and the Newham gasworks at Truro. In the whole region the only passenger-carrying line likely to be re-opened for that purpose is the route from Totnes to Ashburton. From 1968 this is to be run as a summer attraction by the Dart Valley Light Railway.

The changing pattern of markets and fairs

About the middle of last century there were numerous places in Southwest England where old-established markets and seasonal or annual fairs were still held (Fig. 54). Since then the geographical pattern of stock marketing has been greatly affected by major trends in transport. The phase of railway development resulted in an increase in importance of sites near the stations, so that a great number of local markets and fairs ceased to exist. On the other hand, and most notably in the Culm Measures country, several railside markets were created, to the detriment of old market towns. With the completion of the North Devon railway from Crediton to Barnstaple in 1854, markets were established at such wayside stations as Eggesford and South Molton Road, which drew away the trade from the hill town of Chulmleigh where, however, the 'Old Fair' is still held in July. These railside locations temporarily maintained the degree, albeit in a different pattern, of the geographical dispersal of markets in the area between Exeter and Barnstaple (Fig. 55).[1]

Southwest England is traditionally a stock-exporting region, and until fairly recent years a feature of the rail traffic which originated within the region was the number of special stock-carrying trains. Halwill Junction and Exeter were among the busiest dispatching centres. Now, however, much of this trade is carried on by road, and the railside stock-yards have been closed. Sales through the Fatstock Marketing Corporation and direct to large butchering concerns have provided farmers with the means of disposing of stock other than in the local auction mart; but the greatest factor affecting the geographical distribution of markets has been the development of road transport. The increase in the number of haulage contractors, the greater capacity of their vehicles and the extension of their trade by means of direct farm-to-market service have tended to produce a

[1] The information for the year 1929 is taken from *Markets and Fairs in England and Wales*, Ministry of Agriculture and Fisheries Economic Series No. 23 (1929).

concentration into fewer centres, with a corresponding growth of the bigger markets, especially those which offer extensive covered accommodation and up-to-date facilities. As a result of this trend, markets have closed not only in remote villages but also in such old towns as Crediton, Okehampton, and Bodmin. On the other hand, road transport has reinforced the vitality of certain town-markets and road-junction sites in the large area west of a line from Bideford through Okehampton and Tavistock, an area now completely deprived of railways. It is also very important in relation to the seasonal or periodic auctions that are held on and around Exmoor, Dartmoor, and Bodmin Moor.

The holiday industry

In their embryonic stage in the eighteenth century, certain coastal resorts in Southwest England benefited from the improvements in roads and vehicles and from the limitations on travel abroad imposed by the wars with France. Invalids seeking a recuperative environment found it in the mild winter and attractive scenery of the south coast, and sea-water bathing gradually came into fashion for medical treatment and for families who could afford a visit to the seaside. In Devon, Exmouth and Teignmouth were the first places to be favoured, and they were followed during the second half of the century by Sidmouth, Dawlish, and Torquay. Penzance, however, was the first of the Cornish towns to assume the character of a marine resort. On the north coast of the region, Bude, Lynmouth, and Ilfracombe began to develop in the early nineteenth century. Torquay's growth was greatly stimulated by the arrival of the railway, and the population more than trebled between 1841 and 1871, to nearly 22,000. About the middle of the century Paignton's population was still considerably less than that of Teignmouth, but it trebled between 1861 and 1901, a period during which Ilfracombe also grew rapidly. In the latter part of this phase the cult of the large hotel began to spread, and in Cornwall is exemplified at Newquay, Tintagel, Padstow, and Mullion. A more characteristic development in numerous resorts, however, was the expansion of terraced housing and the boarding-house type of accommodation. By about 1900 all the principal resorts were served by rail, and this remained a primary factor in their prosperity until the rapid modern increase in motor transport.

The transformation of the patterns of coastal settlement by the growth of the holiday industry has varied in degree and character. At Torquay, Paignton, and Newquay the functions of the industry are everywhere and patently dominant, but in some other towns, such as Brixham and St Ives, the character and core of an old fishing settlement survives. Woolacombe and Polzeath exemplify comparatively recent housing and hotel development, while another type of growth is illustrated at Challaborough in south Devon, Croyde in north Devon, and along the towan coasts of west Corn-

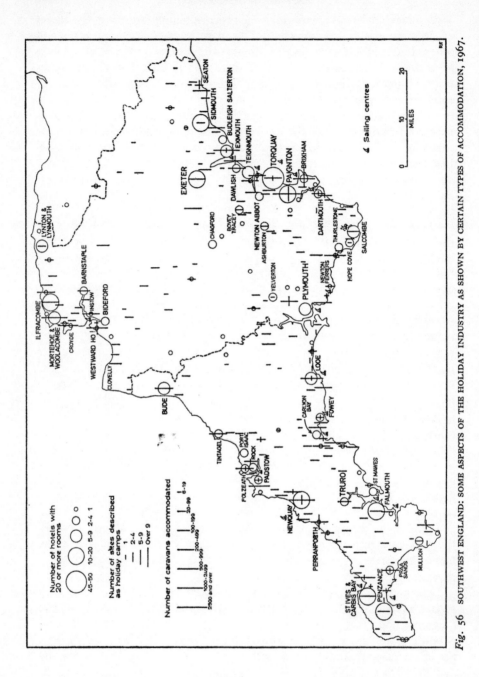

Fig. 56 SOUTHWEST ENGLAND: SOME ASPECTS OF THE HOLIDAY INDUSTRY AS SHOWN BY CERTAIN TYPES OF ACCOMMODATION, 1967.

wall, where chalets and caravans predominate. Some aspects of the variety of accommodation are shown in Figure 56, which indicates the places where hotels of large and medium size are a considerable element, and the localities with caravan and chalet sites. In the increase in hotel space, the tendency in recent years has been to extend or convert existing premises rather than to provide large new buildings. An interesting project, however, is to take shape on the western end of Plymouth Hoe, where a capacious new hotel is to be completed by 1970. Some of the chalet sites which are rather more elaborate than the average and possess some communal facilities are described by the operators as 'holiday camps', but there are only a few of the large, highly-organized type, for example at Seaton and Paignton. Static holiday caravans are far more numerous than the touring type.

Five areas of Southwest England are especially popular for holidays— the coastland between the estuaries of the Dart and the Exe (which receives well over one-half of the visitors to Devon), the coast of east Devon, north Devon, and the Newquay–Perranporth and Penzance–St Ives districts. Many places have excellent conditions for sea bathing, but the resorts with sandy beaches, as at Exmouth, Teignmouth, Paignton, Newquay, and Woolacombe, are more favoured by families with young children than are those with mainly pebbled shores, such as Sidmouth and Budleigh Salterton. In some respects the appeal of parts of the north coast of the region, with its more invigorating climate and opportunities for surfing, is different from that of the southern bays and estuaries, which lend themselves to sailing, boating, and fishing. For an increasing number of visitors, however, the holiday desiderata extend more widely than a single coastal sojourn, and a tour by car or coach offers the enjoyment of a variety of scenery and forms of relaxation.

Visitors to Devon and Cornwall now number nearly 4,500,000 per annum. Since the Second World War the sources of the holiday-makers have widened considerably, a reflection of the greater spread of recreational opportunity throughout the populace, holidays with pay and the prosperity of industry in the Midlands. At present 30 per cent of the visitors come from London and the southeastern counties, nearly the same proportion emanates from the Midlands and the eastern counties, and 20 per cent from northern England. There has been a great change in the roles played by the principal forms of transport. The proportion of visitors who come by private car has rapidly increased to about 80 per cent, while that carried by train has declined to 10 per cent.

Problems raised by the seasonal nature of the holiday trade are inherent in the concentration upon a period of not much more than two months in summer. During the peak towards the end of July and in early August, when there are about 500,000 holiday-makers in the region, there is great pressure on all types of accommodation, often extending far inland from

s.e.—7*

the most popular resorts. Even with the considerable use of imported casual staff, much of the labour is local, and winter unemployment thus remains a serious problem. No sudden great increase in the winter trade can be expected, but benefit would accrue to the region both as regards employment and accommodation if the main season could be lengthened and spread to a greater extent over April to June and September–October, and if more secondary holidays and out-of-season refresher breaks were spent in the Southwest. The greater use of accommodation suitable for conferences during the period from autumn to spring would also help. In the summer, and especially on wet days, towns a few miles inland such as Exeter, Newton Abbot, and Truro experience an influx of holiday-makers from the resorts, and it is possible that the development and addition of more attractions and amenities in such centres will result from the need to cater for the tourist trade.

In the last fifteen years there has been a great increase in non-traditional or informal accommodation, including caravans, chalets, holiday flatlets, and tents. Planning authorities have found it necessary to define saturation areas, where there is already sufficient provision for caravan and chalet holidays and where further development of this nature will be limited or discouraged. Very recently, however, another problem has appeared, for although the rate of augmentation of caravans has slackened, tenting holidays and camping out in fields have greatly increased. This is irrespective of the long-established types of farmhouse or cottage holidays and bed-and-breakfast accommodation in the rural areas. Of late, too, the practice of overnight roadside parking has presented new problems for the authorities. Major difficulties facing the regional planners are how to control or influence these various recent trends without deterring the holiday-maker, and how to allow development without inflicting damage on some of the resources on which the prosperity of the industry is based, not least the splendid scenery, the pleasant countryside, and the picturesque settlements.

Population trends in Devon

During the early eighteenth century the vitality of many of the Devonshire towns depended on the prosperity of the woollen industry, but there were exceptions such as the port of Bideford, which had a large trade in tobacco from some of the North American colonies, and the expanding settlement at Dock. The value of Plymouth's down-Channel situation had already been demonstrated during the war against Spain (1588–1603), and the port was used by discoverers and transatlantic migrants as a convenient point of departure. In the 1690s, however, a new naval base was established two miles west of Plymouth, and within seventy years the settlement around the docks was approaching the size of the older town clustered on the northern and western flanks of Sutton Pool (Fig. 57). Dock took on great importance during the wars with France, and by 1801 its population had grown to 24,000, compared with Plymouth's 16,000. After the wars, however, its expansion slowed down, and Plymouth went ahead as a trading, industrial, fishing, and service centre. In 1881 Plymouth had 74,000 people, but Devonport had only 49,000. The growth of Exeter was slower than that of Plymouth, but the collapse of the woollen industry did not bring it to a halt. During the late eighteenth and early nineteenth centuries the city's nodality in an age of increasing travel, its varied trade, and the considerable immigration led to residential development on an appreciable scale. The beginnings of this phase are discernible in a representation of Exeter at about the middle of this period (Plate 12).

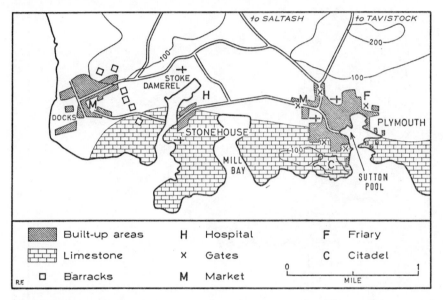

Fig. 57 THE PLYMOUTH–STONEHOUSE–DOCK AREA IN THE 1760s. The northern part of Mill Bay (Sour Pool) had by then been largely drained.

From the 1840s many of the small country towns in Devon began to decline, a process that was hastened by agricultural depressions and the effects of the railways upon local trade, markets, and industry. The incidence of changes in the prosperity of mining was felt much less than in Cornwall, and only appreciably in the localities of large mines such as those near Tavistock, a town which reached its peak in population in the 'sixties. The rate of population increase in Devon as a whole slackened after 1851, and the process of rural depopulation in many parts of the county has persisted down to the present time. Over a long period this trend, particularly in large areas of mid and west Devon, has been attributed to remoteness, poor communications, lack of amenities, limited opportunities for employment, and poor housing. Some districts appear to have been caught

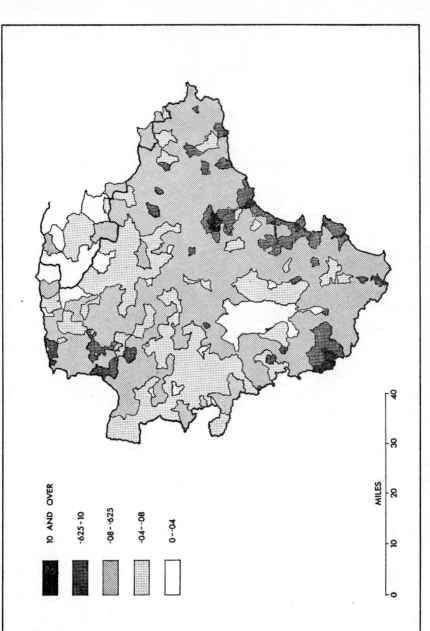

Fig. 58 DEVON AND WEST SOMERSET: DENSITY OF POPULATION PER ACRE, 1961.

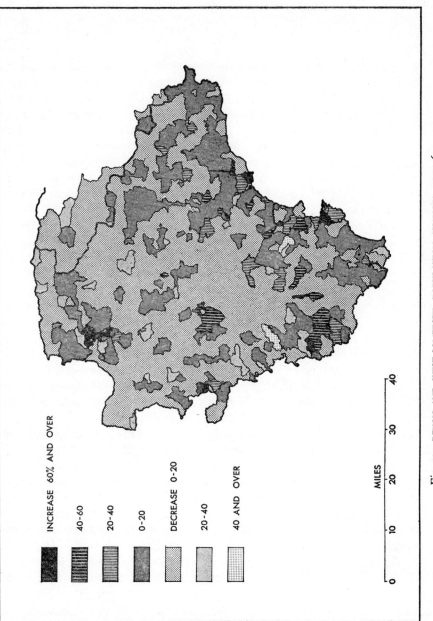

Fig. 59 DEVON AND WEST SOMERSET: POPULATION CHANGES, 1951–61.

in a vicious circle; they needed services and amenities, but with a decreasing population these became even more difficult to provide. Although in certain respects conditions in the rural areas have markedly improved since the Second World War, especially in housing and the provision of public utilities, other factors have affected the situation, including the truncation of the railway system and the infrequency of bus services; and the labour force in agriculture has been greatly reduced by an increase in efficiency and mechanization. The amount of new building obvious enough in some rural parts of Devon may be misleading in terms of the population and functions of the settlements. Some of it may be replacement housing, or specifically for retired people, and in any case it probably has a lower occupance ratio than that of former times. Especially in villages near the large towns, the commuting and retired elements may be so considerable a proportion of the total population as to make the village even more dependent on the town.

The lowest densities of population in Devon are on Dartmoor (Princetown is exceptional because of the location of the convict prison there), Exmoor, and the poorer areas of the Culm Measures country (Fig. 58). Save in the Barnstaple and Bideford districts in the core of north Devon, and the Ilfracombe locality, all the higher densities are registered in the southeastern half of the county, and most extensively in and around Plymouth, Exeter, and the Torbay towns. Fairly high densities are also recorded throughout the tracts from Torquay to Newton Abbot and, through Teignmouth and Dawlish, to the coast of east Devon. As is shown on Figure 59, the population of many parishes in Devon was still decreasing between 1951 and 1961. Plymouth, Ilfracombe, and Dartmouth were noticeable exceptions to the general trend of increases in urban areas. The principal districts with a marked increase were the settlements with a large commuter element tributary to Plymouth, most of the coastal towns from Torbay eastwards, and the district around Barnstaple.

Immigration into Devon in the present decade will probably prove to be at a higher rate than anticipated, and the increase in population in the county will continue to mask the emigration of young people. In recent years various suggestions have been made for the possible transfer of over-spill population from London or for the planned immigration of people of working age into districts in Devon. Plymouth, Exeter, Ivybridge, Honiton, the Tiverton–Cullompton area, and Barnstaple have been mentioned in relation to overspill, and in the two last-named feasibility studies have been carried out. Planning suggestions for the future development of Devon's towns may, however, be as important as discussions about overspill. A possible step towards the greater vitality of the rural areas is indicated, for example, by the proposal to develop 'key' inland towns as centres for rural communities. These would have an adequate range of facilities, amenities, and basic services, and would provide a certain amount of industrial and

other employment which would offset the decrease in the labour requirements of agriculture.

Population trends in Cornwall

With few exceptions, changes in the distribution of population in
Cornwall during the seventeenth and eighteenth centuries were brought
about by shifts in the emphasis on mining. The increase was predominantly
in the western half of the county, especially the area west of Truro, while
from some districts in the east there was a drift to the Plymouth area and
other towns. Following variations in the fortunes of mining and quarrying
in the late eighteenth and the nineteenth centuries, local fluctuations in
population occurred, one of the most remarkable increases being in the
copper-mining locality of Gwennap, which by 1841 was the most populous
parish in Cornwall. Prosperity in mining and quarrying was also reflected
in new building in such old towns as Truro, Helston, Penzance, Liskeard,
and Bodmin, in the expansion and creation of ports, and in the progress of
Camborne and St Austell from small villages to sizeable towns. The steady
growth of Bodmin during the nineteenth century was largely due to its
central position and its functions as the county town, and the location there
of the barracks, prison, workhouse, and hospital. None of the Cornish
towns has emerged as a large, dominant centre, however, for the shape and
physiography of the county tend to partition it, and to limit the influence
of each town to a comparatively small area.

The population of many of the agricultural parishes fell as a result of the
depression and poor harvests of the 1840s, but from the 'sixties the decline
in mining was the major cause of the decrease in Cornwall's population, a
trend which has continued in almost every decade since. On the other hand,
in the second half of the nineteenth century the china-clay area began to
show a considerable increase, and over the turn of the century increases
were also appreciable in the resorts and in the districts near Plymouth. In
the present distribution (Fig. 60) the largest area of thinly populated
country extends south from the poor soils on the Culm Measures across
the high land of Bodmin Moor; and most of the other low-density patches
are on the infertile downs and moors. The other rural areas generally have
only a moderate density, and contrast with the high-density localities of the
principal resorts, the industrial areas of west Cornwall and the china-clay
subregion, the Truro–Falmouth district, the inland centres of Bodmin,
Launceston, and Liskeard, the Tamar valley area, and the southeastern
district closely connected with Plymouth. As in Devon, the population of
many of the rural areas still shows a declining trend (Fig. 61). In the period
1931–51 the resorts of Newquay, Looe, and Bude showed fairly large
increases, as did also the districts of Torpoint and Saltash near Plymouth.
At present the fastest-growing towns are probably Saltash, Bodmin,
St Austell, and Newquay. The recent discussions of possible locations for

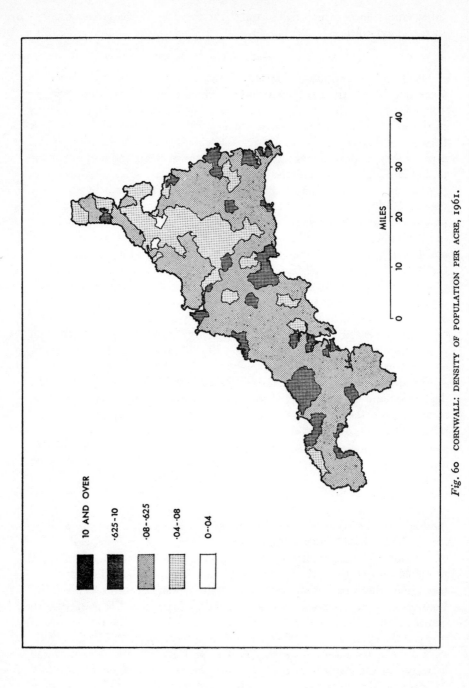

10 AND OVER

·625–10

·08–·625

·04–·08

0–·04

MILES

0   10   20   30   40

Fig. 60 CORNWALL: DENSITY OF POPULATION PER ACRE, 1961.

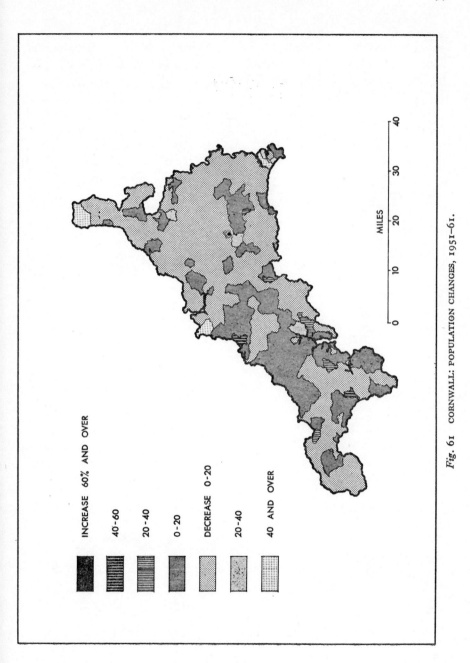

Fig. 61 CORNWALL: POPULATION CHANGES, 1951–61.

overspill population in Cornwall appear to have centred mainly upon
Bodmin, Camborne–Redruth, Liskeard, and Launceston. In 1967 pro-
posals were announced whereby, within the next ten years, Bodmin will
house 1,500 people from London, and will accommodate new factories
for firms moving from the metropolitan area.

CHAPTER 10

East Devon: The Heartland of Devon: Exeter: The Bovey Basin - Newton Abbot - Teignmouth: Torbay

East Devon

BETWEEN the Chalk hills of west Dorset and the lower part of the Exe valley lies a series of generally flat-topped hills whose west-facing escarpments overlook in succession the valleys of the Axe, Sid, Otter, Culm, and Clyst. At their northern end most of these hills merge into a high, wide plateau which forms the major divide between the Somerset Plain and the drainage systems of east Devon (Fig. 62). In the extreme east of the latter county there are small areas of Chalk, but of the three principal hill tracts which form the southern, and lower, extensions of the plateau, two are of horizontal Greensand beds with hard calcareous grits or chert-bearing sandstones uppermost, and one—the most westerly—is of Bunter pebbles. Much of the hilly area above 700 feet can be described as an upland plain whose superficial deposits are those of a composite erosion surface; they include sand, rounded gravels, chert rubble and clay-with-flints. The Great and Little Haldon Hills, which form a ridge lying three to five miles west of the lower Exe, are composed of the Blackdown Beds of the Upper Greensand, with surface deposits not only of coarse Eocene gravels and Oligocene shingle, but also of periglacially disturbed clay-with-flints and chert. Thus although the Haldon Hills form part of the framework of the Heartland subregion (Fig. 63, p. 204), their physical affinities lie closely with east Devon.

Despite the considerable depth of their valleys, none of the rivers Axe, Sid, and Otter makes a sharp break in the neatly curving shoreline of east Devon, for each has a pebble bar across its outlet to the sea. The Axe valley appears to conform to the trend of a Miocene syncline, although much of its upper section is floored with Liassic clays. Triassic sandstones and red Keuper marls are more in evidence along the valleys of the Sid and Otter. Scattered around the hills and valleys are the sites of many small workings from which chert, flint, and sand were formerly extracted for road metal and building purposes, and pits which yielded marl for agricultural use. Today there are a few sand, gravel, and concrete works. The Bunter pebbles and gravels are extensively quarried on Rockbeare Hill and at Black Hill on the ridge west of the lower Otter; together, these

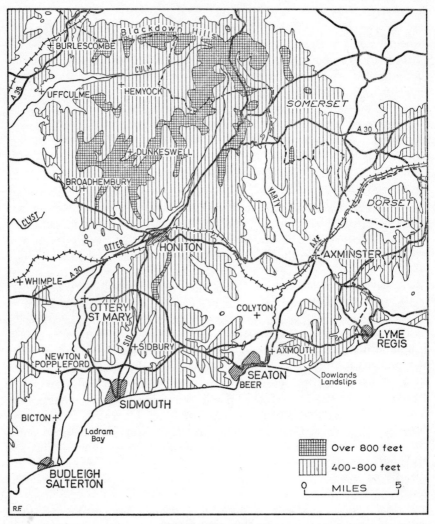

Fig. 62 EAST DEVON.

workings give employment to over 200 men. In the northwest of the subregion there are limestone quarries at Burlescombe, the extraction of sand and the making of concrete are carried on near Uffculme, and Burlescombe has a new factory which produces concrete roofing-tiles. Historically, however, the best-known sites of quarrying in east Devon are the underground workings in the Cenomanian Limestone at Beer, where fine building-stone was produced from the Old Quarry intermittently from the Roman period to the nineteenth century. The equally extensive New Quarry was opened in 1883, but only the processing of lime is still carried on there.

In general the grits, sands, gravels, pebbles, and clays on the hills of east Devon give acid, podzolized, and hungry soils which support principally heather and gorse with much intrusive bracken; but on the Chalk there are fescue pastures with some arable. In the upland parishes the ratio of tillage to total area under crops and grass falls as low as one-sixteenth. The gentler slopes carry tracts of rough grazing and patches of poor cultivation, but the sides of the ridges and plateaux are often too steep for even pastural farming and in many cases are now under small plantations. Although the poverty of the soils and the inadequacy of natural drainage on the flat-topped Haldon Hills have made conditions difficult for afforestation, large areas have been planted with conifers by the Forestry Commission.

The *Agrostis* pastures on the heavy Liassic clays east of Axminster are of indifferent quality, but the grasslands on the Keuper marls in the valleys of the Yarty, the lower Axe, the Sid, and the Otter are better, and the warm red sandy soils on the Trias in the latter areas support a considerable amount of arable. Some of the almost flat, red-soil localities in the Otter valley have the highest proportion of tillage—between one-quarter and one-third of the total acreage of crops and grass. In some districts of east Devon mixed farming is characteristic; but the area as a whole has a high percentage of permanent grass and a great emphasis on dairying, in which Friesian cattle now preponderate, although the Ayrshire, Channel Island, and Shorthorn breeds are locally important. Milk-producing farms in the southern half of the east Devon subregion supply the creamery at Seaton Junction, which has a peak intake of about 30,000 gallons per day. A milk factory serving the northern parts of east Devon is situated at Hemyock. Among the various subsidiary enterprises which are combined with dairying, the most important places are taken by poultry and pig keeping and grain growing. Barley is now the principal crop. There are a number of fruit farms and, although generally small, some of the orchards yield high-quality dessert apples. In the districts of lower rainfall and drier soils, and chiefly on the larger farms of upwards of 100 acres, the production of early fat lambs is an important enterprise, using the Dorset Horn and Dorset Down breeds.

Holdings in east Devon range from specialized poultry and pig farms and small dairying units of less than 60 acres to large mixed farms. Very few units exceed 300 acres, however, and in many parishes the majority of the holdings are within the range of 30 to 150 acres. Noteworthy among the estates is one of the biggest in Southwest England—the east Devon estate of Lord Clinton, amounting to about 19,000 acres. The former home of the family at Bicton is now the Devon College of Agriculture.

The only market in the extreme east of Devon is that held weekly at Axminster, a small town (population 3,700) clustered around its church and route focus on a bluff overlooking the river Axe. Industries here include the making of portable buildings, agricultural and other engineering, the manufacture of carpets, and the production of machine tools and steel type. The two last-named employ respectively 410 and 550 people. Colyton, another old town huddled around its church, is smaller than Axminster, but it has a grammar school. A new factory at Colyton produces porcelain and ceramic components for electrical equipment.

The two towns in the Otter valley exhibit interesting points of comparison and contrast in their site, situation, and development. Both Honiton and Ottery St Mary lie above the left bank of the river, but the former has a far more important situation and is the principal node of communications in east Devon. The large volume of through traffic by road has necessitated the provision of a by-pass on the A30 (Plate 8). Honiton's wide main street extends for about one mile, and much of the pattern of the town conforms to this linear core; but the oldest part of Ottery St Mary is clustered about a focus of local routes near the church. The modern spread of settlement in the neighbourhood of the two towns includes rather diverse components. A large area in the south of Honiton is occupied by the Heathfield military camp. In the Ottery district there has been considerable residential development at West Hill, about two miles distant from the town. Honiton retains its weekly market and it is the more important shopping and service centre, although Ottery St Mary has the local grammar school, an old foundation. At both towns and at Dunkeswell there are timber-working industries, comprising saw mills and the making of portable and sectional buildings. Honiton pottery is well known, and the craft of making pillow lace is still carried on in the district. A new engineering works is to be started at Honiton, and a site is reserved for future industrial development. Ottery St Mary has a manufacture of micro-electronic equipment, a brickworks, and a firm which in 1950 transferred its entire production of switchgear from London to the Otter Mill and now has nearly 400 employees. Among the few other industries situated in east Devon are the manufacture of electronic instruments at Seaton and a joinery works at Newton Poppleford. Budleigh Salterton has a firm which employs 100 people in the making of agricultural tractor and implement replacement parts and accessories, and at Hemyock an engineering concern is engaged in the production of storage installations for factories.

Along the coast the westward geological sequence progresses from blue Liassic shales to red Permian sandstones, and cliffed sections alternate with truncated valleys. The normal geological succession is broken in two principal ways—by landslips and faulting. Between Lyme Regis and Seaton, complex slips occurred at various times down to 1840; and the marked indentation of Seaton Bay has probably been caused by erosion along the line of faults which brought the red marls of the Trias alongside the Greensand.

Almost all the coastal settlements lie at or near the mouths of the three main rivers. Seaton and Beer, to the west of the mouth of the Axe, grew in popularity for holidays and residence after the arrival of the railway in 1868. With a fair proportion of buildings of the late Victorian and the Edwardian eras, and its modern holiday camp and sea-front flats, Seaton's character is markedly different from that of Sidmouth, where the pattern of the old town and of the 'cottages' and terraced residences of the eighteenth and nineteenth centuries lies behind an esplanade and sea wall which overlook a shingle beach (Plate 9). Flanking the lower Sid are splendid hills and cliffs—Salcombe Hill to the east and High Peak to the west. Beyond this the land falls fairly rapidly to the mouth of the Otter and the pebble beach of Budleigh Salterton. The core of this town retains its Fore Street–High Street alignment alongside a stream, but modern residences, including many of the villa type, now occupy most of the neighbouring slopes. The proportion of retired professional people in these coastal towns is among the highest in Devon; at Sidmouth and Budleigh Salterton about 36 per cent of the residents are of pensionable age.

The Heartland of Devon

The appellation 'Red Devon', although equally applicable to some other parts of the eastern third of the county, is particularly associated with the area from Tiverton southwards to the coast. Much of the land which is drained by the middle and lower Exe and its tributaries the Clyst, Culm, and Creedy is indeed on the red Permian rocks, but there are also considerable tracts on the Culm Measures. Taken together these areas may justifiably be described as the Heartland of Devon, not only because they have some of the finest farmland in the county, but also because of their geographical situation. Running through them are all the main routes that converge towards Exeter (Fig. 63). In and around the city the Permian sandstones, marls, and breccias dovetail with the Culm Measures, and further diversity arises from the patches of Permo-Carboniferous extrusives known as 'the Exeter traps', most of which occur in three tracts —to the southwest of the city, to the northwest of Crediton, and in the Silverton–Thorverton district. The soils over the area as a whole are comparatively easily worked, so that although the agricultural basis is of dairying and mixed farming there are considerable tracts of arable.

Holdings of 50 to 150 acres are most common, but in some of the red-land parishes one-half of the farms are larger than this. In the dairying

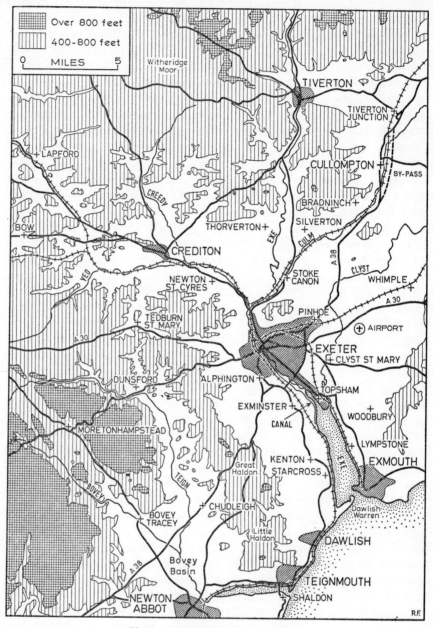

Fig. 63   THE HEARTLAND OF DEVON.

enterprises Friesian cattle are now by far the most numerous, but the Channel Island and Ayrshire breeds are fairly well represented, and a few farmers maintain herds of South Devons. Some localities show a considerable degree of specialization in pigs and poultry. Although sheep are kept throughout the subregion, on the red-land farms there is emphasis on the production of early fat lambs.

Whereas on the generally hilly country of the Culm Measures within the Heartland the tillage averages only about one-seventh to one-fifth of the total acreage under crops and grass and in some parishes is as low as one-tenth, in numerous parishes on the red land the proportion is one-quarter to one-third, and in a few is above one-half. A little wheat is grown in most parishes, but nowhere does it account for more than one-quarter of the acreage under cereals; barley is now predominant, not only on the traditional malting-barley lands to the southeast and north of Exeter but throughout the subregion. The soils on the red sandstones are particularly suitable for the growing of swedes of a superior flavour for human consumption. This is a farm enterprise, and from September to April the crop has a considerable distant market, mainly in London, the Midlands, and the North of England.

Along and to the east of the Clyst valley, red marls and sands predominate, and the latter are worked in the vicinity of Clyst St Mary. The wide valley floor, in the past much subject to flooding, affords reasonably good pasture, and market gardening is carried on around some of the villages sited just above the alluvial plain. At Whimple 160 people are engaged in the manufacturing and processing of cider, an industry which is based upon the many acres of orchards around the village (Plate 10); all together, more than 400 people are on the staff of this firm in Devon. The Exeter airport is situated at Clyst Honiton, and two miles to the north is an even more recent intrusion into the rural landscape—the largest sub-grid electricity transformer station in the Southwest at Higher Burrowton. This is supplied with power from the Hinkley Point nuclear plant near Bridgwater.

Considered in relation to routes in the Heartland subregion, the Clyst valley has to be crossed, whereas the Culm valley offers a corridor followed by the main road and railway from Taunton to Exeter. Because of the heavy traffic on the A38 road, a by-pass—at present the biggest road-works in Devon—is being built to the east of Cullompton. This town (population 3,600) lies immediately to the west of and above the floor of the Culm. Its church is eloquent testimony to the former wealth of the woollen trade here. Textile concerns at work today belong to firms at Wellington (Somerset) and Tiverton. Together with another branch at Uffculme, 160 people are engaged in production for the woollen mills at Wellington, and the mending of silk nets is carried on for John Heathcoat & Co. Ltd. of Tiverton. Other industries at Cullompton are tanning, leather dressing, glove making, and joinery, and road distribution services also give considerable employment. One hundred and fifty people work at Higher King's Mill, where a variety of coloured papers is made on two machines. This factory is owned by a group whose other mills include those at or near Silverton and Stoke Canon (also in the Culm valley) and Watchet (Somerset). The Silverton Mill has a staff of 340 and four machines which make mainly book papers from esparto grass and wood pulp. Two hundred and fifty persons are employed at the Hele Mill near Bradninch; this is owned by a large combine which operates many other paper mills in

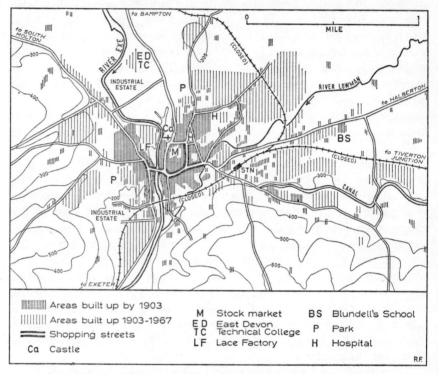

Fig. 64   TIVERTON: SITE, SITUATION, AND MODERN GROWTH.

Great Britain. A variety of good-quality papers is made on the three machines at Hele. At Stoke Canon 120 people work in a two-machine mill which produces medium-quality papers. Other industries in the middle and lower Culm valley are at Tiverton Junction, where a large abattoir and processing plant gives employment to 270 persons, and at Hele and Stoke Canon, where there are cider factories.

In the middle course of the Exe, where for about two miles the valley opens out considerably, the town of Tiverton (population 14,000) stands at the confluence with the tributary Lowman and surrounds an important bridging point at an intersection of main roads (Fig. 64). There is a weekly market, as also at Tiverton Junction. In its architectural character, Tiverton now exhibits great contrasts between its old church, the mansions and almshouses built by merchants in the heyday of the woollen trade, the supermarkets in the shopping centre, and the several housing estates which have been developed since the Second World War. Educational progress has been maintained since 1604, when the public school was founded by Peter Blundell; the latest establishment is the East Devon Technical College. In 1816 John Heathcoat, a lace manufacturer of Loughborough (Leicestershire), decided in view of the Luddite anti-machine riots there to move to Tiverton, where the bobbin-net lace industry thus took root. 'The Factory', as it is familiarly known, has been much extended, and now produces net in nylon, rayon, and silk as well as dress fabrics. Not only does the firm carry on this as Tiverton's chief industry, with a pay roll of about 2,000, but also it has an engineering division which employs more than 450 people and comprises a foundry, factories which make saw-milling and agricultural machinery, and a distributive enterprise concerned with farm machinery and tractors. Together with an American company, it has also established a manufacture of elastic yarn for the textile industry. Other firms at Tiverton are engaged in brewing (which gives employment to 230 persons), the milling of corn and timber, the manufacture of toilet requisites and accessories, and the making of vehicle body-work and equipment, an industry whose special products include refrigerated transporters. The industrial estate at Kennedy Way, in the north of the town, is fully booked; and another industrial area is being developed at Howden, where a large bottling and kegging plant has already been established.

Those parts of the Culm Measures country which lie within the Heartland and are tributary to the Tiverton, Crediton, and Exeter districts have an annual rainfall 10 inches below that of west Devon, and they have better-drained slopes, fewer and smaller patches of moor, more numerous (though small) cider-apple orchards, and richer meadows. The steepest of the valleysides, such as those lying to the west and northwest of Exeter, are left under woods or permanent pasture, but although there is some rough grazing the grassland generally is above average for the Culm Measures country. This is especially true of fields on low hill shoulders and south-facing slopes, where too it is possible to grow fairly good crops of barley, oats, wheat, and roots. Much better, however, and with more arable and orchards, is the land on the long tapering triangle of Permian rocks which runs westwards through Crediton and Bow.

The only town situated on the main route between Exeter and north Devon is Crediton, whose High Street, broadening westwards from the church, is a shopping centre for a large rural area. To some extent Crediton (population 4,900) is a dormitory town, for it is only eight miles from the heart of Exeter. Its market closed in 1962, but as the centre of an important dairying district it has a creamery where the peak daily intake of milk is

34,000 gallons, and butter, cream, and milk powder are produced. Other industries are corn milling, cider making, poultry processing, and the manufacture of confectionery, and pharmaceutical lozenges and pastilles, the last of which gives employment to 125 people. At a branch factory of Heathcoats of Tiverton, 100 women are engaged in the making of children's garments. Elsewhere in the Heartland northwest of Exeter the few village or wayside industries comprise agricultural engineering, the milling of timber, corn and feedingstuffs, and the making of portable buildings.

Between Tiverton and Cullompton and the coast at Exmouth and Teignmouth the general pattern of dairying and mixed farming is diversified in several ways. Glasshouse cultivation is important at Cullompton. Considerable areas of the red lands bear cereals, potatoes, and fodder roots. Many parishes still have some apple orchards but, as in other parts of Devon, in recent years numerous farmers have grubbed out old fruit trees which are no longer an economic proposition. Below Exeter and immediately to the west of the river, the Exe meadows afford some of the best cattle-pasture in Devon, and the Exminster Marshes have long been famous for summer fattening. Although this area has the lowest rainfall in Southwest England, the water table is obviously too high for arable farming. The well-drained, easily worked loams and valley gravels lying at slightly higher levels on either side of the estuary are suitable for nurseries; and there are several areas of market gardens too, notably at Topsham and between Kenton and Teignmouth. In the latter district—in this connection generally referred to as 'the Dawlish area'—violet growing has long been a speciality, although the acreage now is much smaller than in the inter-war period. Wallflowers, ranunculus, anemones, and polyanthus are the other leading flower crops, and fruit—especially strawberries—and vegetables are also grown.

Apart from agriculture, the chief means of employment on the western side of the Exe estuary are the large hospitals at Exminster and Starcross. The estuarine waters are increasingly popular for sailing; and there are large caravan and other camps at Dawlish Warren, whose easily accessible beach is much used by day trippers from Exeter as well as by holiday visitors. Two miles west of the Warren, and in a valley opening on to another sandy beach, lies the resort and residential town of Dawlish (population 7,800). At right-angles to this valley, and a little way inland from the high red cliffs on either side, settlement has spread along the main roads to east and west.

Much of the land above the east bank of the Exe is now almost continuously built up from Exeter to Topsham. From the riverside bluffs by the church in this interesting settlement, one looks over the length and full width of the lower Exe as it expands to two miles wide below its confluence with the Clyst. The pattern, history, and functions of Topsham have been almost entirely related to its position on the Exe and its connections with Exeter, the tributary Clyst having been of little significance. Merchants who visited Holland in the heyday of the Devonshire serge trade brought back the style of building houses with curvilinear gables,

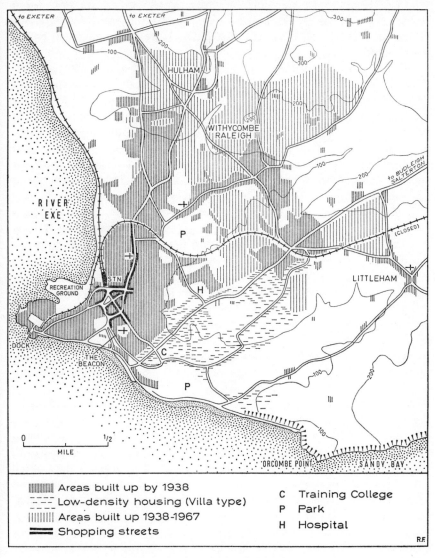

Areas built up by 1938
Low-density housing (Villa type)
Areas built up 1938-1967
Shopping streets

C Training College
P Park
H Hospital

R.F.

Fig. 65 EXMOUTH: THE MODERN GROWTH.

and a series of such residences is a charming feature of The Strand. From the quay the old main street (Fore Street) rises to the first gravel terrace and continues in the High Street towards Exeter. Modern building has filled in many of the spaces between the bank of the Exe and the higher gravel-capped sandstone ridge which forms the interfluve between Clyst and Exe. Today Topsham's functions are mainly those of a local shopping centre and a residential and dormitory settlement. The frequent bus and train services carry considerable commuter and excursion traffic between Exeter, Topsham, and Exmouth. Near Lympstone, and between the railway and the main road, is situated the large training centre of the Royal Marines.

Some of the attractive Georgian buildings of the early phase of Exmouth's growth as a watering place have survived on The Beacon. With its long beach and esplanade, Exmouth is a popular resort and a lung for the Exeter district. There is now a large caravan camp above the cliffs at Sandy Bay, to the east of the main beach. The rapid development of the town in late Victorian and Edwardian times was accompanied by the building not only of much terraced housing outwards from the shopping centres of The Strand–Rolle Street–Chapel Street, but also, on the higher ground, of many villa-type dwellings for the well-to-do residential element (Fig. 65). Exmouth is a favourite place for retirement, and it is also a considerable dormitory for Exeter. The population is increasing quickly and has now reached nearly 22,000. With the creation of the Borough of Torbay, the towns there are independent of the County Council, and Exmouth thereby becomes the largest town in the administrative county of Devon. With the object of diversifying the range of employment, several industries have been introduced, the principal being the making of shoes and leather goods, and light engineering, with staffs now numbering respectively 150, 100, and 120. Other local industries comprise saw milling, brick making, boat building, and engineering.

The City of Exeter

Immediately below its junctions with the rivers Culm and Creedy, the Exe enters a narrow corridor which cuts through the structural grain of the shales and sandstones of the Culm Measures. Also deeply incised into these rocks are several streams, and one of these—a left-bank tributary of the Exe known as the Longbrook—has carved a steep-sided valley in a zone of weakness between the Culm Measures on the one hand and the igneous mass of Rougemont and the Permo-Triassic sandstones, marls, and breccias on the other. To the south of the Longbrook (Fig. 66) is a small plateau surfaced with valley gravels. The eastern part of this plateau, lying at about 120 feet, is almost flat, but from its northern corner the eminence of Rougemont protrudes some 70 feet above the general level. The western half slopes more markedly towards the Exe and terminates in a series of clifflets in the Permo-Triassic rocks overlooking the river.

The choice of this plateau as the site of the Roman town of *Isca* had very important consequences for Southwest England. Not only did the settlement command a river crossing (later the permanent bridging point) and a head of navigation only 10 miles from the sea; it was also on a contact point at or near which there were interlocked several different

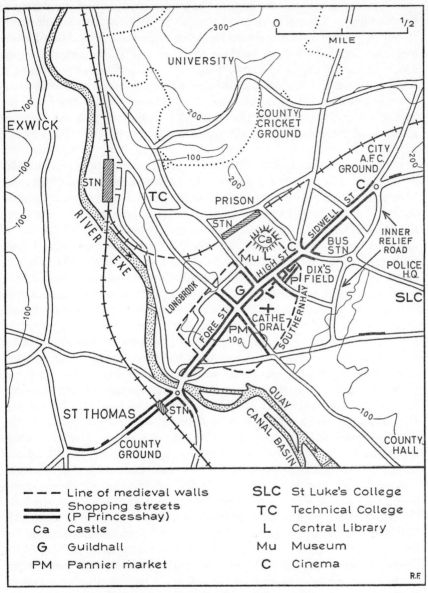

Fig. 66 EXETER: THE CENTRAL AREA, 1967.

kinds of rock and soil, wooded slopes and marshes, land of various qualities for arable and pasture, tributary valleys and an estuary, steep and gentle slopes, and broken and flat country. In effect a fragment of the highland zone of Britain was wedded to the hills and valleys of the lowland zone. For nearly two thousand years the site has been a meeting place of routes coming from the ridges, the gaps in the encircling hills, and the valleys of the Exe basin. Thus the situation of Exeter has proved to be admirably suited to the functions of a centre for much of mid, south, and east Devon, and has been effective in knitting together and expressing the varied activities and interests of those districts. Furthermore, of fundamental importance to the later history of the city itself was the fact that the provision of a walled perimeter around the Roman town defined the core within which the Cathedral, the Castle, the Guildhall, and the principal commercial areas were eventually to be contained (Fig. 66, Plates 11 and 12).

Within the walls, the Cathedral and its precincts and the Castle site with the adjacent Rougemont Gardens remain as distinctive historical enclaves. The present Castle buildings, the oldest of which dates from 1774, lie inside the Norman gateway and curtain wall. For long they accommodated the Devon County Council offices and are still used for the Devon Assizes and Quarter Sessions. In 1963, however, the County offices were largely transferred to a new site, County Hall on Topsham Road. By virtue of its status as a county of a city, Exeter holds its own courts at the Guildhall, a medieval building which was unscathed by the enemy air attacks on the city in 1942. The areas which were devastated by bombing have largely been rebuilt in a mixture of derivative and modern styles, and one of the few innovations has been the provision of a pedestrian shopping precinct in Princesshay. The first stages in the clearance of obsolescent property and the renewal of unbombed but outmoded districts have been completed. A scheme is now being worked out for the redevelopment of the Newtown area which lies to the east of Sidwell Street and the inner relief road. Behind the Guildhall is a partially cleared area which is ripe for rebuilding and could contain either a modern civic focus (new administrative offices are, however, to be situated in Dix's Field) or a variety of cultural and recreational centres, and hotels. Linked with the problem of planning this area is that of traffic congestion in the heart of the city. Since 1938 a by-pass crossing the Exe at Countess Wear, some $2\frac{1}{2}$ miles down river from the centre of Exeter, has diverted much of the long-distance through traffic from the city's main streets, and more recently an inner relief road has been provided, part of which cuts across the west quarter to Exe Bridge (Plate 13); but to complete this portion of the internal road system a dual carriageway and two new bridges to replace the old are urgently required. In the longer term, a new ring road will almost certainly be needed.

Exeter still possesses many examples of Georgian and Regency domestic architecture, notably in Southernhay and Barnfield Crescent, just outside the southeast wall, and in villas, terraces, and crescents elsewhere. Two extra-mural areas—Paris Street (where a new bus station is situated) together with Sidwell Street (which lies on a gently sloping ridge east of the High Street), and Cowick Street in St Thomas immediately across Exe Bridge—have developed as shopping centres, as has also the Fore Street of Heavitree. The districts of St Thomas and Heavitree were incorporated into the city in 1905 and 1911 respectively. About a mile to the north of the centre of Exeter, the University has rapidly expanded on and around the Streatham Estate site, and other educational developments in the city include the Technical College and the College of Art, and the enlargement of St Luke's Training College and the St Loyes College for the Training and Rehabilitation of the Disabled. The principal spreads of modern housing have taken place on the mostly gentle slopes to the east and southeast of Exeter, but both the low-lying flat land (now being relieved of the danger of occasional flooding) and the hillsides west of the Exe are also largely built up. By a boundary award of 1965, the settlements of Pinhoe, Topsham, and Alphington have been ingested into the city's area (Fig. 67). The dormitory zone, however, extends far beyond the present boundary, and the daily influx of workers comes from within a radius of 20 miles from Exeter.

The predominance of the 'service trades'—79 per cent of the insured population in the Exeter area—underlines the facts that the city is a hub and a generator of commerce and services for a large part of Devon, the administrative capital of the county, and an educational, ecclesiastical, and residential centre. Also prominent are the preparation of food and drink and—linked with Exeter's importance as a route focus and as a service centre for a large rural area—engineering (mechanical, electrical, and agricultural) and the repairing and maintenance of vehicles. Exeter accommodates the Devon County Show on a permanent site at Whipton near Pinhoe, and it has a modern stock market and abattoir at Marsh Barton on the Alphington Road. Weekly markets for fatstock and store animals are held on separate days, and shows and special sales are organized throughout the year. Between 1950 and 1967 the annual throughput increased from 78,000 to 278,000 head of stock, 90 per cent of which arrive and leave by road transport.

Despite the absence of heavy industry, Exeter has a variety of occupations in mills, factories, workshops, and depots. Within the city walls there is only a little industry, including printing works and a shirt factory, but a firm which employs about 350 people in the making of ecclesiastical furnishings and academic robes has works in various parts of Exeter. In connection with a flood protection scheme, part of the left bank of the Exe is being cleared, and few industries are now left in this locality. There is a paper mill at Trew's Weir. Across the river and in the area to the south of the canal basin and the gasworks are a firm which manufactures tallow, feeding meals, and fertilizers and an engineering works. One firm whose main activity is the production of iron castings of up to

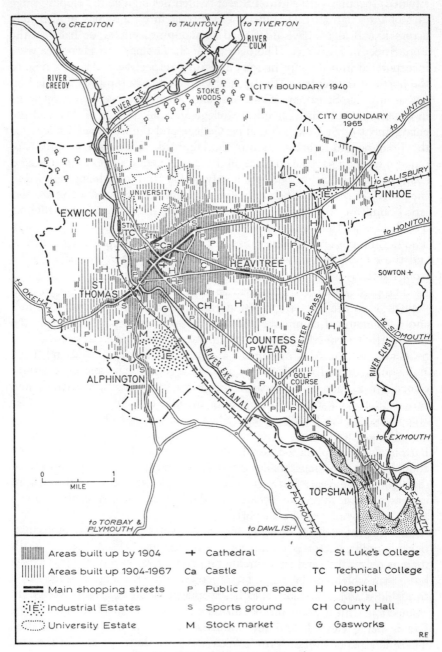

Fig. 67   EXETER: THE CITY AREA, 1967.

six tons employs about 250 people, including 150 in the foundries and 50 in the machine shops. Another, staffed by about 200 persons, is engaged in the production of vessels and tankage for the oil and chemical industries, heavy structural steelwork, and building construction.

Farther south, at Marsh Barton, is a trading and light industrial estate covering 160 acres, on or near which nearly 80 concerns have been established since the late 'forties. There are numerous distribution depots, and several firms are engaged in haulage services, plant hire, and engineering, including the reconditioning of electric motors and control gear, and the repairing of radiators. Factory work includes leather finishing, the fabrication of steelwork, and the making of precision machine tools, Venetian blinds and foundation garments, the last-named giving employment to 130 persons, mostly women. Important recent additions to the industries at Marsh Barton are factories for the textile engineering division of Heathcoats of Tiverton and for Centrax of Newton Abbot; the latter employs about 250 people in the production of compressor and turbine blades. The individually sited industries in the St Thomas district include a provender mill, a shirt factory with a staff of 140, the majority of whom are females, and a cork and flooring-timber works established by a firm which in 1940 moved from its former situation at Dover because of the enemy air attacks on that town. There is a large bakery at Exwick.

Industrial sites adjacent to the inner relief road in the St Sidwell district are occupied by a printing firm whose staff numbers 190, a luggage factory with a pay roll of 170, and a foundation-garment factory; the last two employ mostly women. There are also electrical and motor engineering firms. The trading estate at Pinhoe Road, towards the eastern limit of the city, is taken up chiefly by distribution depots. A firm which, with its subsidiaries, has a staff of 450, has here a bottling dairy and a cream and cheese factory; the peak intake of milk is 20,000 gallons per day. Nearby are the Pinhoe brickworks, an engineering firm, and a grain silo. Other industries within the city's area include brewing at Heavitree and brick making at Exmouth Junction. At Topsham there are timber drying, boat building, the manufacture of clock mechanisms, and the curing of sprats which are brought from various fishing harbours on the south coast of England. The Exeter and Devon County authorities propose to co-operate in the development of an industrial site at Sowton.

The port of Exeter extends from the city's quay and basin to the mouth of the Exe. Within this area the only significant discharging points are Exeter (by means of the canal), Topsham Quay, and Exmouth Dock. In 1966, 390 ships representing 51,000 net registered tons, entered the port; most of these were coastwise vessels bringing petrol from refineries in southern England, gravel and pebbles dredged from the English Channel, and coal from Northeast England. Between one-fifth and one-quarter of the total number of ships arriving come from foreign ports and bring in timber from Scandinavian and Baltic countries, fertilizers, cider apples, and bulk cider for processing (from Caen), Danish lager, wood pulp from Scandinavia, and oystershells crushed for use in poultry food (from Denmark and Sweden). The only exports are of sprats from Topsham, and coke breeze, stone, barley, and milk powder from Exmouth.

Exmouth Dock was opened just over one hundred years ago; it now accommodates vessels of up to 750 tons deadweight. In recent years shipping activity has increased appreciably; whereas in 1954 there were 27 foreign and 86 coastwise arrivals, in 1964 the corresponding totals were 44 and 154. For many years the principal cargoes have been timber, fertilizers, apples, cider, and coal; to these has recently been added sea-dredged pebbles (over 46,000 tons in 1965), which are graded at the dockside and used as aggregates in the building industry. Of late years also, Exmouth has been importing wood pulp for the Culm valley paper mills and has captured a large part of the former trade of Watchet (Somerset) in this respect. Topsham Quay was little used between the 1930s and the early 'fifties, when a grain warehouse was built there. Since 1959 this store has been used for Danish lager, off-loaded at the Quay and thence distributed in the Exeter district. The only other imports at Topsham are occasional cargoes of timber.

The Exeter Ship Canal takes vessels of up to $10\frac{1}{2}$ feet in draught, 120 feet in length and $24\frac{1}{2}$ feet in beam. Most of the ships that use the canal discharge petrol—about 23,000 tons per annum—and timber at Exeter. The recovery in traffic on the canal after the Second World War was gradual, but increased fairly steadily to the period 1955–61. More recently, however, traffic has somewhat decreased, largely because of a decline in the carriage of petrol to the city by sea as a result of the effectiveness of road competition.

The Bovey Basin–Newton Abbot–Teignmouth

During the Oligocene period the Bovey Beds—comprising coarse and fine gravels, sands, clays, and lignite—were laid down in a lake basin. Most of the sands and gravels accumulated in deltas in the northwestern part of the Basin or were massed towards the perimeter; but the finer clays were carried as far as the eastern and southern sides of the lake. The coarse soils generally support poor pasture, scrubby heath or plantations, while in the clay areas much of the surface is pitted with past and present workings (Fig. 68). One of the former clay pits has been filled in and restored to agricultural use, and a scheme is in hand for transforming the disused Decoy pit into a visual amenity and a recreational centre for Newton Abbot.

Commercially, the Bovey Basin is best known for its ball clays, a name derived from the cubes or 'balls' of clay, 9 to 10 inches in side and weighing 30 to 35 pounds each, which were cut from the floor of open pits. Within the Basin there are more than forty seams of clay which range in thickness from 1 to 20 feet, and this district yields most of Devon's output of ball clay. In 1951, 222,000 tons were produced, compared with 40,000 from the Petrockstow Basin in the north of the county; and in 1966 the corres-

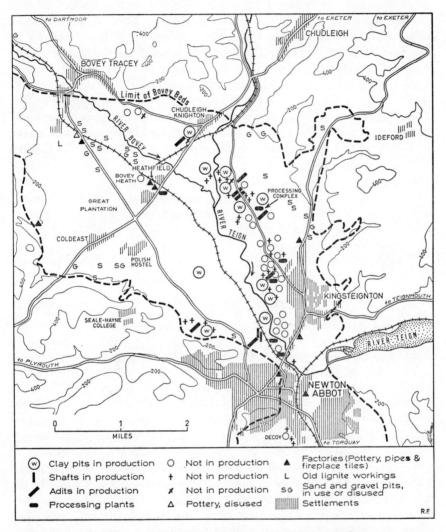

Fig. 68   THE BOVEY BASIN: THE BALL-CLAY INDUSTRY, 1967.

ponding figures were 470,000 and 54,000 tons. Together, the three producing firms in the Bovey Basin employ between 700 and 800 men in the extracting of clay, and the biggest concern has a complex of processing works, saw mills for the production of pit props, and its own transport organization.

The clays occur broadly as two groups—the 'whiteware' group comprising black, dark blue, and light blue types, which are highly plastic clays yielding, after firing, a white or cream body; and the 'stoneware' group, consisting of siliceous clays with an appreciable quartz content. Extraction is by both quarrying and mining, the former being preferred except where the depth of the seam is such as to make mining the more economical method. In quarrying, the overburden is first removed by means of drag-line excavators, and the clay seams exposed are then worked by hand-operated compressed-air spades, drag-line excavators or rotary-bucket excavators. In mining, the vertical shaft method has given way to drift (adit) systems which are worked to a depth of about 600 feet (Fig. 69). Since the Second World War the extraction of the clays has become highly mechanized, and an important recent development in mining has been the introduction of clay-cutting machines. Output is still steadily increasing;

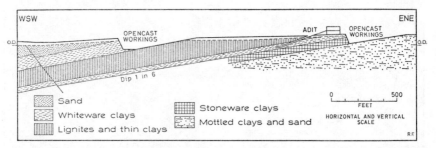

Fig. 69   THE BOVEY BASIN: A SECTION OF SOME OF THE BALL-CLAY WORKINGS, 1967. With acknowledgments to Watts, Blake, Bearne & Co. Ltd., Newton Abbot.

but even at the present high rate of production there is little fear of rapid exhaustion, for the life of the reserves is estimated to be about 100 years.

Drying, grinding, pulverizing, and calcining are the principal forms of processing carried out by the clay-producing firms. Ball clay is used chiefly for the manufacture of earthenware, sanitary ware, tiles, and electrical insulating porcelain. Most of the clay for the home market is sent by road and rail to the Staffordshire potteries, and a certain amount of processed clay is required by various other industries including the preparation of rubber, plastics, linoleum, fertilizers, and adhesives. In the Newton Abbot–Bovey Tracey district ball clays are used in factories which produce wall and fireplace tiles, pottery, and vitrified pipes. The tile works at Heathfield employ about 200 people. Clays for export—now over 70 per cent of the output—are despatched by road to Teignmouth for shipment to European ports, and to Fowey, Avonmouth, or Birkenhead for destinations in other parts of the world. Italy and West Germany are the most important of the European markets.

Sporadic attempts to work the lignite deposits have been made since the early sixteenth century. Until the arrival of cheap coal by rail, lignite was used in the local potteries. Partly because of the shortage of coal in the late 1940s working started again, this time with the object of producing briquettes; and lignite 'cobbles' were shipped from Teignmouth to the Channel Islands where they were used for heating glasshouse boilers. At present there is no mining of lignite, but small quantities are produced incidentally in the extraction of clay. Sand and gravel are worked at several places in and around the Bovey Basin, concrete is made, and there are limestone quarries at Stoneycombe (2 miles south of Newton Abbot) and at Chudleigh. Except for a variety of factories at Newton Abbot, there are few other sizeable industries in the district. At Bovey Tracey there is a branch of the Paignton factory of Standard Telephones and Cables Ltd. and a firm of provender millers who, with their subsidiaries, have a staff of about 100. There are several food-processing plants and various large depots, notably at Heathfield.

The busy town of Newton Abbot, with a population of about 18,600,[1] has a significant situation near the southern outlet of the Bovey Basin and at a focus of valleys, main roads and railways at the head of the Teign estuary (Fig. 70). Topographically, some of the older components of the settlement are distinctly arranged, with villas on the hills and on the perimeter of Forde and Courtenay Parks, and terraced housing behind the main streets. Recent clearance and planning schemes are a prelude to the renewal of parts of the central area and the creation of a more effective public and civic focus within the commercial core. This lies around the river Lemon, a tributary of the Teign, and the flat ground here enhances the attractiveness of the town as a shopping centre. For some years after the air raids of the Second World War had devastated large tracts of the centres of Exeter and Plymouth, Newton Abbot enjoyed a special trade boom, and the modernization of many premises which ensued has helped to maintain its popularity.

Several of the other functions of the town are indicative of the importance of its situation. The weekly market, which has a throughput of about 80,000 animals per annum, serves a large area of south Devon and eastern Dartmoor, and many seasonal shows and sales are held. There are warehouses for various agricultural products, and firms concerned with farm machinery, engineering—including the manufacture of hydraulic pulp-presses—and repair work. Seale-Hayne College, three miles north-west of the town, is one of the leading centres of agricultural education. Except for Prince Rock at Plymouth, the Newton Abbot power station of the Central Electricity Generating Board is the only one in south Devon. The repairing of railway rolling stock—for many years a staple industry—was replaced in 1960 by the maintenance of diesel engines which were then being introduced into the Western Region. In the environs of the

---

[1] The continuous built-up areas in and around the urban district have a total population of 23,900.

town there is a diversity of old and new industries. At Bradley Mills, on the western side of Newton Abbot, tanning was carried on for nearly 200 years, and fellmongering until the Second World War when, because of the shortage of skins, the firm concentrated on combing, for which it now uses mainly high-grade Australian wools. To this has been added the machine processing of man-made fibres, and the whole enterprise occupies about 200 people.

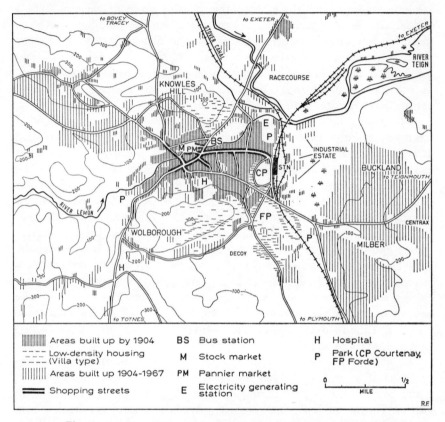

Fig. 70   NEWTON ABBOT: SITE, SITUATION, AND MODERN GROWTH.

The chief spread of settlement around Newton Abbot in recent years has occurred on the slopes east and southeast of the town, where a considerable proportion of the housing has been provided for workers at the Centrax engineering factory (Plate 14), which was established in 1955 and now employs about 2,000 persons. This has specialized in the production of aircraft-engine parts, gas turbines, generator sets, and turbine and compressor blades, but the range of output is now more diversified and includes high-efficiency boilers, axles, and gear transmissions. In Newton Abbot there is a variety of light industries, including a leather-craft factory where 100 people are employed, a bakery employing over 100 persons, a firm making confectionery and ice cream whose staff numbers approximately 100 at the peak period in the summer, and a manufacture of reversible coats which provides work for 140 women. The last three of these industries are among the numerous enterprises which occupy the Brunel Road industrial estate and all together employ nearly 1,000 persons.

As with the Exe, a sand spit partially closes the mouth of the Teign; but in contrast to the threat of the destruction of Dawlish Warren by the sea, the problem here is not erosion but the shifting of sand in the estuary. The nucleus of the town of Teignmouth lies behind the open space of 'The Den' at the northern end of the sand spit (Plate 15). Recently-built flats and the proposed new street layout will diversify the character of the central parts of the town, but modern housing development has already taken place on all the slopes behind. Shaldon, on the western side of the bridged estuary, retains pleasant buildings of the Georgian period, but it too has expanded considerably. Teignmouth's sea-front has a spacious promenade and a sandy beach, separated from that at Dawlish by a series of red cliffs, stacks, and sandy coves through which runs one of the most picturesque main railway lines in England. Although it is perhaps best known as a summer resort, Teignmouth is also a considerable shopping and residential town. There are few industries, but ship- and boat-building is still noteworthy, now using timber and fibre glass and producing trawlers and fast motor-cruisers. As a new fish quay has been provided, Teignmouth may develop as a modern fishing port. The total seaborne trade of the harbour, which can take vessels of up to 1,000 tons carrying capacity, is of the order of 390,000 tons per annum, three-quarters of which is accounted for by shipments of ball clay. There is an increasing export trade in scrap metal, the product of pressing down old vehicles. Imports consist largely of coal (73,000 tons in 1966) and timber. Calcinated-seaweed fertilizer is imported from Brittany.

Torbay: a new County Borough

On the western and southern flanks of the small dissected plateau which lies to the south of the Teign estuary, Permian rocks give way to Middle and Lower Devonian limestones, sandstones, grits, and slates. Amid this older series is a broad outlier of Permian sandstones around Paignton, but it is the headland masses of Devonian limestone which delimit Torbay, with Hope's Nose on the north side and Berry Head on the south. Sheltered within the arc are the harbours and strand of Torquay, the long sandy beaches and Permian clifflets of Paignton, and the harbour of Brixham. On the red land behind Torbay dairying and arable farming are important enterprises, but there is also local emphasis on the fattening of beef cattle and sheep; and in the sheltered districts tributary to the

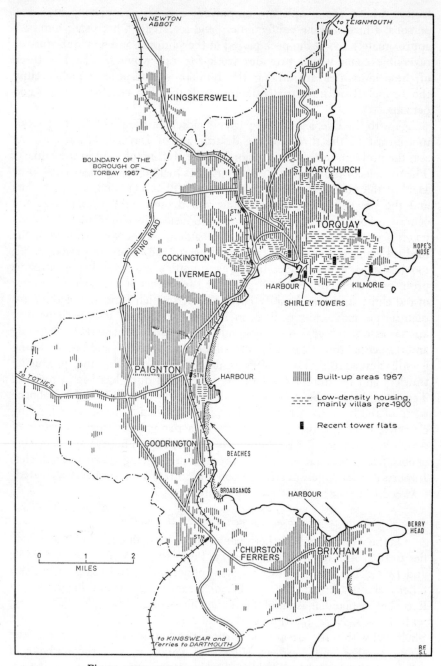

Fig. 71   THE COUNTY BOROUGH OF TORBAY: SETTLEMENT.

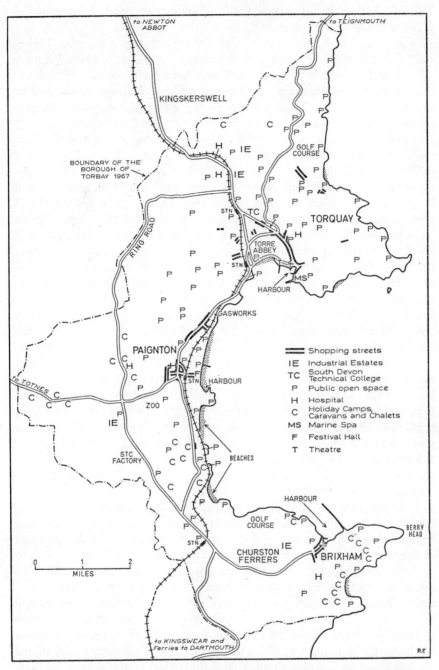

Fig. 72   THE COUNTY BOROUGH OF TORBAY: COMMERCE, INDUSTRY, AND AMENITIES.

Teign, farming is interspersed with horticulture and fruit growing. Cider is made at Netherton.

From medieval times there were fishing stations along the Torbay coast, but the older agricultural settlements such as Tor Mohun, Paignton village, and Churston Ferrers stood well back from the sea, as did also the higher part of Brixham which was a nucleated village surrounded by its own open fields. Even as late as the eighteenth century Torquay consisted of little more than a quay with fishermen's cottages, although Lower Brixham had grown considerably as a fishing port. Since that time the Torbay littoral has been developed as a series of resorts and residential districts. From Torquay, settlement has extended northwards in the directions of Teignmouth and Newton Abbot, and along the coast towards Paignton, which itself has also spread inland (Fig. 71 and Plate 16). A large number of very attractive gardens, parks, and other open spaces have, however, been laid out and preserved for public enjoyment (Fig. 72). Southwards from Paignton modern development has been almost continuous as far as Broadsands, about two miles from Brixham. Renewal of parts of the central areas in the Torbay towns may take various forms; a major scheme of redevelopment has been carried out between Torbay Road and Hyde Road, Paignton, where a pedestrian precinct, supermarket, and multi-storeyed car park have been provided in the Crossways shopping centre. Other noteworthy changes in the Torbay scene in recent years include the proliferation of a variety of holiday chalet and caravan camps, especially at Paignton and Brixham; the building of tower blocks of luxury flats at Torquay (Plate 17); and the addition of the Paignton Festival Hall to the amenities of the resort. There is a proposal to redevelop the locality of the Marine Spa and Beacon Cove at Torquay and to include a lido. The extent, continuity, and population—now close on 100,000—of the built-up areas from Torquay to Brixham prompted the scheme for a merger of the local authorities and the creation of a County Borough of Torbay (Torquay itself was incorporated as a municipal borough in 1892). It has been said that this change, which becomes effective in 1968, will establish a local government structure which will express the growing unity of the Torbay district and encourage the planning and development of the area as a tourist centre of national importance.

With its mild, equable climate and its position well sheltered from the north and east winds, Torquay acquired, during the late eighteenth and early nineteenth centuries, a reputation as being suitable for invalids and as a winter retreat. Stages in the improvement in transport facilities were marked by the completion of the inner harbour in 1806, the construction of the turnpike roads from Newton Abbot and Teignmouth and of the Torbay Road to Brixham in 1842, and the arrival of the railway in 1848; and Torquay became more widely known as a winter and spring resort and an attractive residential town. A commercial centre evolved around and near the harbour, and development of the magnificent marine façade and the hilly background speeded up. Nineteenth-century building included a series of handsome terraces and crescents; and certain areas were laid out in large residences with spacious grounds, groups of trees, and shrubberies, an arrangement which incidentally added considerably to the sylvan element in the Torquay scene, but which presents peculiar problems for redevelopment in changing modern conditions. During the present century much of the building programme at Torquay has consisted of smaller dwellings, both privately owned and on Corporation estates. Modern housing predominates in Paignton, but the core of the resort, centred upon the Torbay Road, retains a distinctive character. During the last twenty-five years Torquay has become more markedly a summer resort, and to an even greater extent this is also true of Paignton. There is, however, a numerous retired population, and of the total residents of Torbay, one in four is of pensionable age.

Between the wars the port of Torquay had a considerable import trade, especially in building materials during the boom periods of housing development. Timber (mainly from Northern Europe), cement from the London area, slates, bricks, and sand dredged from the river Dart were the principal cargoes. Coal—chiefly from Northeast England—was also an important item, and other cargoes included vegetables and groceries. This trade was already declining before the Second World War, which almost put an end to commercial traffic through Torquay harbour. Since then, timber has been the only considerable import. The principal maritime activity is now yachting, for which Torquay is one of the chief centres in the Southwest. Cross-Channel passenger traffic was re-established in 1967 by means of a two-way steamer service connecting Torquay with the Channel Islands and Cherbourg.

For some years Paignton harbour has had no sea trade, but it is used by many pleasure boats. Much of Brixham's fame has rested upon the fishing industry. With the completion of the outer quay in 1804, full use was made of the harbour site which, because of the shelter from westerly gales given by Berry Head, was the best-favoured on Torbay for the development of a modern fishing port. Brixham is well known as the former home of the red-sailed two-masted trawlers, and its fishermen played an important part not only in the Southwest but also in the North Sea trawling grounds. After a long period of decline, fishing has revived, and 42 trawlers are now based upon the port. The recent arrangements for co-operative marketing by the fishermen who own and man the vessels have already resulted in greater prosperity, and there is a scheme to provide a new fish market and wharf to aid the redevelopment of the industry.

Although most of the industrial enterprises in the Torbay towns are on a small scale, in total they offer a fairly wide variety of employment. Those at Torquay include the making of perfume, pottery, joinery and concrete metal working, the polishing of marble and other stones, and the manufacture of coin-in-the-slot television meters and electronic equipment (which employs about 100 people). At Paignton there are the Hollicombe gasworks, a crab-meat factory, a winery, and engineering works. Boat building is carried on by several firms around Torbay, and one of these has four deep-water slipways at Brixham. Most of the limestone from the Berry Head quarry goes to the lower Thames area for use in blast furnaces and the manufacture of cement, and into the production of agricultural lime. Brixham has a number of other industries, including a foundry, engineering, and the making of roller blinds. A jetty is used for the discharging of oil.

During the Second World War Torquay benefited from the arrival, for reasons of security, of training establishments, offices, and light industries. Some of the latter were temporarily accommodated but have since moved to new factories on the Old Woods trading and industrial estate. A firm which makes electrical measuring instruments and pyrometers opened a new works here in 1960 and now employs 150 people. The biggest single industrial enterprise in the Torbay district, however, is Standard Telephones and Cables Ltd., whose factory on the outskirts of Paignton was opened in 1956 and has since been extended. It produces valves, capacitors and film circuits, and has over 2,500 workers. Since 1945 about 4,000 new jobs have been provided in the Torbay area by means of the introduction of industry, and to some extent the district has also profited from developments at Newton Abbot. In the field of technical education, the establishment of the South Devon Technical College at Torquay has been advantageous for the whole area.

CHAPTER 11

Exmoor: North Devon:
The Culm Measures Country: Dartmoor

Exmoor

THE county boundary between Devon and Somerset has been ignored in this description of Exmoor, and 16 parishes of west Somerset have been included in the region (Fig. 73); thus constituted, Exmoor extends from Heddon's Mouth in the west to the Vale of Porlock in the east, and south to include the upper part of the Exe catchment; except for the northeast the region is roughly coextensive with the area of the Exmoor National Park. The southern boundary of the Park near Bampton is close to the geological junction where the Devonian rocks appear at the surface from underneath the Culm Measures. The Devonian rocks, which were deposited during the alternations of marine and Continental conditions, occupy continuous tracts of country running southeastwards from the sea across Exmoor; the local names which label them reveal their forms and hint at their modes of origin—Foreland Grits, Lynton Slates, Hangman Grits, Ilfracombe Slates, Morte Slates, Pickwell Down Sandstones, the Baggy Sandstones, and Pilton Slates. The linear arrangement of the outcrops is the legacy of the Hercynian orogeny; this folded the Devonian rocks into high mountains and gave the northern limb of the resulting synclinorium a strike from northwest to southeast and a regional dip to the south—the direction also in which the rock sequence successively outcrops. The subsequent tectonic history of the eastern part of Exmoor is one of block-faulting which created deep basins. These received in turn the waste materials from the adjacent high Cornubian ranges which were being actively destroyed under arid conditions. One such basin is the Vale of Porlock, which became filled with débris of ever finer grade from breccias in the lower levels through sandstones to marls; all these were deposited unconformably on the Devonian basement during New Red Sandstone times. The occurrence of an equally important tectonic episode in the north has been suggested as a result of recent geophysical work. A major thrust beneath Exmoor is the most reasonable explanation for the progressive southward decrease of gravity anomalies and an upward and outward overthrusting of the Devonian rocks to the north is suspected; this may amount to more than 8 miles of horizontal tectonic transport.

It is the high-standing, folded, and faulted Devonian basement that the ensuing vicissitudes and physiographies of the Mesozoic, Tertiary, and Pleistocene eras have wrought and fashioned into the attractive shapes and forms of land which tourists flock to see and which the National Park Committee attempts to preserve from spoliation. A good deal of the land rises sheer from the sea in massive and awe-inspiring cliffs to a number of level or near-level surfaces which rise in step-like formation inland to great shouldered hills like the Chains (1,575 feet), Dunkery (1,705 feet), and the southwestern facing rampart of hills which extends from Shoulsbury Common in the direction of Dulverton. These plateau surfaces are not related to structure, since the strata are severely plicated and are by no

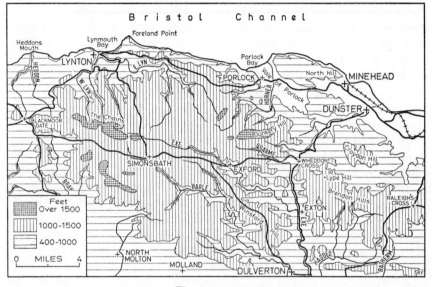

Fig. 73 EXMOOR.

means horizontally disposed, neither do they appear over one particular outcrop but cut both inclined strata and successive rocks; they are indeed the remnants of planation surfaces moulded under varied past climates and former base-levels of erosion. In any wide view of Exmoor from a high point (Plate 19) it is this plateau form which impresses, because the goyals and combes which deeply furrow the planation surfaces are often hidden. The watershed in Exmoor runs east to west from the Chains to Dunkery, and the 70 inches and more of rain which fall over this high and large catchment gather into rivers having short distances to fall the thousand feet and more between the high surfaces and the sea. The most remarkable thalweg of the larger rivers is that of the West Lyn which, on the last mile of its course, falls some 400 feet through a rocky boulder-strewn gorge. Within a few yards from the sea the West Lyn is joined by the East Lyn, a strike stream with a thalweg a little less steep in its lower reach, but one, nevertheless, with a larger catchment. Lynmouth, the only settlement in the lower reaches of these two rivers, is perched precariously on the valley floor and 'the river has more than once claimed its own' (Plate 20). The lower planation surfaces are generally absent from the northern margin of Exmoor, the land falling away wonderfully over steep cliffs to the Bristol Channel; many small streams which rise within a mile or two of the coast find their way to the sea by cascading over water slides and by plunging over remarkable coastal waterfalls. In contrast to these convexly shaped lower reaches are the middle and upper reaches of the rivers which are concave in profile and more gently sloping; they also have flood plains and exhibit valley-in-valley forms.

On the south side of the region lies the vast upper part of the Exe catchment. The Exe river and the Barle, its principal tributary, flow parallel to one another in a southeasterly direction, at first in deep, though generally broad, valleys (Plate 19); subsequently both rivers follow sinuous courses in entrenched meanders. Near Exton the Exe joins the south-flowing river Quarme and this southerly direction is maintained, the Barle adding its waters to the trunk stream south of Dulverton. On the east side a large number of streams drain the south-facing Brendon Hills, but they funnel into either the river Haddeo or river Batherm; these rivers join the Exe near Bury Castle and Bampton respectively. It is this maze of streams which gives the Brendon Hills a gentler and greener look than Exmoor proper, even though a summit height of 1,391 feet occurs at Lype Hill and some of the hills are over a thousand feet high. An important series of faults cross the Brendon Hills, whose displacements of strata in some cases are considerable, but they do not give rise to the marked relief features found farther north. There, the faults have been ultimately responsible for extending an area of low relief far inland—the Vale of Porlock. The resulting break of slope between this vale and the great bulk of Dunkery is not only abrupt but also of considerable magnitude. The Horner Water and its tributaries have cut back a number of deep combes in this fault-line scarp and their thickly wooded valleysides interdigitate between the heathy slopes above and the pattern of fields and farms below. The low-lying Vale of Porlock has been finally formed by excavation of the infilling of New Red Sandstone breccias, sandy limestones, and marls by rivers which at present reach the sea with difficulty through the cobbled, arcuate, storm-beach of Porlock Bay. Terraces and river gravels at heights up to 500 feet are an interesting testimony to the long process of removal which made this lowland, while the coarse, angular deposits of head which have accumulated at the foot of steep slopes suggest that some of the erosion took place under periglacial conditions. In time, an improving climate made possible the use of this erstwhile tundra by man and his animals.

The pattern of river dissection provides one key to the interpretation of the historic land use, as clearing and enclosure extended along the valleys. In this way land was added to land to sustain almost self-sufficing family farms and small agricultural communities. The higher slopes and unenclosed moorland 'up over' were integrated into this farming system as 'from the time whereof the memory of man doth not extend to the contrary' the inhabitants of the bordering hamlets and farms had turned out their animals to pasture on this waste and had collected fuel and turf from it. As more and more of the medieval woodland was being cleared in the wake of settlement, the Norman kings became concerned about the consequent disturbance of the wild animals. To preserve this wild fauna, certain areas of the kingdom were by law designated Royal Forests; Exmoor, being one of them, was placed in the charge of an official, sometimes called the Warden, but more frequently the Forester. Nevertheless, the ancient practices of the bordering farmers were recognized, and thus developed the rights of 'common' which survived even though the land became a Royal Forest.

For centuries Exmoor Forest remained under the commoners and foresters but its boundaries were not inviolate. At a perambulation in 1300 several areas in the north and in the south were disafforested and by 1400 a further loss in the north had occurred. The next blow at the sovereignty of the moor came in 1814 when the ancient demesne land of the Crown of England on Exmoor was disafforested and offered for sale. In 1818 the greater part of the Forest passed by purchase into the hands of John Knight, who set about the reclamation of Exmoor by ploughing up the virgin land, establishing new farms and driving new roads across the moor. Inspired by the work of John Knight in the old Forest, the eyes of many landowners were now cast on the surrounding commons. A further attack on the open land took place between 1840 and 1872, when measures were taken for the enclosure of some 30 Exmoor commons. Public opinion and anger rose against this wholesale enclosure in the 1860s and, after the dismemberment of Wootton Courtenay in 1872, Exmoor settled down again to a period of stability. These assaults had made great inroads onto the open moorlands of Exmoor but had not entirely destroyed its character and for more than half a century few further changes were made. Even the two World Wars were endured with little damage done and Exmoor survived them as a wild upland of immense pleasure and delight to the walker, the horseman, the hunter, the tourist, and the holiday-maker.

In an attempt to preserve this countryside, the State in 1954, very much after the fashion of the Norman kings centuries before, designated Exmoor a National Park, the intention being 'the preservation and enhancement of natural beauty' for the benefit and recreation of all people for all time. The Act notwithstanding, Exmoor is farming country; the land is privately owned and man's mechanical power over Nature is ever increasing. With persistent encroachments being made on Britain's limited rural land area, a

government supported ploughing-up campaign and a commercial afforestation policy, the remaining open moorland of Exmoor faces yet other—
maybe final—assaults. The average loss of moorland over the past decade
has been estimated at a little over a thousand acres a year. In 1965, of the
170,000 acres (about 265 square miles) in the National Park, the open
moorland amounted to 50,665 acres, of which 36,865 acres were heather
moorlands and heath and 13,800 acres grass moorland.

Exmoor is essentially a land of hill farms which, both in origin and form,
are of two kinds—the older traditional hill farms and those set out by the
Knights in their nineteenth-century large-scale reclamation. Access to many
of the former is along narrow, twisting lanes, scored down to the bare rock
in places, sunk deep between the fields and eloquent of the time when the
pack-ponies with their swinging panniers were the major means of transport.
Flat ground that is neither the exposed hill-top nor the wet marshy valley-
floor is rare in Exmoor and most of the farms are on valleysides. The most
effective way to build on a slope is to excavate and set the building in the
hillside with its face to the sun. Formerly a typical farm was low-walled and
thatched, with the cow-shippon a part of a long structure built of the grey
slaty shale, the first stone to come to the hand of the early builders. Later
shippons, barns, and stables are of larger stones quarried from small pits
usually visible near the farm; all are joined close together to enclose the
sloping yard presenting on three sides blank walls to wind, weather, storm,
and foe alike. Small irregular fields enclosed by cast-up earthbanks cluster
close to the farm, very much of the same shape and size as when cleared
from the waste of heather by the pioneer settlers. In these small fields
wheat, barley, oats, and rye were grown formerly, as each farm had to be
virtually self-supporting. Farther away from the farm are much larger
straight-sided fields; these have been more recently enclosed from the moor
and were the former open land of common rights on which the whole
economy of the holding once depended.

Even larger straight-sided fields are characteristic of the immediate
vicinity of the large farm houses built in the 1840s and 1850s by John and
Frederic Knight. They are, for Exmoor, spacious farm houses, long, plain,
heavily built of local stone and slate-roofed, typical of the grace and
solidarity of that Georgian Age. Around them grow tough sycamore and
beech windbreaks and beyond lie the very large fields (Plate 19). These are
enclosed by straight-sided banks dyked with level courses of tamped-in
upright stones and crowned with a sod spine, on top of which the beech
hedges stand; it is claimed that these break the force of the wind in this
storm-swept land for many times the length of their own height. The work
of keeping both bank and hedge in good repair is highly skilled and very
laborious. Good sound roads link farm to farm and, 'two gated' through
the perimeter wall, give access to the outside world. It was in the 1850s,
after attempts in the first few optimistic years of reclamation to grow cereals

on the four-course rotation had failed, that the Forest farms settled down to the traditional Exmoor form of family farming, in which the main income is derived from the sale of store cattle and sheep. The stock itself, however, was increasingly to be changed by additions from without. The Exmoor Horn sheep may still predominate but there are large flocks of Closewools, Scottish Blackface, Cheviots, Border Leicesters, and others as well. The same is true of other stock; the traditional red cattle of Devon are frequently seen (Plate 21) but other breeds such as Galloways have been introduced and more are likely. The Ministry of Agriculture's experimental hill farm at Liscombe is currently comparing breeds and crosses, including Charollais, Herefords, and Friesians. To sustain this hill-farming economy, good pastures are of great importance and the provision of enough feed for long and often hard winters involves a careful rotation of the ploughable land. Usually roots, then oats, are followed by a reseeding to a ley of 5–7 years, alternately grazed and mown for hay and silage. The Exmoor soils are notoriously short of lime and phosphate and fairly liberal dressings of these are required to keep the land in good heart.

The stock from these Exmoor farms eventually finds its way to the markets and fairs held at various places on Exmoor. Very large numbers of sheep are sold at the autumn sales at Blackmoor Gate and the sales at Exford and Molland are also important. In the east of the region sales of stock are made at Raleigh's Cross and at Wheddon Cross near Cutcombe which, in addition, has become a wool-collecting centre for north Devon and west Somerset. At Bampton, in the south, there is a fortnightly market and summer and autumn sales of sheep and store cattle, but the great event of the year there is the Pony Fair. This occurs in October and follows the annual 'drift' of the moor for these wild creatures.

The beauty of Exmoor was discovered after a few well-to-do and literary tourists had found a quiet retreat here during the Napoleonic Wars, when much of Europe had been closed to them. The easier accessibility of the interior made possible by the roads constructed by the Knights, together with the general improvement of all roads in the modern era, has led to a great increase in the number of visitors and to a considerable extension of the catering and accommodation trades. This is so, not only in the few coastal towns such as Porlock, Lynton, and Lynmouth but also in the inland villages, hamlets, and farms. To preserve the peace and beauty of the landscape which tourists of many kinds come to enjoy and to reconcile their needs with those of the farmers and foresters is the very worthy but complicated task of the National Trust and the Exmoor National Park Committee.

North Devon

Lundy, an island lying 18 miles due west of Morte Point, is a cliffed table-land rising as high as 471 feet. Although its average width is only half a mile it extends north–south for 3 miles, and its prominence and position have attracted the attention of divers settlers from the Mesolithic period onwards. Except for the Morte Slates in the southeast corner, Lundy is formed entirely of granite. The west coast is exposed and fearsome in its grandeur, but the east is softened by combes and varied vegetation. The northern quarter affords only moorland grazing for deer and goats; south of this, however, there is pasture which supports several hundred sheep, ponies, and cattle. Two hundred and eighty acres are enclosed, and a few acres are under cultivation near the settlement in the southern quarter. Only about 20 people, including the crews of the two lighthouses, live permanently on the island. The landing beach in the southeast corner is used by many excursionists during the summer and by Lundy's own motor-vessel which sails regularly from Bideford.

The coastal areas of north Devon may be divided into three sections— the hog-backed cliffs, small bays and coves of the north coast proper, the alternating headlands and beaches from Morte Point to Saunton Sands, and the dune and pebble tracts bisected by the double estuary of the Taw and the Torridge (Fig. 74). In the north the two principal settlements are in some ways contrasted. Combe Martin is a linear village in the Umber valley which, aligned SE–NW, is well sheltered, and contains easily worked soils derived from the slates, shales, and limestone in the Ilfracombe Beds of the Middle Devonian. Strawberries, for long an important crop here, are still grown on about 23 acres of the small holdings, but the emphasis in horticulture has shifted from a marked specialization towards general market-gardening for the north Devon towns. Of the distant markets for horticultural crops—South Wales, the Midlands, and the North of England —the last two provide outlets for the winter anemones. In recent years horticulture has declined in area and intensity, and Combe Martin is becoming more dependent on the holiday trade and the retired residential element.

Ilfracombe's harbour lies in a well-sheltered cove, from which the core of the town extends east–west for about half a mile (Plate 22). During the growth of the resort in Victorian and Edwardian times much of the housing spread both contourwise and up the steep surrounding slopes. With its attractive scenery, several beaches, and pleasure grounds, Ilfracombe is very popular as a holiday centre and for excursions by sea from Bristol and South Wales; but as the town has so far acquired little industry, its employment is ill balanced. Manufactures of fancy leather goods and polyurethane products were established in 1963, however, and since 1966 a Board of Trade advance factory has been occupied by a concern which makes electronic equipment. Accommodation is now being built for a firm which expects to employ 150 people in the production of fabric used in zip-fastener webbing.

Two miles west of the coastal junction of the Ilfracombe Beds and the

Morte Slates at Lee, the cliffs trend south from Bull Point. Between
Mortehoe and Baggy Point, 4 miles to the south, is the resort of Woolacombe, whose long main beach is backed by a narrow tract of dunes at the
foot of the sombre hills on the Pickwell Down Sandstones. The thin belt
of the sandstones and shales of the Baggy and Marwood Beds passes in
Croyde Bay to the wider Pilton series—blue-grey slates with bands of lime-

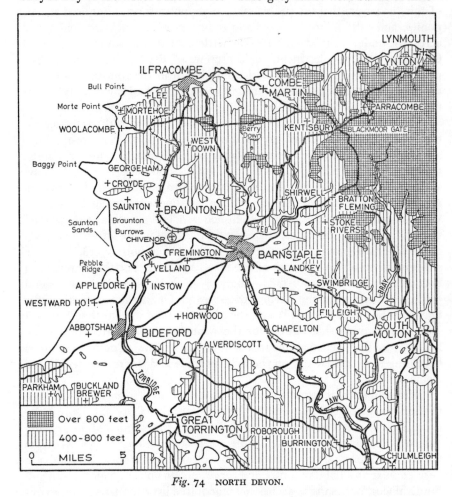

Fig. 74 NORTH DEVON.

stone and sandstone—which extends eastwards through Barnstaple. South
of a line from the Taw estuary to the vicinity of South Molton a chain of
ridges running from west to east announces the presence of the Culm
Measures.

From Saunton Down southwards a 3-mile stretch of dunes overlooks a
wide sandy beach. Behind the dunes (Braunton Burrows) lies a large
triangular tract of alluvium, the southern part of which is highly valued as

fattening pasture. Laid out on the deep, friable loam of the northern part is Braunton Great Field, which still displays features of strip cultivation. Flowers—chiefly narcissi, irises, and anemones—and glasshouse tomatoes are grown to the east of the Burrows. The large village of Braunton has several industries, including the winning of sand and gravel, the making of concrete products and portable buildings, and the manufacture of absorbent

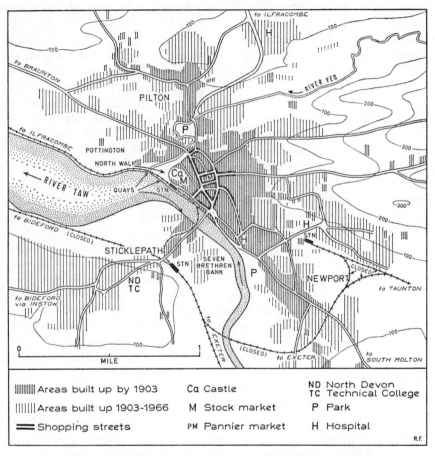

Fig. 75 BARNSTAPLE: SITE, SITUATION, AND MODERN GROWTH.

cotton wool and consumer products based on cotton wool. The factory for the last-named industry was built in 1962 and gives employment to about 100 people. At nearby Chivenor the manufacture of doors, panelling, joinery, and furniture fittings was established in 1964. A large tract of the right-bank estuarine flats of the Taw is occupied by a Royal Air Force station.

The situation of Barnstaple at the head of the estuary commands a busy road and rail crossing of the river (Fig. 75). Because of the large amount of road traffic the thirteenth-century bridge was widened in 1964 without, however, altering its sixteen-arched structure. Barnstaple is a major shopping, service, and supply centre for north Devon; and it has a large pannier market and a weekly stock market. A degree of urban renewal has recently been achieved, and the construction is in progress of a new regional hospital and a modern civic centre, the latter at North Walk. Barnstaple's status as a regional centre is enhanced by the importance of its local administrative functions and the presence of the North Devon Technical College. Its maritime trade has suffered because of the silting of the Taw, but since 1955 activity has somewhat revived with the dredging of sand and gravel, of which about 80,000 tons per annum are discharged at the quays.

Three of the old-established industries at Barnstaple are the making of leather and fabric gloves, bobbin net and warp knitted products (in which over 100 persons are engaged), and pottery, for which the clay is dug at Fremington. Another is represented by a firm which makes doors, and furniture for ships, laboratories, libraries, and offices, and has a staff of about 300. Other industrial occupations include the manufacture of foundation garments, the timber trade, concrete making, contracting, and engineering. A factory on the road to Fremington employs 170 persons in the production of high-pressure valves and couplings; and an industrial estate at Braunton Road has a bakery and factories making food machines, shoes, and packaging machinery. The employment figures for these industries are within the range of 150 to 300 each. In 1965 work started on the development for industrial use of the Seven Brethren site on the south bank of the Taw, to which the foundry, formerly at Newport, has now been moved; 100 men are engaged here in producing castings for the building and engineering trades. The most recent addition to the industries on this site is the manufacture of sewn and welded rubber goods. Another industrial estate, covering 100 acres at Pottington, is being developed by the Devon County Council.

Fremington Quay, situated about halfway to the confluence of the estuaries of the Taw and the Torridge, is a discharging point for domestic coal from Goole—approximately 5,000 tons per annum—and an outlet for ball clay from the Petrockstow district, at the rate of about 12,000 tons per annum. A little farther west is the Central Electricity Generating Board's East Yelland station, which is fed by shipments of coal from South Wales and Scotland. Oil tankers supply a nearby depot which serves much of north Devon and north Cornwall. There is a military camp at Fremington and an Amphibious Experimental Establishment at Instow. The small resort of Instow has a sandy beach and is a centre for sailing; but Appledore, situated on the left bank of the Torridge estuary-mouth, has several industries, including the making of feedingstuffs, gloves, and concrete roofing-tiles (using sand extracted from the estuarine foreshore), and boat building. The harbour possesses two dry docks, and shipbuilding employs about 500 men in the construction of tugs, trawlers, small tankers, barges, and sand-suction dredgers of up to 1,100 tons. Salmon fishing is still important, and of the 36 boats used for this purpose on the two estuaries, 22 are at Appledore.

By means of its fifteenth-century bridge the estuary-head town of Bideford spans the Torridge (Plate 23). Most of the settlement is on the western side, but the other part known as East-the-Water is growing rapidly. Bideford has a pannier market, and a weekly stock market is held in new premises opened at Bank End in 1960. Although the town is smaller than Barnstaple (populations 13,000 and 20,200 respectively)[1], its import trade is larger and more varied, with upwards of 200 ships discharging cargoes during the year. These vessels are generally of the order of 150 to 600 tons. The principal coastwise shipments comprise sand and gravel (52,000 tons per annum), coal (16,000 tons per annum), and fertilizers, and the cargoes of foreign origin are timber from Scandinavia and oystershells from Denmark. Fishing is less important than the building and repairing of small vessels which range from launches, cutters, and fishing boats to ferries and minesweepers.

The largest of the glove-making firms at Bideford also owns the factory at Appledore and one of those at Great Torrington, and employs altogether 325 people. An interesting old industry is the production of 'mineral black', which is now used for colouring cement. Other industries include saw milling, contracting, agricultural engineering, and concrete making. There are also factories which make toys (over 100 persons are employed here), children's clothing, women's dresses, laminated wood, and paints. In the establishment of new works in recent years there has, however, been a marked emphasis on engineering. One firm is engaged in capstan repetition work and the making of precision-engineering parts; another does special-purpose machine building, tool-making and reconditioning, and manu-factures precision components and assemblies. A new factory is being provided for a firm, at present at Appledore, which makes electrical terminals.

To the south of the joint outlet of the two estuaries the sandy beach of Westward Ho! is backed by a pebble ridge which extends NNE–SSW for more than two miles and screens a series of sandhills and flats known as Northam Burrows. The ridge has suffered from erosion caused by high seas whipped by westerly gales, but various remedial measures are now being taken. The name of Westward Ho! was inspired by Charles Kingsley's novel bearing that title (1855), and the site has since been variously developed as a resort.

By virtue of its position, communications, and outlook, the area bounded approximately by Saunton, Swimbridge, Great Torrington, and Parkham may be regarded as the core of north Devon. Much of the land lies well

---

[1] These are the populations of the boroughs and their adjacent, continuous built-up areas.

below the average height both of the hill country to the north and of the surface of the Culm Measures of mid and west Devon, and is comparatively fertile and also well drained, except where it is subject to valley-floor flooding. The coastal tract provides a measure of shelter, and rainfall in the low-lying districts is less than in the rest of north Devon. Where the Taw valley is of appreciable width, many fields are used for the summer pasturing of sheep and cattle and for cereal and fodder crops. The floor of the Torridge is much narrower, but around and to the west of the river dairying is prominent on numerous medium-sized farms. Although the rearing and fattening of sheep and cattle are important in the area generally, there is much greater emphasis on dairying. Ayrshire and Channel Island breeds are occasionally found, but Friesian cattle are most commonly used, on holdings which range from a few acres up to such large units as a 365-acre mixed farm at Lower Yelland on the Taw estuary. Over the whole area the arable is devoted mainly to barley, with various fodder crops now occupying second place. Apart from those in the towns, industries in the district are but small in total. Agricultural engineering is carried on at a few places, and there are saw mills at Chapelton and a gritstone quarry near Landkey. Roadstone is quarried near Muddiford, north of Barnstaple.

About 6 miles up the Torridge from Bideford, the town of Great Torrington (population 2,900) stands on a hill from which roads splay steeply down to bridging points on the floor of the valley. Torrington has a weekly market, and a large creamery which relies on the collection of 98,000 gallons of milk daily and employs 350 people in the production of butter, cream, baby food, and milk powder. The glove-making industry is represented by three firms. Torrington is gradually attracting new industries; recently a Swedish-glass factory has been started and a large new abattoir, meat storage plant, and factory have been opened.

Some of the steep valleysides in the country to the north of Barnstaple are in places thickly clad with woods, and patches of rough pasture occur on the slopes and ridges on the sandstones. The soils on the slates and shales generally support both arable and pasture, and corn growing, dairying, and stock rearing are all important. As this tract rises to Exmoor the acreages under cereals decrease and oats exceed barley; and the pastural farming grades through an increasing emphasis on sheep and Devon beef cattle to a predominance of sheep breeding. The Devon Closewool remains typical of the flocks in the area west of Exmoor, but breeds have been diversified, notably by the introduction of the Border-Leicester type into north Devon in the 1940s and by crossing it with the Exmoor Horn and the Devon Closewool. As also from Exmoor itself, great numbers of young ewes are 'sold downhill' for the production of fat lambs.

South Molton (population 3,000) has a weekly market in premises which have recently been enlarged, and holds many auctions including a fair in August when as many as 16,000 sheep may be on offer. At Hacche Mill,

1 mile north of the town, is a firm which makes heating and electrical components; and other occupations in or near South Molton include agricultural engineering, cider making, and saw milling. Accommodation is to be built in the town for a Watchet (Somerset) firm for the purpose of sorting and packing high-quality papers used for sterilized packaging in hospitals. In the transitional zone between Exmoor and mid Devon, drainage on the Devonian rocks is generally better than that on the Culm Measures, so that there is fairly good permanent pasture. The Exmoor Horn and the Devon Closewool are the predominant breeds of sheep, and many farms have the Devon 'red rubies' and cross-bred beef cattle, although dairying has markedly increased during the last twenty-five years. Arable is found mainly in the wider of the valleys and on south-facing slopes which warm up and dry out quickly in spring.

The Culm Measures Country

Carboniferous rocks known as the Culm Measures account for nearly 30 per cent of the surface of Southwest England. The Lower Measures make up a narrow zone on either flank—to the north and south—of the vast area occupied by the Middle and Upper Culm, whose main constituents are almost everywhere shales, interbedded with resistant sandstones and grits. The interfluves of the Culm country rise generally to levels between 400 and 600 feet, but in three areas the surface is much higher—a large tract in the northeast, ascending to nearly 1,000 feet; Broadbury, with hills ranging from 830 to 920 feet and rising above the average level of the plateau to the west of Okehampton; and part of the Hartland district in the west, lying between 700 and 730 feet (Fig. 76). Dissection in the Culm country is frequently expressed by deep, steep-sided valleys, many of which are oriented east–west and are tributary to the north-flowing Taw and Torridge. Most of the valley floors have been shunned by settlements, routeways, and cultivation. In the whole area only one valley—that of the middle Taw—carries a double thread of major routes.

The indurated sandstones and grits give shallow, stony soils, but on the shales a heavy subsoil makes much of the land cold and difficult to drain, especially on the flats and the slight and convex slopes that are typical of the plateau. In wet and mild conditions there may be an abundance of grass, but it is inadvisable to keep cattle out on this for long because of the danger of heavy poaching; and stock, especially sheep, may quickly develop fluke and other diseases. A lengthy drought, however, can produce a different set of problems for the farmer, particularly in the working of the arable, for the heavy soils may be wind-dried and sun-baked to a hardness approaching that of cement.

Farming difficulties in the Culm Measures country vary in intensity according to the depth of soil and subsoil, the amount of rainfall, the degree of exposure, and, emphatically, the effectiveness of drainage. Variations in

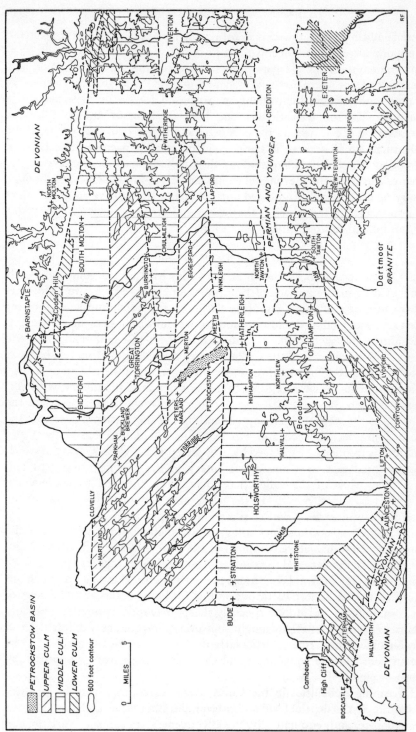

Fig. 76   THE CULM MEASURES COUNTRY: GEOLOGY.

these conditions not only account for purely local diversity, but also collectively provide an indicator for a geographical subdivision of the area. The other main criteria for such a division are position and the degree of remoteness, and the strength of the relationship of the several sectors of the Culm country with other subregions of Southwest England. Using these criteria, it is possible to recognize at least ten sub-areas (Fig. 77). To the north of Tiverton mixed farming and dairying give way to stock rearing in the upland transitional to Exmoor, which is linked with the Heartland of Devon by the Exe valley. East of a line from Tiverton to the western end of the Permian tongue and continued thence southeastwards to Dunsford, the Culm Measures group themselves intimately with the Heartland. On the margins of Dartmoor the Culm areas constitute an integral part of the foothills,

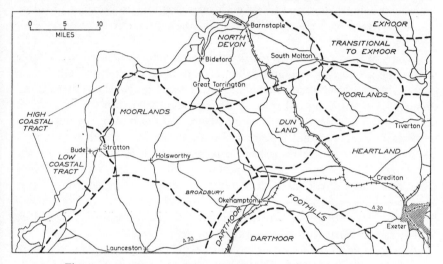

Fig. 77   THE CULM MEASURES COUNTRY: GEOGRAPHICAL DIVISIONS.

while north Devon, as defined earlier in this chapter, claims the comparatively low-lying, northwestern sector of the Culm country. The coastal margins (subdivided into the high tracts and the lower area around Bude) and the district tributary to Launceston are in various degrees also distinct from the remainder of the Culm country—a great expanse of mid and west Devon and north Cornwall. This falls into three sections, of which one— the 'dun' country of mid Devon—is distinguished not only by the better quality of its land but also by its position, for it is a zone of transition between north Devon and the Heartland subregion, and it separates the two areas of Culm 'moorlands'. These are the upland to the northwest of Tiverton and north of Witheridge, and the much larger area extending west and northwest from Broadbury to the coastal margins. Patches of moor, less frequently described as 'down', and varying considerably in extent, occur throughout these areas.

The vegetation of some of the moorlands has long been dominated by
Molinia, with *Eriophorum* too in the worst parts. During the inter-war
period much of the grassland was invaded by *Molinia* and *Juncus*, and many
formerly improved fields relapsed into moor or marsh. Although much land
was put under the plough during the Second World War, the policy of
improvement by ploughing, with its inevitable destruction of the grass-root
mat, has weakened in favour of the application of modern principles of
grassland management. Spraying, harrowing, rotavation, the intensive use of
fertilizers, the increased intensity of stocking, controlled-grazing techniques,
reseeding, and efficient drainage systems have resulted in an appreciable
reduction of rush infestation and an increased output from numerous
pastures. The Culm moorlands, however, still have a comparatively high
ratio of rough grazing; and tracts with relatively low proportions of tillage
and of stocking with sheep still exemplify the difficult areas of heavy soils
and poor drainage.

Many of the farms which display the better-quality grassland, or arable
above the average in area and value, are found in localities which have a
favourable combination of shelter and lower rainfall, a southerly aspect, and
moderate or gentle but adequately drained slopes. Within the area which
drains to the middle Taw are contained some of the best of the traditional
fattening pastures of mid Devon; and some of the land which is described
as 'top-quality dun' carries mixed farms on which both stock and corn are
important. The tongue of red Permian rocks which thrusts westwards from
Crediton peters out in the Culm country; along its margins, some farms
comprise both red and dun land. In the coastal areas, many farms on the
seaward slopes show the benefit of comparatively good natural drainage
and support a variety of tillage and stock.

In recent years the Culm country has experienced a comparatively high
rate of turnover in the ownership and tenancy of farms, in which immigrant
and sometimes temporary farmers have played a part. Family farms of
between 50 and 100 acres are still common, however, while units of up to
50 and from 100 to 200 acres are also numerous. Throughout the range
the emphasis is predominantly pastural (Plate 24), with various degrees of
specialization in dairy, store, and fat beasts and divers combinations of
milk, store cattle, and sheep production. All-grass units of up to 150 acres
are not uncommon. For dairying, the Friesian breed is now most widely
used, although Ayrshire and Channel Island herds are occasionally found,
and the South Devon cattle are comparatively strongly represented in the
Launceston district. Despite the stress on dairying, beef cattle are still
important throughout the Culm country and not infrequently are a major
enterprise on farms of medium and large size. Various breeds and mixtures
of sheep are used, but the Devon Closewool and Border-Leicester cross are
pre-eminent in the northern sectors of the area, while the Devon Longwool
is most commonly found in the west and southwest, and the Greyface in the

Dartmoor foothills. Wool grading and packing enterprises are situated at several places, including Launceston, Burrington, and North Tawton. In the Culm country generally, the principal crops are grass as hay and silage, cereals, kale, and fodder roots. On many farms in the wetter areas, oats and mixed corn were for long almost the only cereal crops, but even here the principal place has in recent years been assumed by barley, which in most of the parishes of the subregion now occupies well over half the area under tillage and in some more than 80 per cent.

The creamery at Lifton, which employs 260 people, is capable of dealing with a daily intake of 45,000 gallons of milk collected by lorry from farms in west Devon and east Cornwall. Butter, full cream, and separated milk powders are manufactured, and infant milk food is packed for the Government under the National Dried Milk Contract and for other concerns. The same firm has a factory at Lapford with 200 workers and a peak daily intake of 45,000 gallons of milk during the summer. Production is similar to that at Lifton, with the addition of full cream and skimmed condensed milk. At certain times of the year both creameries send milk to London and elsewhere for the liquid milk market, and occasionally they sell skimmed milk back to farmers for pig rearing or fattening.

Largely because of centralization and changes in methods of transport and disposal of stock, many of the formerly numerous town, village, and wayside markets and fairs have ceased in modern times. Hatherleigh's private-enterprise centre, however, has expanded rapidly and in 1966 had a throughput of over 210,000 animals. A large market for fatstock, and another for stores, dairy cattle, and pigs, are held on separate days each week, and there are many special and seasonal shows and fairs during the year. Holsworthy holds fatstock and store sales on successive days, and other important weekly markets are at Launceston, Hallworthy, and Week St Mary.

The small Petrockstow Basin, which extends NNW–SSE for about $4\frac{1}{2}$ miles with a width of approximately three-quarters of a mile, is floored by mid-Tertiary sediments—the 'Marland Beds'—composed of argillaceous sands, thin irregular veins of lignite, and deposits of ball clay. Although not so extensive in area and depth as those of the Bovey Basin, the clay deposits are sufficiently large to have been worked at several places over a long period. The principal pits, both open and underground, are now in the localities of Merton and Meeth, where altogether about 120 men are employed in the working of clay. Exports are very largely to the United States and Canada, and these are loaded at Fowey and Avonmouth. Clay for the European market is sent to Fremington Quay for shipment.

Forestry is a considerable occupation in certain areas of the Culm country, for example in the districts of Halwill and Eggesford. In addition to the working of timber under the Forestry Commission, there are saw mills on the former airfield at Winkleigh and at Buckland Filleigh. Timber products are made at several places within the area bounded by Okehampton, Holsworthy, and Torrington—portable bale elevators at Northlew, farm buildings at Stibb Cross, and farm equipment and portable buildings at Buckland Filleigh. Most of the other industrial activity in the Culm country arises from or is concerned with agricultural products and requirements, building and contracting, road haulage, and the maintenance of vehicles. Agricultural engineering enterprises are centred in several of the towns and villages. Launceston has an abattoir and meat-product factory, and industries producing packing-cases, portable buildings, and carpets. Animal feeding-stuffs are prepared at Lifton, and cider is made at Winkleigh. Hatherleigh has a new abattoir and a concrete-making plant which uses sand and gravel brought from Bideford. Basalt is quarried at Greystone near Launceston, and there are brickworks at Whitstone. At Holsworthy a factory to accommodate the manufacture of electronic equipment is projected, but the industry of making hospital clothing may be transferred to larger premises at Stratton. Industries recently introduced are the manufacture of plastic babywear at Lewannick near Launceston, and of injection-moulded plastic letters at Bude, where also a Board of Trade advance factory is to be built.

Throughout the Culm country the high degree of dispersal of population and the paucity of major centres has emphasized the remoteness of many settlements, and has made the modern provision of piped and cabled services an expensive and lengthy procedure. For many years isolation by distance, poor communications, lack of amenities, and the toil of farming difficult land have been factors in the decrease in the population of large districts. The most interesting town in the whole subregion is undoubtedly Launceston, whose hill site about 2 miles west of the Tamar and well above the main river and its several tributaries in the neighbourhood, gave a point of control over routes converging from the directions of Okehampton, Tavistock, and Holsworthy as well as those from Cornwall (Fig. 78). It was the only walled town in the county. The urban core contains the commercial and market centres and the magnificent church of St Mary Magdalene, which is unusual in the quantity and quality of the finely worked granite in its fabric.

To some, the interior of the Culm country may appear to be rather monotonous and unexciting; but whether or not this is so, those who wish for visual stimulation will not be disappointed by the Atlantic façade. Two miles north of Boscastle, beds of chert in the Lower Culm Measures stand solidly in Fire Beacon and High Cliff (731 feet). Near Cambeak, cliffs of intensely contorted slates mark the passage to the Middle Culm Measures; and northwards from here, extreme contortion, produced by the crumpling, faulting, and overthrusting of alternate beds of sandstone and shale, is displayed in some of the coastal stretches (Plate 25). At Bude a wide gap in the cliffs marks the outlet of the river Strat; but to the north, resistant buttress-reefs formed by the harder of the shale and sandstone beds add strength to the cliffs. The coastal margin is an elevated platform gashed by short, deeply incised valleys, many of which have been truncated, giving waterfalls to the shore. Bude's extensive beaches, together with the grassy commons between the shore and the town, are a major asset for the resort. Situated some two miles inland, the old agricultural and former market

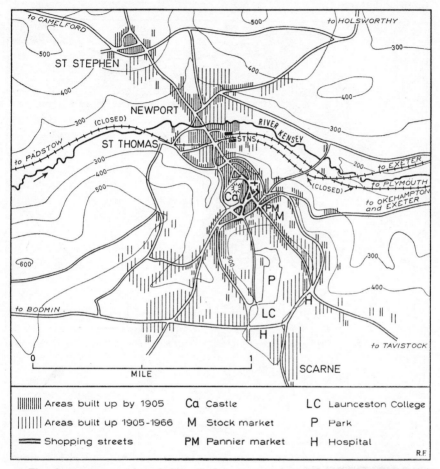

Fig. 78 LAUNCESTON (population 4,600): SITE, SITUATION, AND MODERN GROWTH.

centre of Stratton is in contrast but complementary to Bude (combined population 5,200), and the local administration is under a joint urban council.

Dartmoor

The boundaries of the Dartmoor National Park, as delineated in 1951, conform closely to those of a well-recognized geographical subregion covering 365 square miles (Fig. 79). About two-thirds of this area is made up of granite, and the rest, contained within a belt surrounding the granite and

varying in width, consists of small exposures of other igneous rocks as well
as more considerable tracts of metamorphics and sedimentaries. The inner-
most high moors—the real wilderness of Dartmoor (Plate 26)—are flanked
by extensive commons outwardly and irregularly fringed by the multiform
patterns of enclosures which have thrust up the valleys and on to the
moorland slopes.

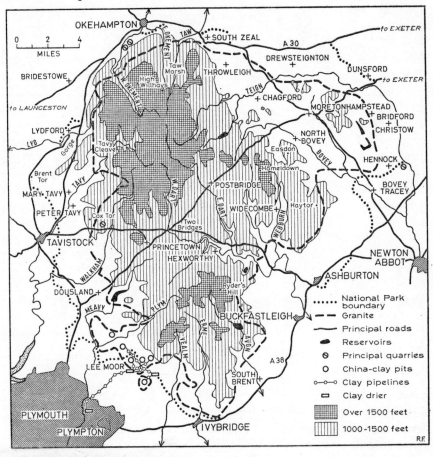

Fig. 79   DARTMOOR.

In the north, rounded hills sweep up to the greatest heights on Dartmoor
in Yes Tor and High Willhays (2,038 feet). The surface of the southern
mass is more gently rolling and not so impressive, Ryder's Hill (1,692 feet)
being the only marked eminence. In the eastern part of Dartmoor proper,
the Shapley–Hameldown whaleback is easily distinguished by virtue of its
height (1,736 feet at Hameldown Tor), length, and north–south alignment;
the East Webburn valley separates it from the southeastern group of tors.
Farther east the highest point on the marginal upland between the rivers

Bovey and Teign is only 1,170 feet; nevertheless even the small tors and rounded hills of this area are locally dominant over the late Tertiary planation surfaces which, at about 800 and 1,000 feet, are fairly extensive in the Moretonhampstead district.

The granite tors on Dartmoor are in various stages of degradation; they differ very considerably in profile, and range in height from a few inches to about 50 feet above the ground. Those which overlook the edges of the upland are particularly impressive, but others are almost as prominent, especially where they are skyline tors on narrow ridges or the tips of spurs (Plate 6). Occasionally a tor is found on the aureole of metamorphic rocks; these were hardened to a resistance to weathering greater than that of the unaltered rocks farther away from the granite, and so they are higher and display residual hill-top masses. Examples occur on the eastern margins of the Dartmoor subregion, as at Skat Tor near Christow, and on the western edge, as at Cox Tor. The prominent hill of Brent Tor (1,130 feet), some 4 miles north of Tavistock, is, however, a steep-sided thrust mass of lava 200 feet thick.

Rotted granite does not normally stand in steep slopes, so a section across many Dartmoor valleys is typically an open V; but steep-sided gorges such as Tavy Cleave do occur where streams have cut deep into wide, vertical joints in sound, hard granite. There are also valleys which are broad and almost flat-bottomed, and in some of these the boundaries of the valley floor appear to lie along constricted zones of weakness in closely jointed or perhaps fractured rock. Such a section is well represented in Taw Marsh. As the rivers come off the granite and delve into the metamorphic zone, their valleys close in rapidly and deepen into ravines or gorges. The river Lyd, with its cascade tributary 'The White Lady', and the Teign valley above Dunsford offer fine examples.

The term 'Dartmoor Forest', still applied to the inner area, recalls that in medieval times the land was preserved for the king's hunting and was subject to the royal forest laws; it does not imply that the hills were covered with trees. Nevertheless it is probable that there were woods in many of the Dartmoor valleys until they were cleared by medieval farmers and also by tinners for the smelting of ores. The lower middle reaches of several valleys, particularly the Teign and Dart, are still beautified by woods of birch, beech, and oak. During the eighteenth and nineteenth centuries many small shelter belts and copses were planted on Dartmoor farms, but in marked contrast to all these are the modern plantations, mainly of conifers, which have made a sombre intrusion into the moorland scene. The Forestry Commission now has approximately 4,700 acres of land, and altogether the privately managed areas of woodland amount to about 7,000 acres and give employment to 120 men.

For many centuries the grass and heather moors have supported an economy based mainly upon stock rearing. They naturally carry most stock during the summer, but considerable numbers of animals are kept on Dartmoor for eight or nine months in the year and some of the hardiest breeds are there all the year round. Scotch Blackface sheep and black Galloway cattle have become a familiar sight on the high pastures, though mixed breeds are also commonly seen. At lower levels the 'improved' Dartmoor sheep and the Devon cattle are strongly represented, but on various parts of the moor the range of breeds has been considerably extended, for example by the introduction of Cheviot and Kerry Hill sheep, and Hereford cross, Aberdeen-Angus, belted Galloway, and Welsh black cattle. Many of the ponies are rounded up annually and then sold off. Periodic disposals of stock take place at several sites, such as Chagford, on the moorland margins; and the need to reduce stocking before the arrival of winter is met by autumn sales of store stock, as of sheep at Dousland and Bridestowe.

The 1,600-acre farm belonging to the prison at Princetown is exceptional in size and function. A thousand acres have been reclaimed and enclosed; the remainder is moorland grazing. The main enterprise is the rearing of stock—principally sheep—but a small dairy herd is kept, and potatoes, kale, swedes, and cabbage are grown. Around farmsteads nestling in the moorland valleys a few fields are used for hay, kale, and roots. The outer fringe of the commons and the foothill country, where there are many more enclosed fields, supports a more intensive stock farming, with numerous Dartmoor sheep and beef-type cattle; and many farms possess grazing rights on the moor. Dairying and the rearing of dairy replacements are locally important, and in these enterprises the South Devon, Channel Island, Friesian, and Ayrshire breeds are well represented. There is also a certain amount of arable, especially in the comparatively dry eastern and southeastern areas. Within the district bounded approximately by Throwleigh, Dunsford, and Bovey Tracey, the occurrence of easily worked, free-draining soils has favoured a marked specialization in main-crop potatoes.

Of the areas of Dartmoor appropriated for military training (amounting to 33,420 acres) the largest includes most of the high northwestern quarter. On the southern edge of that district the grim-looking village of Princetown is dependent on the existence of the convict prison. Since 1891 large reservoir systems have been constructed on Dartmoor in order to meet the increased demand for water in Plymouth, south Devon, and the Torbay towns. The North Devon Water Board extracts water from Taw Marsh, and there has been a proposal to make a reservoir in the West Okement valley. The Central Electricity Generating Board has a small hydro-electric station at Mary Tavy.

In the southwest of Dartmoor are large quantities of kaolin, which are being worked within a tract lying between about 700 and 1,000 feet. From Lee Moor, the main producer, the clay is sent by pipeline to be refined and

dried at Marsh Mills on the lower Plym. The Lee Moor pits and the processing plant together give employment to about 800 men. Almost three-
quarters of the output goes overseas—clay destined for the United States
market is sent by rail to the port of Fowey, and consignments for Europe
are dispatched by road to Plymouth and Par for shipment. The other chief
sales are to the British paper and pottery industries. In the Torycombe
valley near the clay workings a new plant will produce about 26,000,000
calcium-silicate bricks per annum. Shaugh Lake pit yields pottery clays and
is linked by pipeline to drying kilns at an associated plant at Heddon; these
two workings employ about 100 men. The bulk of the clay is sent to the
Potteries by road. A smaller concern at Brisworthy also produces pottery clay.

Since the early nineteenth century granite has been quarried at various
times at Haytor, Foggintor near Princetown, Blackingstone near Moretonhampstead, and Merrivale, 4 miles west of Two Bridges. The firm which
owns the last-named quarry uses it for the working of all their imported
granite, in addition to that produced on the spot. Highly polished cladding-
slabs are the principal product. At Meldon, on the northwestern tip of
Dartmoor, are large quarries where most of the stone extracted has been
dolerite. About 130 men are employed in the British Rail quarries, five-
sixths of whose production (367,000 tons per annum) is used for track
ballast. At another quarry at Meldon, hornfels is produced and concrete is
made. Quarrying at Crockham in the lower Teign valley yields about
100,000 tons of basalt and 60,000 tons of top rock per annum, and provides
material for a nearby concrete works and for road metal. All together, 135
men are employed in this enterprise. A factory at Dunsford produces edge
tools and has a considerable export trade. At Moretonhampstead there are
saw mills, and sectional buildings are made. Okehampton (population
3,800) has a light-engineering concern which makes electrically operated
check weighers, the milling of grain for animal feedingstuffs, saw mills,
and factories making gowns, mattresses, and mineral waters.

Villages are rare on Dartmoor itself, and for centuries the scattered
farmsteads and hamlets were linked with the peripheral churches and
villages or towns by lanes and moorland tracks. During the late eighteenth
century the first real roads were made, including that from Chagford and
Moretonhampstead via Postbridge to Tavistock. The easier accessibility of
Dartmoor in modern times has led to a considerable catering and accommodation trade in the towns, villages, farms, and cottages. Hotels and inns
are found not only in the route centres around Dartmoor, but also at
several points on the moor itself, for example near Haytor and North
Bovey and at Two Bridges. Princetown caters for numerous tourists and
day trippers during the summer. The growth of the holiday and tourist
traffic, together with an increasing public interest in the scenic grandeur
and the antiquities of Dartmoor, poses problems for those who administer
the National Park, as does also any proposal for development in the form of

afforestation, new waterworks, and rural electrification. The primary purpose of the National Park Committee is 'to preserve the natural beauty of the district and give opportunities for open-air recreation', and a balance must somehow be maintained between three main interests—the protection of the landscape, natural and man-made, and of the remoteness and sense of solitude which are inherent in the character of much of Dartmoor; the livelihood of the people in the region; and the demands for more recreation, greater accessibility and exploitation in this age of crowded towns, wider travel facilities, and public and commercial development.

CHAPTER 12

South Devon: Plymouth: Southwest Devon – Southeast Cornwall

South Devon

THE country bounded by the lower courses of the rivers Dart and Yealm rises from the coast to the Dartmoor foothills in a series of wide steps; but these former platforms are much dissected, and their edges have been rounded off by the development of numerous valleys. All the principal rivers—the Dart, Avon, Erme, and Yealm—rise on Dartmoor, and are deeply incised across the structural grain of south Devon.

Compared with their great extent in the northern half of the county, the Carboniferous rocks are poorly represented. They are at their widest in a 10-mile tract lying NE–SW between the river Bovey and Buckfast, but this belongs to the Dartmoor foothills rather than to south Devon. It quickly passes southwards to the Upper Devonian, but on the extreme southern edge of Dartmoor the granite is directly flanked by an east–west belt of the Middle Devonian, a series of shaly slates with interposed limestones and volcanic rocks. To the south, much of the subregion is made up of the Meadfoot Beds; the Staddon Grits are thin, but they stand out here and there as resistant ridges and are identified in the local land-use by the presence of patches of rough pasture. An anticlinal formation accounts for the repetition of the Meadfoot and Staddon Beds to the south of an inter-vening broad, but much dissected, tract of the Dartmouth Beds which extends east–west from Dartmouth to beyond Newton Ferrers. The extreme southern bastion of Devon against the sea consists, however, of a mass of ancient schists in the area between Start Point and Bolt Tail.

The east–west ribbed morphology of the subregion, the rejuvenation of the lower courses of the rivers, the marine transgression which produced the rias and resulted in much deposition, and the uneven dissection of both coastal and inland areas have all had profound effects on the pattern of communications (Fig. 80). On the northern flank of the subregion, main routes conform to the morphological mould. In the south, the only coastal road runs along the sand and shingle bar at Slapton. For the rest, roads keep inland and well above the estuaries where, as in south Cornwall, the width of the rivers and the depth at which the rock channels lie have inhibited the provision of bridges.

Presenting a magnificent sequence of headlands, cliffs, estuaries, and bays, the whole of the coastal area from Brixham to Plymouth Sound has been designated a tract of outstanding natural beauty; also included are all the estuaries and the lower valleys of the Dart and the Avon, making up a

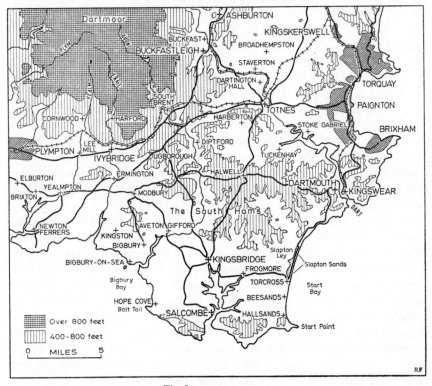

Fig. 80 SOUTH DEVON.

total area of 128 square miles. The most remarkable feature of the discordant coast of Start Bay is Slapton Ley, a lagoon which was formed by the damming of three small streams by a shingle beach in which Chalk flints predominate. Along the southward extension of the shingle bank there is much evidence of erosion by both man and the sea, especially near the three old fishing settlements of Torcross, Beesands, and Hallsands. The removal of 650,000 tons of shingle for use in the Keyham extensions to Devonport Dockyard in the period 1897–1902 led to the disappearance of Hallsands beach, and as a result of a great storm in 1917 most of the 25 houses in the village were destroyed by the sea. In 1923 the construction of twelve cottages as part replacement was started at North Hallsands, and recently these have been modernized. Beesands too shows the effects of erosion, particularly in the gradual effacement of the low cliff in front of the settlement. The opportunities offered by the wealth of coastal features in this part of south Devon, by the varied landforms and ecological habitats in the area, and by the diversity of settlement patterns both on the coast and inland, favour the work of the Slapton Ley Field Studies Centre, which is situated within a 400-acre Nature Reserve.

'The South Hams' is the name traditionally applied to the country lying between the lower Dart and the Erme; it signifies 'the land of enclosed pastures' south of Dartmoor. Although the soils vary considerably, in general those on the slates, limestones, and volcanics are warm, well-drained, light to medium reddish loams; and on the schistose belt in the extreme south the soils are better than is usually the case on such rocks. The dissection of the subregion by many valleys helps to diversify the patterns of land use, the steep valleysides being traditionally left in permanent pasture or flecked with woods. Here and there considerable tracts of the valley floors have been reclaimed into rich meadows. The arable lies mainly on the rounded slopes (Plate 27), but with the use of modern machinery cultivation has extended down the steeper gradients. On the windswept levels the landscape is almost treeless, but over the whole subregion there is a closely woven mesh of hedgebanked enclosures which are associated with small or medium-sized farms. The most typical holdings are mixed farms within the range of 50 to 150 acres, although there are numerous smaller units. Few farms exceed 300 acres.

As the climate is mild and much of the land is of moderate height and favourable aspect and is well-drained, there is a high proportion of fairly good pasture. Throughout the area great emphasis is put on dairying, although stock rearing and fattening still play an important role. The South Devon cattle, sometimes described as a triple-purpose breed—for milk, butterfat, and beef—are maintained on many farms, but Friesian herds are now most numerous, and considerable numbers of Channel Island cattle are also kept. Totnes is the main centre in south Devon for the collection, distribution, and dispatch of milk. About 250 people are employed by its creamery, which is served by some 1,300 farms. The peak intake is of 65,000 gallons per day in May, and there is a large output of clotted cream. Employment is given to 400 persons by the bacon factory at Totnes, which is supplied not only from south Devon but also from east Cornwall, whence comes 40 per cent of the throughput of pigs. Numerous farms in south Devon have pigs, and sheep are kept even more generally. South Devons predominate, although the Dartmoor and Longwool breeds are also found. In most parishes tillage occupies between one-quarter and one-third of the total acreage under crops and grass. Roots for winter stock-feed, a little wheat, and some oats are grown, but in recent years barley, traditionally

s.e.—9*

an important crop in the South Hams, has taken up to as much as one-half to two-thirds of the tillage. In certain sheltered districts, especially where sea influences penetrate along the estuaries, there is a small-scale specialization in the growing of fruit or flowers. Among the few tracts still under orchards of commercial value, are areas tributary to the Dart immediately above and below Totnes. In several localities appreciable quantities of broccoli are grown as a cash crop, and second-early potatoes find a local market in the holiday season. Glasshouse cultivation of flowers and vegetables is carried on commercially near several towns and villages.

Stock marketing in south Devon is now centred in less than half a dozen towns. The eastern area is partly served by Newton Abbot, but weekly markets also take place at Totnes, Kingsbridge, and Plympton. All these hold spring, summer, or autumn sales of store cattle and sheep, and there are end-of-the-year fatstock shows. Periodic sales of stock are held at Ashburton, and South Brent has a fair in September for the sale of sheep and horses.

Ashburton (population 2,900) is clustered along and astride the river Yeo, a small tributary of the Dart. It owed its earlier importance firstly to a central position in a tract of varied land use on the shales, limestones, and volcanic rocks, secondly to the rise of the woollen and mineral trades and industries on southern Dartmoor, and thirdly to its situation at the halfway stage on the main road between Exeter and Plymouth. By-passed since the 1930s, and with little industrial activity except the quarrying of roadstone and limestone in the vicinity, the town is mainly a residential and local shopping centre. Near the confluence of the Yeo and the Dart stands Buckfast Abbey. The site, first chosen for a monastic settlement in the eleventh century, was acquired by French members of the Benedictine order in 1882, and the present church was built in the period 1907–32.

In the Buckfast–Buckfastleigh district there are basalt and limestone quarries, an industrial plating works, a wool-grading store, and woollen factories. At the Buckfast Lower Mills about 100 people are engaged in the manufacture of carpet yarn, and at Buckfastleigh a large woollen mill employs about 140 persons and exports much of its output of cloth. Nearby, another factory worked by the same firm carries on woolcombing and fell-mongering, and specializes in rugs and dressed sheepskins. Staverton— about 4 miles down the Dart valley—has cider making and is the head-quarters of a large firm of building and engineering contractors whose joinery works here give employment to 170 people. Dartington Hall is a centre for progressive education and the arts, and its estate comprises farms, woodland, saw mills, and a factory for the making of tweeds.

The site of the old part of Totnes stands on a hill of igneous rock above the right bank of the Dart, and commands the estuary-head bridging point (Fig. 81). As the tidal reach of the river extends up to Totnes, the quays are accessible to sea-going vessels which bring in timber, principally from

Finland, Sweden, and Poland. About 22,000 tons are imported per annum, and the timber yard and saw mills provide employment for over 100 men. There are two wood preservation plants, and at Seymour Wharf is a large manufacture of roof trusses and laminated beams and arches. Other industries at or near Totnes include the making of confectionery and smoked foods, boat building, and agricultural engineering.

Roads linking Totnes with the coastal settlements and the estuarine towns avoid the main river valleys. Dartmouth is approached by a route across a plateau, and the other principal road serving it keeps to the shore along Slapton Sands before striking inland to Kingsbridge. For contacts

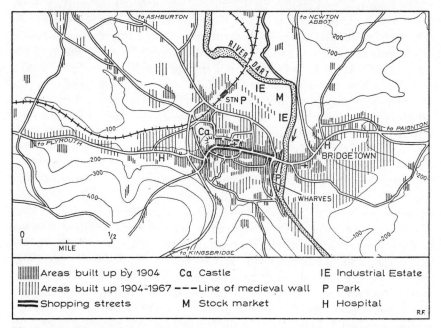

Fig. 81   TOTNES (population 5,600): SITE, SITUATION, AND MODERN GROWTH. Bridgetown was incorporated in the borough in 1835.

with the Torbay towns and for through routes to the east it is greatly dependent on the ferries to the main road and railhead at Kingswear. Some of the significant phases in Dartmouth's history are recalled by the twin Tudor castles guarding the cliff-flanked entrance to the Dart, the wealth which accrued from commerce in the seventeenth and eighteenth centuries (expressed in such buildings as the arcade of the Butterwalk) and—as elsewhere in the coastal tract of the South Hams—memories of the preparations by the United States forces for the Normandy landings in 1944. Formerly anchored in the deep, almost land-locked harbour was the Royal Navy's training establishment, H.M.S. *Britannia*; but in 1905 the ship was replaced by the new-built College. This is a prominent feature high above the right bank of the estuary and distinct from the modern spread of the town, which has had to contend with steep slopes up to about 400 feet above sea-level (Plate 18). Maritime activity in the Dartmouth area is now principally concerned with yachting, and there is a marina and a boatel. The Noss Works employ about 150 people in marine and general engineering and the building of luxury yachts. At Dartmouth there are potteries, and a new industrial estate is being developed at Townstal, where engineering has recently been established.

Fishing along the coast of south Devon is of only minor account. Crab and lobster catching is carried on from a few settlements, such as Hope Cove, Beesands, and Hallsands. To the east of the outlet of the river Avon are the separate estuarine towns of Kingsbridge and Salcombe (Plate 28). The former, situated at a nodal point at the head of a branching ria system, is an agricultural centre and a tourist and shopping focus for much of the South Hams. It has little industry, but engineering, the weaving of tweeds, and the making of fireplaces are carried on. There are boat-building yards at Frogmore Creek (three miles east of Kingsbridge) and also at Salcombe, which is a holiday and residential town, and a sailing centre. Farther west a stretch of the coast has been developed for holiday purposes at Bigbury-on-Sea and Challaborough; and Newton Ferrers, along the estuary of the Yealm, has a sailing school, boat building, and a marine biological laboratory.

Other than those already mentioned, industrial concerns in south Devon are but few and are widely dispersed. Basalt is quarried at East Allington (3 miles northeast of Kingsbridge), limestone at Brixton, and both near Yealmpton. At Steer Point near Brixton a large brick-making plant has recently been reconstructed on the most modern lines. The Ivybridge paper mill employs about 200 people in the manufacture of fine-quality papers on two machines and produces 90 tons per week; but the works at Tuckenhay now make only rag pulps for other paper mills, at the rate of 40 tons per week. South Brent and Yealmbridge have furniture factories, and feeding-stuffs are milled at Ermington. In the localities of Ivybridge and Lee Mill especially, several firms are concerned with the assembling and distribution of agricultural machinery. Lee Mill also has a joinery works.

The City of Plymouth

A much-dissected series of limestones and slates provides most of the terrain on which the city of Plymouth is built. Middle Devonian limestones make up the southern part of the block of land—roughly 4 miles square—which lies between the estuaries of the Plym and the Tamar and within the pre-1967 boundary of the city. Upper Devonian slates and grits occupy most of the remainder, but midway across the square there is a band of igneous rocks. All these series are generally aligned east–west, and conforming to this structural framework is a succession of steep-sided valleys separated by well-defined ridges which here and there are scored by short streams. The site occupied by the small fishing and agricultural settlement which formed the nucleus of medieval Plymouth lay near the outlet of one such stream cut into the contact zone between the limestones and slates. This settlement huddled on the sheltered northwestern side of Sutton Pool, an inlet to the north of the point where the Cattewater—as the mouth of the Plym estuary is known—begins to open out to Plymouth Sound; and as the 'Old Town' of Plymouth took shape it still looked towards this harbour of Sutton (Fig. 57, p. 191, and Plate 29). At the head of the harbour, an area of about 50 acres centred upon the Barbican and bounded by The Hoe, Old Town Street, and Trielle Street, contains most of the surviving historic buildings, including a number from the sixteenth and seventeenth centuries. Within a larger area, formerly demarcated by the town wall and punctuated by Hoe Gate, Frankfort Gate, Old Town Gate, and Friary Gate, are the church of St Andrew and the Guildhall.

The whole of the marine frontage from the Plym estuary westwards to the right-bank tributaries of the lower Tamar and the settlements of Cremyll, Torpoint, and Saltash, bears the imprint of Plymouth's maritime history through peace and war. The seventeenth-century Citadel fortress commands the entrances to the Cattewater and Sutton Harbour. On and around the limestone plateau of Plymouth Hoe are the tercentenary Armada memorial, a statue of Sir Francis Drake, part of Smeaton's Eddystone lighthouse (rebuilt here in 1882–4), the Royal Naval war memorial (1924–54), and the Marine Biological Laboratory. The Hoe looks south to Drake's Island, Plymouth Sound, and the Breakwater, a great shelter 1 mile in length which was built between 1812 and 1840.

To the north of the Narrows—the outlet of the Tamar to Plymouth Sound—the estuarine waters are known as the Hamoaze, which is a superb anchorage used almost exclusively by naval craft. Extending for about 4 miles north–south, it has several inlets of tributary estuaries, notably the Lynher river, on the western side; but it is the left bank of the Hamoaze that carries the principal activities and structures of the great naval base. Noteworthy buildings in the Stonehouse district include Sir John Rennie's Royal William Victualling Yard (1826–35), the Royal Naval Hospital (1762 onwards), and the Royal Marine Barracks (from 1784, but mostly nineteenth century). Northwards, the Royal Naval Dockyard dominates the left bank of the estuary for a distance of 2½ miles and, with post-war extensions, now covers an area of 320 acres (Plate 31). It has twelve dry docks and a large building slip. In recent times large-scale work has included the modernization of H.M.S. *Eagle*, a task which took four years. At present the Dockyard is easily the leading employer in the Plymouth district, having on its pay rolls about one-fifth of the industrially insured population.

In addition to all the ship-building, repairing, and refitting that is carried out at the Dockyard, the Plymouth area has the several functions of a naval depot (H.M.S. *Drake*) and a supply and training base. The Group Headquarters of the Royal Marines is at Stonehouse, the Royal Naval Engineering College (H.M.S. *Thunderer*) at Manadon, and a training establishment (H.M.S. *Cambridge*) at Wembury. Since the Second World War the training units of H.M.S. *Fisgard* and *Raleigh* have occupied large sites to the west of Torpoint. Some of the finest views of the Hamoaze are obtained from crossing points from Plymouth into Cornwall. For many years two principal ferries—to Torpoint and Saltash—were used for the conveyance of passengers and road vehicles across the Tamar, and the rail link with Cornwall was achieved in 1859 with the completion of one of Brunel's most famous works, the Royal Albert Bridge. Adjacent to this is a high-level road bridge to Saltash, opened in 1961; but with the increase in traffic to and from Cornwall it is possible that this structure will soon have to be widened and that a sister bridge will eventually have to be provided. The Saltash ferry has been dispensed with, but the diesel-driven Torpoint ferries are still in use.

In 1914 the three towns of Plymouth, Stonehouse, and Devonport were merged into a single county borough, the status of a city was granted in 1928, and the first Lord Mayor took office in 1935. Although by this time 'the three towns' had become a continuously built-up aggregate, the centres of Plymouth and Devonport each retained a recognizable identity and a distinct character. Much of the fine and varied architecture of John Foulston —of the period 1811–40—was intact, and some of this has survived, notably at Devonport; but during the aerial bombardments of the Second World War, and especially those in 1941, the centres of both Plymouth and Devonport were largely destroyed. Reconstruction of the core of Plymouth began in 1947 with the foundation of two new axes—Royal Parade from east to west and Armada Way running north–south from near the main railway station to The Hoe. The latter is free from through vehicular traffic. With the restoration of the Guildhall and the fifteenth-century church of St Andrew, and the grouping of the new civic, business, and shopping blocks around the central streets, the reconstruction scheme has been largely completed (Fig. 82, Plates 29 and 30), with the result that the civic functions and loyalties of the whole city are markedly concentrated upon a single focus.

After the Second World War Plymouth had to face four other major tasks—restoring war-damaged property, providing new housing, solving traffic problems, and attracting industry. Much of the city's area in 1928 (5,719 acres) was already closely built up. It was obvious that the first major expansion would have to be northwards, and in 1938 the boundaries were extended in that general direction, increasing the area to 9,525 acres. The housing problems which existed at that time—including much overcrowding in certain wards—were greatly aggravated by the wartime devastation, and it was fortunate that large areas were available for future development. Underlining the part played by the Plymouth authorities in carrying out post-war housing programmes is the fact that one-third of the houses within the pre-1967 boundaries are council-owned.

The new neighbourhood units which were planned and created in the post-war years include Efford, Ham, Honicknowle, Southway, Whitleigh, and Ernesettle. These have been laid out as housing estates, interspersed with open spaces and rural reservations and, in some cases, groups of

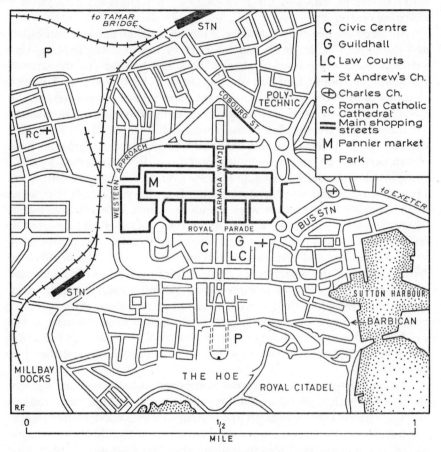

Fig. 82 PLYMOUTH: THE NEW CENTRAL AREA, 1967.

industrial sites. The Honicknowle units were intercalated in the long gap which down to the 'forties existed between the earlier settled districts of Crownhill on the east and Higher St Budeaux on the west. Housing development is continuing northwards and eastwards and has now encompassed the old villages of Tamerton Foliot and Egg Buckland. In overcoming the difficulties presented by the alternation of steep-sided ridges and deep valleys, the planners and developers have cause for satisfaction in the pattern of the housing units, their sunny aspects, and their attractive views (Plate 32).

As they contain an amalgam of people from various parts of 'the three towns' as well as a proportion of recent immigrants, the housing estates may have not only a fresh social cohesion but also a common allegiance to the new centre of Plymouth. Some of the inner areas have presented special problems in redevelopment for the purposes of housing and local services; at Devonport these have been partly solved by the building of a series of tower blocks of flats and the revitalization of Marlborough Street as a shopping centre.

Although the pre-1967 boundary of the city reached to Tamerton Foliot and Roborough in the north and the river Plym in the northeast, a considerable commuting element already lived well beyond. To the west of Plymouth, the borough of Saltash (population 8,300) as well as Torpoint (6,500) and Millbrook, are to some extent dormitories for city workers; and building activity in southeast Cornwall, especially at Saltash, has been much intensified since the opening of the Tamar road bridge. Of the dormitory districts on the Devonshire side of the city, Plympton and Plymstock have shown particularly rapid growth in recent years. Both are served by main roads into Plymouth (the new Laira Bridge over the Plym to Plymstock was opened in 1962) and are indeed no farther from the city centre than some of the housing estates which were already within the pre-1967 boundary. Plymouth's claim to annex a tract of southwest Devon was accepted at national government level in 1965 and confirmed in 1967, but only for those areas of Plympton and Plymstock which are already built up or are likely to be developed in the near future (Fig. 83). Not only does this acquisition add about 34,000 to Plymouth's population, raising it well towards 250,000, but also, by enfolding the left bank of the Plym estuary, it gives complete reality to the name of the city. Each of the principal settlements in the newly gained area has a shopping centre, but Plympton is in need of a new urban heart, and the city has now taken over the task of implementing this project.

As the largest urban unit in the Southwest and as a modern regional centre, Plymouth has developed and acquired numerous important functions and the 'service' employment groups contain well over one-half of the working population. Education plays a prominent part in the life of the city, and although there was keen disappointment that Plymouth was not included among the sites of the new universities created in the early 'sixties, its large College of Technology has recently been nominated as one of those to be granted Polytechnic status, and a nautical college is under construction. There are also colleges of art and housecraft, and an adventure training centre on Drake's Island. A teachers' training college— the Church of England College of St Mark and St John—is to move from Chelsea and will be re-established at Derriford. Plymouth is a major hospital centre too, and a new regional unit is to be built at Derriford. The historical and romantic appeal of the city, its maritime character, its programme of reconstruction, and its convenient situation in relation to south Devon, Dartmoor, and Cornwall, have all been factors in the growth of a tourist and holiday trade which will probably be much further developed. With the expansion of these various functions, as well as the acquisition of new industry and commerce, the increasing volume of traffic both within and on the approaches to the city has emphasized the need for relief or ring roads, including the provision of a major by-pass at Plympton. Plymouth is well served by several road-haulage organizations, and the replanning of rail traffic in the area includes the development of a new and extensive freight terminal at Friary. If a new airport is provided to serve the city—the long-used site at Roborough is small by modern standards and cannot be extended —it will probably be situated in south Devon and not within the city's boundaries. The provision of an airport in south Devon is at present, however, a contentious subject.

Down to the 'forties, Plymouth had a somewhat limited range of old-established industries including brewing, timber and metal working, tar distilling, and the manufacture of chemicals, foodstuffs, and clothing. The problems of unemployment and the drifting away of young people, together with the need for diversification in order to avoid over-dependence on work at the Naval Dockyard, led to campaigns to attract new industries; and the first phase, begun in 1946, resulted in the establishment of three large concerns. One of these—Tecalemit at Longbridge—now employs 2,300 people in the making of engineering products with special emphasis on lubrication and hydraulic equipment. At Ernesettle the Rank–Bush–Murphy factory gives employment to 1,600 persons in the assembling of television sets; and at Honicknowle the dress-making firm of Berkertex has a staff of nearly 1,000. A second, more intensive, phase began in 1955. In all, during the post-war period 27 companies have established factories which employ more than 10,000 workers. Before dealing further with the modern expansion on the factory estates of Plymouth, however, it is necessary to take into account developments both within the older areas of the city and in the newly acquired districts of Plympton and Plymstock (Fig. 84).

Plympton has two estates for industries and depots, at Newnham and Valley Road, and its industries now include boat building—which employs 120 people—engineering, metal working, motor-body building, and the manufacture of portable buildings. A Government training centre has been established for the redeployment of labour to new skills. The principal activities in the locality of Plymstock are limestone quarrying, the making of concrete, and a large cement works which, reconstructed in 1961, produces about 500,000 tons per annum and employs 180 persons. A new gasworks for the Plymouth area is being built at Breakwater Quarry.

There are about a dozen boat-building firms in the district from Plympton and the Cattewater to Cremyll. A factory in Alexandra Road employs 330 people in the manufacture of meat products. For many years

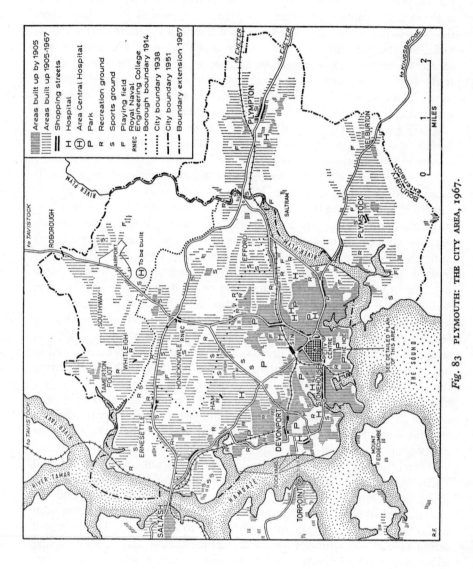

Fig. 83 PLYMOUTH: THE CITY AREA, 1967.

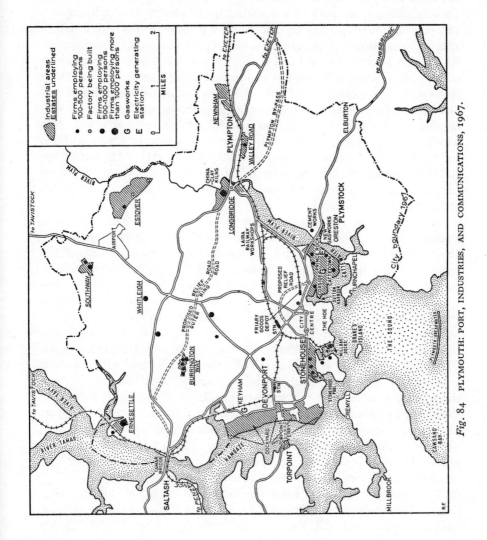

Fig. 84 PLYMOUTH: PORT, INDUSTRIES, AND COMMUNICATIONS, 1967.

Prince Rock has been the site of an electricity generating station, and in 1960 the second phase of the construction of a new power plant was completed. Engineering works include a firm which moved to a new factory at Prince Rock in 1963. Plymouth's pure soft-water supply was a factor in the establishment in 1911 of a manufacture of lubricants which employs 100 people. Cattedown has tar distilleries, a printing works with a staff of 180, and a manufacture of fertilizers which provides work for 140 people. At Coxside are the gasworks and a firm of constructional engineers which employs 200 persons. About the same number are engaged in a clothing factory. A milling concern at Millbay produces animal foods and flour and has a staff of 140; and in the locality of Stonehouse are breweries which employ 200 people, and two modern factories, established in 1960 and 1961, which produce dresses and foundation garments and have pay rolls of 300 and 140 respectively. Glove making at Stoke (Devonport) has 220 employees, and to the northeast a baby-food factory at Hartley, established in 1931, has 620. The building of vehicle bodies and the making of boxes are carried on at Richmond Walk near Stonehouse.

Resulting from the second phase of post-war industrial expansion, manufactures of bedding and machine tools—the latter now employing over 300 persons—were set up on the Ernesettle estate. Most of the factories at Burrington started work in the early 'sixties, and their employment figures are within the range of 100 to 300 each. The principal activities are the making of swimwear, quality instruments for use in educational establishments and industry, electronic measuring equipment and components, pneumatic and hydraulic equipment, and power capacitors, and light engineering which specializes in the production of signalling gear. Factories at Southway are concerned with the manufacture of thermostatic controls and office equipment; established here in 1961 and 1962 respectively, they now employ 750 and 450 people. A shoe-making factory at Whitleigh has a staff of 930. The last of the industrial estates, at Estover, has a large reserve area for future development; one factory already employs 280 persons in the manufacture of precision tubing, and of two others in process of construction, one will probably give employment to over 200 people in the making of precision gear-cutting tools.

Plymouth formerly had some significance as a port of call for ocean liners, which used to lie in Cawsand Bay or in the shelter of the Breakwater while passengers and mails were transferred to tenders based upon Millbay Docks. In the 'thirties there were about 500 liner calls per annum, but the post-war recovery in this traffic was only partial. In 1953 about 17,000 passengers landed from 157 liners, but this activity greatly diminished after 1961 with the cessation of calls by the French line which had been the principal visitor, and the last Millbay tender was withdrawn from service in 1963. More recently, however, a number of luxury-cruise liners have been calling at Plymouth. Fishing, though now of only minor importance, is still carried on by trawlers and inshore vessels which land their catches at Sutton Harbour for disposal at the Barbican wholesale fish market. The twelve trawlers that are permanently based upon Plymouth operate in the area between Start Point and the Lizard peninsula.

In 1963 the merchandise handled at the port of Plymouth amounted to nearly 1,475,000 tons, and in 1966 the total was over 1,630,000 tons. If the demand arose, this maritime trade could be greatly increased; but the hinterland offers comparatively little for export. In 1966 the principal shipments were of china clay from southwest Dartmoor (286,000 tons), stone (56,000 tons), and coke breeze (22,000 tons). Coastwise cargoes of clay are mainly destined for various British paper-mills and are taken to Kent, Lancashire, and Scotland. The chief overseas markets for clay are in countries in Western and Southern Europe. Shipments of stone go mostly to the London area.

The importance of Plymouth as a populous city and a major distributive centre is reflected in its import trade, which is larger and more varied than that of any other port in the Southwest; in 1966 incoming cargoes amounted to 1,242,000 tons. First place is taken by petroleum products (744,000 tons) which come from overseas as well as by coastwise shipping. Coal is still an important item (275,000 tons); most of it emanates from Northeast England and South Wales. Timber (50,000 tons) is chief among the cargoes landed for the building trade, and is brought mainly from Northern Europe and Canada. Gypsum for the Plymstock cement works is imported from Eire and France. Western Europe is the principal source of the imports of fertilizers, and there are also considerable shipments from Northeast England and Cheshire. Grain (62,000 tons) comes chiefly from the United States, Western Europe, and the U.S.S.R. Imports of vegetables include onions and cauliflowers from Brittany, which is also the source of large consignments of strawberries, chiefly in May.

Surveyed from east to west, the first group of wharves in the port of Plymouth is around the Cattewater. The Victoria Wharves, on the northwest side of this area, are visited weekly by large coastal vessels which bring in general cargoes, and they are the outlet for china clay which arrives in bagged form from the drying plant at Marsh Mills. Cattedown Wharves and part of the Cattewater nearby have several deep-water berths and normally take the largest vessels using the port—tankers of 15,000 tons deadweight. Petroleum products are discharged into depots and storage-tank terminals, and a new pipeline runs from the wharves to the electricity generating station at Prince Rock. The other imports here consist mainly of fertilizers and gypsum. Opposite Cattedown are Pomphlett Creek, where stone is shipped, and a timber-landing point at Oreston. A flying-boat base, which was of special importance during the Second World War, was formerly situated at Mount Batten, which marks the western end of the Cattewater.

At Sutton Harbour potatoes and horticultural produce are discharged at the Northeast Quay, and Baltic timber is off-loaded at Shephard's Wharf. Bayly's Wharf deals mainly with coal for the gasworks at Coxside and for distribution to local depots, and exports coke breeze and spent oxide. Millbay's trade consists principally of importing grain, timber, coal, fruit, and vegetables. Plymouth's main commercial yard for ship repairing, which employs about 150 men, is situated at Millbay, which is also noteworthy for a considerable development of berths and facilities for yachts; this reflects the established, and growing importance of Plymouth as a yachting centre. Around the shore from Millbay westwards, commercial traffic is quite small. A distribution depot for petroleum products is, however, being established at Stonehouse Pool. Further north the only non-naval cargoes are off-loaded at Tamar Wharf and consist of coal for the gasworks at Keyham.

Southwest Devon–Southeast Cornwall

Four miles southeast of Launceston the incision of the Tamar valley becomes more marked as the river traverses the Lower Culm Measures and cuts deeply into the Upper Devonian slates and the interposed igneous rocks. Wooded tracts enhance the beauty of the steep valleysides and the gentler slopes above, notably to the south of Dunterton and north and east of Gunnislake. From a point about 2 miles south of Tavistock to the fullest width of its valley near Bere Ferrers the Tavy too is sharply incised in a narrow, winding trench which is virtually devoid of settlement, and almost continuously wooded.

In the agriculture of southwest Devon generally, there is a fairly even balance between dairying, livestock, and mixed farming. There is a preponderance of Friesian and South Devon cattle, and most of the sheep are of the Devon Longwool, Dartmoor, and cross breeds. Pigs and poultry are kept on numerous holdings. Barley is the predominant crop, and accounts for almost all the acreage under cereals. Although units of between 50 and 150 acres form a substantial proportion of the total number of holdings, on the margins of Dartmoor smaller dairying enterprises as well as mixed farms of various sizes add to their grazings by means of common rights. Between Tavistock and Launceston a dissected plateau rises northwards to a narrow moor-clad ridge whose highest part reaches 966 feet; but the lower slopes at 300 to 500 feet have a deep soil overlying the lavas, and carry mixed and stock farms above the average in size. Some of the best permanent pasture in Devon is found within this tract, notably in the parishes of Lamerton and Milton Abbot.

After the Dissolution of the monasteries, the lands and buildings of Tavistock Abbey, which had been the largest and wealthiest in Southwest England, were granted to the Russells, ancestors of the Duke of Bedford, whose planning and building during the nineteenth century gave the centre of Tavistock much of the character which it still possesses (Plate 33). Today the town is important as a market, shopping, distributive, and route centre.

It has weekly pannier and stock markets, and especially noteworthy are the St John's Fair in September, the Goose Fair in October, and the West of England and Tavistock fatstock show in November. Although still small, the amount of industry in the district has recently been increased by the development of sites at Westbridge and Pixon Lane. In and near the town there are now firms engaged in agricultural and precision engineering, sheet-metal work, and the making of portable buildings, joinery, and confec-

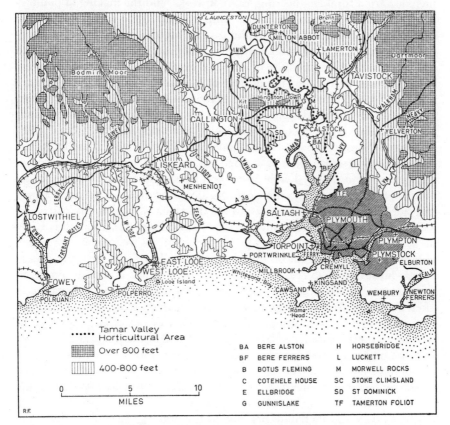

Fig. 85 SOUTHWEST DEVON—SOUTHEAST CORNWALL.

tionery. The principal products of the quarrying concerns are basalt, slate, rustic stone, garden paving, and concrete. A firm at Grenofen, southeast of Tavistock, is engaged in the fabrication of goods from plastic sheeting and polythene. Tavistock's population contains a considerable retired and residential element, as well as commuters who work in Plymouth.

South of Luckett the Tamar passes through a 4-mile tract within which there is much evidence of former mining; and attention has recently been given to the further exploration of the mineralized zone in and around the valley. It seems that the areas lying between Gunnislake and Kit Hill (Fig. 85) and possibly also on the Devonshire side of the Tamar offer the most likely fields for a redevelopment of mining in this district. The small town of Callington is situated on an interfluve southwest of the moorland area of Kit Hill (1,091 feet). Since the cessation of mining it has been mainly a local shopping and market centre, but its monthly stock market ceased in 1965 and only autumn sheep sales are now held. Industries at present active include agricultural engineering, cabinet works, and the making of poultry-house units and equipment (which employs about 100 men), and plastic components. Also carried on in the district are the quarrying of a close-grained granite on Hingston Down, the chief products being roadstone and concrete; and the manufacture of chip baskets at Calstock, plastic babywear at Gunnislake, and sectional buildings at Luckett. Animal feedingstuffs are milled at Stoke Climsland, and marine engineering is carried on at Calstock.

The district of specialized cultivation commonly known as 'The Tamar Valley' extends on both sides of the river, but interruptedly, from Horsebridge southwards to Saltash and Tamerton Foliot. Within these limits the really intensive cultivation is carried on in tracts which in some cases measure not more than 1 mile from west to east; and most of the acreage under special crops lies on the Cornish side. Over much of the area, aspect and slope are the factors that determine the extent to which any particular locality is suitable for horticulture (Fig. 86 and Plate 34). Rainfall is fairly high, averaging about 45 inches per annum, and its frequency is of prime importance for successful cropping on the shallow soils. Lengthy downpours, however, exacerbate the problem of erosion, especially on steep slopes, some of which are as much as 34 degrees; and soil reclamation is often necessary. Where the gradients are particularly steep the toil involved in working and redistributing the soil may now be out of all proportion in relation to the availability of labour and the yield of the plots, and in recent years a number of holdings which have become vacant on the most difficult slopes have not been taken up again and are reverting to scrub or woods.

Many holdings are favoured not only by the protection afforded by the hill masses to the north but also by the influence of the sea penetrating far up the estuary and its tributaries and by the drainage of cold air down the valleys and away southwards via the Hamoaze. Further, the southerly aspect and the steepness of many of the slopes ensure that the soils warm up very speedily under spring sunshine which averages $4\frac{1}{2}$ hours per day in March and 6 in April.

Neither of the two old-established tree fruit crops—apples and cherries —is of great importance today. Although the Land Utilisation Survey described the district in the 'thirties as 'The Tamar Valley Fruit Region', immediately before and after the Second World War early daffodils were considered the most important crop; and the balance between the several flower and fruit crops has changed again since then. Nevertheless it is probable that even now the area is best known for its major fruit, straw-berries, which usually appear on the market before the end of May. The chief sales are in London and towns in the Midlands, the North of England, and in Scotland. About 250 of the Tamar valley holdings have strawberries as their main crop, and in recent years the area planted has remained steady at about 300 acres. Only about 70 acres are now under other small fruit.

It is probable that, taken together, flower crops now represent the most valuable horticultural investment in the area, with approximately 350 acres

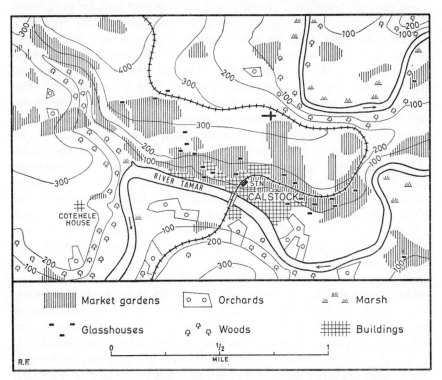

Fig. 86 MARKET GARDENS AT CALSTOCK IN THE 1960s. With acknowledgments to Callington Grammar School and The Second Land Use Survey of Britain.

in bulbs. Narcissi have long been regarded as the chief of the Tamar valley flowers; but as competition from other areas has grown and as prices have been almost static in recent years, the acreage has somewhat decreased. Much of the production, as also that of anemones, is directed to distant markets, especially the Midlands and the North of England. As with fruit, the principal forwarding points are Saltash, Calstock, Gunnislake, and Bere Alston. A considerable acreage is devoted to anemones, a crop which for numerous producers has had a stabilizing effect in that it provides work and income during the autumn, when otherwise they would have to find entirely different employment. Recently several growers have given an increasing

proportion of their land to irises. Although approximately 370 acres are
under vegetables, the Tamar valley is not a great commercial vegetable-
producing area. The physical conditions which favour its fruit- and flower-
growing industries do not give it an advantage for vegetable cultivation
over other horticultural districts where in any case the land is worked more
easily and is held in bigger units. Largely in response to the demand from
Plymouth, however, some growers regularly assign a proportion of their
land to peas, beans, lettuces, and cabbages.

In 1955 the number of growers taking part in horticultural production
in the Tamar valley area was nearly 1,000, comprising those who were
entirely concerned with the special crops, also numerous farmers who
allotted some land to horticulture, and a fairly large number of part-time
growers. In 1965 the number was 650, of whom about 400 were probably
wholly engaged in the cultivation typical of 'The Tamar Valley'. The
decrease is attributed partly to the amalgamation of holdings, partly to the
abandonment of difficult 'gardens' (as many of the plots are known), but
mainly to increasing economic pressures. Competition from overseas and
from forced and processed supplies is a major factor affecting the prices,
and especially the high early returns, which the growers must obtain in
order to do considerably more than offset the heavy expenses which are
necessarily involved in their form of husbandry. Efforts to maintain and
improve the production of their high-value crops are aided by the work
and advice of the Ellbridge Experimental Horticulture Station near Saltash.

Most of the holdings are worked by one man or family, but extra female
labour is employed for picking and packing. The majority of the units on
which the growers are concerned solely with horticulture are of 3 to 10 acres,
but some are even smaller. In general, outdoor holdings of less than 4 acres
do not now provide a living, and the men have some other form of work as
well. The only stock carried on the small holdings are, occasionally, pigs
and poultry. Of those farms which devote an appreciable proportion of their
land to horticultural crops, the largest are of 40 to 100 acres. Both within
and on the margins of the Tamar valley area, however, there are a number
of farms of much larger acreage, and these are concerned with the types of
enterprise found over much of southwest Devon and southeast Cornwall—
dairying, mixed farming, and the fattening of stock.

With the exceptions of the granite mass of Kit Hill–Hingston Down, a
local outcrop of the Culm Measures to the south of Callington, and a discontinuous series of igneous rocks within a tract running WNW–ESE from
Menheniot to the Tamar, almost the whole of southeast Cornwall consists
of Devonian slates, shales, and grits. In the area east of a line from Liskeard
to Portwrinkle the Upper Devonian slates predominate in the northern
two-thirds and the Lower Devonian series in the south. The area west of
this line is also subdivided geologically, with slates of the Middle Devonian
taking up the northern part, and grits and slates of the Lower Devonian

occupying the remainder. Much of southeast Cornwall is a dissected table-land averaging 400 to 500 feet in height and segmented by the southeast-flowing tributaries of the Tamar (the rivers Lynher and Tiddy), the south running rivers Seaton and Looe, and the Fowey, first in its west-ward course after it leaves Bodmin Moor and then in its southward section from Glynn near Bodmin. Most of the valleys are deeply incised and steep-sided, but those in the Upper Devonian slates rather less sharply. The narrow valley floors and the low levels that are subject to flooding are avoided by habitation, and in general the settlements and cultivation are on the gentle slopes of the topland or interfluves, while the valleysides are used either as permanent pasture for store stock or as woodland. With its mild climate, fairly high rainfall of 40 to 50 inches per annum, and deep valleys offering shelter and downwash soils, southeast Cornwall is noteworthy for its tracts of timber of rapid growth (Plate 35).

In the Rame peninsula the topland carries a rich reddish loam, very good for the growing of corn and swedes and for pasture for sheep and beef cattle. Over the rest of southeast Cornwall the soils are light to medium loams, free-draining but hungry, requiring much lime and fertilizer. Although leys are traditional on the ploughable land, the mild and damp conditions favour high grass-productivity, and the stress is strongly upon mixed livestock farming. In many parishes the total tillage is only one-quarter of the acreage under crops and grass, and in some is even less. For sheep rearing and fattening the breeds used are mainly the Devon Long-wool, South Devon, and Devon Closewool; the Longwools are commonly crossed with Suffolk or Down rams for fat-lamb production. To some extent South Devon cattle are still employed for beef and milk, but there has been a marked increase in dairying, using principally the Friesian and, in smaller numbers, the Channel Island and Ayrshire breeds. Especially in the eastern parts of the area, pig keeping has increased in importance. A little wheat and oats are grown, but barley is predominant and in several parishes occupies all the acreage under cereals. Forage crops consist mainly of kale, rape, and turnips. Potatoes are chiefly second earlies, lifted in July and August for the holiday trade, and main-crop varieties, dug in October; but some sheltered localities, most of them cliff pockets, have a small pro-duction of early potatoes in June. Others, with a favourable aspect, have small areas under soft fruits and flowers similar to those of the Tamar valley horticultural district. Save in that area, many of the holdings in southeast Cornwall are within the range of 50 to 300 acres, and commonly between 75 and 150.

The western part of the subregion is to some extent served by the stock markets held weekly at St Austell and fortnightly at Lostwithiel. At the eastern end, Saltash also has a fortnightly market; but far more important for the whole of southeast Cornwall is the agricultural centre of Liskeard, where there are two weekly markets, one of which is for attested stock. In recent years the throughput of animals has increased considerably, to about 72,000 per annum. Lostwithiel and Saltash, however, are the milk-collecting centres and the creameries there employ about 150 and 100 people respectively. Lostwithiel's tributary area includes most of mid Cornwall as well as the southeast as far as Looe, and the daily intake reaches a maximum of 60,000 gallons in May. Large quantities of liquid milk are dispatched by tanker, but dried milk powders are manufactured and, as at Saltash, liquid skimmed milk is sold back to the farmers for stock rearing and feeding purposes. Saltash creamery has a peak intake of 34,000 gallons per day. Clotted cream is a speciality here, but most of the milk is sold in Plymouth and other towns in west Devon and in east Cornwall.

Lostwithiel (population 1,900) is a small centre in the link zone between the china-clay district and southeast Cornwall. In medieval times it was the county and stannary town of Cornwall, but these functions passed to other towns. It declined as a port while Fowey grew in importance; it was outstripped by Launceston, Bodmin, and Truro for administration and by St Austell for trade, and it lies outside the mining and quarrying areas of modern times. Lying on a small plateau to the south of Bodmin Moor and between the deep valleys of the rivers Seaton and Looe, Liskeard (population 4,700) has a nodal importance for both main and local routes, channelling them westwards to Bodmin and Lostwithiel, eastwards to Plymouth and Tavistock, and south to Looe. Industrial establishments in the locality include saw mills, welding and engineering works, and a store for the grading and baling of wool. At Moorswater, in the valley 1 mile west of the town, a new industrial estate accommodates firms engaged in the processing of photographs and in precision engineering, the latter employing over 100 persons. Extractive industry in southeast Cornwall consists of quarrying granite, basalt, and gabbro, and there is a considerable output of concrete and coated stone. The principal workings (including Hingston Down) all together give employment to well over 100 men. Scattered about the area are a few other industries, such as saw milling at Bodmin Road, and precision repetition work at Doublebois. An estate at Burraton, Saltash, has printing and calendar making; and in the Torpoint district engineering and the manufacture of diamond and tungsten carbide tools are carried on. At Millbrook about 100 people are employed in the production of polystyrene plastering-board and flexible sheeting for the insulation of walls and ceilings. At Trago Mills, between Liskeard and Bodmin, there is a commercial trading estate which offers direct sales to the public.

The coast of southeast Cornwall is much frequented by weekend visitors from Plymouth as well as by summer holiday-makers. West of the long beach of Whitesand (or Whitsand) Bay the littoral scene is diversified by steep-sided valleys with picturesque settlements, notably Looe and Polperro; and Looe Island, the largest off the coast of Cornwall, adds further variety (Plate 37). Although the decline in fishing led to the closure of the cannery at Looe in 1962, the industry has recently revived a little, with good catches of pilchards and mackerel. Shark fishing has become very popular as a sport for visitors, and is now a major summer activity at Looe, adding to the boating, yachting, and beach attractions. Boat building is carried on, principally at Looe and Polruan near Fowey. The charm of the estuarine area and the old town of Fowey (population 2,400), which for many years has been an important centre for yachting, makes it a resort with unusual appeal. In 1965 a trading estate was opened at Fowey, and the first factory accommodates firms which produce plastic mouldings, and pottery and woodwork novelties. To the north of the town the activity at the china-clay loading jetties is a reminder of the importance of the links between Fowey and the St Austell district, which have grown closer in recent years.

CHAPTER 13

Bodmin Moor: Northwest Cornwall: The China-clay District: The St Austell – Truro District, Roseland and The Fal

Bodmin Moor

THE limits of a large granite boss outline the subregion of Bodmin Moor, an area of approximately 80 square miles (Fig. 87). As with Dartmoor, the northern hill mass is the highest part, rising to Rough Tor and Brown Willy at 1,311 and 1,375 feet respectively. Although sparse compared with those on Dartmoor, the tors on Bodmin Moor are almost as dominant over the broadly undulating surfaces, and are most rugged and impressive in the north and the southeast, where steep-sided hills reach heights of 1,296 and 1,213 feet in Kilmar Tor and Caradon. The inner areas are not so steeply graded, and the central southern mass, which achieves a maximum elevation of only 1,112 feet on Brown Gelly, consists largely of gently rounded ridges aligned NNW–SSE (Plate 36). The relief and drainage pattern are very much in sympathy with lines of weakness in the granite. Where the stre __ s plunge into the surrounding metamorphic zone their valleys contract and deepen, and occasionally have small gorges or waterfalls. Marsh-filled basins are most extensive in the north, especially on the outer flanks of the Rough Tor mass. Blanket bog of the Dartmoor type is scarcely represented, but in places sphagnum peat is several feet thick, and shallow peat is widespread. Occasional water-filled hollows occur, such as Dozmary Pool, with which is associated the story of Sir Bedivere and the great sword Excalibur. Dozmary is at least as well known as Cranmere Pool on Dartmoor and, with a circumference of 1 mile, is much larger. Water authorities already have intakes, such as De Lank and Crowdy Marsh, and they are looking increasingly to Bodmin Moor for additional sources of supply, as in the new Siblyback reservoir on a tributary of the Fowey; this is also to be used as an amenity centre.

A considerable output of fine-grained silver-grey granite comes from the

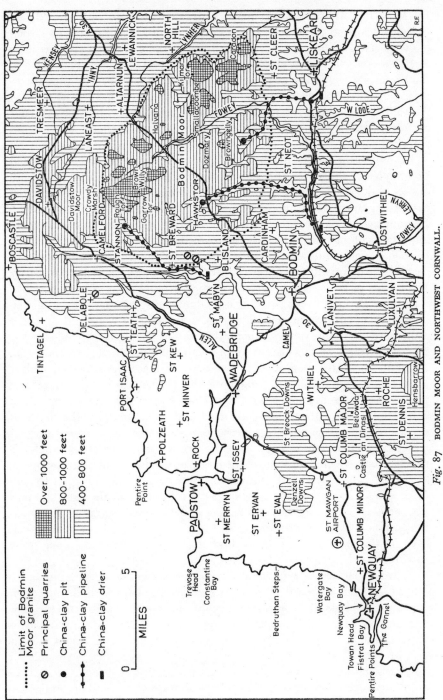

Fig. 87 BODMIN MOOR AND NORTHWEST CORNWALL.

De Lank and Hantergantick quarries situated between St Breward and Blisland. Much of the kaolinized rock on Bodmin Moor lies under a covering of peaty alluvium, but nevertheless the working of china clay has been carried on in several pits, chiefly in the western and southern areas. Each of the three pits which are at present in production is linked by pipeline to drying installations several miles distant. Tin streaming has left its mark in the valleys of Bodmin Moor, especially along the Fowey, but the evidence of former mining is largely concentrated in the southern and eastern marginal zones.

Although the old-established roads from Devon into Cornwall avoided Bodmin Moor altogether, the central tract of the moor lying between the hill masses of the north, south, and southeast offered a more direct route and the easiest alignment for a modern road; it is traversed by the Launceston–Bodmin section of the A30. With its heavy through traffic, this is far more important commercially than are the roads that cross Dartmoor. It may not be such a scenic route, but in fair weather it does afford panoramic views of parts of the moorland, not always appreciated by those who regard it merely as a means of crossing the obstacle of high ground as quickly as possible.

Today Bodmin Moor presents a predominantly pastural scene, broken by patches of cultivation in the lower areas, by strips of woodland along the southward-draining valleys where they leave the upland, and by the afforested tracts of Davidstow Moor, Halvana, and Smallacoombe—300, 495, and 900 acres respectively. The early occupancy was based mainly upon stock farming; but during both the prehistoric and the medieval phases the slopes of some of the high Downs carried a certain amount of cultivation. Both within the moor itself and on its margins the limits of enclosure and tillage have to some extent fluctuated since medieval times with changes in economic conditions. In recent years considerable amelioration has been effected on some of the larger of the moorland farms by means of the Livestock Rearing Improvement Scheme and the subsidies for hill cattle and sheep; and on some holdings the renovation of the natural sward has been carried out by the introduction of better-quality grasses. Reclamation projects, with controlled grazing of enclosed land, have shown that, even on the high slopes, parts of Bodmin Moor can be made much more productive.

For the farmers the physical adversities are not so much cold—prolonged snowfall and hard winters are rare—as the high rainfall, the severe exposure to winds, the wetness and acidity of the peaty soils, and the slow and, in places, impeded drainage. Compared with other hill-farming areas in England, however, Bodmin Moor is of only moderate height and its climate is mild, so that the nature and growth of the pasture is suitable for emphasis on the rearing of cattle rather than on that of sheep. Much of the moorland vegetation consists of a *Molinia–Agrostis* sward, and in comparison with Dartmoor tracts of heather are small. There is a patchy interspersal of bracken, gorse, sedge, and dwarf rush. Many farms have extensive grazing rights on unfenced areas, and the solution of problems connected with such rights awaits decisions at national level on the future of the common lands. As conditions are, the open ground may be overgrazed, especially in dry summers, and if so, little food remains for the winter. On land which is enclosed and the sole right of the occupier, summer grazing does not normally eat out the pasture, and a proportion is saved as winter feed. With the general diminution in the supply of grazing during the autumn, calves are sold off in October and the dry cows are out-wintered, with supplementary feeding only where necessary. Any young stock remaining on the farms are in-wintered from November onwards. The cattle are chiefly Galloway, Devon, and cross breeds, and the sheep mainly Blackface and Devon Longwool, with some Dartmoor, Exmoor, Cheviot, and Clun. An increasing number of ponies compete for the grazing on the open moor.

The principal crop is grass as hay and silage, and the small acreages under tillage are devoted to fodder crops and cereals, which here comprise barley, mixed corn, and oats. In the marginal tracts lying between 500 and 800 feet, large holdings are interspersed with smaller farms. Although help has been forthcoming from the Marginal Production Scheme, some of the small units have insufficient capital to develop a livestock-rearing system and have to rely on dairying and pig and poultry keeping, supplemented by catering for holiday visitors. The problem of the small farms is particularly acute on the southeastern margins of the moor, where a number of holdings, established by mining families during the nineteenth century, are so small—within the range of 5 to 50 acres—as to be uneconomic. Amalgamation has been suggested as the solution to this problem.

Almost all the market towns within easy range take some part in the disposal of stock from Bodmin Moor and the marginal areas. Some of the peripheral villages too have annual fairs and auctions. Thus St Breward holds fairs in April and July (for the disposal of store lambs) and a sale of sheep and cattle in October; the Old Cardinham sheep sale is held in August, and St Pratt's Fair takes place at Blisland in September. The most noteworthy sales-centre on the edge of Bodmin Moor is, however, that developed by private enterprise in recent years at Five Lanes, to the south of Altarnun, where there is a covered cattle-yard which can accommodate 1,000 calves. The market is held fortnightly, and it is also the venue of several fairs and seasonal sales of cattle and calves, sheep and lambs, and horses and ponies.

Northwest Cornwall

From early times a special significance has attached to the locality of Bodmin by virtue of the transpeninsular routes which here cross the narrow divide between the valleys of the Camel and the Fowey, utilizing the gap which separates the Hensbarrow Downs from Bodmin Moor (Fig. 87, p. 275). Aligned east–west, the town's main street (Plate 38) carries the A30 and, at either end, has a convergence of routes from southeast Cornwall (Liskeard and Fowey) and the northwest (Padstow and Wadebridge). While Bodmin is an important gateway to northwest Cornwall, it also has close relations with areas to the south and east. In 1838 the centre of the county assizes and administration was transferred here from Launceston, and despite the later concentration of the administration in Truro, Bodmin retains the assizes and has the headquarters of the Cornwall District of Constabulary; it is still 'the county town'. As a result of army re-organization, however, it has lost the depot of the former county regiment as well as the Joint Services' School of Linguists. Its functions as a service centre are variously evidenced by the two hospitals, a weekly newspaper, and a grammar school which takes pupils from as far away as Wadebridge and Padstow. The recent growth of the town is linked with the development of industrial and trading sites at Dunmere Road and at a former military camp known as the Walker Lines. There are several distribution depots, and among the industries already established are tool making, the manufacture of spectacle frames, and the production of precision components and copper tubes; the last-named gives employment to about 200 people.

In contrast to the Culm Measures which constitute the coastal frontage north of Boscastle, rocks of the Devonian series make up almost the whole of the cliffs to the south. The tracts of dunes in northwest Cornwall are less extensive than those southwest of Newquay; and not only is the coast much broken in detail but also it is divided into two main sections by the only long estuary on the whole of the northern side of Cornwall (Plate 39). Mining has been comparatively sparsely represented in the subregion, and quarrying is very localized; with but a small industrial imprint, the man-made landscapes exhibit very different scenes from those typical of west Cornwall and the china-clay district. Of all the Cornish resorts, Newquay is especially remarkable for its rapid growth and the predominance of the holiday trade in its economy. Another feature of modern development in northwest Cornwall has been the construction of airfields, particularly on the broad platform of marine origin that lies between Padstow and Newquay.

Strongly characteristic of the coastline of the subregion is the multiple alternation of bays or coves eroded in the Devonian slates and shales, and headlands formed by the more resistant grits and igneous rocks. From Wadebridge westwards to the coast a bed of tuff provides a base on which rest the Upper Devonian rocks whose sequence begins in a wide compound syncline around the Camel estuary. In this series slates are predominant, but northeast of the estuary bands of igneous rocks lying east–west help to diversify the relief, and in places dykes stand out as low, but steep-sided ridges. Small igneous masses provide the resistant tips of the headlands near Padstow, but the magnificent coastal complex at Tintagel consists mainly of slates, phyllites, and lavas whose structural arrangement owes much to overthrusting.

South of Trevose Head, rocks of the Middle Devonian series make only a short contribution to the coastal features. All the remainder—from Bedruthan Steps to beyond Newquay—is furnished by the Lower Devonian succession, beginning with the Staddon Grits. Dartmouth Slates constitute the cliffs overlooking the long beach of Watergate Bay, but a brief tract to the north of this and a much longer one to the south are made up of the Meadfoot Beds of slates and grits. Differential erosion of these beds largely accounts for the picturesque scenery at Newquay, where the cliffed promontory of Towan Head separates Fistral and Newquay Bays, and the two Pentire Points (East and West) flank the narrow inlet known as The Gannel.

In the estuarine area of the Camel and along the coast to the west, the landscape is varied by accumulations of sand. The estuary suffers from a surfeit of sand, notably in the Doom Bar towards its mouth; but, as with the shores of northwest Cornwall, it has long been a source of sand for use in agriculture. In recent years extraction has been by dredging, mainly at the mouth of the estuary and on the Padstow side.

Around Padstow Bay and to the northeast the markedly steep slopes to the sea are characterized by a stepped profile, which has been interpreted as the consequence of marine erosion related to a series of former Pleistocene sea-levels. Coastal settlements, but few in number, originally huddled in the shelter afforded at the head of small inlets, but with the development of the holiday trade and the arrival of a residential element Polzeath and Port Isaac have expanded; and in the far north of the coastal strip the population and the tourist trade of the Tintagel–Boscastle district have increased considerably. The castle site at Tintagel, with its legendary Arthurian associations, attracts more than 120,000 visitors each year. Port Isaac is still to some extent engaged in mackerel fishing and the catching of lobsters and crabs; a co-operative has recently been formed for the purpose of marketing mackerel. Padstow, formerly an important harbour with a large fishing fleet, now has only about nine inshore vessels; it is mainly a residential and holiday centre (population 2,700). On the opposite side of the estuary, Rock is a residential settlement with a high proportion of retired people and it has grown in importance as a sailing centre.

The lowest bridging point on the river Camel is five miles farther upstream, at Wadebridge (population 3,600). Here a number of local routes, as well as those from Padstow and Bodmin, converge to the point where the main road (A39) from north Devon to west Cornwall is borne by a fifteenth-century bridge which has recently been doubled in width. The trading and industrial interests of Wadebridge lie with both the estuarine and the inland areas. It has a weekly market and holds numerous shows and sales of stock during the year; and it has the permanent site of the Royal Cornwall Show. Wadebridge formerly had a waterborne trade, including the shipping of agricultural produce and the importing of timber and other building materials and coal. But as the quays can now be reached only by small coasters on spring tides, the trade in these products is done by road. The town is important as a centre for agricultural and other supplies; and the industries include engineering and foundry work and boat building, which has recently concentrated on large trimarans. A Board of Trade advance factory is to be built at Wadebridge.

In the southern part of the subregion, Newquay has grown from a small settlement dependent on the pilchard fishery to a residential and shopping town and holiday resort whose permanent population is now about 12,000. During the peak period of the summer trade, however, approximately 60,000 people are in residence. The resort, the most popular holiday town in Cornwall, is ostentatiously a creation of the nineteenth and twentieth centuries, with some of the clifftops and the slopes behind built up in hotels and guest- and boarding-houses (Plate 40). But although much of the land to the east and south has been developed, the cliffed scenery of the district has largely been preserved and enhances Newquay's other assets for the holiday trade—the splendid beaches, the bracing climate, the rocks and caves along the coast, and the surf-lined sea. The accessibility of the resort has been increased by the establishment of regular air services to St Mawgan airport, which has the distinction of being the only civil air terminal situated on an operational station of the Royal Air Force.

Mining activity in northwest Cornwall was almost confined to the northern and western margins of the Hensbarrow granite and the Padstow district where, down to the nineteenth century, copper, lead, iron, and antimony were the principal products. This century wolfram has been extracted at Castle an Dinas near St Columb Major. Delabole has what is claimed to be the oldest and biggest slate quarry in England (Plate 41). The great pit has reached a depth of more than 500 feet, and the waste dumps are now being reworked; but there appears to be little fear of the rapid exhaustion of reserves, for a core hole has proved the existence of slate of high quality at 265 feet below the present lowest level of working. Probably the best-known products are the grey and grey-green roofing slates, but several others, including slabs, building and hedging stone, concrete, powders and granules, are also important.

In 1965 two industries—the manufacture of knitwear and metal window-frames—were started on the Valley Truckle estate at Camelford. An advance factory may be taken over for the making of hydraulic-brake components, and there is a project for a factory where coils and transformers for electrical and electronic equipment will be made. A firm at Delabole is engaged in the manufacture and design of agricultural and general machinery, hydraulic lifts, and quarrying and mining equipment. More than 100 people are employed by a creamery near Davidstow. The greater part of the milk intake here, which reaches a peak of 30,000 gallons per day in June, is held for cheese-making; and much of the by-product whey is used on a large farm nearby, concerned mainly with the production of pigs for bacon.

As they are almost wholly exposed to the Atlantic winds, the plateaux of northwest Cornwall are treeless tracts; but considerable blocks and patches of woodland are found in the valleys away from the coast, notably to the southeast of Wadebridge and northwest of Bodmin along the river Camel and its tributary the Allen, where there are saw mills and a manufacture of portable buildings. The general pattern of farming in the subregion is geographically uneven, being broken most obviously in two tracts of poorer land. In the north of the area and towards Bodmin Moor the greater elevation and exposure induces a high rainfall. Tillage is only between one-ninth and one-quarter of the area under crops and grass, and the pastures are here and there flecked with patches of coarse grass. To the south of the Wadebridge–Padstow district, on the long east–west ridge of the St Breock–Denzell Downs which in places rise to 700 feet, heather moor formerly covered much of the extensive outcrop of the Staddon Grits. In this area, however, agriculture has made considerable inroads, especially on the southern side; and the possibilities of improvement have been demonstrated in recent years by the success of a reclamation project and the maintenance of a high rate of stocking on land lying at about 600 feet.

Soils on the slates which occupy large parts of northwest Cornwall are moderately fine-textured brown earths; and although rainfall over much of the area averages about 40 inches per annum, the land dries out quickly due both to good natural drainage and the effects of strong winds. Much of the subregion is under mixed farming with varying degrees of emphasis on the rearing and fattening of stock, dairying, and the growing of corn. Farmers in the northern districts tend to rely considerably on Longwool sheep and Devon cattle, but in the south there is a fairly high proportion of South Devon sheep. Throughout the area dairying enterprises use principally the Friesian breed, although the South Devon cattle are well represented, and Ayrshire and Channel Island herds are kept on a number of farms. Save in the comparatively high areas already noted, tillage is rather more than one-third of the total acreage under crops and grass. Some winter wheat is grown in the south, and in some parishes elsewhere there are appreciable acreages of mixed corn; but in many parts of the subregion barley now occupies about two-thirds to three-quarters of the total tillage. The Wadebridge–Padstow district, comparatively gently sloped and low-lying, has a fairly high proportion of arable, now as well as traditionally devoted mainly to cereals. Although potatoes are a cash crop in several localities, the general exposure of northwest Cornwall has restricted the growing of 'special' crops to small areas. Shelly sands have long been used to lighten and fertilize the soils in the subregion, often at the rate of as much as ten tons per acre every year. As a result of this treatment, many acres are probably now over-limed and suffering from induced mineral deficiencies.

Dairying is carried on almost throughout the range of holdings, but in some localities small units of less than 30 acres are particularly concerned with this enterprise and with pig and poultry keeping. A number of farms well above the general range of 30 to 150 acres are found in districts either where corn-and-stock enterprises are strongly characteristic or where there is a high percentage of permanent grass and the holdings are predominantly devoted to rearing. Stock markets are held weekly at Wadebridge and St Columb Major, but the only other serving northwest Cornwall from within is that held monthly at Delabole. Boscastle, however, has sheep sales in July and September.

The China-clay District

The extracting and processing of china clay are the basic modes of employment on and around the Hensbarrow granite mass, to which they impart a remarkable regional individuality (Fig. 88 and Plate 42). Much of the industrial terrain is characterized by deep open pits, glittering mounds of sandy waste, and a variety of buildings where clay is refined, dried, and stored. Certain streams that rise in the clay area run milky-white, but the small lakes in disused pits are greenish-blue, and the heather and the yellows of broom, gorse, and lupin shrubs on the slopes add colour to a landscape that is sometimes considered dreary but nevertheless has a stark beauty of its own. Blocks of farmland and patches of moor are interspersed with a heavy but irregular overlay of industry and housing. St Austell has spread rapidly in recent years, and village clusters, such as St Dennis, Roche, and Bugle, have grown as clay workers' settlements. The scatter of dwellings elsewhere is only in part derived from the early dispersal of farmsteads. As first mining and then clay working augmented the settlement patterns, many small holdings of cottage dwellers were carved piecemeal from the rugged ground on and around the granite. The present-day legacy of this process of enclosure is seen especially in the parishes of Roche, St Austell, St Dennis, and St Stephen-in-Brannel, where two-thirds of the holdings are of less than 20 acres. They may have a little cultivation, but more typically are given over to pasture carrying a few head of stock. Some holdings possess grazing rights on adjoining tracts of moor.

Although the northern part of the Hensbarrow Downs has been somewhat improved, about one-quarter is still rough grazing, which ranges downwards from moorland at over 1,000 feet to marshy pasture, such as the poorly drained tracts on Goss Moor at about 400 to 450 feet. Farm holdings in the Hensbarrow area are predominantly pastural, the stock most commonly kept being dairy cattle, principally of the Friesian, Channel Island, and South Devon breeds. The weekly market at St Austell serves most of the district. Over the greater part of the area, tillage accounts for only between one-sixth and one-fifth of the acreage under crops and grass.

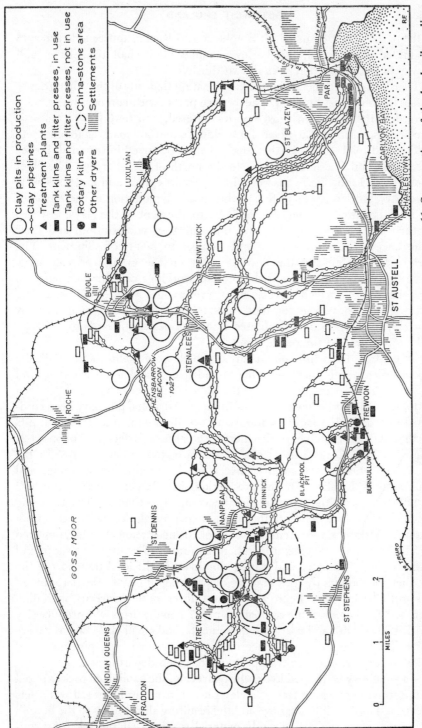

Fig. 88   THE HENSBARROW CHINA-CLAY DISTRICT: DIAGRAMMATIC MAP OF THE PRINCIPAL WORKINGS, 1966. Some sections of the local railway lines are now disused.

In the parishes of St Austell, St Stephens, and Roche, appreciable acreages are under mixed corn, but barley occupies about half the tillage, and elsewhere the proportion rises to two-thirds.

Hensbarrow experienced more kaolinization than any of the other granite masses in Southwest England. The western part of the main boss was greatly affected, but the eastern third was less altered, and here fresh granite is quarried, especially at Luxulyan, for building stone and material for concrete making and road works. Little transformation occurred in the small bosses —Belowda and Castle an Dinas—to the north of Hensbarrow. The chief resources of kaolin lie in masses which vary in extent and carry a sandy, clayey overburden up to 30 feet in thickness. Exploitation of these masses has been favoured not only by the large total extent of the clays, but also by their high average quality and uniformity of composition, and their occurrence so near the surface and so close to points of shipment. The fairly high rainfall and the flow of water on the granite provide large quantities of clear water; and the present workings can draw on supplies from disused pits which serve as storage reservoirs. Most of the producing pits are now above the 500-foot contour, but the movement of clay by pipeline, road, and rail is facilitated by the slopes southwards to the edge of Hensbarrow and the coastal tract.

In contrast to the idle pits, many of which were shallow and small, the modern pits rapidly increase in depth and size. The deepest working level so far reached is over 400 feet, but the clay-bearing rocks have not yet been bottomed. At Caudledown, south of Bugle, five original pits have been combined into a single vast excavation; and the Blackpool and Halviggan pits northwest of St Austell have also merged, creating a surface void of 60 acres. English China Clays Ltd., 5,000 of whose 9,500 employees live in the St Austell area, is the major concern in the production, refining, and marketing of the clays. On the production side, 85 per cent of Cornwall's output comes from the principal member company—English Clays Lovering Pochin & Co. Ltd. The group has its own central electricity generating station at Drinnick and a remotely controlled sub-station at Bugle, powered by a turbo-prop jet engine; it maintains a number of engineering shops and research establishments; and it is predominant in the local transport of the products of the pits by road and the dispatching of clay to the harbours of Par and Charlestown. There are about a dozen other concerns, including china-clay and china-stone companies, paper-making firms who produce clay for their own filler and coating requirements, and small-scale clay recovery units. The larger of these concerns have their own pits, pipelines, and 'kilns' or dryers, and also transport and research departments.

In what may be termed hydraulic quarrying, the kaolinized rock exposed in the stope or working face of a clay pit is broken up by hosed water jets (monitors) under high pressure, and the resulting slurry flows to the bottom of the pit. Here the coarse sandy material is separated and taken by conveyor belts or inclines to the waste heaps ('sky-tips'). The slurry is pumped to the surface for de-watering, and after refining, the clay passes to drying units and the finished product is stored. Unkaolinized granite in the pits is broken down by blasting and transported to the surface; this waste material is known as 'stent'. Modern programmes of mechanization in the china-clay industry have included the provision of more and improved machinery in the pits, the use of filter presses and mechanical dryers, the building of large storage silos, and the laying of pipelines to the drying installations, especially those to the west of St Austell and at Par.

The yield of clay amounts to between 10 and 20 per cent of the kaolinized rock that is extracted; the remainder goes on to the spoil heaps. Although the tips are the principal source of sand and gravel in Cornwall, and about 80 per cent of the waste material is suitable for use in making concrete, consumption is of necessity comparatively low, amounting to less than one-tenth of the spoil that is currently dumped. Among the important by-products of the china-clay area are, however, a variety of washed and graded sands for civil engineering purposes, concrete for general use, reconstituted stone, complete industrialized housing-units, and pre-cast concrete buildings for agriculture and industry. There appears to be promise of further development in the production of heavyweight precision concrete castings. A small amount of the waste material goes into poultry grit, and some of the sand is used for decorative purposes.

Among the other products of the clay district is Molochite, a calcined china-clay low in iron content. This is employed extensively in the making of highly refractory fire-bricks for electric furnaces, blast-furnace linings, and pottery kilns. China stone, which in places occurs side by side with the clay, but is found mainly within a two-mile tract between the villages of St Stephens and St Dennis, consists of partially decomposed granite which is quarried and is then put through crushing plants and pulverizing mills. The fine powder produced from processing is a fluorine-free stone flux, invaluable in the manufacture of ceramics.

Leading the home consumers of china clay is the British paper-making industry which, using the clay as a coating and a filler, accounts for about 60 to 65 per cent of this market. Consumption in the Potteries constitutes another 30 per cent, and other uses for china clay in this country are as a filler or extender in the rubber industry, and as a constituent in the manufacture or preparation of medicines, cosmetics, plastics, paints, fertilizers, linoleum, textiles, and cement. The export trade in china clay was severely reduced by the great depression of the early 'thirties and by the Second World War; but in the years immediately following, it made a remarkable recovery and has since expanded rapidly. In 1961 exports were just over 1,000,000 tons, and the rate of increase has so quickened that in 1966 1,700,000 tons were shipped overseas. Over 75 per cent of Cornwall's output is sent to markets that are world-wide. The United States of America is one of the largest of the overseas customers, but sales there are lower than in the 'twenties, having been reduced by the depression of the 'thirties, the increase in her own production of clay, and the effects of the Second World War. Sales to several European countries, however, have increased, despite much competition. Among the principal customers are West Germany, Italy, and the Scandinavian countries, where much of the clay is used in the manufacture of paper.

Although some of the clay for use in this country is dispatched from St Blazey and Burngullow by liner- and tanker-trains, the three harbours of Charlestown, Par, and Fowey—all within easy range of the clay pits—serve as the major outlets for the Hensbarrow district. Charlestown is a small harbour formed by two piers and it contains a tidal basin secured by lock gates. It has four berths for vessels of up to 500 tons and 12 feet in draught. Its trade is almost entirely coastwise, consisting principally of shipping china clay—which is brought to the harbour by road transport—to paper mills in the Medway and lower Thames districts. Inward cargoes comprise coal, coke, timber, and occasionally, processed seaweed fertilizer from Brittany. During the 'thirties Charlestown foundry was re-equipped and virtually rebuilt by the firm of English Clays Lovering Pochin.

Par's tidal basin lacks the deep-water berthing facilities that are available at Fowey, but its position gives it a certain advantage over the latter, which is 5 miles farther away from the main source of clay. Par is served almost entirely by road transport and by the pumping of clay along pipelines to dryers on and near the harbour. In recent years large drying and refining plants have been built in the harbour area; and work completed in 1960 almost doubled the capacity of the port and also improved the cargo-handling plant for English China Clays Ltd. (who acquired control of this private port in 1946). This has resulted in a higher rate of turn-round of vessels for both the home and the continental trades. Par is obviously well suited to these types of trade, in which large vessels are not generally required. At present the port can accommodate twelve ships at a time and is handling more than 1,600 vessels per annum, a rate which substantiates her claim to be the busiest of the small harbours of the United Kingdom (Plate 43).

During the present decade the tonnage of shipments at Par has already risen considerably; in 1962 it amounted to 697,000 tons of clay, compared with 377,000 in 1957. In 1966 Par's total trade comprised 953,000 tons, of which all but 72,000 consisted of china clay and stone; and the peak in the shipments per week stood at 31,000 tons. Par is the chief point for the coastwise dispatch of clay, but there has also been a marked increase in the foreign trade, notably to Europe and not only by short sea routes. Imports consist of felspar, coal, timber, and oil, nearly all of which is for the use of the parent company. On the harbour side there is a stone-pulverizing plant, and Par also has saw mills and an engineering firm which is engaged in the maintenance and distribution of industrial equipment and tractors.

The port of Fowey has this century greatly enhanced its modern function as a deep-water harbour, with four jetties for the loading of china clay. There is no other trade. Within the general Conservancy control of the Fowey Harbour Commissioners, the management of the jetties is vested in British Rail, and the facilities are entirely rail-fed. In 1963-4 improvements were made in transport arrangements, and clay trains run from the producing localities to St Blazey, where they are remarshalled for dispatch to Fowey. It is now proposed (1967) to lease the port to English Clays Lovering Pochin & Co. Ltd., and the transport system will probably be re-organized. For voyages from Fowey to European ports, cargoes are commonly of the order of 750 to 1,500 tons, but for carriage to distant markets ships of up to just over 10,000 tons are employed. Vessels of this tonnage, and of 460 feet in length and 28 feet in draught, are about the maximum size that can be berthed at present, but further improvements are envisaged in order to accommodate ships of up to 15,000 tons deadweight. Meanwhile it has been possible to raise the bulk loading rate from 240 to 320 tons per hour. Although the modern phase in the development of Par resulted in a falling-away of Fowey's share of the coastwise trade, her exports have increased rapidly in recent years, and the rate of shipment per week has reached new records. In 1966 one week's dispatch amounted to over 23,000 tons, and the total shipments of clay were 720,000 tons, compared with 470,000 in 1962.

In the Hensbarrow subregion there is a growing, albeit small, measure of diversity of employment. At St Blazey 100 people work for an engineering firm which manufactures special-purpose machines, there is a paint factory at Penwithick, and at St Austell approximately 200 persons work in a brewery. In addition to engineering and a factory which is mainly engaged in the production of broccoli crates for west Cornwall, more industry has been established at Holmbush, including a shirt factory (which employs 100 girls), and works for the manufacture of automatic control equipment and the assembly of electrical components. The acceleration in the growth of St Austell (Fig. 89) is, however, mainly a reflection of the prosperity and vitality of the china-clay industry, and of the enhancement of the functions of the town as the undisputed capital of the Hensbarrow district, a hub of routes, a shopping centre, and a focal point of local administration and, notably with its Technical College, of education too. Other facets of the modern increase in the importance of the town are seen in its close relationship with the coastal area from Mevagissey to Fowey (in 1968 the latter will merge with St Austell in a new borough), and its participation in the holiday trade. In 1963 work started on the first stage of implementing an ambitious scheme to redevelop the town centre and almost to double the existing area occupied by shops; the work should be completed in 1969. The new part of the commercial core includes a pedestrian precinct (Aylmer Square), super-

markets, and a multi-storeyed car park. As with the new group offices of
English China Clays Ltd.—John Keay House, opened in 1966—it is appro-

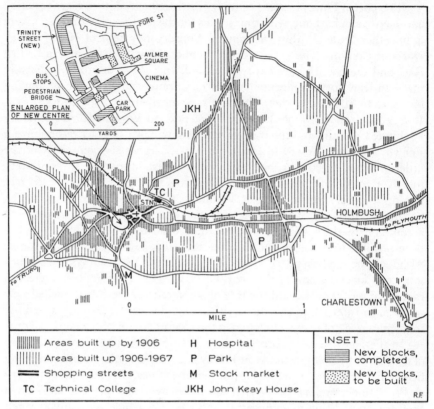

Fig. 89   ST AUSTELL: THE MODERN GROWTH.

priate to the functions and character of St Austell that the construction
should have been carried out by the building division of that group.

The St Austell–Truro District, Roseland and The Fal

Between the austere industrial landscapes of the white-coned china-clay
district and the mine-scarred areas of west Cornwall, is a zone of almost
complete contrast. Here are fertile farmlands, closely wooded valleys, and
a long branching estuary; a fine deep-water anchorage in Carrick Roads,
and yachting waters set amid superb scenery; docks and wharves where a
major industry—ship repairing—helps to sustain the maritime pulse of
Cornwall; and the city of Truro, the county's administrative centre, situated
at the head of navigation and astride the main routes that pass through
southern Cornwall (Fig. 90).

The oldest rocks in the area between St Austell Bay and the estuary of
the Fal lie within a NE–SW tract extending from Turbot Point to Gerrans

Bay, and constitute a discontinuous series, probably of Devonian age. Along the coast the boldest, highest promontories—Dodman Point (Plate 44) and Nare Head—are formed respectively of resistant phyllites and dolerite. To the north and west the heterogeneous mass gives way to the grits, sand-stones, and slates of the Grampound and Portscatho Beds. The Falmouth Series is best represented in a tract from Truro to Chacewater, but farther south, on the western flank of the Carrick Roads, the Mylor shales pre-dominate. The northern limit of the subregion is marked by the passage to

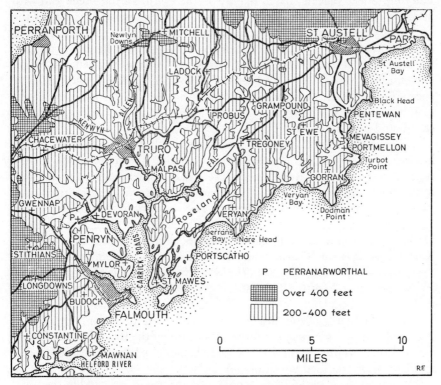

Fig. 90   THE ST AUSTELL–TRURO DISTRICT, ROSELAND AND THE FAL.

the Meadfoot Beds, which consist of slates with seams of siliceous material. These beds of hard rock surround the Hensbarrow granite mass and, from a narrow tract between St Austell and the coast near Black Head, they give rise inland to a succession of east–west ridges which are, however, incon-spicuous save in the largest and highest on Newlyn Downs, at 490 feet. The western limit of the subregion is almost everywhere indicated by the appearance in the landscape of evidence of past or present mining and quarrying within and around the Carn Marth and Carnmenellis granite masses.

Although the subregion displays a diversity of micro-climatic conditions, in general the rainfall averages 40 to 45 inches per annum and the humidity is high. Over the greater part of the area the soils consist of relatively fertile medium loams which, lying on a slate or shaly subsoil, are shallow and free-draining. The farming is mainly of a mixed type, with various degrees of emphasis on fatstock production, dairying, and arable. Roseland—the district extending from Tregoney to the south coast and Carrick Roads—was traditionally a fattening ground for cattle and sheep, but, as with the area stretching eastwards to St Austell Bay, it is now devoted more to dairying. Sheep rearing, based mainly on the South Devon breed and with small to medium-sized flocks is, however, still important. In parts of the large district more closely connected with Truro there is a somewhat higher proportion of milk-producing enterprises, although even here, and notably on some large farms of up to about 350 acres, herds of Friesian and South Devon cattle are kept for both beef and milk; and numerous holdings carry sheep. For the weekly marketing of stock, these parts of Cornwall are served mainly by Truro, where there are also many sales and shows of cattle, sheep, and pigs during the year.

Some mixed corn is grown in the subregion, but in recent years barley has been the predominant cereal crop, occupying a particularly high percentage of the tillage in Roseland and the area eastwards, and in the districts to the north and east of Truro. Mixed farms of 50 to 300 acres form a substantial proportion of the total units. The subregion generally is not a flower-producing area; but there are exceptions, one being the largest flower-farm in Southwest England which is situated on the slopes of the Kenwyn valley near Truro. Some fruit, early potatoes, and a variety of vegetables are grown in the Budock–Mawnan district and along the slopes on the western side of the Fal estuary, where there are good conditions of shelter, aspect, and freedom from frost. East of the estuary the virtual absence of market-garden types of crop is accounted for not only by a lower degree of favour from such conditions, but also by the lack of a tradition of horticultural production and marketing that might have developed if the area had been provided with railways.

Except on the exposed parts, where settlement is sparse, and in the tract southwest of Truro, where the pattern of close dispersal quickly becomes akin to that of the west Cornwall industrial district, old single farmsteads or clusters of two or three are fairly evenly distributed throughout the subregion. Many are on the plateaux and interfluve slopes, and avoid the steep-sided valleys. There are few large villages; and even some of these derive their origin and form from the foundation of a borough, as at Grampound and Tregoney. In recent years, however, some villages have grown appreciably with the development of the holiday trade; and the same applies to several of the coastal settlements. The retired, residential element has also been a significant factor in the modern growth of a number of places, perhaps most obviously at St Mawes.

In the area east of Truro and the Fal estuary, industries are few and sparsely distributed. Farm buildings are made at Grampound Road, and the tannery at Grampound produces sole leather, using oak bark for the preparation of the liquor required in the process, and leather for artificial limbs. Several old fishing settlements are dotted along the east-facing shores of the bays. The building of crabbers and cabin cruisers is carried on at Portmellon, but the largest harbour is at Mevagissey, where the fishing fleet comprises trawlers, pilchard drifters, long-liners, and mackerel boats. In 1966 the fishermen here formed a co-operative for marketing purposes.

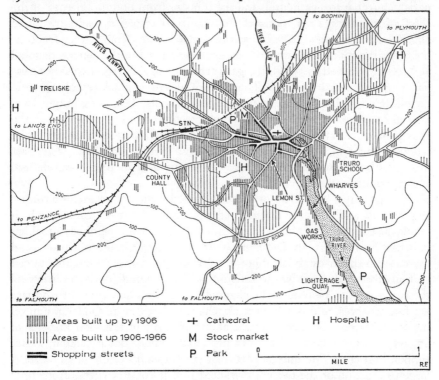

Fig. 91   TRURO: SITE, SITUATION, AND MODERN GROWTH.

Unfortunately the canning factory closed in 1967; it had facilities and staff for handling 1,200 stones of pilchards per day, and for a time had a considerable export trade to West Africa.

Truro, with a population of 14,300, stands at a converging point of ridge and valley routes in a bowl-shaped area at the confluence of the rivers Kenwyn and Allen (Fig. 91). Below this the river widens and, for a length of about 3 miles before it merges with the Fal, is known as Truro river. The jurisdiction of the port of Truro, however, extends southwards over the waters of the Fal for a further 4 miles. Silting deprived the medieval port of Tregoney of the possibility of rivalling Truro, which in any case was better situated in relation to the mining industries of west Cornwall, for which it became one of the trading outlets and 'coinage' towns. In parts of the central area, notably in Lemon Street, the city retains the dignity of buildings associated with its growth from the seventeenth to the nineteenth century as a trading and residential town and a social and cultural focus for much of Cornwall. Successively the turnpike roads and the railways enhanced Truro's functions as one of the most important towns in the county; and her status rose in other respects with the establishment in 1876 of a diocese separated from that of Exeter, the enlargement (1880–1910) of St Mary's parish church into a cathedral, and the transfer from Bodmin in 1912 of the chief administrative functions of the county. In 1966 the administrative offices for Cornwall were re-housed in a new County Hall. Other facets of the city's functions as a service centre are evidenced in the general hospital at Treliske (opened in 1966), the gasworks, one of the largest weekly news-papers published in Cornwall, and various educational establishments, including a number of largely independent schools. Truro is a hub of local as well as of major roads, and the volume of traffic has necessitated the provision of a relief road through the southern part of the city. The redevelopment of Pydar Street, to the west of the Cathedral, is in part linked with the growing importance of the city as a shopping, warehouse, and distributive centre.

The principal industries at present carried on at Truro include timber engineering and joinery, biscuit making, and a knitwear factory which employs about 100 people, mostly women. Linked with the old sail-making industry is that of manufacturing tents, including circus 'big tops'; and there is also an old-established pottery. In 1967 the Government announced that an advance factory was to be built at Truro. Dredging is necessary all the year round to keep open the channel to the city's quays. In Truro there are five wharves, and down river are the new Lighterage Quay and an oil depot at Malpas. Oil accounts for about one-half of the total imports of 47,000 tons per annum, the other principal cargoes being cement, grain, timber, and coal. The only export is of small quantities of coke breeze. A large proportion of the oysters marketed in this country comes from beds in the waters administered by Truro and Falmouth. The district has become very popular for sailing; and boat-building or repairing yards are active at several places along the Fal estuary and its inlets, especially on the western side. Sail making is carried on at Penryn and Falmouth.

Penryn, an old borough long ante-dating Falmouth, occupies the spine of a short ridge falling eastwards to the harbour. The trade by sea now consists chiefly of imports of oil—about 58,000 tons per annum—and coal (10,000 tons). There is an oil depot at Ponsharden. Scores of quarries in the area to the west and southwest of Penryn testify to its past importance as the chief source of Cornish granite for building purposes. Penryn was for long the centre for the dressing of the stone, and great quantities were shipped from 'The Granite Port'; but during the past twenty years the St Breward district on Bodmin Moor has become more important for the quarrying of granite for building stone, and the granite-dressing industry at Penryn virtually came to an end in 1966. Today, firms in the Long Downs–Mabe–Constantine district are concerned with the quarrying and dressing of granite for monumental purposes and, to a lesser extent, for building; and stone is crushed for hard core, chippings, and concreting aggregates. There is a considerable output of concrete products. Among the industries at or near Penryn are timber and joinery works, the manufacture of foundation garments, and—at Long Downs—the making of wooden buildings. A substantial proportion of the modern industrial activity, however, has been generated by firms concerned with engineering —general, marine, electrical, and electronic—the last of which employs about 150 persons. An engineering firm whose work includes the manufacture of special-purpose machines occupies a site on the new industrial estate at Kernick Road.

Aligned NW–SE along the foot of a ridge and running parallel to the shore, a long main street formed the waterside artery of Falmouth down to the nineteenth century; but the town has since extended its core at right-angles to this shopping street, in the traffic centre and commercial area known as 'The Moor'. Housing development has spilled over the ridge and has spread to the north and west. Open spaces, however, have been devoted to beautiful gardens; and to the south, Pendennis Point has been preserved from modern building and has a panoramic drive around the castle and headland. To the west of Pendennis the beaches, promenade, and hotels which face south over Falmouth Bay form the frontage of the resort. In effect there are four Falmouths—the older part of the town with its long waterfront facing northeast; the docks; the residential areas; and the resort (Plate 45). Apart from the docks and the holiday trade Falmouth's industries are few, but are gradually increasing in number and size. Civil engineering and constructional contracting are carried on, and an industrial estate is being developed at Tregonniggie, where the first factory is occupied by fishing-reel manufacturers who employ 200 people, three-quarters of them women. A new printing-works is being established, and an advance factory has been taken by an engineering firm. With a technical college and a school of art, Falmouth has a growing importance in the field of education.

The port has a small coastwise trade, consisting principally of incoming cargoes of refined oil products (about 50,000 tons per annum) and coal. Ship repairing, engineering, and foundry work are of outstanding importance in the employment groups; but the functions of ships' agents and chandlers, and the operation of pilot cutters and tugs are also carried out in the port. Of the four docks which existed in 1958 one was then rebuilt and named the Queen Elizabeth Dry Dock; this is 850 feet long and 130 feet wide, and is the largest privately-owned dry dock in this country. With approach dredging to give 30 feet of draught at low water, it has proved possible to bring in tankers and other vessels of up to 90,000 tons for repair. There are in addition, a number of ship-repairing berths adjacent to the basin from which the dry docks lead; and the total wharfage is now over 8,000 feet. At certain times in the past the rather irregular nature of the business caused sharp fluctuations in the amount of work available, but the ship-repairing organization has introduced a system of regular employment, and the majority of the work-people—about 1,650—are now permanently engaged.

CHAPTER 14

The West Cornwall Industrial Area:
The Lizard Peninsula:
The Land's End Peninsula

The West Cornwall Industrial Area

CARNMENELLIS is the name applied generally to the highest and much the largest of the granite masses in this penultimate subregion of west Cornwall; but as the hill specifically bearing that name rises only to a smoothly rounded summit at 825 feet, it is not a spectacular physiographical feature. Nor are the gently rounded hills nearby, with summits at about 600 to 700 feet; but away to the north and southwest some of the smaller bosses, for example Carn Brea and Tregonning Hill, are sufficiently high and steep-sided to stand out quite conspicuously (Fig. 92).

The character of much of the subregion has been moulded by the exploitation of that part of the main mineralized zone of Southwest England which here forms a NE–SW traverse about 8 miles wide. In places the surface carries peculiarly tortured landscapes expressive of the working of tin and copper over a long period, and is riddled with abandoned shafts and studded with old engine-houses, spoil-heaps, and stream-works (Plate 46). The application of the term 'industrial' to the west Cornwall subregion is, however, justified not only by the activities, past and present, of mining and associated works, but also by the development and establishment of other industries, especially in the core district of Camborne–Redruth.

Both the north and the (shorter) south coasts of the subregion have features which distinguish them from those of the Lizard and Land's End peninsulas. At either end of the north coastal strip is a tract of sandy beaches backed by dunes known as 'towans'. One series stretches from Hayle to Godrevy; and farther north the beaches extending for 4 miles from Perranporth to Holywell rise inland to a belt of dunes which is widest and highest in Penhale and Gear Sands. Interposed between the two main tracts of sand is a rugged stretch of slate and sandstone cliffs, deeply gashed at Portreath, Porthtowan, Trevaunance Cove, and Trevellas Porth, and punctuated by the promontories of Godrevy Point and St Agnes Head. The south coast of the subregion extends only briefly along Mount's Bay, but comprises two contrasted sections. Eastwards from Penzance to Marazion and the castle-crowned granite boss of St Michael's Mount (Plate 47), a long stretch of beach is backed by low, flat, and, in places, marshy ground. This is succeeded by an irregular, cliffed coast, occasionally fronted by beaches, as at Praa Sands (Plate 48). In modern times parts of

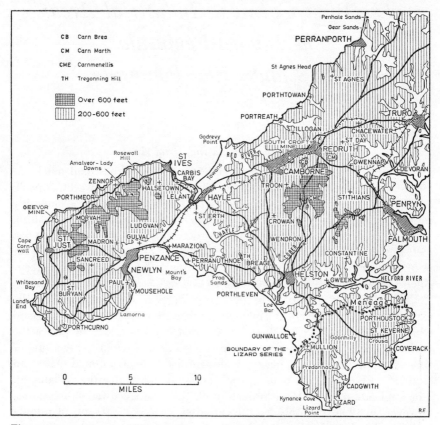

Fig. 92   THE WEST CORNWALL SUBREGION AND THE LIZARD AND LAND'S END PENINSULAS.

the coasts have been variously built up for residential and holiday purposes —in a mixture of styles at the resort of Perranporth, in bungalow or chalet types near Porthtowan and Hayle, and in medium-sized houses and bungalows at Praa Sands; and caravan parks or camps have been established at or near most of these places. The seaside settlements, and also many inland places—save only the least attractive—depend greatly on the holiday trade; and all the coastal tracts of the west of Cornwall provide lungs for the Camborne–Redruth district.

Only one mine—South Crofty at Pool (Plate 49)—is now working; it employs about 380 men and produces approximately 1,000 tons of tin concentrate per annum. A scheme is in hand to unwater the flooded East Pool and Agar mine nearby and also the lower levels of the North Tincroft mine. For some years the waste material coming down the Carnon valley from Gwennap has been exploited, and recently there has been more activity in recovering tin on sites near Redruth and along the Red river, as at Tuckingmill and Roscroggan. Tin-bearing sand is being dredged in St Ives Bay, and separation takes place at a dressing plant at Lelant Wharf. Hopes have long been held in west Cornwall that mines would be re-opened or new shafts sunk, and in recent years the prospect of a firm rise in the price of tin and of a diminution in the output from certain overseas countries has encouraged the exploration of many sites. In 1967 a shaft was sunk at Pendarves near Camborne.

From at least the early nineteenth century the fame of the Camborne–Redruth district rested not only upon mining, but also upon the affinitive industries which produced drills, fuses, and engineering equipment. Today the biggest single industrial enterprise in the west Cornwall subregion is the production, at Camborne, of compressed-air equipment for use in mining, civil engineering, and industry in general. The firm concerned—Holman Brothers Ltd.—was founded in 1801 and has expanded into a group which has one large and two smaller factories in the Camborne district and employs all together about 2,750 people in Cornwall. Through subsidiary and associated companies and agents it has also spread its activities and interests throughout the world. At Camborne the group has concentrated most of its manufacturing and its administrative functions on a central site, though one of its member companies occupies a factory at Pool. The group's range of production at present consists of reciprocating and rotary-screw air compressors, pneumatic tools of all kinds, positive displacement pumps, and automated control systems. Over 50 per cent of the group's production in the United Kingdom is exported. The district plays an important part in technical education, for the Camborne School of Metalliferous Mining is the largest centre in the Commonwealth for the training of mining engineers, and in recent years the Cornwall Technical College at Pool has expanded rapidly.

The most characteristic of the domestic building forms in west Cornwall are two-storeyed granite houses of the late eighteenth and the nineteenth centuries; but the monotonous nature of some of this housing is here and there somewhat relieved by buildings of the Georgian period or in villa styles, and by chapels which are often of substantial and imposing structure. Modern factories and housing estates, and new and renovated shop façades have helped to diversify the appearance of the Camborne–Redruth district, and at Camborne the administrative building of the Holman group provides a new element of contrast with the vernacular scene. The A30 road by-passes Redruth but still threads through the intermediate settlements of Illogan

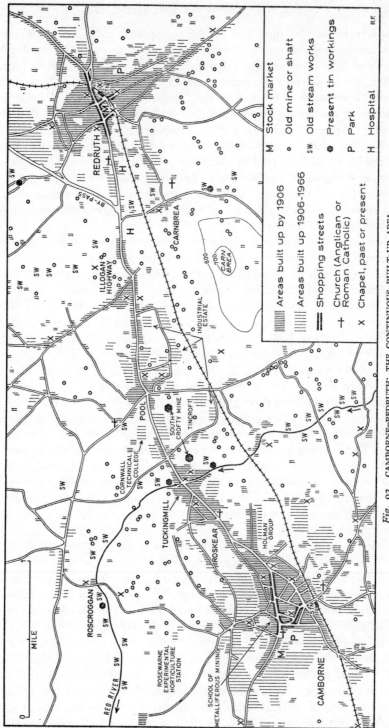

Fig. 93 CAMBORNE–REDRUTH: THE CONTINUOUS BUILT-UP AREA.

M   Stock market

o   Old mine or shaft

SW   Old stream works

●   Present tin workings

P   Park

H   Hospital

▦   Areas built up by 1906

▨   Areas built up 1906–1966

▤   Shopping streets

†   Church (Anglican or Roman Catholic)

X   Chapel, past or present

R.F.

Highway, Pool, and Tuckingmill to Camborne, and is almost entirely built up for about 5 miles (Fig. 93).

Camborne–Redruth urban district is administered by a single council, which has taken a leading part in the provision of new housing, additional supplies of water as in the Stithians Dam scheme (completed in 1965), and sites for industrial purposes. By 1966 the factories established in the urban area since the Second World War had already provided jobs for about 2,500 people, and in that year the Government announced that an advance factory was to be built. Although the new industries have considerably widened the range of employment, there is still a need for work for semi-skilled and unskilled men.

In 1947 an old mining area of 22 acres at Pool was cleared and prepared as an industrial site, and the first factory—a branch of Heathcoats, the textile firm at Tiverton, Devon—was opened in the following year. It has rapidly expanded, and employs about 350 men and 250 women. The planned area of the industrial estate at Pool has been increased to 60 acres, and accommodates firms concerned with electromechanical repairing, fur processing, and printing and bookbinding; the last two are staffed by 100 and 150 persons respectively. In 1964 a factory wherein nearly 100 people, mainly men, are engaged in leather and textile sewing and in light engineering, migrated here from Redruth; and a firm of radio and television manufacturers established a large works which gives employment to about 350 persons, the majority of them women. Other industries in the locality of Pool include saw milling, engineering, and the making of tools and drawing dies.

At Tuckingmill the factory left vacant by the cessation of the fuse-making industry has been taken over by manufacturers of agricultural machines and implements, whose other works are at Blackwater, to the north of Redruth; all together, 140 people are on the staff of this firm. Camborne has a factory where over 100 women are employed in the making of foundation garments, and a firm which specializes in the rebuilding of machine tools. The industrial activities in and around Redruth have been augmented since the Second World War, but the old-established brewery and bacon factory are still among the large employers, each with a staff of about 100. Other concerns are engaged in engineering, steel fabrication, and the making of knitwear, electrical fittings, concrete, and pottery. Near Portreath two firms give employment to 100 and 200 persons respectively, mostly females, in the manufacture of women's clothing. Apart from the industries in the Camborne–Redruth district and at Hayle, those in the west Cornwall subregion are small in number and size, and are sparsely distributed. Of all the valleys tributary to the Fal, those in the district from Stithians to Devoran and Chacewater formerly had the closest links with the mining areas; and engineering and the making of castings are still carried on at Devoran.

In recent years the harbour at Portreath has been used mainly as a depot for coal brought by road, rail, and, very occasionally, coastwise vessels; but it is now being replanned for housing development. Hayle has more maritime trade than that of all the other harbours on the north coast of Cornwall put together. Formerly Hayle was important for the smelting of ores, and it had a large trade with South Wales, a famous foundry, and other industries connected with shipping and mining. Nowadays the only export is of scrap metal, chiefly to South Wales, but inward cargoes include oils from Fawley and Milford Haven (22,000 tons per annum), potatoes from Northern Ireland (9,000 tons), cement from the lower Thames district (7,500 tons), timber from Finland and Poland, and sulphur from Bayonne. Coal, at 125,000 tons the biggest item and mainly for the Central Electricity Board's generating station, comes principally from Barry, Goole, Blyth, Whitehaven, Workington, and Ayr. For many years the firm that owns and operates the port has carried on the importing of coal and timber and the trade of builders' merchants for much of west Cornwall. Around or near the harbour are firms engaged in assembling scrap metal, extracting bromine from sea water, boat building, and engineering. In 1954 a company of constructional engineers and steel stockholders moved to Hayle, and another new industry —the making of outboard motors—was set up in 1960. At Copperhouse (the eastern part of Hayle) there were formerly smelting works and a foundry; today about 300 people are employed in a factory which makes screens for granular materials and supplies perforated metal to more than fifty industries.

Small woods clothe the sides of several valleys in west Cornwall, and there are a few plantations and estate parks; but in general the landscape carries very little woodland, for the mining industries devoured much of the local timber. The countryside is by no means wholly bleak and open, however, for there is a close multiform mesh of field boundaries, although rows of trees are not as numerous as low hedges and banks of earth, stone, and turf. In many localities the old pattern of rural settlement has been greatly augmented and partially blurred by a scatter of two-storeyed terraces, cottages, and villas, together with bungalows and smallholders' dwellings. This later dispersal, although apparently rather haphazard and amorphous, nevertheless assumed here and there specifically geometric forms that are still discernible in mining villages and short cottage-rows, in small clusters of buildings at road junctions, and in encroachments of smallholdings over the granite slopes. There are still patches of moor, particularly on badly drained land and on exposed heights with rocky surfaces and thin soils, but most of them are small areas of 'croft' or rough grazing, which is an element in a number of holdings today.

Through a narrow zone extending from Newquay and Perranporth to Truro, the mixed farming on a basis of cattle, sheep, and arable that is characteristic in mid Cornwall rapidly gives way westwards to a dominantly dairying type, with concentration upon the Friesian and Guernsey breeds for high yields of milk and cream. During the peak period in summer the large creameries at St Erth and Camborne and the smaller ones at Penryn and Scorrier (northeast of Redruth) together deal with a daily intake of about 105,000 gallons of milk; they give employment to some 430 people. The availability of skimmed milk from cream and butter-making on the farms encouraged the rearing and fattening of pigs; and the small size of many of the holdings was another factor conducive to the development of this enterprise, as also to that of poultry keeping. Sheep ratios in west Cornwall are generally low, and in a few parishes there are no sheep at all. With the exception of the 'special' crops mentioned below, the working of the arable is mainly directed to the growing of stock feed, the principal items being barley, mixed corn, kale, and roots. The hay crop, important for winter conservation, is carefully gathered in despite the difficulties sometimes experienced in damp and quickly changing weather conditions.

Small holdings form a remarkably high proportion of the number of agricultural units, and in the parish of Camborne–Redruth those of less than 15 acres make up two-thirds of the total of about 700 holdings. Farms of various sizes within the range of 15 to 100 acres are, however, a substantial element in the aggregate for the subregion. The majority of the comparatively few farms of 100 acres and upwards are in localities which experienced only a moderate or low intensity of mineral working and which therefore had few of the small-scale enclosures characteristic of the mining areas. Weekly markets serving west Cornwall take place at Penzance, Helston, Camborne, Redruth, and Truro, though considerable numbers of stock are now disposed of through other sale channels.

In respect of crop production west Cornwall is most widely known for its broccoli, spring cabbage, early potatoes, and flowers. Research work on these 'special' crops is carried on at the Rosewarne Experimental Horticulture Station at Camborne. This aspect of agriculture is common to parts of the Lizard peninsula and the Helston district, the west Cornwall subregion and the Land's End peninsula; and the most productive district in the whole of Cornwall lies within the zone that links these last two areas and extends around and behind the head of Mount's Bay from Mousehole to Perranuthnoe. A tract 2 miles long and half a mile wide that runs east from Gulval has a micro-climate and an aspect that are very favourable for intensive agriculture, and is known as 'The Golden Mile'.

The Cornish winter cauliflower (broccoli) crop is grown on about 7,000 acres, most of which lies within the area extending westwards from Redruth and Helston as far as St Ives and Mousehole. It is often a farm rather than a market-garden crop, and consists almost entirely of the Roscoff type, which was introduced here in the 1920s. The cutting period extends from November to May, but a marked peak normally occurs from the middle of February to early in March, when as much as 30,000 tons may be marketed. Consignments by rail go mainly to the northern and midland towns of England and to Glasgow, while those by road, which in recent years have accounted for well over half the total tonnage, are sent principally to London. In 'The Golden Mile' the clearance of the first part of the broccoli harvest is often followed by the planting of early potatoes, and the marketing of this crop is concentrated into late May and early June. All the western parishes in the subregion have appreciable acreages, but the distribution in the eastern areas is more patchy.

Daffodils, narcissi, anemones, and violets make up the bulk of the flowers that are produced commercially in west Cornwall, although polyanthus, wallflowers, and irises are of supplementary value. Most of these are open-air crops, but some flowers—and also tomatoes—are grown under glass, notably in the locality of St Erth. Particularly in the instance of daffodils and narcissi, flower production is tending to be an enterprise carried on by specialist, large-scale growers. Anemone growing, however, appears to be an exception. For many years the greater part of the acreage devoted to this crop in Cornwall has lain within the district westwards from Camborne and Helston to St Ives and Mousehole. Most of the blooms are marketed by the end of January, although in favourable conditions the season may extend to about Easter. This enterprise has often been regarded as typically that of small growers on pieces of land ranging from one-quarter of an acre to 2 acres, and this has been emphasized now that some of the larger growers, for whom anemones were a side-line crop, have given it up altogether. In recent years virus infection and other troubles affecting anemones in west Cornwall have increased, and the future of this part of the flower industry is rather uncertain.

The Lizard Peninsula

'The Lizard' is the name popularly assigned to the whole of the peninsula which lies south of Helston and the Helford river, but the northeastern third of the area is traditionally known as Meneage. Geologically, the peninsula comprises two main areas which are sharply contrasted. Forming the southern and larger portion are the igneous and metamorphic rocks of the Lizard series (Fig. 92, p. 296). These are separated from the northern part by an irregular fault-and-thrust line and a narrow brecciated or crush zone which extends 7 miles inland from the east coast. Farther north the Helford river is entrenched in the least resistant of the shales and grits of the Gramscatho Beds, which themselves pass into a narrow belt of the Mylor Beds flanking the granite of the Carnmenellis mass.

Of the group of serpentine rocks which form most of the southern portion of the peninsula, the largest constituent is a coarsely crystalline type known as bastite serpentine. This occupies much of the central area including the large tract of Downs which bears the name Goonhilly. On its northern and western limits it merges into a streaky, finer-grained rock— the tremolite type—whose largest mass stretches from Mullion southwards through Predannack Downs to Kynance Cove, where colourful exposures of the serpentines are richly varied. A third type—a compact fine-grained rock called dunite serpentine—occurs mainly on the northern, outward margins of the tremolite. Within the eastern sector of the Lizard peninsula, gabbros not only form a single extensive mass but are also profusely injected into the serpentine as dykes. Considerable parts of the girdle of gneiss and schists which encircled the intrusive serpentines have been removed by marine erosion, and these types of rock are now limited to the northern flank of the serpentine and gabbro and to certain coastal tracts. In the extreme south the reefs and skerries are of gneiss, and close by are the crumpled schists at Old Lizard Head, representative of the oldest rocks in the peninsula.

The plateau surface that extends from Lizard Point to the northern valleys has little relief. Its age and origin have been much debated, as has also the development of the radial drainage system of the Lizard, which is independent of that of Carnmenellis. Gravel deposits extending over nearly half a square mile at about 360 feet on the summit of Crousa Downs may indicate the marine origin of the erosion platform. This lies between 200 and 350 feet for the most part, but rises as high as 370 feet on Goonhilly, where is situated the Post Office earth station for receiving and relaying communication signals via space satellites (Plate 50).

Although exposure has played a part in limiting the areas under woods, these are not confined to the Helford river area and the other sheltered valleys of Meneage. There are several plantations, and since 1954 the Forestry Commission has had a small experimental forest at Croft Pascoe on Goonhilly. Rocky surfaces characterize parts of the Downs on the serpentine and also of Crousa Downs near St Keverne, where the land is strewn with a residue of blocks of weathered gabbro. Soils on the serpentine include some derived almost entirely from the underlying rock and others derived partly from foreign material. Supporting only heather, gorse, and coarse grass, the Downs have almost no agricultural value and are practically devoid of habitation. Poor drainage, exposure, and thinness of soil are the principal factors that have restricted the area suitable for farming in the Lizard peninsula. In some localities the limit of cultivation has been forced almost to coincide with the boundary of the serpentine, in others the physiographical nature of the surface has exercised a more powerful control over the land use.

Soils on the gabbro vary in depth and quality, but in general they are far superior to those on the serpentine, and much of the gabbro in the St Keverne district carries fertile land, especially on the eastern side. Areas of good agricultural value are found on the brown loams between St Keverne and the Helford river and in the northwest, especially on the greenstones contained within the Mylor Beds around Helston and Porthleven. In the southern half of the peninsula, farming is carried on not only on the good land on the schists, but also in a number of valleys and on favoured interfluves and seaward-facing slopes on the granite–gneiss and, here and there, even on the serpentine. Throughout the peninsula there is a strong emphasis on dairying, for which the Friesian and Guernsey breeds are generally used. Pigs are kept on most of the holdings. The growing of the principal crops—barley, mixed corn, oats, and kale—is an integral part of the stock-feeding programme. Especially in certain sheltered, south-facing localities on the eastern side of the peninsula, however, there is a degree of specialization in the production of flowers, broccoli, and early potatoes. Most of the farms in the subregion are small, but some are in the range of 150 to 300 acres.

The agricultural areas are fairly well studded with farmsteads, but villages are few, being mainly either embodiments of road junctions on the margins of the plateau or clusters in and around small coves, more especially those along the comparatively sheltered east coast. There is but one town—the old borough of Helston—which is widely known for its Flora Day with the Furry Dance (Cornish *fer*, a fair) held on or about the eighth of May. Coinagehall—the name of the main street—recalls Helston's long association with the mineral-producing districts to the north and west, and its former function as a stannary town. The site of the core of the settlement is the eastern side of the narrowest part of the Cober valley; and the importance of its situation lies partly in its command of the bridge carrying the road from Penzance to Falmouth, which is joined by other main roads from the west and north (St Ives and Hayle, Camborne and Redruth) before it passes through the town. Helston's nodality is completed by the road to Porthleven, which crosses the Cober by another bridge, and by its control of the principal entry to the Lizard peninsula. The only other, but minor, road access to Meneage is by way of Gweek, at the head of the Helford estuary.

Although deprived of the branch railway from Gwinear Road, completely closed since 1964, Helston continues to serve an area which extends well outside the Lizard peninsula itself. It has various functions as an agricultural and trading centre, and there is a weekly market in which entries of cattle and pigs average 300 and 700 respectively. Since 1967 a Government-sponsored advance factory has been occupied by a firm manufacturing fancy leather goods. In recent years a large settlement has sprung up at Culdrose (between 1 and 2 miles southeast of the town), where a Royal Naval aerodrome is equipped as a helicopter training unit. This establishment has been a major factor in the recent growth of Helston, whose population is now about 8,500.

One mile south of Helston the river Cober flows along the Loe valley into the sand- and shingle-barred freshwater pool known as 'The Loe', where it has long been depositing alluvium and silt derived from the waste of old mineral workings several miles upstream. As a plan in 1837 for making a harbour at the mouth of The Loe came to nothing, the valley and the 2-mile stretch of the pool do not provide a maritime function for Helston; but Porthleven, at the mouth of a smaller valley about 2 miles to the west, is busily occupied with marine work. In the early 1960s boat-building was re-established by a firm who leased the whole harbour, and the range of constructional work now extends to trawlers, cutters, pilot launches, and hydrofoil craft. Several inshore trawlers, drift-net vessels, and crabbers are based at Porthleven, and there is a factory which prepares crab-meat products. The processing of broccoli by deep-freeze methods and the making of netting and tarpaulins are also carried on. Sea trade is small, being limited to importing fertilizers and exporting granite chippings which come from the Goodygrane quarries near Constantine.

Helston and Porthleven are popular as holiday centres, and many of the settlements around the Helford river and in the Lizard peninsula also rely greatly upon trade brought by the many visitors who are attracted by the estuary and the beaches, and the beauty and diversity of the cliffs and coves. Among the few industries or crafts that are carried on in the peninsula is the cutting, shaping, and polishing of the colourful bastite serpentine, mainly for ornamental purposes. This is an individual or workshop craft, catering mostly for tourists and located chiefly at Lizard Town. In sharp contrast to the Land's End peninsula and the west Cornwall industrial area, the Lizard has never been important for mining, but from about 1750 to 1820 soap rock was worked for use in the manufacture of pottery. Stone now quarried in the diabase, hornblende-schist, and gabbro near St Keverne is used mainly for road metal. The workings—at Porthoustock and Dean Point—are along a sheltered tract where the crushed stone is easily loaded into coastwise vessels, which take it to ports in southern England. Some of the villages and hamlets in the Lizard peninsula are still engaged to a certain extent in fishing (Plate 51), and a trading society has recently been formed by the fishermen of Porthleven, Mullion, Cadgwith, and Coverack, together with those of Falmouth. The cultivation of oysters has long been carried on in the Helford river area, and the Duchy of Cornwall has an oyster farm at Porth Navas.

The Land's End Peninsula

Standing respectively at the northern and southern entrances to the Land's End district are the towns of St Ives and Penzance, between which the chief link is provided by the main road skirting the neck of the peninsula (Fig. 92, p. 296). The conversion and renovation of old buildings has modi-fied but not destroyed the character of the core of St Ives which extends in a half circle around and behind the harbour (Plate 52). Its maritime façade screens a maze of narrow streets and clusters of fish cellars, courtyard houses, and small dwellings with a store on the ground floor, which used to be typical of many Cornish fishing havens. Several longliners, trawlers, and crabbers are still based on the harbour, but for many years St Ives has been as well known for its artists as for its fishing. Since the 1880s, when artists were first attracted by the grandeur and beauty of the scenery, the light and colour in the environment, the picturesque settlements, and the comparatively inexpensive living, the total number in the St Ives and Newlyn–Lamorna districts has risen to about 200; and the area is now famous not only for its painters and sculptors, but also for pottery craftsmen.

The beaches at St Ives and Carbis Bay are a major asset for the large holiday business. One of the few industries is accommodated in a factory near 'The Island', which employs about 200 people in the making of nylon overalls and drill clothing. Former mining activities in the St Ives district are recalled not only by the ruins of stacks and engine houses, but also by the place-name Stennack—a locality where many of the miners lived—and by the nineteenth-century planned village of Halsetown. This was built as a mineworkers' settlement by James Halse, a St Ives solicitor with mining interests. Many of the cottages fell into disrepair, but in recent years a considerable number have been restored.

Significant phases in the building up of modern Penzance are attested by a variety of Georgian houses, St Mary's Church, and the Market House (both erected in the 1830s), and by the Victorian components of the western and eastern extensions of the town. This century, housing development has added considerably to the built-up area (Fig. 94), and in 1934 the borough boundaries were extended so as to encompass not only Newlyn, but also Paul, Mousehole, Heamoor, and Gulval. The population of the borough is now about 19,000. Penzance acts as a shopping, service, and administrative centre for much of the far west of Cornwall—new government offices have been built near the Morrab Gardens—and it is a holiday resort favoured by a very mild climate and by the long beaches and the beautiful setting of Mount's Bay. It is the railhead and the hub of some half a dozen roads which form a fan-shaped pattern within the Land's End peninsula. Penzance provides the points of departure for the helicopter and the shipping services to the Isles of Scilly, but the maritime trade of the harbour is only small. Apart from the shipments of flowers and potatoes from Scilly, incoming cargoes are mainly coal from Northeast England, cement from the lower Thames area, various fertilizers from Germany and Holland, processed seaweed fertilizer from Brittany, and boxwood for use in the making of crates for broccoli and flowers. In 1966 it was decided to transfer the supplying of coal to the gasworks from sea to rail transport. A group concern employs about 120 people in ship repairing and allied work, and has recently extended the dry dock, which takes coastal commercial craft of up to 1,500 tons. Industries introduced into Penzance in the past few years include precision engineering and the making of frictionless guides for fishing rods. Among the concerns established on an industrial estate at Eastern Green are a light engineering firm which specializes in gardening equipment, and a factory where the making of children's shoes gives employment to about 120 people. An advance factory has been built on this estate, and is being taken over by the shoe-making firm.

Newlyn has small engineering industries producing, for example, hold-

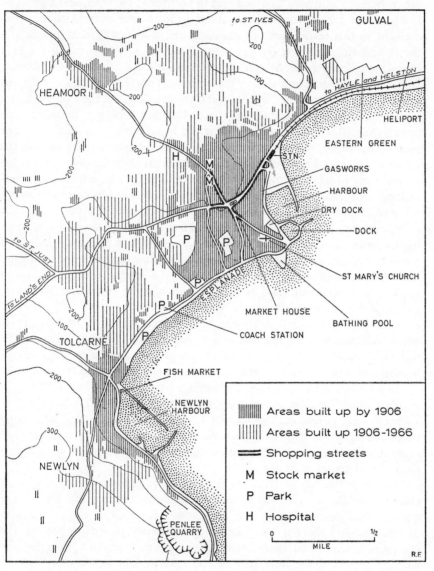

Fig. 94 PENZANCE: THE MODERN GROWTH.

ing fixtures for machine tools; but it is mainly dependent upon roadstone quarrying and the fishing industry. The working of diabase hornfels at the Penlee quarry is augmented by that of granite at Castle an Dinas north of

Gulval. Large quantities of concrete and bituminous coated materials are produced, and the whole enterprise gives work to 160 men. Shipments of stone, amounting to approximately 400,000 tons per annum, go to about a dozen ports in southern England and to Germany, Holland, and Eire. The fish landings at Newlyn, valued at about £300,000 per annum, make it pre-eminent in this respect among the harbours of Cornwall, and matched in Southwest England only by Brixham. Trawling is carried on all the year round, longlining from March to October, and the catching of lobsters, crabs, and crayfish mainly during the summer. Very few herrings now appear in the waters that are fished by the west Cornwall fleet, but the chief mackerel season extends from February to June. Pilchard fishing is mainly in the period from March to October. About 100 boats work from Newlyn at one season or another, but many of these are small. In recent years most of the larger vessels based here, including deep-water trawlers, have been operated by one firm which employs about 300 people in fishing, engineering, net-making, and transporting fish by lorry. At or near Newlyn there are several other industries based upon fishing—the processing of fish paste and crab meat, canning, and the making of ice and fish fertilizer. One of the process-ing factories can deal with as much as 3,000 stones of pilchards daily, and 1,400 stones can be handled at a cannery. Problems raised by variable and intermittent landings have been largely solved by the re-organization of marketing arrangements and by the provision of more processing, large-can, and deep-freeze storage facilities. Newlyn now has the means of preserving over 300 tons of fish, and deep-frozen fish are used as bait by the longliners when fresh mackerel, pilchards, and squid are not available. Occasionally fish is brought by road from other Cornish harbours as far away as Mevagissey and Looe, and even from Devon for processing at Newlyn.

In addition to being famous for fishing, Newlyn Harbour is well known as the site of the tidal observatory where the Ordnance Datum is fixed. Farther west, points on the Land's End peninsula are used for linking transoceanic cables with land lines, as at Porthcurno (where the telegraph company also has an engineering training school), and for radio communica-tion with ships, as at St Just.

Although the Mylor Beds are fragmentarily represented on the north coast of the Land's End mass, their continuous terminal line lies on the eastern flank, extending in the shape of a reversed S from Lelant to Mousehole; and short tracts of land near Penzance, as well as parts of the coastal area west of St Ives, consist of sheets or masses of epidiorite. The western areas are the only part of the mainland of Southwest England where granite is directly and extensively attacked by the ocean; but the cliff scenery is not wholly that of granite, for metamorphic rocks also appear, for example to the north of Cape Cornwall. Though impressive, the cliffs are not among the highest in the region; but the crenulated coast exhibits a great variety of small coves, 'zawns' or narrow inlets, short craggy or tor-topped headlands, and masses of columnar or castellated granite. Whitesand Bay and Porthcurno have considerable beaches.

The granite of the Land's End peninsula is mostly medium- to coarse-grained, but an inner boss of fine-grained rock underlies the northern Downs, and here the undulating surface is comparatively free from rugged carns and large boulders. Stream patterns in the peninsula have been much influenced by lines of faulting and joints. On the northwestern side a series of narrow benches or flats is cut by many short streams running at right-angles to the main watershed; and the valleys are sufficiently deep to be a factor in the irregularity of the course taken by the road from St Ives to St Just. Most of the longer streams in the peninsula flow southeastwards, and as they end in deeply incised funnels (Plate 53) they cause the roads running across the southern plateau to keep well inland.

Above 430 feet the land stands out boldly, and the main watershed extends almost the whole length of the peninsula southwestwards from Rosewall Hill. To the north of it is a landscape of tiny walled enclosures, with small groups of farmsteads fairly evenly spaced across the narrow, windswept platform, and a few larger knots of settlement in the villages of Zennor, Porthmeor, and Morvah. On the plateaux to the south and on the gentler of the slopes along the southeast-flowing streams there are numerous farmsteads; even here, however, there are but four village clusters— Madron, Paul, Sancreed, and St Buryan. Except for Newlyn, Mousehole is the largest of the old fishing settlements, most of which are situated along the sheltered southeast coast.

Especially above 400 to 450 feet there are considerable areas where, through the centuries, the margins of enclosure and cultivation have fluctuated. Medium-quality land is interspersed with, or grades rapidly into, rough grazing and croft, which in places is virtually waste ground but may include old enclosures from the moor. Some of the farms incorporate a fairly large proportion of rough pasture and in terms of size are thereby considerably larger than the 45 acres which is the average area of the holdings in the Land's End peninsula. In the lower, plateau-and-valley areas, mixed farming is characteristic, with dairying as the outstanding and almost universal enterprise. The rainfall of 40 to 45 inches is moderately high, and as winters are mild there is a long grass-growing season. A high stocking rate is permanently maintained, especially of the predominantly Guernsey cattle. Many holdings have pigs, but the sheep ratios are among the lowest in Southwest England. Of all the subregions, the Land's End peninsula is now the only one where mixed corn is the principal cereal crop.

On the eastern flank of the peninsula a narrow belt of soils on the Mylor Beds and the greenstones broadens around Penzance and then links up with the intensely cultivated area at the head of Mount's Bay. Although conditions during the Second World War induced a change from a specialized cultivation to a mixed-farming type of rotation on some farms on the eastern tracts of the peninsula, crops of broccoli, spring cabbage, early potatoes, and flowers are still important. 'Special' crops are grown elsewhere in the Land's End area in sheltered localities with a favourable aspect such as that of south-facing, steep valleysides.

Small masses of china clay occur in several places, but at present the only workings are near St Just. Clay is quarried at Lower Bostraze and concrete blocks are made at Leswidden. For many years St Just and Pendeen were the focal points of the western mining localities; and the former—the largest settlement west of St Ives and Penzance—ranks as an urban district and functions as a local shopping and minor service centre. An airport nearby is used by a firm which operates mainly scenic flights. Apart from mining and quarrying there are few industries or crafts in the western part of the peninsula, St Just itself having only a foundry and a pottery. Geevor mine, 2 miles to the north, employs 280 men and has an output of about 700 tons of tin concentrate per annum. Diamond drilling has been in progress in the Cape Cornwall section, and there is renewed interest in the disused Boscaswell and Levant mines. The latter is being unwatered, with the object of prolonging the Geevor levels. In recent years exploratory work has been proceeding which may lead to a resuscitation of mining elsewhere in the Land's End peninsula. Sites to the south of St Ives have been investigated, and coastal and off-shore drilling is in progress in the Penzance–Newlyn area. In 1960 an application was made to re-open a mine at Carnelloe, but this was refused, mainly for the reason that the industry would spoil the scenery in the locality of Zennor and Gurnard's Head; and in 1966 a suggestion that the site of the Ding Dong mine, 4 miles northwest of Penzance, should be reworked was opposed on the grounds of the scenic quality and the archaeological value of the district.

CHAPTER 15

The Isles of Scilly

THE general disposition of the group of islands and reefs which constitute the Isles of Scilly was largely determined by the way in which lines of weakness running NE–SW and NW–SE assisted the deep weathering of the granite, which may have started in Tertiary times. In detail, however, the islands have been shaped by the subsequent stripping of much of the growan by subaerial (especially periglacial) and marine processes; the multiform sculpture of the granite exposures in tors and coasts; the post-Eocene oscillations in sea-level; and the formation of sandbars, beaches, and dunes. The most recent of the changes in sea-level is attested by the submergence of features of human occupancy, such as boundaries of ancient fields. Some of the waters between the larger of the northern islands are so shallow that at very low tide and in calm weather it is possible to walk from one island to another.

Five islands are now inhabited—St Mary's, Tresco, St Martin's, Agnes with Gugh, and Bryher (Fig. 95). More than three-quarters of the total population of about 1,900 live on St Mary's. Not only is this the largest island (2½ square miles), but it also has the highest proportion—about one-half—under cultivation and the biggest single settlement, Hugh Town (Plate 54). By 1855 the difficult island of Samson was occupied mostly by elderly people, who were then evacuated; and St Helen's and Teän became uninhabited even earlier. Some of the Eastern Isles were formerly used by the people of St Martin's for pasturing sheep, kelp-burning, and collecting driftwood. With the exception of the temporary occupation of Rosevear during the construction of the lighthouse on Bishop Rock, settlement has shunned the jagged, inhospitable islets known as the Western Rocks, which have claimed many lives through shipwrecks.

The geographical position of Scilly both in relation to seaways and to the English mainland has been variously exploited in the past, and the factor of isolation has often been overpowered by the need for trade or by national requirements of defence. The sequent occupancy and economy has thus been more complex than if the islands had been used merely as a detached appendix of Cornwall. Although some of the topographical names and patronyms are of Cornish type, they are interspersed with markedly different elements. For long the economy relied on efforts to wrest a living

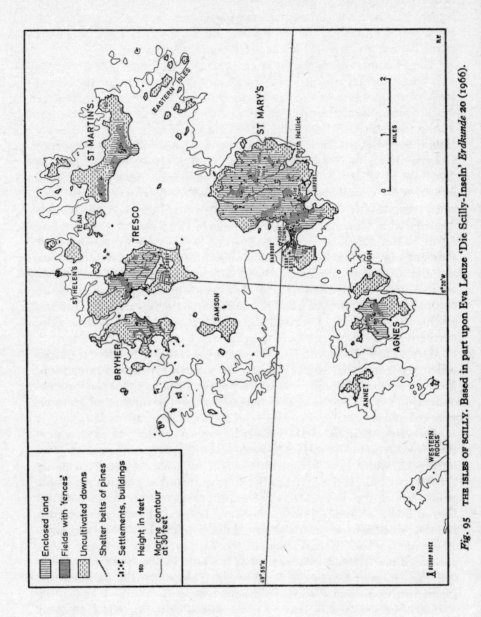

Fig. 95   THE ISLES OF SCILLY. Based in part upon Eva Leuze 'Die Scilly-Inseln' *Erdkunde* 20 (1966).

from the limited resources offered by land and sea, but at times it was boosted or depressed by factors over which the inhabitants had little or no control. Today it is almost entirely dependent on the exploitation of conditions favourable to flower growing and of the attractions to tourists of the natural and man-made character of the islands.

Large numbers of megalithic graves, tumuli, and Bronze Age settlement sites bear witness to a considerable prehistoric occupancy and to the importance of the position of the island group on early trade routes along the western margins of Europe. There is evidence of trade and settlement during the Romano-British period also, but the recorded history of Scilly from then to the sixteenth century is remarkably thin. Early and medieval Christianity on the islands was centred upon St Helen's (originally the name was St Elid) and Tresco, and Saxon and Norse influences intruded into what were, perhaps throughout the Dark Ages, sparsely distributed and predominantly Celtic and monastic settlements. Ennor Castle, which in medieval times commanded the harbour in Old Town Bay, was in bad repair by the early sixteenth century, when Scilly generally was in a poor state and only St Mary's and Tresco were inhabited. But during the wars and the expansion of trade in Tudor times the position of the islands became important nationally, and they were fortified against attack or occupation by Spain. The principal defences of the late sixteenth and the seventeenth centuries, on Tresco and St Mary's, guarded respectively the northern and southern entries to the safe anchorages. On the north coast of St Mary's a new settlement, Hugh Town, grew in the shelter of Star Castle, which was completed in 1594; and a quay was provided there in 1601. Meanwhile the Godolphin family from Cornwall had been granted the lease of Scilly in 1571. They brought in new settlers, and Bryher and St Martin's were repopulated.

Following the lease of the islands to Augustus Smith in 1834, a new church was completed at Hugh Town and the quay was extended. The settlement, which now occupies the whole of a narrow, sandy isthmus between two hills, is the centre of the services maintained within the island group, having the Town Hall as the headquarters of the Council of the Isles of Scilly, a comprehensive school, the hospital, the shops and banks, and the principal harbour. It also has all the main hotels with the exception of one on Tresco. In 1949 most of the sitting tenants in Hugh Town purchased the freeholds, but otherwise the universal landlord of Scilly is still the Duke of Cornwall, from whom Tresco is held on lease by Lieutenant-Commander T. M. Dorrien-Smith.

Since the seventeenth century the economy of the islands has passed through several distinct phases. Until the 1720s the increase in population was sustained by the subsistence economy of farming and fishing; but with the growth from 822 persons in 1720 to nearly 2,000 by 1793 came the pinch of poverty, especially on the off-islands. Activities which helped to carry Scilly through this difficult period were kelp-burning, the export of fish, smuggling, and piloting, which increased with the number of vessels making use of the shelter afforded by the islands and awaiting a shift of wind. The war period from 1793 to 1815 was comparatively prosperous, for service pay, defence work, billeting, and pilotage all brought in money, and there was a considerable export of potatoes. With the ending of the wars most of these sources of income ceased or declined, and there was much distress in the islands until 1834; but then a new era opened as Augustus Smith pursued the task of reforming the economy. By 1851 the population had increased to 2,606, the highest figure ever recorded.

Until the 'seventies maritime occupations played a prominent part in the economic recovery. Shipbuilding, overseas trade, fishing, the provisioning of vessels, and pilotage (local and distant) were all important until they were adversely affected by changes in shipping. From the late nineteenth century the emphasis in employment moved markedly from the sea to the land, and the commercial growing of flowers became established as the mainstay of Scilly, with large markets in London, the Midlands, and the North of England. Nowadays, in an average season, the exports amount to between 40 and 50 million flowers.

The physical factors which limit agriculture on Scilly are not so much height—only at one point on St Mary's and at St Martin's Head does the land attain 160 feet—or rainfall which, averaging 32 inches per annum, is only moderate, as exposure and the roughness of much of the surface, especially those areas which are described as 'downs'. Most of the cultivable soils are light to medium loams overlying the growan and clay ('ram'). The heavy manuring required by intensive cultivation is partly supplied from the available cattle dung and the seaweed which is gathered in the autumn and winter; but other land-feeding practices now common are the ploughing in of rye grass and the application of large quantities of expensive fertilizer.

Scilly's main advantage for flower growing lies in her mild and equable climate. To the flower growers the really dangerous element in the weather is strong, cold, salt-laden winds, against which nature offers insufficient protection. The islands are by no means without trees, but most of these have been planted in patches or belts for shelter purposes. Before the flower industry started, the fields on Scilly were commonly enclosed by granite-boulder walls ('hedges'), and many of these are still useful; but since then 'fences'—mostly of pittosporum, escallonia, veronica, euonymus, and tamarisk—have been generally planted to shelter the rectangular flower-plots ('squares'). Contrasts between the sheltered farmlands and the open downs are clear on all the inhabited islands (Plate 55).

The flower-producing period begins with the picking of narcissi and normally extends from November to May. From mid April, when the narcissus–daffodil season is almost over, until mid May the dispatches of flowers consist chiefly of irises, tulips, stocks, and ixias. The overall range of production is lengthened a little farther by violets and calendulas. Casual labour is not in such good supply as formerly, but during the peak period all available hands are required on the holdings of the 200 or so growers. All the inhabited islands are concerned in the commercial growing of flowers, but about 75 per cent of the total for export is produced on St Mary's, and two-fifths of the rest comes from the Tresco Bulb Gardens, where there are 40 acres in bulbs. This is part of the largest agricultural unit on Scilly—the 160-acre Tresco Farm; the other units range from garden smallholdings to a 39-acre farm on St Mary's. A holding of four to six acres of bulbs alone is regarded as the minimum necessary to provide a livelihood, and the main group of holdings consists of those which have five to eight acres in bulbs.

Following the flower season comes the work of cleaning the ground by spraying, cultivation, and rotation. In order to hasten flowering during the next season, as much as five to eight tons per acre of imported straw is burnt in June and July on ground containing second- and third-year bulbs of 'Soleil d'Or' narcissi. Many bulbs are lifted for treatment—up to about one-third or even one-half of them each year. Planting is done from June to October, and ideally bulbs are in the ground for three years. It is difficult, however, to recognize or to adhere to a standard rotation. For many years eelworm has been a common pest, and its appearance has usually entailed the lifting of bulbs irrespective of their duration. Flower growers have other problems too, including the spread of garlic and of fungi which attack the bulbs, especially in mild, humid conditions. Most serious, however, is the fact that in recent years flower prices have been almost static, while competition has grown from overseas and from mainland producers who use techniques of forcing and pre-cooling bulbs. Perhaps the survival and development of the flower industry on Scilly will depend on four factors—a lengthening of the season, a greater concentration on high-quality flowers, a more persuasive publicity, and a higher degree of co-operation on the marketing side, of which there is already some evidence. As it is, bulbs occupy about 600 of the 1,600 acres which make up the total farmland on Scilly; and flowers from bulbs are the biggest business in the agriculture of the islands, accounting for 60 to 70 per cent of the gross output from the land.

Early potatoes play a part in rotations, and in recent years have slightly increased in importance. They are planted in December and January and dug in the second half of April and in May. Exports of potatoes amount to about 300 tons per annum. Other crops are mangolds, swedes, and kale for cattle feed. Most farms carry at least a few cattle which, with the exception of a small number of Friesians, are all of the Guernsey breed. With the increase in the number of visitors to Scilly, dairying has become a useful supplementary enterprise on many farms; but the supply of milk from the island cattle does not meet the demand at the peak of the holiday trade, and cream has to be imported. After the season ends, however, and

Scillonians themselves take a holiday, there is a surplus of milk and some is sent to Cornwall. Many holdings run poultry, but very few now have pigs. Until 1966 sheep had not been kept on Scilly since the 1930s, when they were last pastured on St Martin's and Bryher; but one farm on St Mary's now has a small flock. The considerable mechanization of the cultivation and of farm transport on Scilly has resulted in a great decrease in the number of horses during the past twenty years.

Communications between the islands are maintained by launches; those with the mainland are by ship, aeroplane, and, since 1964, helicopter services from St Mary's. In 1956 a new motor-vessel, the *Scillonian*, replaced the steamship of the same name which had run on the Hugh Town–Penzance route for many years. A second vessel, the *Queen of the Isles*, made her first voyage in 1965. She can carry 80 tons of cargo and 300 passengers, or about half the maximum number accommodated on the *Scillonian*. Both ships are used for the export trade in flowers and potatoes, the carriage of supplies, and the passenger traffic from the mainland. Since 1966, however, part of the flower crop has been dispatched by helicopter, and the *Queen of the Isles* has at times been employed in charter voyages elsewhere in British waters.

Scilly's attraction to the holiday-maker is not confined to the enjoyment of a mild climate and an island environment, the bathing, boating, and fishing, and the excursions from one island to another. There is a variety of scenery, not least along the coasts, with their white sandy beaches, boulder-strewn shores, and sheltered coves alternating with headlands of massive granite. Hills and slopes roughly covered with gorse and heather contrast with the neat landscape of horticulture. The old-style building in granite and thatch ended many years ago; but if some of the modern work is less picturesque, all is offset and relieved by the wealth of colour in the sea and the vegetation, colour enhanced by the clarity of the light and the seawater and varying from the tracts of gorse, heather, and bracken and the carpets of bluebells and cushions of sea pink to the shining drapery of mesembryanthemums. The Abbey Gardens on Tresco contain thousands of varieties of plants, many of them rare and from distant parts of the world, and add an exotic quality to the island scene. To some extent this is also true of the antiquities on Scilly, ranging from prehistoric settlements and burial places to castle and battery sites, and figureheads from wrecked vessels.

The mild winter and the early spring attract numerous visitors, but the main holiday season extends from mid March to mid October. At the peak of this period some 1,750 tourists are resident, of whom about 150 are campers on sites that are necessarily restricted in number and area. Each year about 20,000 people spend a holiday on the islands and the number of day trippers is approaching 100,000. For many of the inhabitants of Scilly the development of this trade has stabilized a two-season economy on the basis of flower growing and providing for visitors. However, the number of summer holiday-makers is nearing the maximum that the islands can take with the present accommodation, and the increase in tourism, together with the rise in demand for buildings and amenities, has raised the question of how to permit a certain amount of development while protecting the character and landscapes of Scilly. This problem will now have to be seriously tackled.

SELECTED REFERENCES

CHAPTER 1

Balchin, W. G. V. *Cornwall* (London 1954)
Davies, A. 'The personality of the South-West' *Geography* **39** (1954), 243–9
Devon and Cornwall: A Preliminary Survey (Exeter 1947)
Halliday, F. E. *A History of Cornwall* (London 1959)
Hoskins, W. G. *Devon* (London 1954)
Lewis, W. S. 'The South-West' in *Great Britain: Essays in Regional Geography* ed.
    A. G. Ogilvie (Cambridge 1930 edition), 93–113
Morgan, M. A. 'South-West England' in *Great Britain: Geographical Essays* ed.
    J. B. Mitchell (Cambridge 1962), 191–209
Pounds, N. J. G. 'The historical geography of Cornwall' Unpublished Ph.D. thesis,
    University of London (1945)

CHAPTER 2

H. Dewey's *South-West England* (2nd edition, 1948), in the Geological Survey series *British Regional Geology*, summarizes the geology of the area treated here. It contains a list of the published geological maps, and a comprehensive bibliography. The special district memoirs of the Geological Survey that relate to sheets of the 1-inch-to-1-mile maps are also listed; they contain detailed descriptions of the areas covered, but portions of north Devon have not been described in sheet memoirs. For the Southwest there are several Economic Memoirs—Special Reports on Mineral Resources.

The Royal Geological Society of Cornwall which has recently celebrated its one-hundred-and-fiftieth birthday is the second oldest body of its kind in Britain. A wealth of detailed information about the geology of Cornwall and particularly of its mines is to be found in the Reports and Transactions of the Society. From 1958 to 1961 the Society published 'Abstracts of the Proceedings of the Conference of Geologists and Geomorphologists working in the South-West of England'. The activities of this group are now published in the *Proceedings of the Ussher Society* (Camborne 1962–). The Geological Sections in the *Reports and Transactions of the Devonshire Association* deal with many aspects of the geology of Devon.

Among other works the following deserve individual reference:
De la Beche, H. T. *Report of the Geology of Cornwall, Devon and West Somerset*
    (H.M.S.O. 1839)
Bott, M. H. D. et al. 'The Geological interpretation of Gravity and Magnetic
    Surveys in Devon and Cornwall' *Phil. Trans. Royal Soc. London Series A.*
    No. 992 **251** (1958), 161–91
Clayden, A. W. *The History of Devonshire Scenery: an essay in Geographical
    Evolution* (Exeter 1906)
Dinely, D. L. 'The Devonian System in South Devonshire' *Field Studies* **1** (1961),
    1–20
Dines, H. G. *The Metalliferous Mining Region of South-West England* (H.M.S.O.
    1956)
Exley, C. S. and Stone, M. 'The Granitic Rocks of South-West England' in *Present
    Views of Some Aspects of the Geology of Cornwall and Devon* ed. K. F. G.
    Hosking and G. J. Shrimpton (Penzance 1964)
Hosking, K. F. G. 'The Relationship between the Primary Mineralization and the

318

structure of South West England' in *Some Aspects of the Variscan Fold Belt* ed. K. Coe (Manchester 1962)

House, M. R. and Selwood, E. B. 'Palaeozoic Palaeontology in Devon and Cornwall' in *Present Views of Some Aspects of the Geology of Cornwall and Devon* ed. K. F. G. Hosking and G. J. Shrimpton (Penzance 1964)

Rogers, I. and Simpson, B. 'The Flint Gravel Deposit of Orleigh Court Buckland Brewer' *Geol. Mag.* **74** (1937), 309–16

Simpson, S. 'Culm Stratigraphy and the Age of the Main Orogenic Phase in Devon and Cornwall' *Geol. Mag.* **96** (1959), 201–8

Tidmarsh, W. G. 'The Permian Lavas of Devon' *Quart. Journ. Geol. Soc.* **88** (1932), 712–75

CHAPTER 3

Arkell, W. J. 'The Pleistocene rocks at Trebetherick Point, north Cornwall; their interpretation and correlation' *Proc. Geol. Ass.* **54** (1943), 141–70

Balchin, W. G. V. 'The erosion surfaces of north Cornwall' *Geog. Journ.* **90** (1937), 52–63

— 'The erosion surfaces of Exmoor and adjacent areas' *Geog. Journ.* **118** (1952), 453–76

— 'The denudation chronology of South West England' in *Present Views of Some Aspects of the Geology of Cornwall and Devon* ed. K. F. G. Hosking and G. J. Shrimpton (Penzance 1964), 267–82

Brunsden, D. 'The origin of the decomposed granite' in *Dartmoor Essays* ed. I. G. Simmons (Devon. Ass., Torquay 1964), 97–116

Dearman, W. R. 'Wrench-faulting in Cornwall and South Devon' *Proc. Geol. Ass.* **74** (1963), 265–89

Dineley, D. L. 'Contortions in the Bovey Beds (Oligocene), South West England' *Biuletyn Peryglacjalny* **12** (1963), 151–60

Everard, C. E. 'Mining and shoreline evolution near St Austell, Cornwall' *Trans. Royal Geol. Soc. Cornwall* **19** (1959–60), 199–219

Everard, C. E., Lawrence, R. H., Witherick, M. E., and Wright, L. W. 'Raised beaches and marine geomorphology' in *Present Views of Some Aspects of the Geology of Cornwall and Devon* ed. K. F. G. Hosking and G. J. Shrimpton (Penzance 1964), 283–310

Green, J. F. N. 'The history of the river Dart, Devon' *Proc. Geol. Ass.* **60** (1949), 105–24

Gregory, K. J. 'Dry valleys and the composition of the drainage net' *Journ Hydrology* **4** (1966), 327–40

Guilcher, A. 'Nivation, cryoplanation et solifluxion quaternaires dans les collines de Bretagne et du nord de Devonshire' *Rev. de Géomorph. Dynamique* **1** (1950), 53–78

Jukes Brown, A. J. 'The valley of the Teign' *Quart. Journ. Geol. Soc.* **60** (1904), 319–34

Kidson, C. 'Dawlish Warren, Devon: Late stages in sand spit evolution' *Proc. Geol. Ass.* **75** (1964), 167–84

— 'The coasts of south and southwest England' in *Field Studies in the British Isles* ed. J. A. Steers (London 1964), 26–42

Kidson, C., Brunsden, D., Orme, A. R., and Waters, R. S. 'Denudation chronology of parts of South-Western England' *Field Studies* **2** (1964), 115–32

Ledger, R. 'Beach erosion at Bude, North Cornwall' *Trans. Royal Geol. Soc. Cornwall* **19** (1963–4), 392–406

Linton, D. L. 'The problem of tors' *Geog. Journ.* **121** (1955), 470–87

— 'Tertiary landscape evolution' in *The British Isles* ed. J. Wreford Watson, with Sissons, J. B. (London 1964), 110–30

Linton, D. L. and Waters, R. S. 'The Exeter Symposium: Discussion' *Biuletyn Peryglacjalny* **15** (1966), 133–9

320 SOUTHWEST ENGLAND

McFarlan, P. B. 'Survey of two drowned river valleys in Devon' *Geol. Mag.* **92** (1955), 419–29

Mitchell, G. F. 'The St Erth Beds—an alternative explanation' *Proc. Geol. Ass.* **76** (1965), 345–66

Orme, A. R. 'Abandoned and composite sea cliffs in Britain and Ireland' *Irish Geography* **4** (1962), 279–91

— 'The geomorphology of southern Dartmoor and adjacent areas' in *Dartmoor Essays* ed. I. G. Simmons (Devon. Ass., Torquay 1964), 31–72

Palmer, J. and Neilson, R. A. 'The origin of granite tors on Dartmoor, Devonshire' *Proc. Yorks. Geol. Soc.* **33** (1962), 315–40

Savigear, R. A. G. 'Some observations on slope development in north Devon and north Cornwall' *Trans. Inst. Brit. Geographers* **31** (1962), 23–42

Stephens, N. 'Some Pleistocene deposits in North Devon' *Biuletyn Peryglacjalny* **15** (1966), 103–14

Stephens, N. and Synge, F. M. 'Pleistocene shorelines' in *Essays in Geomorphology* ed. G. H. Dury (London 1966), 1–51 (especially 16–26)

Te Punga, M. E. 'Periglaciation in southern England' *Koninklijk Nederlandsch Aardrijkskundig Genootschap* **74** (1957), 401–12

Waters, R. S. 'Differential weathering and erosion on oldlands' *Geog. Journ.* **123** (1957), 503–13

— 'The bearing of superficial deposits on the age and origin of the upland plain of east Devon, west Dorset and south Somerset' *Trans. Inst. Brit. Geographers* **28** (1960), 89–97

— 'Involutions and ice wedges in Devon' *Nature* **189** (1961), 389–90

— 'Altiplanation terraces and slope development in Vest-Spitsbergen and South West England' *Biuletyn Peryglacjalny* **11** (1962), 89–101

— 'The Pleistocene legacy to the geomorphology of Dartmoor' in *Dartmoor Essays* ed. I. G. Simmons (Devon. Ass., Torquay 1964), 73–96

— 'The geomorphological significance of Pleistocene frost action in south-west England' in *Essays in Geography for Austin Miller* ed. J. B. Whittow and P. D. Wood (Reading 1965), 39–57

— 'The Exeter Symposium: Dartmoor Excursion' *Biuletyn Peryglacjalny* **15** (1966), 123–8

Weller, M. R. 'The erosion surfaces of Bodmin Moor' *Trans. Royal Geol. Soc. Cornwall* **19** (1959–60), 233–42

Wooldridge, S. W. 'The physique of the South West' *Geography* **39** (1954), 231–42

— 'The Radstock Plateau—a note on the physiography of the Bristol district' *Proc. Bristol Naturalists' Soc.* **30** (1961), 151–62

Floods and Water Supply

Brierley, J. 'Flooding in the Exe valley' *Proc. Inst. Civil Engineers* **28** (1964), 151–70

— 'Discussion on flooding in the Exe valley' *ibid.* **32** (1965), 109–16

Harrison, A. J. M. 'The 1960 Exmouth floods' *The Surveyor and Municipal and County Engineer* (4 Feb. 1961), 127–32

Kidson, C. 'The Exmoor storm and the Lynmouth floods' *Geography* **38** (1953), 1–9

Ministry of Housing and Local Government. *Dartmoor Rivers Hydrological Survey* (London 1966)

Smith, R. I. *An outline of British Regional Hydrology* Publication of the Nature Conservancy, Speyside Research Station, Aviemore, Inverness-shire (1965)

Worth, R. H. 'The physical geography of Dartmoor' *Trans. Devon. Ass.* **62** (1930) 99–115

CHAPTER 4

Climate

Archer, C. H. 'The wettest areas of south-western England' *Weather* **11** (1956), 35–9
Bleasdale, A. and Douglas, C. K. M. 'Storm over Exmoor on August 15, 1952'
    Met. Mag. **81** (1952), 353–67
Bonacina, L. C. W. 'The Widecombe Calamity of 1638' *Weather* **1** (1946), 122–5
— 'The scenery of Devonshire in relation to the weather and climate' *Weather* **6**
    (1951), 131–5
— 'The Exmoor Cataclysm' *Weather* **7** (1952), 336
Burton, S. H. 'The "Chains" of Exmoor' *Weather* **7** (1952), 334
Climatological Atlas of the British Isles (H.M.S.O. 1952)
Douglas, C. K. M. 'Some features of the local weather in South-east Devon'
    Weather **15** (1960), 14
Glasspole, J. 'Fluctuations of Annual Rainfall' *British Rainfall* (H.M.S.O. 1921),
    288–300
Hogg, W. H. 'Climatic Factors and Choice of Site, with special reference to Horti-
    culture' in *The Biological Significance of Climatic Changes in Britain* ed.
    C. G. Johnson and L. P. Smith (London 1965), 141–55
Manley, G. 'The effective rate of altitudinal change in temperate Atlantic climates'
    Geog. Rev. **35** (1945), 408–17
— *Climate and the British Scene* (London 1952)

Soils

Barrow, G. *The Geology of the Isles of Scilly* (Memoir of Geological Survey,
    Sheets 357, 360, 1906)
Beche, H. T. De la 'On the connection between geology and agriculture in Devon'
    Journ. Royal Agric. Soc. England **3** (1842), 21–35
Cailleux, A. 'Phénomènes periglaciaires et férruginisations à Harpford Common'
    Biuletyn Periglacjalny **15** (1966), 121–2
Clayden, B. *Soils of the Middle Teign valley district of Devon* Nuffield Farm Project
    (Exeter 1962)
— 'The relationship of soil development to site on Culm shales' *Proc. Ussher Soc.*
    1 (1963), 54–5
— 'The soils of the Middle Teign valley district of Devon' *Bulletin of the Soil
    Survey of England and Wales* No. 1 (Harpenden 1964)
— 'The soils of Cornwall' in *Present Views of Some Aspects of the Geology of
    Cornwall and Devon* ed. K. F. G. Hosking and G. J. Shrimpton (Penzance
    1964), 311–30
Clayden, B. and Manley, D. J. R. 'Devonshire' *Soil Survey of Great Britain* Report
    Nos. 15–19 (1962–7)
— 'The soils of the Dartmoor granite' in *Dartmoor Essays* ed. I. G. Simmons
    (Devon. Ass., Torquay 1964), 117–40
Coombe, D. E. and Frost, L. C. 'The nature and origin of the soils over the Cornish
    serpentine' *Journ. Ecol.* **44** (1956), 605–15
Curtis, L. F. 'The soils around Simonsbath' *Exmoor Review* **3** (1961), 16–18

    Soil classification follows that used in:
Mackney, D. and Burnham, C. P. 'The soils of the West Midlands' *Bulletin of the
    Soil Survey of England and Wales* No. 2 (Harpenden 1964)

Vegetation

Coombe, D. E. and Frost, L. C. 'The Heaths of the Cornish Serpentine' *Journ.
    Ecol.* **44** (1956), 226–56
Conolly, A. P. et al. 'Studies in Post-Glacial History of British Vegetation' *Phil.
    Trans.* **B234** (1950), 397–469

Annual Reports of the Forestry Commissioners (H.M.S.O.)

Godwin, H. 'Radiocarbon Dating and Quaternary History in Britain' *Proc. Royal Soc.* B**153** (1961), 287–320

Hepburn, I. *Flowers of the Coast* (London 1952)

Keble Martin, W. and Fraser, G. T. *Flora of Devon* (Arbroath 1939)

Mathews, J. R. 'Geographical Relationships of the British Flora' *Journ. Ecol.* **25** (Cambridge 1937), 1–90

— *Origin and Distribution of the British Flora* (London 1955)

Pearsall, W. H. *Mountains and Moorlands* (London 1950)

Proctor, M. C. F. 'The phyto-geography of Dartmoor bryophytes' in *Dartmoor Essays* ed. I. G. Simmons (Devon. Ass., Torquay 1964), 141–71

— *South-West England* Pamphlet prepared for Tenth International Botanical Congress (Exeter 1964)

Rouse, G. D. and Edlin, H. L. 'The Forests of South-West England' *Forestry* **31** (1957), 27–51

Simmons, I. G. 'An outline of the vegetation history of Dartmoor' *Trans. Devon. Ass.* **94** (1962), 555–74

— 'The Blanket Bog of Dartmoor' *Trans. Devon. Ass.* **95** (1963), 180–96

— 'Pollen Diagrams from Dartmoor' *The New Phytologist* **63** (1964), 165–80

Willis, A. J. et al. 'Braunton Burrows: The Dune System and its Vegetation' *Journ. Ecol.* **47** (1959), 1–25 and 249–88

CHAPTER 5

A valuable aid to the study of the early settlement of Cornwall is the very large collection of Parish Histories, transcriptions and miscellaneous manuscripts made by Charles Henderson between 1920–33 and now housed in the Royal Institution of Cornwall Museum, Truro, and currently being published in part by them. Details about the early settlement of Cornwall and Devon are recorded chiefly in the *Journal of the Royal Institution of Cornwall* (1818–), the *Proceedings of the West Cornwall Field Club (Archaeological) New Series* (1952–61), *Cornish Archaeology* (1962–), *Proceedings of the Devon Archaeological Exploration Society* (1929–), *Reports and Transactions of the Devonshire Association* (1863–), and in *Devon and Cornwall Notes and Queries* (Exeter 1900–).

There are three general archaeological surveys:

Hencken, H. O'N. *Archaeology of Cornwall and Scilly* (London 1932)

'Archaeology in Cornwall 1933–1958' Twenty-fifth Anniversary Number *Proc. W. Cornwall Field Club* **2** (1957–8)

Fox, Aileen *South West England* (London 1964)

For the prehistoric period see:

Willock, E. H. 'A Neolithic Site on Haldon' *Proc. Devon Arch. Expl. Soc.* **2** (1936), 244–64 and **3** (1937), 33–44

Houlder, C. H. 'A Neolithic Settlement on Hazard Hill, Totnes' *Proc. Devon Arch. Expl. Soc.* **21** (1963), 2–31

Liddell, D. M. 'Excavations at Hembury Fort' *Proc. Devon Arch. Expl. Soc.* **1** (1930–1), 40–64, 90–121 and **2** (1935), 135–76

Radford, C. A. R. 'Prehistoric Settlements on Dartmoor and the Cornish Moors' *Proc. Prehist. Soc.* **18** (1952), 55–84

Megaw, J. V. S. et al. 'The Bronze Age Settlement at Gwithian' *Proc. W. Cornwall Field Club* **2** (1961), 200–14

Fox, Aileen 'Celtic Fields and Farms on Dartmoor' *Proc. Prehist. Soc.* **20** (1954), 87–102

— 'South-Western Hill-Forts' in *Problems of the Iron Age in Southern Britain* ed.

S. S. Frere. Occas. Paper No. 11 London University Institute of Archaeology (1961), 35–60

Brooks, R. T. 'The Rumps, St Minver' *Cornish Arch.* **3** (1964), 26–34

Cotton, M. A. 'Cornish Cliff Castles' *Proc. W. Cornwall Field Club* **2** (1958–9), 113–21

Saunders, A. D. 'Excavations at Castle Gotha, St Austell' *Cornish Arch.* **2** (1963), 49–51

For the Roman period see:

Fox, Aileen *Roman Exeter* (Manchester 1952)

— 'Roman Exeter (Isca Dumnoniorum)' in *The Civitas Capitals of Roman Britain* ed. J. Wacher (Leicester 1966)

Fox, Aileen and Ravenhill, W. 'Old Burrow and Martinhoe' *Antiquity* **39** (1965), 253–8

— 'Early Roman Outposts on the North Devon Coast' *Proc. Devon Arch. Expl. Soc.* **24** (1966), 3–39

— 'Excavation of the Roman Fort at Tregear, Nanstallon near Bodmin, Cornwall' Interim Reports *Cornish Arch.* **5** (1966), 28–30 and **6** (1967), 32–4

Thomas, A. C. 'The Character and Origins of Roman Dumnonia' in *Rural Settlement in Roman Britain* ed. A. C. Thomas. C.B.A. Research Report **7** (1966), 74–98

For the Celtic period see:

Doble, G. H. *Cornish Saints Series* 1–49 (1923–48)

Fox, Aileen 'Some evidence for a Dark Age Trading Site at Bantham, near Thurlestone, South Devon' *Antiq. Journ.* **35** (1955), 55–67

Radford, C. A. R. 'The Dumnonii' *Trans. Devon. Ass.* **79** (1947), 15–30

— 'Tintagel: the Castle and Celtic Monastery' *Antiq. Journ.* **15** (1935), 401

Ravenhill, W. 'The Settlement of Cornwall during the Celtic Period' *Geography* **40** (1955), 237–49

— 'Rural Settlement in Cornwall and Devon' *Brit. Ass. for the Adv. of Science* **15** (1959), 342–5

Thomas, A. C. 'Imported Pottery in Dark Age Britain' *Medieval Arch.* **3** (1959), 89–111

— 'People and Pottery in Dark Age Cornwall' *Old Cornwall* **5** (1960), 1–9

— *Christian Antiquities of Camborne* (St Austell 1967)

For the Saxon and Medieval periods see:

Beresford, M. W. 'Dispersed and Grouped Settlement in Medieval Cornwall' *Agric. Hist. Rev.* **12** (1964), 13–28

Gover, J. E. B. 'The Place-Names of Cornwall' Unpublished MS, Truro Museum

Dudley, D. and Minter, E. M. 'The Medieval Village at Garrow Tor, Bodmin Moor, Cornwall' *Medieval Arch.* **6–7** (1963), 272–94

— 'Treworld, Boscastle' *Medieval Arch.* **8** (1964), 282

Finberg, H. P. R. *The Early Charters of Devon and Cornwall* (Leicester 1953)

Gover, J. E. B., Mawer, A., and Stenton, F. M. *The Place-Names of Devon* (Cambridge 1931)

Linehan, C. D. 'Deserted Sites and Rabbit-Warrens on Dartmoor' *Medieval Arch.* **10** (1966), 113–44

Minter, E. M. 'Houndtor Down' *Medieval Arch.* **6–7** (1962–3), 341–3 and **8** (1964), 282–5

Hoskins, W. G. and Finberg, H. P. R. *Devonshire Studies* (London 1952)

Hoskins, W. G. *The Westward Expansion of Wessex* (Leicester 1960)

— 'The Highland Zone in Domesday Book' in *Provincial England* (London 1963), 15–52

Finberg, H. P. R. 'The Open Field in Devonshire' *Antiquity* **23** (1949), 180–7

Ravenhill, W. 'The Domesday Geography of Cornwall' in *The Domesday Geography of South-West England* ed. H. C. Darby and R. Welldon Finn (Cambridge 1967)

Welldon Finn, R. 'The Domesday Geography of Devon' in *The Domesday Geography of South-West England* ed. H. C. Darby and R. Welldon Finn (Cambridge 1967)

Shorter, A. H. 'Field Patterns in Brixham Parish, Devon' *Trans. Devon. Ass.* **82** (1950), 271–80

CHAPTER 6

Alexander, J. J. 'The Early Boroughs of Devon' *Trans. Devon. Ass.* **58** (1926), 275–87
— 'The Beginnings of Tavistock' *Trans. Devon. Ass.* **74** (1942), 173–97

Alexander, J. J. and Hooper, W. R. *The History of Great Torrington in the County of Devon* (1948)

Beresford, M. W. and St Joseph, J. K. S. *Medieval England* (Cambridge 1958)

Campbell, S. 'The Haveners of the Medieval Dukes of Cornwall and the Organisation of the Duchy Ports' *Journ. Royal Inst. Cornwall New Series* **4** (1962), 113

Carus-Wilson, E. M. *The Expansion of Exeter at the Close of the Middle Ages* (Exeter 1963)

Chope, R. P. 'The Aulnager in Devon' *Trans. Devon. Ass.* **64** (1912), 568–97

Davis, O. W. 'Barnstaple in the Seventeenth Century' *Architectural Rev.* **4** (1898), 99–105

Dolley, R. H. M. and Elmore Jones, F. 'The Mints "Aet Gothabyrig" and "Aet Sith(m)estbyrig" ' *Brit. Numismatic Journ.* **28** (1956), 270

Dolley, R. H. M. and Metcalf, D. M. 'The Reform of the English Coinage under Eadgar' in *Anglo-Saxon Coins* (London 1961), 136–68

Finberg, H. P. R. 'The Borough of Tavistock its origin and early history' *Trans. Devon. Ass.* **79** (1947), 129–52
— 'The Boroughs of Devon' *Devon and Cornwall Notes and Queries* **24** (1951), 203–9

Henderson, C. *Essays in Cornish History* (Oxford 1935)

Hoskins, W. G. 'English Provincial Towns in the Early Sixteenth Century' *Trans. Royal Hist. Soc.* **6** (1956), 1–21

Lewis, G. R. *The Stannaries: A Study of the English Tin Miner* (Harvard Univ. Press, Cambridge 1924)

Maclean, J. 'The Tin Trade of Cornwall in the Reigns of Elizabeth and James, compared with that of Edward I' *Journ. Royal Inst. Cornwall* **4** (1874), 187–90

Pool, P. A. S. 'Penzance: A brief history of the town and borough' *Penzance Old Cornwall Soc.* (1965)

Roddis, R. J. *Penryn, History of an Ancient Cornish Borough* (Penryn 1965)

Watkin, R. H. *The History of Totnes Priory and Medieval Town* (Torquay 1914 and 1917)

Welch, C. E. 'A Survey of Some Duchy Manors' *Devon and Cornwall Notes and Queries* **29** (1962), 161

Westcote, T. *A View of Devonshire in MDCXXX* ed. G. Oliver and P. Jones (Exeter 1845)

Whetter, J. C. A. 'Cornish Trade in the 17th Century: An Analysis of the Port Books' *Journ. Royal Inst. Cornwall* New Series **4** (1964), 388–413

Witherick, M. E. 'The Mediaeval Boroughs of Cornwall—An Alternative View of their Origins' *Southampton Research Series in Geography* **4** (1967), 41–60

CHAPTER 7

Agrarian landscapes

Hoskins, W. G. 'The reclamation of the waste in Devon, 1550–1800' *Econ. Hist. Rev.* **13** (1943), 80–92

Pounds, N. J. G. 'The Lanhydrock Atlas and Cornish agriculture about 1700' *Annual Report of the Royal Cornwall Polytechnic Soc.* (1944), 1–15
— 'Sandingways to the sea' *Devon and Cornwall Notes and Queries* **22** (1942–6), 289–91
Shorter, A. H. 'Ridge and furrow in Devon and Cornwall' *ibid.* **24** (1950), 3–6

Trends in agriculture from the eighteenth century to the Second World War

Dicks, T. R. B. 'The south-western peninsulas of England and Wales: studies in agricultural geography 1550–1900' Unpublished Ph.D. thesis, University of Wales (1964)
Fraser, R. *General View of the County of Cornwall* (London 1794)
— *General View of the County of Devon* (London 1794)
Fussell, G. E. ' "High Farming" in Southwestern England 1840–1880' *Econ. Geog.* **24** (1948), 67–73
— 'Four centuries of farming systems in Devon; 1500–1900' *Trans. Devon. Ass.* **83** (1951), 179–204
Marshall, W. *The Rural Economy of the West of England* (London 1796)
— *A Review of The Reports to the Board of Agriculture* (London 1817)
Shorter, A. H. 'Flax-growing in Devon in the eighteenth and early nineteenth centuries' *Devon and Cornwall Notes and Queries* **24** (1950), 41–4
The Land of Britain ed. L. D. Stamp. The Report of the Land Utilisation Survey of Britain. Roberson, B. S. Part 91, Cornwall (1941). Stamp, L. D. Part 92, Devon (1941)
Vancouver, C. *General View of the Agriculture of the County of Devon* (London 1808)
Worgan, G. B. *General View of the Agriculture of the County of Cornwall* (London 1815)

Modern trends in agriculture

Brown, A. J. 'Barley growing in Devon' *Agriculture* **72** (1965), 544–8
Cole, Helen M. 'Some economic aspects of early crop production in South West England' Aberystwyth Symposium (1966)
Devon Farming The Devon Agriculture Study Group (Exeter 1952)

The last section of this Chapter also draws upon many of the Reports of the Department of Agricultural Economics, University of Exeter, especially the following:
Barley Production in Devon and Cornwall in 1964 Farmers' Report 2 (1966)
Brewer, J. L. and Davies, E. T. *An Economic and Physical Study of Cattle and Sheep Production in Devon and Cornwall in 1961–63* Report 151 (1965)
Burnside, Estelle and Rickard, R. C. *An Economic Study of Pig Production in South West England* Reports 129, 140, 147, 152 and 158 (1962–6)
Cole, Helen M. and Adkins, Jane N. *Commercial Anemone Production in South West England 1959–62* Report 132 (1962)
Davies, E. T. *A Study of Store Cattle and Sheep Production in Devon and Cornwall in 1965–66* Farmers' Report 4 (1967)
Harrison, J. E. and Tyers, K. G. *Main Crop Potatoes in South West England 1960* Report 130 (1962)
Roscoe, Betty J. and Langley, J. A. *Milk Production in South West England* Report 135 (1962)
— *Some Economic Aspects of Milk Production: a Study in South West England* Report 162 (1967)
Store Cattle Production in Devon and Cornwall in 1964–65 Farmers' Report 1 (1966)
Wheat Production in South West England Report 145 (1964)

CHAPTER 8

Manufacturing industries

Hoskins, W. G. *Industry, Trade and People in Exeter 1688–1800* (Manchester 1935)
Shorter, A. H. 'A classification of old mills in Devon and Cornwall' *Devon and Cornwall Notes and Queries* **23** (1949), 277–80
— 'The tanning industry in Devon and Cornwall 1550–1850' *ibid.* **25** (1952), 10–16
— 'The historical geography of the paper-making industry in England' Unpublished Ph.D. thesis, University of London (1954)
— *Paper Mills and Paper Makers in England 1495–1800* (Hilversum 1957)

Mining and quarrying

This section is greatly indebted to the definitive histories by D. B. and R. M. Barton.
Barton, D. B. *A History of Copper Mining in Cornwall and Devon* (Truro 1961)
— *A History of Tin Mining and Smelting in Cornwall* (Truro 1967)
— *The Cornish Beam Engine* (Truro 1966 edition)
Barton, R. M. *A History of the Cornish China-Clay Industry* (Truro 1966)
Bulley, J. A. 'The beginnings of the Devonshire ball-clay trade' *Trans. Devon. Ass.* **87** (1955), 191–204
Jenkin, A. K. H. *Mines and Miners of Cornwall* **1–14** (Truro 1961–7)
Mineral Areas in Cornwall Worthy of Investigation Cornish Mining Development Association (1950)
Rowe, J. *Cornwall in the Age of the Industrial Revolution* (Liverpool 1953)
Trounson, J. H. 'The Cornish mineral industry' *The Mining Magazine* **66** (1942), 195–205

Fishing and shipbuilding

Braddick, L. E. 'The port of Topsham, its ships and shipbuilders' *Trans. Devon. Ass.* **85** (1953), 18–34
Rogers, I. *Ships and Shipyards of Bideford, 1568–1938* (Bideford 1947)
Russell, P. 'Some historical notes on the Brixham fisheries' *Trans. Devon. Ass.* **83** (1951), 278–97
Stephens, W. B. 'The West-country ports and the struggle for the Newfoundland fisheries in the seventeenth century' *ibid.* **88** (1956), 90–101

The modern industrial accession

The Economic and Industrial Development of the South West Prepared for the Joint Committee for the Economy of the South West by Associated Industrial Consultants Ltd. (1965)

CHAPTER 9

Transport

Barton, D. B. *The Redruth and Chasewater Railway 1824–1915* (Truro 1966 edition)
Boyle, V. C. and Payne, D. *Devon Harbours* (London 1952)
Clark, E. A. G. *The Ports of the Exe Estuary 1660–1860* (University of Exeter 1960)
Ewans, M. C. *The Haytor Granite Tramway and Stover Canal* (Dawlish 1964)
Hadfield, C. *The Canals of South West England* (Newton Abbot 1967)
Lewis, M. J. T. *The Pentewan Railway 1829–1918* (Truro 1960)
Noall, C. *A History of Cornish Mail- and Stage-Coaches* (Truro 1963)
Pearse, R. *The Ports and Harbours of Cornwall* (St Austell 1963)

Sheldon, G. *From Trackway to Turnpike* (Oxford 1928)
Thomas, D. St J. *A Regional History of the Railways of Great Britain* 1 *The West Country* (Newton Abbot 1966 edition)

The holiday industry

Bennett, W. J. 'A century of change on the coast of Cornwall' *Geography* **37** (1952), 214–24
Bulley, J. A. 'Teignmouth as a seaside resort (before the coming of the railway)' *Trans. Devon. Ass.* **88** (1956), 143–62
Lewes, F. M. M., Culyer, A., and Brady, Gillian A. *Holiday Transport in Devon and Cornwall* (University of Exeter 1967)
Survey of the Holiday Industry Cornwall County Council (Truro 1966)
The Coasts of South-West England National Parks Commission: Coastal Preservation and Development (London 1967)

Population

A Region with a Future: A Draft Strategy for the South West South West Economic Planning Council (London 1967)
Bennett, W. J. 'The settlement of Cornwall with particular reference to the economic aspects of its development 1750–1950' Unpublished M.A. thesis, University of London (1951)
County of Cornwall Development Plan: Report of the Survey (Truro 1952)
County of Cornwall Development Plan (First Review): Report of Survey (1962)
Devon County Council Development Plan: Analysis of the Survey (1952)
Devon County Council Development Plan (First Review): Analysis of the Survey (1964)
Devon-Plymouth: Industry and Growth Industrial Feasibility Study prepared for the Devon County Council and Plymouth City Council by Associated Industrial Consultants Ltd. (1966)
Marsden, B. S. 'The establishment of the geographic incidence of the retired population in Devon and Cornwall, and an examination of the role of amenities in this distribution' Unpublished M.A. thesis, University of Leeds (1960)
Pounds, N. J. G. 'Population movement in Cornwall and the rise of mining in the eighteenth century' *Geography* **28** (1943), 37–46
Simmonds, N. M. 'The functions and growth of the city of Exeter, 1800–1841' Unpublished M.A. thesis, University of Exeter (1959)
The Barnstaple Feasibility Study Devon County Council Planning Committee (1967)

CHAPTER 10

East Devon

Cornish, V. *The Scenery of Sidmouth* (Cambridge 1940)

The Heartland of Devon

Allen, W. G. *John Heathcoat and His Heritage* (London 1958)
Brown, A. J. 'Exeter' *Agriculture* **60** (1953–4), 593–4
Delderfield, E. R. *Exmouth Milestones* (Exmouth 1948)
Dibb, C. 'Early fat lamb in Devon' *Agriculture* **67** (1960–1), 605–9
Ibbett, W. C. 'Devon swedes' *ibid.* **65** (1958–9), 357–60
— 'Dawlish violets' *ibid.* **65** (1958–9), 515–8

Exeter

Johns, E. M. 'Old and new townscapes in Exeter' *Town and Country Planning* **32** (1964), 296–307
Sharp, T. *Exeter Phoenix* (London 1946)

Shorter, A. H. 'The site, situation and functions of Exeter' *Geography* **39** (1954), 250–61

The Bovey Basin

Scott, A. *Ball Clays* Memoirs of the Geological Survey, Special Reports on the Mineral Resources of Great Britain 31 (London 1929)

Torbay

Russell, P. *A History of Torquay* (Torquay 1960)

CHAPTER 11

Exmoor

Beard, W. D. 'Exmoor Farmer' *Agriculture* **62** (1956), 530–3
Bourne, H. L. *Living on Exmoor* (London 1963)
Burton, S. H. *Exmoor* (London 1952)
— ed. for the Exmoor Society *Can Exmoor Survive? A Technical Assessment* (The Exmoor Society 1966)
Exmoor Review, The Journal of the Exmoor Society (1959–)
MacDermot, E. T. *The History of the Forest of Exmoor* (Taunton 1911)
Miles, R. 'Forestry and Landscape in the Exmoor National Park' *Forestry* **33** (1960), 13–19
Orwin, C. S. *The Reclamation of Exmoor Forest* (Oxford 1929)
Thomas, A. N. 'The Triassic Rocks of N.W. Somerset' *Proc. Geol. Ass.* **51** (1940), 1
Webby, B. D. 'The Stratigraphy and Structure of the Devonian Rocks in the Brendon Hills, West Somerset' *Proc. Geol. Ass.* **76** (1965), 39–60
Whitton, T. H. F. 'A Devon and Somerset Estate' *Agriculture* **61** (1954), 344–8

North Devon

Allington, P. 'Combe Martin: a study of horticultural isolation' *Agriculture* **69** (1962), 279–82
Arber, E. A. N. *The Coast Scenery of North Devon* (London 1911)
Arber, Muriel A. 'Pleistocene sea-levels in North Devon' *Proc. Geol. Ass.* **71** (1960), 169–76
Burton, S. H. *The North Devon Coast* (London 1953)
Langham, A. and M. *Lundy Bristol Channel* (Bradford 1960)
Roe, R. C. 'Bideford' *Agriculture* **59** (1952–3), 343–4
Stuart, A. and Hookway, R. J. S. *Coastal Erosion at Westward Ho! North Devon* A Report to the Coast Protection Committee, Devon County Council (1954)

The Culm Measures Country

Bradshaw, M. J. 'Aspects of the geomorphology of Northwest Devon' Unpublished M.A. thesis, University of London (1961)
Jones, T. W. W. 'North Tawton' *Agriculture* **71** (1964), 136–7
Moore, H. I. and Macfarlan, P. J. 'Problem areas in Devon' in 'A symposium on some problem areas in the South-West' *Journ. Royal Agric. Soc. England* **112** (1951), 9–24

Dartmoor

Dartmoor: National Park Guide No. 1 ed. W. G. Hoskins (London 1957)
Fogwill, E. G. 'Pastoralism on Dartmoor' *Trans. Devon. Ass.* **86** (1954), 89–114
Harvey, L. A. and St Leger-Gordon, D. *Dartmoor* (London 1953)
Johns, E. M. 'The surveying and mapping of vegetation on some Dartmoor pastures' *Geog. Studies* **4** (1957), 129–37
Martin, E. W. *Dartmoor* (London 1958)

Myers, L. 'Granite from Merrivale' *Stone Industries* **1** (1966), 24–7
Rouse, G. D. *The New Forests of Dartmoor* Forestry Commission Booklet 10 (London 1964)
Smith, V. *Portrait of Dartmoor* (London 1966)
Waters, R. S. *Dartmoor* Geography of Great Britain in Colour (London 1959)
Worth, R. H. *Dartmoor* (Plymouth 1953)

CHAPTER 12

South Devon

Burton, S. H. *The South Devon Coast* (London 1954)
Hardy, J. R. 'Sources of some beach shingles in England' *Abstracts of Papers, 20th International Geographical Congress* (1964)
Mercer, I. D. 'The natural history of Slapton Ley Nature Reserve' *Field Studies* **2** (1966), 385–407
Orme, A. R. 'The geomorphology of the South Hams' Unpublished Ph.D. thesis, University of Birmingham (1961)
Robinson, A. H. W. 'The hydrography of Start Bay and its relationship to beach changes at Hallsands' *Geog. Journ.* **127** (1961), 63–77
Russell, P. *Dartmouth* (London 1950)
The Story of Dartington (Paignton 1964)
Watt, A. 'Kingsbridge' *Agriculture* **66** (1959–60), 94–5
Willy, Margaret *The South Hams* (London 1955)

Plymouth

Shorter, A. H. and Woodley, E. T. 'Plymouth: port and city' *Geography* **22** (1937), 293–306
Sillick, C. B. Muriel 'The city-port of Plymouth' Unpublished Ph.D. thesis, University of London (1938)
Tamblin, Jean L. 'The problems of industrial location in Plymouth' Unpublished M.A. thesis, University of London (1965)
Walling, R. A. J. *The Story of Plymouth* (London 1950)
Watson, J. P. and Abercrombie, P. *A Plan for Plymouth* (Plymouth 1943)

Southwest Devon–Southeast Cornwall

Barton, D. B. *A Historical Survey of the Mines and Mineral Railways of East Cornwall and West Devon* (Truro 1964)
Booker, F. *The Industrial Archaeology of the Tamar Valley* (Newton Abbot 1967)
Fuller, D. J. 'Tamar valley strawberries' *Agriculture* **69** (1962), 214–8
Jackson, A. L. 'East Cornwall' *ibid.* **65** (1958–9), 529–30
Johnstone, Katharine H. 'Horticulture in the Tamar valley' *ibid.* **62** (1955), 123–9
Keast, J. *The Story of Fowey* (Exeter 1950)
Rennie, L. 'Tavistock' *Agriculture* **59** (1952–3), 244–5

CHAPTER 13

Bodmin Moor

Burr, H. 'The Cornish Commons' in 'A symposium on some problem areas in the South-West' *Journ. Royal Agric. Soc. England* **112** (1951), 19–24
Jackson, A. L. 'The small marginal producer on Bodmin Moor' *National Agricultural Advisory Service Quart. Rev.* No. 36 (1957), 88–92
Malim, J. W. *The Bodmin Moors* (London 1936)

Northwest Cornwall

Burton, S. H. *The Coasts of Cornwall* (London 1955)
Clarke, B. B. 'The superficial deposits of the Camel estuary and suggested stages in
   its Pleistocene history' *Trans. Royal Geol. Soc. Cornwall* 19 (1961–2), 257–79
Gurnett, L. R. 'North Cornwall' *Agriculture* 70 (1963), 543–4

The China-clay District

Hocking, J. A. 'The china clay trade of the United Kingdom' *Northern Universities'
   Geog. Journ.* 1 (1960), 20–8
Pounds, N. J. G. 'The china clay industry of Southwest England' *Econ. Geog.* 28
   (1952), 20–30
Rowse, A. L. *St Austell Church: Town: Parish* (St Austell 1960)

The St Austell–Truro District, Roseland and The Fal

Carter, W. R. B. 'Truro' *Agriculture* 58 (1951–2), 247–8

CHAPTER 14

The West Cornwall Industrial Area

Boyer, R. S. 'Profitable small farms in west Cornwall' *Agriculture* 66 (1959–60),
   294–7
Cole, Helen M. 'Anemones in the Southwest' *ibid.* 71 (1964), 16–19
Goodridge, J. C. 'The tin-mining industry: a growth point for Cornwall' *Trans.
   Inst. Brit. Geographers* 38 (1966), 95–104
Gullick, C. F. W. R. 'A physiographical survey of west Cornwall' *Trans. Royal
   Geol. Soc. Cornwall* 16 (1936), 380–99
Ibbett, W. C. 'Commercial anemone growing' *Agriculture* 64 (1957–8), 274–8
Johnstone, Katharine H. 'Early potatoes in Cornwall' *ibid.* 63 (1956–7), 124–6
— 'Cornish cauliflowers' *ibid.* 70 (1963), 216–9
Probert, J. C. C. *The Architecture of Cornish Methodism* (Redruth 1966)
Shepherd, F. W. 'Rosewarne' *Agriculture* 65 (1958–9), 201–6
Vale, E. *The Harveys of Hayle* (Truro 1966)
Weaver, M. E. 'Industrial housing in west Cornwall' *Industrial Arch.* 3 (1966),
   23–45

The Lizard Peninsula

Fryer, G. 'Evolution of the land forms of Kerrier' *Trans. Royal Geol. Soc. Cornwall*
   19 (1957–8), 122–53
Toy, H. S. *The History of Helston* (London 1936)

The Land's End Peninsula

Craze, S. P. 'Penzance-Land's End' *Agriculture* 58 (1951–2), 42–3
Hilton, N. 'The Land's End peninsula: the influence of history on agriculture
   Geog. Journ. 119 (1953), 57–72
Ruhrmund, F. 'Newlyn Harbour' *Cornish Rev.* No. 5 (1967), 72–5
Walsh, B. E. 'Valley development on the Land's End peninsula' *Northern Uni-
   versities' Geog. Journ.* 1 (1960), 59–68

CHAPTER 15

Bowley, E. L. *The Fortunate Islands* (Reading 1957 edition)
Christopher, K. 'Opportunities for Scillonian farmers' *Agriculture* 70 (1963), 276–80
Downes, A. 'Farming the Fortunate Isles' *Geography* 42 (1957), 105–12
Grigson, G. *The Scilly Isles* (London 1948)

Jellicoe, G. A. *A Landscape Charter for the Isles of Scilly* (London 1965)

Johns, E. M. ' "Off-islands" of Scilly' *Town and Country Planning* 35 (1967), 234–9

Kay, E. *Isles of Flowers* (London 1963 edition)

Leuze, Eva 'Die Scilly-Inseln' *Erdkunde* 20 (1966), 93–103

Matthews, G. F. *The Isles of Scilly* (London 1960)

Mitchell, G. F. and Orme, A. R. 'The Pleistocene deposits of the Scilly Isles' *Proc. Ussher Soc.* 1 (1965), 190–2

Mumford, C. *Portrait of the Isles of Scilly* (London 1967)

Shepherd, F. W. 'Agriculture in the Isles of Scilly' *Agriculture* 55 (1948–9), 528–36

Vyvyan, C. C. *The Scilly Isles* (London 1960 edition)

INDEX

Figures in bold type indicate where the main information on the subject will be found.